THE BOOK WITHIN THE BOOK

BIBLICAL
INTERPRETATION
SERIES

VOLUME 14

THE BOOK WITHIN THE BOOK

Writing in Deuteronomy

BY

JEAN-PIERRE SONNET

BRILL

LEIDEN · NEW YORK · KÖLN

1997

This book is printed on acid-free paper.

Library of Congress Cataloging-in-Publication Data

Sonnet, Jean-Pierre.
   The Book within the book : writing in Deuteronomy / by Jean-Pierre
Sonnet.
      p. cm. — (Biblical interpretation series, ISSN 0928-0731 ;
v. 14)
   Originally presented as the author's thesis (Ph. D.)—Indiana
University.
   Includes bibliographical references and indexes.
   ISBN 9004108661 (cloth : alk. paper)
   1. Bible. O.T. Deuteronomy—Criticism, interpretation, etc.
2. Bible. O.T. Deuteronomy—Authorship. 3. Moses (Biblical
leader)   I. Title.   II. Series.
BS1275.2S68   1997
222'.15066——dc21   97–12687
                                                                   CIP

Die Deutsche Bibliothek – CIP-Einheitsaufnahme

Sonnet, Jean-Pierre:
The book within the book : writing in deuteronomy / by Jean-Pierre
Sonnet. - Leiden ; New York ; Köln : Brill, 1997
   (Biblical interpretation series ; Vol. 14)
   ISBN 90-04-10866-1 Gewebe

                    ISSN 0928-0731
                    ISBN 90 04 10866 1

PRINTED IN THE NETHERLANDS

A la mémoire de mon père,
Jean Sonnet
לא כהתה עינו ולא נס לחה

CONTENTS

PREFACE XI

NOTE ON ABBREVIATIONS AND SOURCES........................ XV

INTRODUCTION 1

1. Communication Within and Without: Deuteronomy's
   Analogy.. 1
   a. In the History of Interpretation 1
   b. Communication on the Narrative Stage 4
   c. Primary and Secondary Data.................................... 6

2. In the Beginning: Methodological Options................. 9
   a. The Telling of History 9
   b. Dramatic Presentation 12
   c. Deuteronomy's Integrity and Deuteronomy's Inte-
      gration within the Pentateuchal Narrative 21
   d. From Beginning to End 24

1. "THE WORDS THAT MOSES *SPOKE*":
   ORAL COMMUNICATION IN DEUTERONOMY'S
   REPRESENTED WORLD... 27
   1. Oral Communication? 29
   2. Momentum and Counter-Momentum............................. 32
   3. Moses' Prophetic Credentials 35
   4. Buffer Voice, Surrogate Voice 38

2. THE LOGIC OF WRITING IN MOSES' TORAH SPEECH
   (Deuteronomy 5-26) 41
   1. "He Wrote Down" (I)–Deuteronomy 5........................... 42
   2. "You Shall Write" (I)–Deut 6:6-9................................... 51
   3. "He Wrote Down" (II)–Deuteronomy 10 59
   4. "You Shall Write" (II)–Deut 11:18-21 69
   5. "He Shall Write a Copy of this Torah"–Deut 17:18-20 .. 71
      a. "He Shall Write for Himself" 72

b. The Royal Reading as *Mise en Abyme* of the People's
Reception 78

Excursus: The Writing of the Bill of Divorce in Deut 24:1-4   83

3. THE METAMORPHOSES OF THE SĒPER (Deuteronomy
27-28, 29-30) 85
1. Writing "Beyond the Jordan"–Deut 27:1-8 86
    a. Beyond the Jordan 87
    b. The Liminal Character of the Stone Inscription 88
    c. Analogues in the Pentateuch and in the Ancient
       Near East 92
    d. A Communicational Diptych 95
2. *sēper* in Deuteronomy 28 97
3. *sēper* in Deuteronomy 29-30 103
    a. The Interpretative Frame 103
    b. *In Medias Res* 105
    c. The Purposeful Reference to the *sēper* 107
    d. Curiosity and Suspense 110

Excursus: The Sequence in "Fabula" of Deuteronomy's
Middle Speech Units (Deuteronomy 5-28 and 29-30):
A Discussion of Lohfink's Reconstruction 112

4. WRITING THE "BOOK," WRITING THE SONG
(Deut 31:1-32:47) 117
1. Two Approaches to the Art of Telling in Deutero-
    nomy 31 118
    a. An "Esthetic and Systematic" Organization? 119
    b. Temporal Deformations: Up to What Point? 122
    c. Addresses in Sequence 125
2. Before the Theophany–Deut 31:1-13 127
    a. Joshua as the Crossing Character–Deut 31:1-8 128
    b. The Written Torah as Torah Beyond Moses–Deut
       31:9 134
    c. The Written Torah and the Re-Enactment of the
       Horeb Experience–Deut 31:9-13 140
3. The Turning Point of the Theophany–Deut 31:14-32:   147
    a. The Return of the Repressed–Deut 31:14-15 147
    b. In The Tent of Meeting–Deut 31:16-22 148
    c. Leader of a Rebellious People–Deut 31:23 153

d. A Supplemented Torah–Deut 31:24-26 156
e. Moses' Prophetic and Factual Knowledge–Deut 31:
   27-29 167
f. The Power of the Song–Deut 31:30-32:44 173
g. "All Has Been Heard"–Deut 32:45-47 178
4. Conclusion 180

5. "BEFORE HIS DEATH" (Deut 32:48-34:12) 183
1. "And Die There on the Mountain"–Deut 32:48-52   185
2. "So Moses, the Servant of YHWH, Died There"–
   Deut 33:1-34:7 192
3. "So the People of Israel Listened to Joshua"–Deut
   34:8-12 194
4. Conclusion 197

6. MOSES AND MOSES' "BOOK" IN BIBLICAL TIME
AND SPACE 199
1. Patriarchal Death Scenes 202
2. Reading Deuteronomy 31-34 in a Patriarchal Key 204
3. Whose Fatherhood? 207
4. Blessings: Patriarchal vs. Prophetic 210
5. Balaam vs. Moses: What Prophecy? 215
6. Visionary Prophets: Abraham and Moses 218
7. From Burial Place to Crossing Book 223
8. The Mosaic Communication 230

7. "TAKE THIS 'BOOK'": THE TORAH "BOOK" AND
THE BOOK OF DEUTERONOMY 235
1. So Spoke Moses 237
2. Frame-Breaks 238
3. "The Torah I Am Setting Before You" 243
4. The Book Within the Book 246
5. Moses vs. the Narrator: The Limits of the Analogy 250
6. *Explicit Liber Helleaddabarim Id Est Deuterononomium* 252
7. Conclusion 259

Excursus: The Shadow of the Scribes 262

BIBLIOGRAPHY 269

INDEX OF AUTHORS 285
INDEX OF SCRIPTURAL AND OTHER REFERENCES 288

PREFACE

The question of Moses' authorship has been the most provocative issue, and one of the major chapters, in the history of biblical interpretation. The problem derives from two verses in
Deuteronomy 31: "And Moses wrote this Torah" (Deut 31:9);
"When Moses had finished writing the words of this Torah in a
'book'" (Deut 31:24). Traditional interpretation, both Jewish and
Christian, identified the "book" written by Moses with the Book
of Deuteronomy, and even with the Pentateuch itself. Critical historical exegesis dismantled the traditional equation and endeavored to identify Deuteronomy's successive redactors. Scholars have
made reasonable hypotheses identifying stages in the growth of
the text. Yet the literary claim of Deuteronomy as we have it, that
is, in its only non-hypothetical state, is still in want of a critical
assessment. What does it mean, in Deuteronomy's overall plot,
that Moses wrote a "book" and did not, for instance, engrave his
words on a stela, like Hammurapi? What is the plausible content
of this "book" (Deuteronomy's literary construction, also, pre-
cludes the equation of Moses' Torah "book" with the framing
Book of Deuteronomy), and how does this "book" relate to the
Torah that Moses taught beforehand in the plains of Moab? Is
there any link between Moses' writing in Moab and God's writing
at Horeb? How is the theme of the "book" connected with the
issue of Moses' death and the motif of his unlocated burial place?
What is the relevance of the introduction of this theme as a part
of Deuteronomy's closure? Does this theme take on greater significance when viewed from the perspective of the Pentateuch?
What is the significance of Moses' recourse to the very medium
that Deuteronomy embodies—the medium of the book? In many
regards, Deuteronomy seems to revolve around issues of communication. These issues and their literary shaping require an appropriate description, in a framework that differs from both the traditional perspective and the historical critical project.

Using a narrative approach, and comparative data from the
ancient Near East, this study endeavors to answer these questions
by characterizing the process of communication throughout
Deuteronomy. The investigation first delineates the process of

communication *in* Deuteronomy's represented world (Moses' communication to the sons of Israel); it depicts next the Book of Deuteronomy *as* communication (by the narrator to the reader). These two processes are shown to cooperate in a determined way, that gives Deuteronomy its distinctive power. The theme of the "book within the book" serves as the climax for the interaction of these levels of inner and outer communication. Like none of the preceding books in the Pentateuch, Deuteronomy is concerned with the function of literacy and textuality in religion and society. The main characters in the story all appear at some point in the role of scribes. The written record of the Torah progressively becomes a key protagonist in the narrated events. While Moses dies outside of the land, his "book" is launched to accompany the people into the land. Yet what happens on the narrative stage is echoed in the reader's world: the terms of Moses' Torah "book" are equally brought to the reader's knowledge. The function of Moses' "book" is thus carried on by the framing Book of Deuteronomy. The description of the poetic architectonics that enables such a dual disclosure is the formal object of the study. Whereas the Greek tragedies and the Roman orations had accompanying theoretical works, no *Peri Poiētikēs* or *Institutio Oratoria* accompanied the narrative and the speeches of the Hebrew Bible and thus of Deuteronomy. Yet Deuteronomy's plot, in its way of combining oral and written communication, may adumbrate its own narrative theory of divine and human communication. In its telling of the genesis of Moses' Torah "book," Deuteronomy possibly suggests the paradigm of what a book like Deuteronomy is all about. Is Deuteronomy therefore a self-conscious work? "The phenomenon of an artwork mirroring itself as it mirrors reality," Robert Alter writes, ". . . could be traced back as far as the bard within the epic in the *Odyssey* and Euripides' parody of the conventions of Greek tragedy."[1] Could this phenomenon be extended to Deuteronomy's depiction of Moses' writing of the Torah that he delivered orally beforehand? The theme of Moses' authorship still remains a provocative issue.

The dissertation underlying this book was composed under the

[1] R. Alter, *Partial Magic: The Novel as a Self-Conscious Genre* (University of California Press: Berkeley, 1975) xi.

dedicated guidance of Professor J. S. Ackerman (Indiana University) and of Professor M. Sternberg (Tel Aviv University). The former directed my Ph.D. program with the blend of wisdom and pioneering sense that, in my view, makes the study of the Bible at Indiana University so attractive. The latter engaged me, during the two years of redaction in Israel, in a far-reaching intellectual adventure. Working with M. Sternberg is to develop sensitivity to both comprehensive models and close reading, and measure what biblical poetics is all about. I wish also to express my appreciation to Professor B. Levinson who has been both a challenging reader and the most friendly adviser in crucial stages of the program, and to Professor Herbert Marks whose biblical and literary wit has been a constant stimulation, and whose support has a lot to do with the completion of this work. I am also greatly indebted to Professor Norbert Lohfink who helped me launch the project in its right course, and has been a most cordial interlocutor in several of its stages. I should like to thank Indiana University's Institute for Biblical and Literary Studies, my Jesuit Province, and my home institution, the *Institut d'Études Théologiques* (Brussels) which trusted me enough to support me from beginning to end. Finally, I should like to express my gratitude to the editors of the *Biblical Interpretation* series, who made it possible to turn this study about writing into the present book.

NOTE ON ABBREVIATIONS AND SOURCES

The abbreviations used in this work follow those listed in the *Society of Biblical Literature Membership Directory and Handbook* (Decatur: Society of Biblical Literature, 1994) 223-40, with the following exceptions and additions:

ABRT	*Assyrian and Babylonian Religious Texts*
BibInt	*Biblical Interpretation*
BJ	*La Bible de Jérusalem*
Dhorme	*L'Ancien Testament* (La Pléiade)
Joüon-Muraoka	*A Grammar of Biblical Hebrew*
NJPSV	New Jewish Publication Society Version
RLA	*Reallexikon der Assyriologie und vorderasiatischen Archäologie*
TOB	*Traduction Œcuménique de la Bible*
TUAT	*Texte aus der Umwelt des Alten Testaments*
Waltke-O'Connor	*An Introduction to Biblical Hebrew Syntax*

The biblical text is quoted in English translation according to the Revised Standard Version (RSV). Minor changes have been introduced in the personal names and in the place-names, and where a more literal translation was required for the argument. The medieval and early modern Jewish interpreters are quoted from *Torat Ḥaim Ḥumash* (Jerusalem: Mossad HaRav Kook, 1994), with the exception of Bekhor Shor (see bibliography).

INTRODUCTION

> Now as I looked at the living creatures, I saw a
> wheel upon the earth beside the living crea-
> tures, one for each of the four of them. As for
> the appearance of the wheels and their con-
> struction: their appearance was like the gleam-
> ing of chrysolite; and the four had the same like-
> ness, their construction being as it were a wheel
> within a wheel.
>
> Ezekiel 1:15-16

1. *Communication Within and Without: Deuteronomy's Analogy*

As a "wheel within a wheel," to echo Ezekiel's vision (Ezek 1:16),
Deuteronomy is an act of communication within an act of communication. Moses' oral "words" unfold as the written "words" of
the framing book—Deuteronomy. Or, the other way around,
Deuteronomy is an act of communication about an act of communication. The book's narrator starts the narration but almost
immediately hands it over to its dramatis persona, whose direct
speech gives the work its distinctive ring. In this study I intend to
describe Deuteronomy's way of combining the two levels of communication: Moses' address, in the represented world (to the sons
of Israel in the plains of Moab), and the book's address to its
reader. While covering the process of communication throughout
the book, the investigation will focus on chapters 31-34 and, more
precisely, on the theme of Moses' writing of the Torah "book"
(see Deut 31:9, 24). The working hypothesis will be that a meaningful analogy exists between communication in Deuteronomy's
represented world and in Deuteronomy's representing medium.
On both levels, communication is either actually or eventually
achieved by a written "book".

a. *In the History of Interpretation*

Both Jewish and Christian traditional approaches took the relationship between Deuteronomy and the Torah "book" that Moses

wrote for granted. Deuteronomy was written by Moses for the simple reason that Moses wrote the Torah (see Deut 31:9, 24).[1] The alleged evidence was brought into disrepute by historical criticism and replaced by a whole range of hypotheses about Deuteronomy's origins and growth. As to authorship, the narrative claim that Moses was an author became irrelevant, the relevant issue being henceforth the historical identity of Deuteronomy's successive redactors.[2] Dismantling the traditional equation and deserting Deuteronomy's inner claims, historical criticism, however, has created room for a fresh approach to the book's poetics, i.e., to its literary architectonics. A ground-breaking study in that sense is Robert Polzin's *Moses and the Deuteronomist*, which calls attention to Deuteronomy's compositional structure.[3] The poetics of Deuteronomy, Polzin points out, consists in the book's unique combination of reporting and reported speech. "Almost all the book consists of reported speech, mostly in direct discourse and mostly of Moses, whereas only about fifty-six verses are reporting speech, the Deuteronomic [*sic*] narrator's, which form the context for Moses' utterances."[4] In Polzin's analysis, this compositional structure primarily serves a dialectic between viewpoints, opposing Moses to the Deuteronomistic narrator. Polzin's emphasis on the category of point of view, however, prevents him from doing justice to other constituents of Deuteronomy's compositional structure, notably to its link with a narrative plot. The alternation of reporting and reported speech is also, as I will indicate, a narrative device marking off the turns in Moses' communicational enterprise on the last day of his life.

Polzin's study calls for revision on a further point. In his opinion Deuteronomy's poetics consists in a dialectic of "speeches."

---

[1] See, however, the debate in the Babylonian Talmud about the authorship of the Pentateuch's last eight verses (*b. B. Bat.* 14b-15a), and Ibn Ezra's veiled allusions, in his commentary to the Torah, to a post-Mosaic supplementation of Deuteronomy (in Deut 1:1; 3:11; 27:1-8; 31:9).

[2] The tenet of Moses' authorship is periodically revived by neo-conservative exegetes. See most recently E. H. Merril, *Deuteronomy* (The New American Commentary 4; Nashville: Broadman and Holman, 1994) 22-23.

[3] R. Polzin, *Moses and the Deuteronomist: A Literary Study of the Deuteronomic History. Part One: Deuteronomy, Joshua, Judges* (New York: Seabury, 1980).

[4] R. Polzin, "Reporting Speech in the Book of Deuteronomy: Toward a Compositional Analysis of the Deuteronomic History," *Traditions in Transformation: Turning Points in Biblical Faith* (F. M. Cross Festschrift; ed. B. Halpern and J. D. Levenson; Winona Lake, Ind.: Eisenbrauns, 1981) 194.

Moses' communication, however, actually eventuates in the writing of the Torah "book." In other words, Deuteronomy includes the theme and aspect of *written* communication. Accordingly, Deuteronomy's poetics is also to be thought of as a relationship between "books"—the framing Book of Deuteronomy and the Torah "book" that Moses writes within Deuteronomy's narrative (Deut 31:9, 24). The issue of inner and outer, oral and written communication in Deuteronomy thus calls for an overall assessment, complementing Polzin's seminal insights.

The investigation is all the more needed since exponents of critical exegesis somehow perpetuate the pre-critical tenet when they equate Moses' Torah "book" with the Book of Deuteronomy.[5] In assuming the identity of the two records, scholars overlook the basic scale of representation that Deuteronomy brings into play. The representing medium (the Book of Deuteronomy) and the object represented on the narrative stage (the "book" of the Torah) belong to incommensurable planes of representation, as much as the Book of Esther and the letters sent out by King Ahasuerus (see Esth 3:12-15). Often considered the Archimedaean point of Pentateuchal historical criticism, Deuteronomy, paradoxically, is still in want of a critical establishment of its basic literary architectonics. The scene of Moses' writing and the motif of Moses' Torah "book" are the touchstone of the whole issue. Whereas pre-critical tradition overread Deuteronomy's narrative claim, projecting Moses' authorship onto the framing work, and whereas historical criticism has dismissed the same narrative claims, a critical approach attentive to Deuteronomy's poetics can bring out a powerful analogy: in the Pentateuchal canon Deuteronomy is the book that tells about the rise of the (Torah) "book."

---

[5] In recent scholarship see for instance T. Veijola, "The Basic Story in Deuteronomy 1-3," *'Wünschet Jerusalem Frieden': IOSOT Congress, Jerusalem 1986* (ed. M. Augustin and K.-D. Schunck; Beiträge zur Erforschung des Alten Testaments und des Antiken Judentums 13; Frankfurt am Main: Peter Lang, 1988) 254, "[In Deuteronomy] the existence of the Torah as a written document is always supposed, as its identity with Deuteronomy." M. Weinfeld, "Deuteronomy, Book of," *ABD* 2.174, "Deuteronomy is, in fact, the only book of the Pentateuch to be ascribed to Moses (Deut 31:9)." D. T. Olson, *Deuteronomy and the Death of Moses: A Theological Study* (OBT; Minneapolis: Fortress, 1994) 135: "One must identify this book of the *torah* as the book of Deuteronomy itself" (and passim).

b. *Communication on the Narrative Stage*

The concern of Deuteronomy's narrator, like that of any narrator, is to equip his reader with all he will need to know by the
end of his journey. Moses' concern, on the narrative stage, is to
transmit to Israel in Moab all it needs to know to do "in the land
which you are going over to possess" (4:14 and passim). The two
goals are intricately connected. It is by showing Moses as he
attempts to bring home (to the sons of Israel and to the land of
Israel) his ultimate teaching that Deuteronomy brings home (to
the reader) Moses' Torah. The two communicational purposes
cooperate as do wheels within wheels. Deuteronomy therefore
stands or falls on its ability to combine inner and outer communication. That there is in Deuteronomy's represented world an
autonomous issue of communication, conditioning the consistency of the work, is not sufficiently emphasized even in modern
Deuteronomic studies. These studies favor a hermeneutical, read-
er-oriented perspective. In this view, the Book of Deuteronomy
primarily aims to help its reader face historical and existential
challenges by rehearsing the paradigmatic scene of the entry into
the land.[6] The situation of Israel in Moab, receiving YHWH's ultimate Torah on the eastern bank of the Jordan river, mirrors the
historical and existential situation of the people in exile, called
to a new bond with YHWH and to a new "inheriting" of the land.
The book is therefore tailored, in its speeches, legal teaching, and
narrative, to fit the hermeneutical task of such a reader. The
"fusion of horizons," to take over Gadamer's concept, combining
the work's semantic proposition and the reader's existential project, represents the achievement of Deuteronomy's purport. It is
not my intention to play down this dimension of the book's relevance, but rather to correlate it with a more basic pertinence of
the work. The involvement of the reader should not be achieved

---

[6] See G. von Rad's reflections about the "Purpose of Deuteronomy," *Studies in Deuteronomy* (SBT 9; London: SCM Press, 1948) 70, "Six centuries wasted in sin and constant apostasy are cancelled out and Israel is set once more at Horeb to hear Jahweh's word of salvation, which has not yet lost its power." See also P. Beauchamp, *L'un et l'autre testament: Essai de lecture* (Paris: Seuil, 1976) 57-65; L. Perlitt, *Deuteronomium* (BK 5/2; Neukirchen Vluyn: Neukirchener Verlag, 1991) 134-35; T. A. Lenchak, *"Choose Life!": A Rhetorical-Critical Investigation of Deuteron-omy 28,69-30,20* (AnBib 129; Rome: Editrice Pontificio Istituto Biblico, 1993) 27; Olson, *Deuteronomy*, 165-66.

at the expense of Deuteronomy's historiographical claim, that is, its claim to record what took place "in the wilderness, in the Arabah, . . . the fortieth year, on the first day of the eleventh month" (Deut 1:1-2). Nor should the hermeneutic process dismiss the narrative consistency of the history in question—*how* did Moses bring home what he had to bring home. For what is told in Deuteronomy is primarily YHWH's and Moses' way to entrust Israel, once and for all, with everything that is required by the covenant in Moab (whence "once") and by the covenantal life in the land (whence "for all"). In Deuteronomy, like in the rest of the Hebrew Bible narrative, there is no hermeneutic shortcut; the reader has everything to gain by playing by the historiographical and narrative rules of the work.

"Entre le début et la fin du livre," Thomas Römer writes, "il ne se passe pas grand-chose de nouveau si ce n'est l'installation de Josué comme successeur de Moïse (Dt 31, 7s.) et la mort de ce dernier (Dt 34, 1s.)"[7] Römer's statement mirrors the common scholarly assumption regarding Deuteronomy's narrative plot: it is minimal. And it is not thought of as related to Moses' act of communication. Significantly enough, Römer did not single out the scene of Moses' writing (in Deuteronomy 31) as something that happens "entre le début et la fin du livre." The link of Moses' writing with Deuteronomy's overall story is sometimes overshadowed by a division of the book that turns chapters 31-34 into an appendix.[8] In such a perspective, Deuteronomy is a collection of speeches with some extrinsic notices appended. Textual evidence may even be denied, as in Samuel Amsler's "Loi orale et loi écrite dans le Deutéronome." The "marginal" mentions of Moses' writing in Deuteronomy 31, Amsler contends, are the exceptions that confirm the rule: "Pour le Deutéronome lui-même, Moïse n'écrit rien, il parle."[9] The role of Moses' writing in Deuteronomy's

---

[7] Th. Römer, "Le Deutéronome et la quête des origines," *Le Pentateuque: Débats et recherches* (ed. P. Haudebert; LD 151; Paris: Cerf, 1992) 66-67.

[8] E.g., A. D. H. Mayes, *Deuteronomy* (NCNB; Grand Rapids: Eerdmans, 1979) 371, and I. Cairns, *Word and Presence: A Commentary to the Book of Deuteronomy* (ITC; Grand Rapids: Eerdmans, 1992) 267. The labelling of Deuteronomy 31-34 as "appendix" is arguably founded on the book's redactional growth—Deuteronomy 31-34 is considered as a part of the Deuteronomistic frame, embedding the more genuine, Deuteronomic, legal corpus. Such divisions, however, fundamentally thwart the basic thrust of Deuteronomy's narrative.

[9] S. Amsler, "Loi orale et loi écrite dans le Deutéronome," *Das Deuteronomium: Entstehung, Gestalt und Botschaft* (ed. N. Lohfink; BETL 68; Louvain: University

overall plot thus calls for a closer assessment. The ending of
Deuteronomy, I shall indicate, is completely misrepresented if
Moses' writing of the Torah "book" (31:9), and the completion
of this writing (31:24), are left out of the picture. A turning point
in the represented process of communication, the motif of Moses'
writing, is also subtly prepared for by the prophet's previous developments as (re)teller and lawgiver. The theme of written communication goes back to the remotest event that Moses' retelling
brings into relief, the giving of the Ten Words at Horeb (see
Deuteronomy 4-5), and it repeatedly emerges in his injunctions.
Contrary to Römer's claim, I intend to show that something is
definitely going on between Deuteronomy's beginning and end:
a dramatic process of communication.

c. *Primary and Secondary Data*

Will Israel be appropriately equipped with the "words" of the
covenant when Moses completes his direct act of communication?
Will Deuteronomy's reader be equally fitted with the same, essential "words" when he finishes the reading of the book?[10] This is
Deuteronomy's issue, in terms of communication. This is the issue
I want to establish in the present inquiry. Everything Deuteronomy brings together for this communicational purpose will have to
be taken into account. Everything, and nothing else. In other
words, Deuteronomy's proposition is to be construed according

---

Press, 1985) 51; see the echo of Amsler's claim in Lenchak, *"Choose Life!,"* 16-17.
    [10] The term "reader" will be used in these pages in a specific meaning, best
defined by M. Perry: "In speaking of the *reader* and his responses I do not mean
the subjective reactions of any actual reader. I am referring to a 'maximal' con-
cretization of the text that can be justified from the text itself, while also taking
into account the norms (social, linguistic, literary, etc.) relevant for its period,
and the *possible* intentions of the author. What I term as the *reader* is therefore a
metonymic characterization of the text" ("Literary Dynamics: How the Order of
a Text Creates its Meanings," *Poetics Today* 1 [1979] 43; cf. W. Iser's definition of
the "implied reader" in *The Act of Reading: A Theory of Aesthetic Response* [Balti-
more: Johns Hopkins University Press, 1974] 34). Perry's statement expresses a
hierarchy of criteria that will be respected in this study. The reading process
(embodied in the reader's responses) will be described as primarily and ultimately
regulated by the narrative text of Deuteronomy; "the norms relevant for its period" will be approached on comparative grounds, via biblical and extra-biblical
analogues; the *"possible* intentions of the author" will be understood as the *possible* intentions of the final editors of Deuteronomy as the Pentateuch's conclusive
book.

to its primary narrative and historiographical claim, without the interference of secondary data, that is, clues obtained in addition to, and in spite of, the book's "first hand" proposition.

This interpretative rule, excluding secondary data, especially applies to the knowledge associated with the critical investigation of Deuteronomy's genesis.[11] That the redactional growth of Deuteronomy bears a relation to the poetics of the text we now read is beyond doubt. Throughout its development, the work very likely underwent significant metamorphoses as to, for instance, the voicing of the laws it contains, or the medium implied in their transmission.[12] By uncovering these previous stages in Deuteronomy's development, critical hypotheses retrace the hermeneutical challenges faced by redactors and editors in their reshaping and supplementing of the work. Critically approached in this way, the text is endowed with a further dimension—a kind of historical depth. In the present study, however, I will avoid the detour through genetic hypotheses, and I will do so for a theoretical reason. Whatever the actual genesis of a narrative work, and whatever the traces this process left behind in the text, the work in question is supposed to provide within itself (within its literary context of interpretation) the elements required for its intelligibility *as a narrative*. Deuteronomy tells the beginning (see 1:5) and the completion (see 31:24; 32:46) of a process, and it is to be presumed that it efficiently brings the reader from the former to the latter point. The narrative consistency of Deuteronomy will accordingly be probed in these pages on the evidence immediately given by the text.

An example will make this option clearer. Deuteronomy's usage of the word ספר, "record, inscription, book," plays a crucial role

---

[11] The adjectives "synchronic" and "diachronic" will be avoided in the present inquiry because of their confusing character. Anyone who has approached narratives in a "synchronic" way knows how much "diachrony" they imply, in their unfolding of a plot throughout represented time (*dia-chronos*), as in their resorting to an essentially "dia-chronic" representing medium (language, in its discrete and linear character). I will instead designate the rise and growth of a given text as its "genesis" (and talk of a "genetic" approach, or of textual "genetics"), and call "poetics" the representational architectonics of the same text.

[12] On the former issue, see N. Lohfink, "Das Deuteronomium: Jahwegesetz oder Mosegesetz? Die Subjektzuordnung bei Wörtern für 'Gesetz' im Dtn und in der dtr Literatur," *TP* 65 (1990) 387-91; on the latter, see L. Perlitt, *Bundestheologie im Alten Testament* (WMANT 36; Neukirchen-Vluyn: Neukirchener Verlag, 1969) 42-45

in this inquiry. In his essay on the theology of the covenant, Lothar Perlitt contends that the issue of Moses' ספר in Deuteronomy is cleared up when approached genetically. The theme of the written Torah, recorded on a ספר, Perlitt argues, is a distinct Deuteronomistic creation, supplementing the earlier, Deuteronomic, theme of the "listening to the voice."[13] Whereas reception in the original Deuteronomy all came down to the "listening of the voice," it extended to the "listening of the book" in the Deuteronomistic redactional reshaping of the work.[14] Perlitt's hypothesis thus arguably gives access to an intermediary, or even to the genuine stage of Deuteronomy's poetics—a stage featuring exclusively oral communication.[15] By referring to a subsequent redirection of the works's poetics—the inclusion of the theme of written communication, Perlitt's suggestion calls attention to the hidden side of Deuteronomy's present form (and, presumably, helps explain some tensions in the current text). Hermeneutical decisions supposedly underlie the Deuteronomistic recasting, and they are worth retracing. Yet, however interesting, Perlitt's hypothesis cannot serve as a parameter in an investigation such as mine. The fact I will address is that Deuteronomy *combines* the theme of the voice and the theme of the written record and does so, supposedly, to all intents and purposes. Since a narrative text presumably delivers what it promises, it is in Deuteronomy's narrative, and not behind it, that the rationale for the combination of

---

[13] See Perlitt, *Bundestheologie*, 42-45; in the same sense, see F. L. Hossfeld and E. Reuter, "ספר *sefær*," *TWAT* 5.938-39: "Die gesamte Grundschicht von Dtn 5-28 kennt nur die Mündlichkeit... . Damit ist die Entstehungszeit eines *sefær hattôrāh* geklärt: die Vorstellung eines abgeschlossenen, niedergelegten JHWH-Willens ist für späte Dtr charakteristisch."

[14] Cf. the different stance of S. R. Driver (apropos of Moses' first reference to the Torah record (ספר) in Deut 28:58): "The expression harmonizes imperfectly with 31[9] (where Moses is first said to have 'written' the Deuteronomic law); and betrays the fact that Deuteronomy was from the first a *written* book" (*A Critical and Exegetical Commentary on Deuteronomy* [ICC; 3rd ed.; Edinburgh: T. & T. Clark, 1910] 316); see also G. A. Smith, *The Book of Deuteronomy* (CB; Cambridge: Cambridge University Press, 1918) 317.

[15] The appeal to Deuteronomistic supplementation may imply a plurality of redactional processes, since scholarship usually relies on several Deuteronomistic strata. The occurrence of ספר in Deut 30:10, for instance, belongs to a redactional unit (30:1-10) usually assigned to a later Deuteronomistic stratum than the unit that precedes it, 29:15-27, which also refers to the ספר-record (29:20, 26). See H. D. Preuß, *Deuteronomium* (ErFor 164; Darmstadt: Wissenschaftliche Buchgesellschaft, 1982) 160-61; idem, "Zum deuteronomistischen Geschichtswerk," *TRu* 58 (1993) 234-35.

oral and written media is primarily to be sought. The narrative rationale can secondarily be confronted with genetic hypotheses, so as to create multidimensional critical perspectives. In the course of the investigation, however, the description of the poetics of a text and the inquiry on its genesis are to be kept independent from each other. "In the end," Greenstein writes, "a critic must repeatedly decide whether to relate to a phenomenon as a primary or secondary object of interpretation."[16]

2. *In The Beginning: Methodological Options*

The present study will be conducted according to a set of methodological options implied by Deuteronomy's literary model. The model in question is brought to the fore by Deuteronomy's opening verses (Deut 1:1-5), which will thus provide the ground for the following *discours de la méthode*. The work's opening evidences the adherence of the narrative to the (biblical) model of omniscient narration; it signals Deuteronomy's recourse to dramatic "showing" as its main representational option; it anchors the represented story in the greater Pentateuchal narrative; it announces the work's and story's thrust toward completion. These features call for corresponding methodological procedures, which I will now progressively elaborate.

a. *The Telling of History*

> [1]These are the words that Moses spoke to all Israel beyond the Jordan. . . . [3]Moses spoke to the people of Israel according to all that YHWH had given him in commandment to them. . . . [5]Moses undertook to expound this Torah, saying . . . (Deut 1:1-5)

Within the narrative corpus of the Hebrew Bible, another book opens in quite similar fashion: "The words of Nehemiah the son of Hacaliah" (Neh 1:1). The reader must come to the end of the verse—"The words of Nehemiah the son of Hacaliah. Now it happened in the month of Chislev, in the twentieth year, as *I* was in Susa the capital, that . . ."— to realize that the announced "words

---

[16] E. L. Greenstein, "The Formation of the Biblical Narrative Corpus," *AJS Review* 15 (1990) 152.

of Nehemiah" are Nehemiah's overall narration in the first person. Retrospectively, the reader can (although he is not compelled
to) ascribe the very words that open the book to Nehemiah's
authority, "The narrative of Nehemiah the son of Hacaliah"
(NJPSV).[17] Deuteronomy's opening does not allow any similar
reading operations. The Mosaic voice, about to be heard, and the
voice that introduces it, turn out to be irreducible to each other.
The reproduction of Moses' words emanates from an anonymous
narrating voice. In his commentary on the Torah, Ibn Ezra dis-
cretely lets his reader understand that the west-of-the-Jordan point
of view of the narrating voice (Moses in Moab is described as
standing "beyond the Jordan") is incompatible with Moses', since
the prophet never crossed the river in question.[18] The same voice
furthermore warrants the conformity of Moses' teaching to
YHWH's instruction: "Moses spoke to the people of Israel according to all that (כֹּל אֲשֶׁר) YHWH had given him in commandment
to them" (Deut 1:3). Such knowledge, coming from a party other than YHWH and his prophet, points toward the omniscient
narrator who, from Gen 1:1 onward, has conducted the Pentateuchal narrative. Deuteronomy's opening has therefore nothing
in common with superficially analogous prophetic overtures, "The
words of ..." (Jer 1:1; Amos 1:1). Like in Neh 1:1, these overtures
herald prophetic authorship. Not so in Deuteronomy, which,
although harboring the words of Israel's greatest prophet (Deut
34:10), proceeds from "more than a prophet," that is, from the
anonymous and omniscient voice that led the Pentateuchal narrative up to the end of the Book of Numbers.[19]

---

[17] In its opening, the book of Nehemiah thus includes a movement of self-reference (the work introduces itself as "the words of Nehemiah"), and so does the
apocryphal book of Baruch, Καὶ οὗτοι οἱ λόγοι τοῦ βιβλίου οὓς ἔγραψεν
Βαρουχ, "These are the words of the book which Baruch wrote" (Bar 1:1; the
quoted book merges with the quoting book). Deuteronomy's framing book, I
shall indicate in my last chapter, carefully avoids any similar trope of (explicit)
self-reference, in accordance with the narrative poetics implemented by the Pentateuch. For the exception represented by the book of Nehemiah in the Hebrew
Bible's narrative poetics, see M. Sternberg, *The Poetics of Biblical Narrative* (Bloomington: Indiana University Press, 1985) 12-13, 66, 73-74.

[18] Ibn Ezra, on Deut 1:1. See B. Spinoza's elaborating on Ibn Ezra's clues in
Chapter Eight of his *Tractatus Theologico-Politicus* (trans. S. Shirley; Leiden: Brill,
1989) 162-64.

[19] For a presentation of the biblical narrator's privileges and manners, see
Sternberg, *Poetics*, 12-13, 32-35, 58-128. Sternberg's use of the category of omniscient narration in his "drama of reading" has been critized as ideological (see

Deuteronomy is to be read within the poetic parameters established in its opening. It is not a prophetic work, but a narrative about Moses' prophetic communication in Moab; it shares the historiographical claim made in the previous Pentateuchal narrative. When Römer contends that Deuteronomy does not try to conceal its fictitious character and is not concerned with the chronological gap between Moses' and the reader's time,[20] he misses the most basic claim of the Pentateuchal narrative, namely, its claim to tell past history with absolute truth.[21] No doubt, the reader will learn countless lessons from Moses' address, but never as the prophet's direct addressee. Moses never turns to Deuteronomy's reader, even when he mentions future addressees, "who [are] not there with us" (29:14). In other words, everything in Deuteronomy is mediated by historiographic telling; sense and reference primarily reverberate within the represented world set up by the

---

especially M. Bal, *On Story-Telling: Essays in Narratology* [ed. D. Jobling; Sonoma, California: Polebridge, 1991] 61-62; E. A. Castelli, S. D. Moore, R. M. Schwartz, eds., *The Postmodern Bible: The Bible and Culture Collective* [New Haven: Yale University Press, 1995] 112-13, 278-80). Yet the presence of omniscient narration in the Biblical narrative (from Genesis to Kings), as claimed by Sternberg, is itself not called into question (the technique is conventional in Sumerian, Assyrian, Egyptian and Canaanite storytelling).

[20] See Th. Römer, "Quête des origines," 74. Römer's contention is based on the fact that Moses addresses as "you" a double addressee: the Exodus generation, destined to die in the desert (see Deut 1:34-36), and the successive generation, destined to enter the land. "Cette 'ambiguïté' de l'identification des destinataires montre que le Deutéronome ne cherche nullement à cacher son caractère fictif. Perlitt a raison de faire remarquer que la volonté dtr de rendre présente, dans un but parénétique, l'histoire passée ne se soucie guère de la chronologie. Les Deutéronomistes savent que leur public est capable de comprendre cette suppression des époques, et de s'approprier l'histoire présentée [see Perlitt, *Deuteronomium*, 134]. Cet 'accord' entre auteur et lecteur inclut pour le Deutéronome un 'jeu' avec la tradition, mais aussi un 'jeu' avec les générations." Actually, the play between the two generations represents Moses' rhetorical way of addressing his audience as the trans-generational Israel: the sons were, through their fathers, Israel-present-at-Horeb; both groups are therefore addressed as "you" (see N. Lohfink, *Die Väter Israels im Deuteronomium—Mit einer Stellungnahme von Thomas Römer* [OBO 111; Freiburg: Universitätsverlag; Göttingen: Vandenhoeck & Ruprecht, 1991] 20-21). For a symmetrical, trans-generational, use of "we," see the "little credo" in Deut 26:5-10. The phenomenon is rhetorical; it takes place within Deuteronomy's represented world and is not a clue betraying a poetics of avowed fiction. The latter would contradict the Pentateuch's most basic assumption: its claim to tell history.

[21] See E. Auerbach in his famous contrast between the ending of the *Odyssey* and the narrative in Genesis 22 (*Mimesis: The Representation of Reality in Western Literature* [Princeton: Princeton University Press, 1953] 14); see also Sternberg, *Poetics*, 30-32.

book's opening. Instead of blurring generic conventions, and far from being psychologically abused by the text, the reader relates to the represented world as to the world of past history. As I indicated in the previous section, the reader's hermeneutical relationship with Deuteronomy is not achieved at the expense of the work's historiographical claim; it operates along with it. Historiographical narration is Deuteronomy's most basic deal.

b. *Dramatic Presentation*

Deuteronomy could have opened like the Book of Samuel, which first sets up the represented world—ויהי איש אחד ... ושמו אלקנה, "There was a certain man ... whose name was Elkanah" (1 Sam 1:1)—and brings forth the character's words in due course (see 1 Sam 1:8 for Elkanah's first quoted speech). Deuteronomy's initial sentence does introduce the reader to the represented world: "Moses spoke to all Israel beyond the Jordan in the wilderness ... in the fortieth year, on the first day of the eleventh month" (Deut 1:1, 3). Still, the character's forthcoming speech is referred to beforehand: "These are the words that ..." The book opens with the narrative element Meir Sternberg calls a "transformer," i.e. the linguistic element that marks a transition from narrative frame to quoted inset.[22] The standard transformer in biblical narrative is the infinitive construct לאמר, "saying," the equivalent of the modern colon and opening quotation mark in Western languages.[23] The לאמר marker occurs in Deuteronomy's overture, and occurs where expected, that is, at the end of the narrative opening: "Moses undertook to expound this law, *saying*, ..." (Deut 1:5). The quotation shifter, however, has been anticipated at the very head

---

[22] See M. Sternberg, "How Indirect Discourse Means: Syntax, Semantics, Poetics, Pragmatics," *Literary Pragmatics* (ed. R. Sell; Routledge: London, 1991) 63: "All reported discourse is a mimesis of discourse *by* discourse. At the same time ... the two always assume the form of discourse *within* discourse. The (piece of) discourse quoted becomes an *inset* within the *frame* of the reporting discourse, often with the help of an introductory clause or *transformer*." Whereas אלה הדברים, "These are the words," functions in Deut 1:1 as a transformer, introducing a quoted inset, the opening words of Exodus, אלה שמות, "These are the names," pertain to the narrative frame. Yet the relationship of Exod 1:1-2 to Exodus' represented world is indirect: we do not read in Exod 1:2 about the characters acting on the narrative stage, but about their names.

[23] See S. A. Meier, *Speaking of Speaking: Marking Direct Discourse in the Hebrew Bible* (VTSup 46; Leiden: Brill, 1992) 94-140.

of the book—אלה הדברים, "These are the words." Like an index finger, it refers the reader straightaway to the centrality of the words that are about to be quoted. From the outset, Deuteronomy thus announces what will be increasingly confirmed: its appeal to dramatic presentation. By placing in Moses' mouth all of its legal exposition and most of its narrative content (in the peculiar guise of retelling), Deuteronomy makes the most of the "showing" (*versus* "telling") mode of Biblical poetics.[24]

The distinction between "telling" and "showing" has been highlighted by Wayne Booth in his *Rhetoric of Fiction*.[25] It originates in earlier views, such as this remark by J. Warren Beach:

> Authors like Thackeray, or Balzac, or H.G. Wells ... are always *telling* the reader what happened instead of showing them the scene, telling them what to think of the characters rather than letting the reader judge for himself or letting the characters do the telling about one another. I like to distinguish between novelists that *tell* and those [like Henry James] who *show*.[26]

In the Hebrew Bible narrative, Sternberg indicates, "free recourse to exegetical 'telling' [does not] preclude a mastery of the art of dramatic 'showing'"[27]: both modes are present as representational options.[28] Yet dramatic "showing" gains priority as the technique of reenacting, which somehow transforms the reader into "spectator" of the foundational and historical events. By "bringing the

---

[24] With the exception of God's intervention in the theophany (Deut 31:14, 16-21, 23; 32:49-52), Moses is the only speaking character on the narrative stage. As Polzin points out, "the book is more than just Moses' utterances within the narrator's utterances: Moses' utterances continually quote, with direct discourse, other utterances" (*Moses*, 25). Quoted by Moses, God and the people may in turn quote further locutors. For these *cas de figures*, see Polzin, *Moses*, 25-26; idem, "Reporting Speech," 193-211.

[25] W. C. Booth, *The Rhetoric of Fiction* (2nd ed.; Chicago: The University of Chicago Press, 1983) 3-20.

[26] Quoted in Booth, *Rhetoric*, 2.

[27] Sternberg, *Poetics*, 122.

[28] In associating authoritative "telling" with "early narration (and dramatic "showing" with its modern counterpart), Booth (*Rhetoric*, 3-9) tends to overlook the forms of "showing" attested in ancient narrative literature. Booth's appeal to the narrative opening of the book of Job (Job 1-2) should not overshadow the fact that the opening in question gives way to forty chapters of dramatic "showing." See my "'Le livre trouvé': 2 Rois 22 dans sa finalité narrative," *NRT* 116 (1994) 836-61, where I show that the Book of Chronicles, in its narrative parallel to 2 Kings 22, resorts to "telling" where the Book of Kings prefers "showing."

speech-act into the foreground,"[29] biblical narrative enacts the historical drama, exposing the reader to the intricate interplay of
divine and human wills. The art of biblical narrative accordingly
lies "between narration and dialogue," to quote Robert Alter's
seminal work.[30] In Deuteronomy, however, the recourse to direct
speech is almost pervasive, as announced in the opening verse,
"These are the words..." Until chapter 31, the narrative frame
turns out to be minimal, although unmistakable, while the quoted inset proves to be maximal. Moses speaks, bringing to the fore,
in an ultimate speech act, what YHWH entrusted him: "Sur le
devant de la scène parle l'homme sans lequel nous ne pourrions
pas savoir que Dieu a parlé."[31] In so doing, Moses "sets before"
(נתן/שׂים לפני, see 4:8,44; 11:26,32; 30:1,15,19) his audience all it
needs to make the right covenantal choice, and to live according
to it.[32] In Deuteronomy's represented world, this "setting before"
is achieved by Moses' speeches. In the reader's world, this "setting before" is achieved by the reproduction of Moses' speeches.
Dramatic presentation is thus at the core of Deuteronomy's communicational enterprise.[33]

Deuteronomy's appeal to dramatic speech as a modality of narration will elicit, in the present inquiry, determinate interpretative policies:

1. Dramatic speech, which unfolds without the support of narrative comments, has its own way of occupying the represented
stage. In Deuteronomy 29-30, for instance, most of the situation-
al parameters of Moses' speech are found in the speech itself (see
29:9, "You stand this day all of you before YHWH your God: the
heads of your tribes, your elders, and your officers, all the men
of Israel," etc.). No narrator elaborates the details of the scene;
they are provided in the speech itself. Throughout Deuteronomy,
Moses alludes to the act, and to the fact, of his own communication: "this Torah," "this 'book' of the Torah," "these words,

[29] R. Alter, *The Art of Biblical Narrative* (New York: Basic Books, 1981) 67.
[30] Alter, *Narrative*, 63-87.
[31] P. Beauchamp, *L'un et l'autre Testament: 2. Accomplir les Ecritures* (Paris: Seuil, 1990) 314.
[32] See Lenchak, *"Choose Life!,"* 112-18.
[33] N. Lohfink has recently, after these pages were originally written, adopted the categories of "showing" and "telling" in his description of Deuteronomy's "Art des Erzählens" (see "Bund als Vertrag im Deuteronomium," *ZAW* 107 [1995] 218-21).

which I command you this day," etc. Reading Deuteronomy will involve granting these expressions their full dramatic import. Facing these phrases, Deuteronomy's reader is not primarily dealing with a text that imparts self-referential hints, but with a speaking character, who refers to communication *realia* in a world endowed with time and space. In other words, reading will amount to interpreting the speeches in the world they project.

2. Dramatic speech highlights the link of linguistic representation with the linear temporality of hearing and reading. When extensive recourse is made to direct speech, both the narrator behind the scene and the dramatis persona in the limelight concur in bringing everything home according to the sequential order of language. Moses' speeches in Deuteronomy, in particular, develop their line of argument according to a rhetorical progression, with characteristic stages and turning points.[34] Understanding is progressively brought about, at the pace of the speeches' ordered momentum. Like narrative, speech therefore invites an approach along the syntagmatic axis (the *actual* combination of the work's elements), rather than a paradigmatic treatment (directed on the elements themselves, in their *possible* combinations).[35] It is the exegete's temptation to skip the linearity of the reading process (the reader's progressive hermeneutics), and to determine from without, in panoramic view, what is patiently built from within.[36] In an article significantly subtitled "How the order of a text creates its meanings," Menakhem Perry stresses that the verbal elements of the literary text "appear one *after* another, and its semantic complexes (e.g., scenes, ideas, characters, plot, value-judgments) build up 'cumulatively,' through adjustments and readjustments."[37] In the following pages, I will therefore stick as much as possible to the linear unfolding of

---

[34] The rhetorical dimension of Moses' speeches in Deuteronomy has been set into relief by studies such as N. Lohfink, *Das Hauptgebot: Eine Untersuchung literarischer Einleitungsfragen zu Dtn. 5-11* (AnBib 20; Rome: Pontifical Biblical Institute Press, 1963); G. Braulik, *Die Mittel deuteronomischer Rhetorik* (AnBib 68; Rome: Pontifical Biblical Institute Press, 1978); Lenchak, *"Choose Life!"*

[35] About the pair "syntagma"/"paradigm" in Jakobson's theory of language (and about its roots in de Saussure's *Cours de linguistique générale*), see O. Ducrot and T. Todorov, *Encyclopedic Dictionary of the Sciences of Language* (Baltimore: Johns Hopkins University Press, 1979) 106-11.

[36] A survey like G. Braulik's "Die Ausdrücke für 'Gesetz' im Buch Deuteronomium," *Bib* 51 (1970) 39-66, is not entirely free from this tendency.

[37] Perry, "Literary Dynamics," 35.

speech and narrative. The rule will be not to read against, or above, the stream. Things that really matter, it is presumed, will be cleared up in due time and in appropriate fashion. There is more to gain from patient and close reading than from panoramic expounding.

3. Systematization of direct speech in a given narrative amounts to systematization of point of view. What is said by a character is, in most cases, also seen through his point of view. Conveying faithfully the divine revelation (see Deut 1:3), Moses is also a genuine teller, reteller or locutor, with a personal perception of things. "I am a hundred and twenty years old this day; I am no longer able to go out and to come in," old Moses seems to moan; "Moses was a hundred and twenty years old when he died, his eye was not dim, nor his natural force abated," the narrator corrects (34:7). Prophetic faithfulness does not exclude human, all too human, idiosyncrasies. In his *Moses and the Deuteronomist*, Polzin made point of view the key to Deuteronomy's poetics. Resorting to Mikhail Bakhtin's dialogic model, Polzin regards Deuteronomy as the sophisticated conflation of two ideological voices (or points of view), Moses' (in the reported speech) and the Deuteronomist's (in the reporting speech).[38] The book becomes "the repository of a plurality of viewpoints, all working together to achieve an effect on the reader that is multidimensional."[39] Moses' reported voice contrasts with the Deuteronomistic reporting voice as "authoritarian dogmatism" contrasts with "critical traditionalism." In the course of my investigation, I will have to reassess Polzin's thesis on the matter of point of view. Moses, it seems, is more complex and dramatic a figure than Polzin's authoritative dogmatist. Instead of being idiosyncratic, the contrast between reporting and reported speech may well belong to the general contrast between the narrator's omniscience and any character's limitations in the Hebrew Bible.

In Deuteronomy's poetics, the combining of (minimal) omniscient narration and (maximal) dramatic presentation is reflect-

---

[38] See Polzin, *Moses*, 18-24. Polzin primarily refers to V. N. Voloshinov (= M. Bakhtin), *Marxism and the Philosophy of Language* (New York: Seminar Press, 1973) and M. Bakhtin, *Problems of Dostoevsky's Poetics* (Ann Arbor: Ardis, 1973).

[39] Polzin, *Moses*, 27. In Polzin's view, however, the two voices eventually fuse as the book comes to a close: "The ideological composition of the Book of Deuteronomy is essentially monologic" (p. 72).

ed in the framing of the work's sections. The heading in Deut
1:1-5 prefaces the whole book; in its role as a general overture, it
sets up the spatial and temporal parameters of the action and
launches the work's overall poetics—"These are the words." The
reader, however, encounters a similar heading in Deut 4:44-49,
that equally belongs to the book's frame—"And this is the Torah."
He is therefore forced to retrospectively adjust the role of the
opening in Deuteronomy 1 and to record the work's further division. Similar reading operations are prompted by the same type
of headings in 28:69 and 33:1. Deuteronomy thus presents itself
as a string of four Mosaic speeches,[40] each introduced by syntactically analogous superscriptions:[41]

אלה הדברים

אשר דבר משה אל כל ישראל בעבר הירדן (1:1)

וזאת התורה

אשר שם משה לפני בני ישראל ... בצאתם ממצרים (4:44-45)

אלה דברי הברית

אשר צוה יהוה את משה לכרת את בני ישראל בארץ מואב

מלבד הברית

אשר כרת אתם בחרב (28:69)

וזאת הברכה

אשר ברך משה איש האלהים את בני ישראל לפני מותו (33:1)

These are the words
  which Moses spoke to all Israel beyond the Jordan (1:1)

---

[40] The Deuteronomic superscription system was first noticed by P. Kleinert,
*Das Deuteronomium und der Deuteronomiker: Untersuchungen zur alttestamentlichen
Rechts- und Literaturgeschichte* (Bielefeld und Leipzig: Velhagen & Klasing, 1872)
166-67. In recent scholarship, Kleinert's perception of the structure of Deuteronomy has been elaborated by N. Lohfink in various contributions; see for the first,
"Der Bundesschluß im Land Moab: Redaktionsgeschichtliches zu Dt 28,69—
32,47," *BZ* 6 (1962) 32-34, and most recently, "Bund als Vertrag," 218-19. For the
status of Deut 28:69, see H. F. van Rooy, "Deuteronomy 28,69—Superscript or
Subscript," *JNSL* 14 (1988) 215-22, and N. Lohfink's answer, "Dtn 28:69—Überschrift oder Kolophon?," *BN* 64 (1992) 40-52.

[41] It goes without saying that the similar headings that occur within
Moses'speeches (Deut 6:1; 12:1) have no relevance at the level of the overall narrative framing; see Lohfink, "Bundesschluß," 34 n. 11; cf. Olson, *Deuteronomy*,
14-15, who posits a five-superscription frame by including 6:1.

> And this is the Torah
>> which Moses set before the sons of Israel ... when they came
>> out of Egypt (4:44-45)

> These are the words of the covenant
>> which YHWH commanded Moses to make with the people of
>> Israel in the land of Moab
> besides the covenant
>> which he had made with them at Horeb (28:69)

> And this is the blessing
>> with which Moses the man of God blessed the sons of Israel
>> before his death (33:1)[42]

Does the succession of the units in the text entail that the Mosaic speeches also followed each other in their "historical" performance? The categories of "sujet" and "fabula" can help formulate this question with more precision. In the theory of the Russian Formalists, the "sujet" (*sjužet*) is the sequence of motifs as encountered by the reader in a narrative work, in the order and shaping decided on by the author. The "fabula," on the contrary, consists of the same motifs in their "objective" order of occurrence, as progressively and retrospectively reassembled by the reader.[43] In Moses' speech in Deuteronomy 1-4, for instance, "sujet" and "fabula" present inverted temporal sequences. In his retelling of the people's history, Moses reshuffles the order of events, recounting the progression of the people *from* Horeb (Deut 1:6-3:29) before he tells the people's experience *at* Horeb (in Deuteronomy 4). Moses presumably has good (rhetorical) reasons to produce such a "sujet." Along with Moses' audience, the reader of Deuteronomy is also able to reconstruct, in a "fabula," the historical order of Israel's journey. What about the sequence of Moses' speeches, introduced by the four superscriptions? The apparent claim of the narrative is that the recapitulatory and prospective "words" (Deuteronomy 1-4) were delivered prior to the "Torah" (Deuteronomy 5-28), that the conveying of the Torah

---

[42] I will indicate in due time the role of two brief narratorial accounts in Deuteronomy's general structure (Deut 4:41-43 and 32:48-52), introducing respectively the second and the third unit (the headings of which open with a *waw*, "*And* this is the Torah/the blessing").

[43] See especially B. Tomashevsky's "Thématique," in *Théorie de la littérature* (ed. T. Todorov; Paris: Seuil, 1965) 240-42; part of this essay has been reprinted in *Russian Formalist Criticism: Four Essays* (ed. L. T. Lemon and M. J. Reis; Lincoln: University of Nebraska Press, 1965) 61-95.

led up to Moses' "words of the covenant" (Deuteronomy 29-30), and that the process was concluded by the uttering of Moses' "blessing before his death" (Deuteronomy 33-34). Yet, only at the end of the reading process will the reader be able to say whether or not it was so. Only at the end, and probably after intermediate guesses, will he retrospectively produce a "fabula" that might, or might not, parallel the "sujet."

In a contribution significantly entitled "Zur Fabel des Deuteronomiums," Norbert Lohfink makes his case in favor of a "fabula" that, so to speak, permutes the order of the two central units (Deuteronomy 5-28, 29-30).[44] In Lohfink's view, Moses delivered the Torah (Deuteronomy 5-28) *during* the ritual of the covenant referred to in his speech in Deuteronomy 29-30. I will review, and eventually reject, Lohfink's hypothesis in my Chapter 3, when examining the status of the ספר-record in Deuteronomy 27-28 and 29-30. A particular observation, however, is worth anticipating. In Lohfink's opinion, the reordering of the units' sequence is prepared by the form of Deuteronomy's headings. It is his contention that the four superscriptions do not inform us about the sequential order of Deuteronomy's action, but about "Textgattungen"—the literary genre of the four speeches ("words," "Torah," "words of the covenant," "blessing").[45] The effect of this procedure on the "fabula," Lohfink continues, is a kind of "loosening" ("Lockerung"): "Das narrative Grundmuster des Nacheinander könnte durch die Überschriften suspendiert sein."[46] It should be observed, however, that two of the superscriptions do include temporal data bearing on Deuteronomy's represented action. The first heading is concluded by the narratorial statement, "Moses

---

[44] N. Lohfink, "Zur Fabel des Deuteronomiums," *Bundesdokument und Gesetz: Studien zum Deuteronomium* (ed. G. Braulik; Herders Biblische Studien 4; Freiburg: Herder, 1995) 65-78; see also idem, "Bund," 228-33. While adopting the categories of the Russian Formalists, Lohfink points out that Goethe and Schiller used an equivalent "Fabel" category in their mutual correspondence (see "Zur Fabel," 65 n. 1.; "Bund," 229).

[45] Lohfink, "Fabel," 69; see also "Bund," 229.

[46] Lohfink, "Fabel," 69-70. Interestingly enough, Lohfink does not see the uncoupling of "story" and "fabula" at the level of Moses' second and third speeches as a purposeful literary device. He is rather inclined to attribute the phenomenon to genetic factors, i.e., to constraints originating in the "zweifellos höchst komplizierten Wachstumsgeschichte des Texte" ("Bund," 233; see also "Fabel," 74).

undertook (הוֹאִיל) to expound this Torah saying ...” (Deut 1:5).[47]
The Mosaic speech that follows (Deuteronomy 1-4) thus receives
a determinate location in Deuteronomy’s represented time span.
The last heading equally concludes with a similar temporal parameter: “This is the blessing with which Moses the man of God
blessed the sons of Israel *before his death*” (33:1). In other words,
the blessing that follows is the last of Moses’ possible speeches. A
temporal perspective is thus opened in the first superscription
and closed in the last one. As far as these superscriptions and the
speeches they introduce are concerned, “sujet” and “fabula” overlap each other: what comes first in the text comes first in Moses’
represented day; what comes last in the text comes last in Moses’
day (and life). Yet, though a temporal perspective is opened in
the first heading, no guarantee is thus given about the respective
location of the middle units (Deuteronomy 5-28, 29-30) in
Deuteronomy’s “fabula.” The issue has necessarily to be assessed
on actual evidence and in due time (see Chapter Three).

   Whatever the “fabula” that will surface in the end, my description of Moses’ communication act will expressly conform to the
organization of the text marked off by the four superscriptions.
The basic assumption is that these textual indicators, more than
any external patterns transposed to Deuteronomy, lead to the
dynamics of Deuteronomy’s narrative action. The influence of the
Hittite and Neo-Assyrian treaty forms on Deuteronomy, for
instance, is undeniable.[48] Many of Deuteronomy’s themes and
much of its phraseology come under better light when compared
with the treaty literature of the ancient Near East. Yet, when it
comes to the narrative thrust of the text, it is the fourfold division featured by Deuteronomy, and not the generic form of (related) oath and treaty texts, that provides the appropriate guideline.

   Dramatic “showing,” however, does not constitute all of Deuteronomy. Significant switches to the “telling” mode mark the end
of the work.[49] Intrusions by the narrator’s voice at the conclusion

---

[47] About Deut 1:5 as an integral part of Deuteronomy’s first heading, see N.
Lohfink, “Bundesschluß,” 32 n. 2. For the meaning of יאל, Hiphil, as “to under-
take,” see M. Weinfeld, *Deuteronomy 1-11* (AB 5; New York: Doubleday, 1991)
125-26.
[48] The authoritative treatment of this issue is still M. Weinfeld, *Deuteronomy and
the Deuteronomic School* (Oxford: Oxford University Press, 1972) esp. 59-157.
[49] Narratorial intrusions in Moses’ first speech and the brief account in Deut

of Moses' third speech (Deut 31:1 onward), at the close of Moses' Song in Deuteronomy 32, and at the end of Moses' blessing in Deuteronomy 33, re-inscribe Moses' voice in the framing narrative. Special attention will be paid to these narratorial accounts and comments. They tell about Moses what Moses could not tell about himself; they set the dynamics of Moses' speeches within the dynamics of his last words and deeds, following YHWH's last interventions (in Deut 31:14-23; 32:48-52). The end of the story, as well as the end of the work, belongs to the "telling" mode. The framing of history—"There has not arisen a prophet since in Israel like Moses" (34:10)—is the omniscient narrator's prerogative.

c. *Deuteronomy's Integrity and Deuteronomy's Integration within the Pentateuchal Narrative*

Deuteronomy's overture—"These are the words"—launches a distinctive literary work, stamped by its formal integrity. The book is therefore to be read and expounded in a way that enhances its literary autonomy. The interplay of Deuteronomy's own poetic components, from overall plot to lexical texture, is to be presumed totally self-sufficient within the limits of the work. Coleridge's phrase, "each work must contain within itself the reason why it is so and not otherwise," should apply here. On the other hand, Deuteronomy does not open like the Books of Job ("There was a man in the land of Uz"), or Esther ("In the days of Ahasuerus, the Ahasuerus who reigned from India to Ethiopia"), which shift the reader to biblically unprecedented places and times. By summarizing stretches of the narrative found in the Book of Numbers in its opening, Deuteronomy presents itself as something like a rehearsal (and turns out to be a sequel).[50] Whatever the previous status of Deuteronomy (in its genesis),[51] the canonical book is, and discloses, a further unit of Pentateuchal

---

4:41-43 concerning Moses' establishment of cities of refuge in Transjordan complete the picture; they will be treated in Chapter Five and Seven.

[50] In their terseness, the notes in Deut 1:4-5 about the defeat of Sihon, king of the Amorites, and of Og, king of Bashan, act as reminders of a known story—the story which is read in Num 21:21-35.

[51] See for instance the claim in recent Pentateuchal criticism that Deuteronomy represents the first redactional stage of what, after the later preposing of Genesis-Numbers, became the Pentateuch. See especially M. Rose, *Deuteronomist und Jahwist: Untersuchungen zu den Berührungspunkten beider Literaturwerke* (ATANT 67;

narrative. Deuteronomy's matter and manner confirm the situation of the book in the narrative canon (and vice versa): what Moses tells in Deuteronomy 1-4 and in Deuteronomy 5-11, he actually retells;[52] and what he tells in a disorderly fashion, he actually retells on the basis of a known ordered sequence.[53]

Deuteronomy enjoys therefore the special status of these works which "lead a dual existence both as separate, fully realized wholes and as parts of a larger scheme."[54] In my inquiry I shall accordingly enhance the two frameworks in which Deuteronomy can be read. Poetic components will be assessed in their primary setting, that is, within Deuteronomy's narrative and rhetorical economy. They will also be appraised against the background of the preceding Pentateuchal narrative. The discreteness of Deuteronomy will thus be emphasized,[55] just as its closing role within the overall Pentateuch narrative. Within the Pentateuchal context, the principle of temporality in reading (readers progress in a text in the light of what they have already been told) operates exactly as in the smaller context of Deuteronomy. As a matter of principle, whatever comes "before" in the Pentateuchal sequence forms the literary background of what comes "after." Coming to Moses'

Zürich: Theologische Verlag, 1981); idem, "La croissance du corpus historiographique de la Bible—une proposition," *RTP* 118 (1986) 217-26; Th. Römer, *Israels Väter: Untersuchungen zur Väterthematik im Deuteronomium und in der deuteronomistischen Tradition* (OBO 99; Freiburg: Universitätsverlag; Göttingen: Vandenhoeck & Ruprecht, 1990); idem, "Quête des origines," 65-98.

[52] Apropos of Deuteronomy 1-3, L. Perlitt avers: "Es gibt hier keinen erzählenden Stoff ohne Parallele in Num." ("Deuteronomium 1-3 im Streit der exegetischen Methoden," 158). See also Beauchamp, *Testament (2)*, 317, and the chart in C. Dogniez and M. Harl, *La Bible d'Alexandrie: 5. Le Deutéronome* (Paris: Cerf, 1992) 104-105.

[53] See M. Sternberg, "Time and Space in Biblical (Hi)story Telling: The Grand Chronology," *The Book and the Text: The Bible and Literary Theory* (ed. R. Schwartz; Oxford: Blackwell, 1990) 138.

[54] D. H. Richter, *Fable's End: Completeness and Closure in Rhetorical Fiction* (Chicago: The University of Chicago Press, 1974) 177.

[55] In his *Expositional Modes and Temporal Ordering in Fiction* (Baltimore: Johns Hopkins University Press, 1978) 2-5, M. Sternberg examines the strategies of authors who make use of historical sources (e.g., Shakespeare), and authors such as Trollope, Balzac, or Faulkner, who repeatedly carry over "not only settings but whole casts of characters and clusters of incidents from one work to another of the same cycle" (p. 2). He concludes that "writers as a rule take the necessary precautions to render each of their works as expositionally autonomous as possible, even when the carrying over of characters and fictive world involves no divergence from previous conceptions" (p. 3). The rule, as I shall indicate, also applies to Deuteronomy.

words in the plain of Moab, "after he had defeated Sihon the king of the Amorites ... and Og the king of Bashan" (Deut 1:4), the reader is prepared to listen to Moses' telling of the conquest of Transjordan (Deut 2:24-3:22) as a *retelling*, since Num 21:21-35 made him acquainted with the facts of the matter. Coming to Moses' blessing "before his death" (Deut 33:1), the reader will equally remember that other figures in Israel's story also imparted a blessing "before their death" (see Gen 27:7,10; Genesis 49).[56]

As the title of Polzin's *Moses and the Deuteronomist* announces, the context of his Deuteronomy is Noth's "Deuteronomistic History" (DtrH), which runs from Deuteronomy through Kings, and he assumes "from the start that the Deuteronomic [*sic*] History is a unified literary work."[57] However appropriate in a genetic approach, this segmenting of the narrative material represents an abstraction with respect to the organization of the canonical Hebrew Bible. Deuteronomy functions in this organization as a sequel to Genesis-Numbers, bringing to an end the foundational patriarchal and Mosaic history. And it is in its capacity of conclusion to the Pentateuch that Deuteronomy introduces the so-called Former Prophets (Joshua through Kings). The belonging of Deuteronomy to the Pentateuch is not only a matter of position in the canonical sequence; it is also inscribed in Deuteronomy's texture. In the concluding verses of the work, for instance, Deuteronomy's narrator creates significant intra-Pentateuchal connections (see Deut 34:9 as a reference to Num 27:18, 23; Deut 34:11 as an echo to Moses' *geste* in Exodus).[58] Thus the DtrH hypothesis, which is a genetic hypothesis, does not provide

---

[56] There is therefore no relation whatsoever between narrative anteriority or posteriority, and genetic dependency. The literary sequence in the (canonical) Hebrew narrative may ascribe to genetically related texts narrative functions that go against the time-line of the genetic relationship. The Joseph story (Genesis 37-47; Genesis 50), for instance, is often thought of as a very late romance linking the patriarchal and the Exodus cycles. It nevertheless functions as an "early" given for texts coming after it in the narrative sequence (and possibly written before it).

[57] Polzin, *Moses*, 18.

[58] See E. Blum's assessment of Deut 31:14-15,23 and 34:10(-12) (*Studien zur Komposition des Pentateuch* [BZAW 189; Berlin: de Gruyter, 1990] 77-88). In Blum's view, these verses are part of a bigger constellation that includes Exodus 33-34 and Numbers 11-12, emanating from a so-called *D-Komposition* (KD), a post-Deuteronomistic composition of the Pentateuch, still in the Deuteronomistic tradition. F. García López has contended that KD pervades more of Deuteronomy 34 (it arguably comprises 34:1b-4 and 34:10-12) ("Deut 34, Dtr History and the Pen-

the soundest ground for an approach to Deuteronomy's overall poetics.[59] The determination of Deuteronomy's narrator and "implied author" as the "Deuteronomist"[60] represents another importation of secondary data into the text's inner claim. In its canonical and narrative claim, Deuteronomy is not tied to a specific, "Deuteronomistic," voice (pertaining to the so-called Deuteronomistic corpus), but to the voice that so far conducted the Pentateuchal narrative. The undivided character of the Pentateuchal narrative voice shows in Deuteronomy's last verses. The voice that discloses the unmatched status of Deuteronomy's character—"There has not arisen a prophet since in Israel like Moses" (34:10)—associates Moses' uniqueness to his leadership in the Exodus venture—"for all the signs and the wonders which YHWH sent him to do in the land of Egypt, to Pharaoh and to all his servants and to all his land, and for all the mighty power and all the great and terrible deeds which Moses wrought in the sight of all Israel" (34:11-12).

d. *From Beginning to End*

In its role as representing medium and frame, Deuteronomy features a characteristic beginning: "These are the words" (Deut 1:1). The work equally stages, in its opening verses, the beginning of the represented action: "Moses undertook to expound this Torah" (1:5). Dealing with the theme of written communication, my inquiry will focus on a motif essentially attached to the end, and not to the beginning, of the book's text and story. Yet the beginning of a work necessarily has, and possibly brings out, a link with its future completion. A literary work, be it a scroll or, in our "modern" sense, a *codex*, cannot conceal its being just a piece of literature, a discrete unit of written communication between beginning and end. Similarly, Deuteronomy is a separate book within a greater narrative unit. "It is one of the great charms of

---

tateuch," *Studies in Deuteronomy: In Honour of C. J. Labuschagne on the Occasion of his 65th Birthday* [ed. F. García Martínez and al.; VTSup 53; Leiden: Brill, 1994] 47-61).

[59] See the remarks by G. N. Knoppers, *Two Nations under God: The Deuteronomistic History of Solomon and the Dual Monarchies. Volume 1. The Reign of Solomon and the Rise of Jeroboam* (HSM 52; Atlanta; Scholars Press, 1993) 29.

[60] See Polzin, *Moses*, 18-24.

books," Frank Kermode writes, "that they have to end."[61] The material limitations are indeed, to our readers's pleasure, the outer side of the inner necessity to bring things to a conclusion. A narrative beginning is in that sense the first element of what irreversibly, still in many cases silently, drives the reader toward the end. The domination of the end, as Ann Jefferson avers, is a decisive dimension in the act of reading: "Narrative is more than a mere collection of motifs, devices or functions, more than a simple sequence of actions; it is an end-dominated collection or sequence, and this domination of the end will affect the reading of all that precedes it."[62]

Deuteronomy's beginning makes explicit what it could have concealed. The book announces from the outset a definite, and therefore limited, content: "*These* are the words that Moses ...." We know furthermore from the start that, within a day, Moses achieved what he had to achieve: "On the first day of the eleventh month, Moses spoke to the people of Israel according to all (ככל אשר) that YHWH had given him in commandment to them" (1:3). No detail whatsoever is thereby given about the ending of the work (history, no less than stories, has unpredictable outcomes). Yet the omniscient narrator makes clear that the process of communication he records is a process brought to completion, "according to all" YHWH commanded to convey. How Moses performed this command is still to be read. In the present inquiry I will pay special attention to the ways and means whereby the announced completion is actually realized. Deuteronomy is the story of a communication process brought to its end, as authoritatively told in 31:24, "When Moses had finished (ככלות) writing the words of this Torah on a 'book,' to the very end," and in 32:45, "When Moses had finished (ויכל) speaking all (כל) these words to all Israel." As it turns out, the completion of Moses' prophetic mission coincides with the demise of the prophet. An unparalleled prophetic age comes to its end and, with it, the Pentateuch: "And there has not arisen a prophet since in Israel like Moses, whom YHWH knew face to face" (34:10). More than any

---

[61] F. Kermode, *The Sense of an Ending: Studies in the Theory of Fiction* (Oxford: Oxford University Press, 1966) 23.

[62] A. Jefferson, "*Mise en abyme* and the Prophetic in Narrative," *Style* 17 (1983) 196.

book in the Hebrew Bible, Deuteronomy brings into play what might be called the poetics of the end.

*

The investigation unfolds in seven chapters, and it does so in two stages. The first six chapters center on the process of communication *in* Deuteronomy, that is, on Moses' transaction with the sons of Israel in the plains of Moab. The seventh and last chapter considers the fuller picture by taking into account *Deuteronomy* as communication—the Book of Deuteronomy in its address to the reader. More precisely, the final chapter describes the interaction of Moses and the book's narrator in their respective communicational enterprises. From One to Six, and then to Seven, the plan is thus to characterize Deuteronomy's poetics of "the wheel within the wheel."

Chapter One focuses on Moses' recourse to *oral* communication, and puts the address in Moab back in its dramatic context. Chapters Two through Four retrace the emergence of the theme of *written* communication in Deuteronomy, following the text-continuum. Chapter Two surveys the references to written communication in Moses' "Torah speech" (Deuteronomy 27-28 not included). Chapter Three deals with the mentions of the ספר, or Torah "record," in Deuteronomy 27-28 (in the "Torah speech") and in Deuteronomy 29-30 (in Moses' "words of the covenant"). Chapter Four examines the most eventful section in Deuteronomy's narrative—Deut 31:1-32:47. Moses' written and oral communication comes to completion, yet only after a dramatic intervention by YHWH. Chapter Five bears on 33:1-34:12 and engages a basic question: why is the end of the communication of the Torah not the end of Deuteronomy? Why does Deuteronomy's overall plot include the story of Moses' demise? From plot, Chapter Six switches to character, widening the narrative framework. The end of Deuteronomy subtly echoes the conclusion of Genesis. The originality of Moses' prophetic mission stands out against the background of the patriarchal saga. Yet Deuteronomy is more than a story about communication; it is communication. Chapter Seven, as I said above, considers the analogy between Deuteronomy's "inner" and "outer wheel," and provides a general conclusion by examining the issue of the "book a within the book."

CHAPTER ONE

"THE WORDS THAT MOSES *SPOKE*"
ORAL COMMUNICATION IN DEUTERONOMY'S REPRESENTED WORLD

> Sprich auch du,
> sprich als letzter,
> sag deinen Spruch.
> . . . .
> Nun aber schrumpft der Ort,
> wo du stehst:
> Wohin jetzt, Schattenentblösster,
> wohin?
> Steige. Taste empor.
>
> Paul Celan, "Sprich auch du"

"These are the words that Moses spoke (דבר)" (Deut 1:1). Deuteronomy's opening ushers in a distinctively oral communication. The issue of *written* communication that constitutes the proper topic of this study, and that will be treated in the following chapters, is part of a larger communication scheme. In Deuteronomy's scheme, as can be surmised from Deut 1:1, (oral) speech is the leading medium.[1] Speech is to be understood here as "represented speech," that is, as Deuteronomy's way of (re)presenting Moses' ultimate "words." The historiographical claim of Deuteronomy is inseparable from the book's representational options —the first of them being the staging of Moses as an orator. This narrative setting can be critically compared with extra-biblical data; it cannot, however, be measured by comparative data—a narrative is also and always idiosyncratic. Outside of the Bible, for instance, no mention has been found indicating that, in the ancient Near East, collections of laws were promulgated orally ("orally" meaning here "without the mediation of a written record"). Yet Moses does precisely that, conveying orally, without

---

[1] As it will turn out, everything transmitted by Moses is first transmitted orally. Commitment to writing occurs as the outcome of previous "words of mouth." The one exception is represented by the Song of Moses in Deuteronomy 32 (see Deut 31:22 and my comments in Chapter Four).

any written reminder, an extensive collection of laws (that YHWH revealed to him at Horeb forty years ago!). Oral procedures, on the other hand, played a definite role in the making of covenants, as is evidenced in the inscription of Sefire (recording the treaty between KTK and Arpad): "Thus have we spoken [and thus have we writ]ten" (I C 1).[2] Covenantal oral procedures are found in Deuteronomy, where Moses notably records God's and Israel's respective oaths (Deut 26:17-19). It is, however, the privilege of a narrative such as Deuteronomy to present and represent things in a particular way, in order to achieve what a narrative can achieve. The represented story can be in total keeping, in partial keeping, or even at odds with the cultural and institutional procedures of the time (as far as we know them). From *Gilgamesh* (Tablet XI) and the Epic of *Erra* to the Book of Job to Joseph Conrad's *Lord Jim*, narratives have shown a special affinity for long speeches, at times presumably longer than life. Narrative characters, God included, are often endowed with impressive oratorical talents. With such a convention the reader is somehow the winner, since reading then amounts to watching the vivid birth of "words." It is my contention that Deuteronomy's poetics is built on such a representational option, and it is in this literary perspective that "speech" will here be described.

In this first chapter, I will review some significant aspects of Moses' oral communication. Moses' "words" are introduced as oral utterance, without reference to any previous, parallel, or, for that matter, future commitment to writing. In true "showing" fashion, the Mosaic speeches set up their own narrative context, and, in so doing, they disclose their dramatic dimension. In their prophetic authority, these speeches all proceed from a foundational scene—the revelation at Horeb—which is (re)told by Moses in due course. At the core of their authority lies a subtle dialectic between YHWH's and Moses' voices.

---

[2] Text and translation in J. A. Fitzmyer, *The Aramaic Inscriptions of Sefire* (BibOr 19; Rome: Pontifical Biblical Institute, 1967) 19. The oral transaction documented in the text of Sefire, however, is not to be confused with the oral procedures enjoined *by* covenantal (written) records—the oral is then contained within and conceived by the textual. On this point, see the survey of vow, pledge and assertion formulae in S. Parpola and K. Watanabe, *Neo-Assyrian Treaties and Loyalty Oaths* (SAA 2; Helsinki: Helsinki University Press, 1988) xxxviii-xli.

1. *Oral Communication?*

In recent scholarship, it has been contended that Moses' act of communication includes writing from the start: Moses began to write as soon as he began to speak. The hypothesis in question hangs on the translation of a single word, the verb באר in Deut 1:5, and has been notably defended by Siegfried Mittmann.[3] Commenting on Deut 1:5 (הואיל משה באר את התורה הזאת), generally translated as "Moses undertook to expound this Torah"), Mittmann questions the link usually established between the Hebrew verb באר and the Akkadian verb *bâru(m)*, "deutlich machen, überführen,"[4] and rather sees in באר "eine spezielle Art schriftlicher Aufzeichnung."[5] Mittmann himself did not connect the issue of the translation of באר in 1:5 with the overall issue of written communication in Deuteronomy, but the connection is suggested by scholars like Christoph Dohmen and Manfred Oeming:

> Möglicherweise will der Autor an dieser Stelle bewußt den Beginn eines Verschriftungsvorganges, wenn auch vage, anzeigen, damit dieser—wenn auch nicht näher präzisierte—Vorgang dann in seinem Ergebnis mit dem Abschluß der Verkündigung festgehalten werden kann, wie dies Dtn 31,24 mit seiner Vorstellung von der Vollendung anzeigt.[6]

Mittmann believes that Hab 2:2, כתוב חזון ובאר על הלחות, provides a semantic parallelism between כתב and באר. "Write down the vision"

---

[3] S. Mittmann, *Deuteronomium 1.1-6.3: Literarkritisch und Traditionsgeschichtlich Untersucht* (BZAW 139; Berlin: de Gruyter, 1975) 14.

[4] See *bâru(m)*, *AHW*, 1.108b-109a (among the nuances under III D: "genau angeben", "genau feststellen", "jmd. einer Tat überführen", "jmdm. bestätigen").

[5] Mittmann, *Deuteronomium*, 14; J. L. Palache, *Semantic Notes on the Hebrew Lexicon* (Leiden: Brill, 1959) 9, conjectures the meaning of "to engrave" from Deut 27:8 and Hab 2:2; D. Cohen, *Dictionnaire des racines sémitiques* (Paris: Mouton, 1976) 2.41, indicates the Akkadian *bâru*, "paraître sûr, prouvé", but, referring to Palache and postulating a connection with the roots BR- ("les notions de 'creuser, percer, couper' se retrouvent dans quelques rac. comportant la séquence BR" [p. 2.80]), he suggests the semantic development of "tailler, inciser, graver" and eventually "expliquer" (!). Among recent translations, see the new edition of *BJ* (1973), where Cazelles translates as "Moïse se décida à graver cette Loi," what he first rendered by "Moïse commença à promulguer cette Loi" in the 1956 edition; see also the *Einheitsübersetzung* (1980): "... begann Mose ... diese Weisung aufzuschreiben."

[6] C. Dohmen and M. Oeming, *Biblischer Kanon: warum und wozu? Eine Kanontheologie* (QD 137; Freiburg: Herder, 1992) 65. See also Mayes, *Deuteronomy*, 116 (about Deut 1:5), 375 (apropos of 31:9).

would be reformulated as "'transcribe' [it] on the tablets." Another hint in favor of such a semantic equivalence is allegedly found in Deut 27:8, וכתבת על האבנים את כל דברי התורה הזאת באר היטב. In Mittmann's view, "You shall write" ("on the stones all the words of this Torah)" is specified by באר, "das demnach auch hier nur eine dem כתב verwandte Tätigkeit bezeichnen kann."[7]

How is Mittmann's hypothesis to be assessed? His rendering of Deut 1:5 does not take advantage of any of the ancient versions. Jerome's Vulgate, which reads *explanare*, the Targum Onqelos, which has פרש ית אולפן, "he made the teaching explicit," and the Targum Neofiti I with למפרשה, "to explain",[8] all echo (whatever the actual dependencies) the Septuagint's rendering of באר as διασαφῆσαι, "to make explicit, to explain."[9] In my view, Perlitt has convincingly refuted Mittmann's reference to a semantic parallelism between באר and כתב, both in Hab 2:2 and in Deut 27:8.[10] Mittmann's interpretation, Perlitt argues, creates a repetition in Hab 2:2—"Write down the vision; 'write' on the tablets"—that has no special relevance in the verse's context. The Septuagint construes the form באר as an adverb, σαφῶς, "explicitly, clearly," and accordingly renders ובאר as an adverbial interpolation, γράψον ὅρασιν καὶ σαφῶς ἐπί πυξίον, "Write the vision, *and clearly*, on the tablets."[11] Such an emphasis on the readability of the inscription is justified by the ending of the sentence, "so he may run who reads it." In similar fashion Perlitt questions Mittmann's reference

---

[7] Mittmann, *Deuteronomium*, 14. A. Lemaire renders ובאר in Hab 2:2 as "und ritze" ("and incise," in the sense of "taking notes" before making a fair copy [= כתוב]), but admits that the sequence of Hab 2:2 would then state the process in the wrong order ("Vom Ostrakon zur Schriftrolle: Überlegungen zur Entstehung der Bibel," *XXII. Deutscher Orientalistentag Tübingen 21-25 März 1981* [ZMDGSup 5; Stuttgart: Steiner, 1985] 116). More recently, Lemaire has rendered באר היטב in Deut 27:8 as "très distinctement," coming over to the traditional interpretation of באר ("Les inscriptions sur plâtre de Deir 'Alla et leur signification historique et culturelle", *The Balaam Text from Deir 'Alla Re-Evaluated: Proceedings of the International Symposium held at Leiden 21-24 August 1989* [ed. J. Hoftijzer and G. van der Kooij; Leiden: Brill, 1991] 54).

[8] Neofiti I specifies: "Moses undertook to explain the '*book*' (ספר) of this Torah, saying ..." The Targum apparently has its way of getting the issue of oral/written communication in Deuteronomy straight; it supposes a Torah "book" written before the start of Moses' oral expounding. Yet this anticipation of the written record undermines Deuteronomy's presentation, namely its determination to let the reader relate to Moses' Torah as to an "oral Torah" (in Deuteronomy's represented world), prior to any commitment to writing.

[9] Targum Pseudo-Jonathan has למלפא, "to teach, to instruct."

[10] Perlitt, *Deuteronomium*, 22-23.

to a semantic parallelism in Deut 2:8. "In 27,8 steht באר ... nicht parallel zu וכתבת, sondern zu היטב, das auch (und nur) in Dtn 9,21; 13,15; 17,4; 19;18; 2Kön 11,18 adverbiell gebraucht wird."[12] The Septuagint construes the double absolute infinitive באר היטב as a double adverb: σαφῶς σφόδρα.[13] The RSV translation of Deut 27:8, "And you shall write upon the stones all the words of this law very plainly" (see also NJPSV) is thus totally justified.[14] In conclusion, *pace* Mittmann, the rendering of באר as "make explicit, expound," and of Deut 1:5b as "Moses undertook to expound this Torah"[15] is supported by the Akkadian *bâru*, by the ancient versions, and by the examination of parallel occurrences. In addition, as pointed out by Amsler, the immediate context apparently excludes the reference to a written medium: "Moses undertook to expound this Torah, *saying* (לאמר) ..."[16] What Moses undertakes is thus an oral exposition, the one that immediately follows, quoted in direct speech.[17]

A mention of an inceptive writing by Moses, like the one Mittmann projects into the text, would have created a specific set

---

[11] See the translation by W. Rudolph, *Micha—Nahum—Habakuk—Zephanja* (KAT 13/3; Gütersloh: Gerd Mohn, 1975) 211, "Schreibe die Offenbarung, und zwar deutlich, auf die Tafeln." E. Dhorme, *La Bible: L'Ancien Testament II* (Paris: Gallimard, 1959) 807 n. 2, discerns the interpolation of an imperative: "Ecris une vision, rends[-la] claire, sur des tablettes."

[12] Perlitt, *Deuteronomium*, 22.

[13] An analogous sequence of absolute infinitives in *casus adverbialis* is found in Deut 9:21, ואכת אתו טחון היטב, "and I crushed it, grinding it very small."

[14] See also Dhorme's translation: "Puis tu écriras sur les pierres toutes les paroles de cette Loi bien clairement"; TOB construes באר as an imperative: "expose-les bien."

[15] As pointed out by Weinfeld, *Deuteronomy*, 126 (with a reference to *GKC* § 120 *g, h*), the literal rendering of MT should be, "Moses undertook, he expounded this Torah." באר is indeed vocalized as a finite verb (בֵּאר). About the asyndetic coordination of הואיל, "to be willing to, to begin," with a finite verb, see Jouon—Muraoka § 177 *d*.

[16] Amsler, "Loi orale," 52 n. 4.

[17] Is the speech in question to be considered a constitutive part of the Torah ("this Torah"), as is sometimes contended? See for instance F. Crüsemann, *Die Tora: Theologie und Sozialgeschichte des alttestamentlichen Gesetzes* (Munich: Kaiser, 1992) 385, "Mit dem letzten Wort (*lēmōr*) wird ab v.6 folgende Rede als Beginn der Tora bezeichnet. Damit ist der hier einsetzende und die ersten drei Kapitel des Deuteronomiums umfassende Geschichtsrüberblick ganz eindeutig Teil der Tora selbst." This view overlooks the precise bearing of the sentence, "Moses undertook to expound this Torah, saying: ..." What is quoted is the *expounding* of "this Torah," not the Torah itself. The formal identification of the announced Torah apparently requires further parameters.

of expectations as to the represented act of communication. It
would notably have engendered a kind of discomfort in the reader's mind regarding the communication in question: do we have
to rely on two channels of communication? Do the oral and the
written messages overlap? Are the quoted words the written or the
oral words of Moses, or both? Deuteronomy, which ties the reader to Moses' oral performance, launches a simpler *contrat de lecture*. All of Moses' communication is (for the time being) conveyed straightforwardly in what Moses says, that is, in what the
anonymous narrator liberally, and reliably quotes. What is read is
what was heard.[18] This initial, basic representational convention,
I will show, is the one that makes the ensuing sophisticated variations possible.

2. *Momentum and Counter-Momentum*

In the first speech act cited by the narrator in Deuteronomy,
Moses tells YHWH's departure order from Horeb: "'You have
stayed long enough at this mountain; turn and take your journey... . Behold, I have set the land before you; go in and take
possession of the land which YHWH swore to your fathers, to Abraham, to Isaac and to Jacob, to give to them and to their descendants after them'" (Deut 1:6-8). By selecting this "turning point"

---

[18] This does not imply in turn that the quotes by Moses (citing himself, God
or the people) are equally reliable. "The Bible," Sternberg writes, "always says the
truth in that its narrator is absolutely and straightforwardly reliable" (*Poetics*, 51);
Moses, as a character, does not share the narrator's reliability. When it comes to
a quotation *by* a character in the Bible (as in any piece of omniscient narration),
the opening of quotes, or, in biblical parlance, the use of the "transformer" לאמר,
"saying," does not warrant the reproduction of what was actually heard. The
appeal to quoted direct speech often proceeds from discursive strategies that have
nothing to do with the purpose of (actual) literal reproduction. For the "direct
speech fallacy," see M. Sternberg, "Point of View and the Indirections of Direct
Speech," *Language and Style* 15 (1982) 67-117; idem, "Proteus in Quotation-Land:
Mimesis and the Forms of Reported Discourse," *Poetics Today* 3 (1982) 107-56. To
be sure, Moses, as announced in Deut 1:3, "spoke to the people of Israel according to all that YHWH had given him in commandment to them (אותו אלהם ...
צוה)." This narrational statement warrants that Moses transmitted what God *commanded him concerning Israel*, no more no less. Such a statement, however, does
not by itself warrant a systematic and literal reproduction of God's utterances
(the model of divine dictation is foreign to Deuteronomy). And in addition to
what he has to convey in prophetic faithfulness, Moses apparently tells many other things in his Deuteronomic speeches.

as the point of departure in his storytelling, Moses aligns his
speech with the initial impetus from YHWH that had driven the
people of Israel toward the promised land. By restating in Moab
what YHWH had said in Horeb, Moses' speech takes over from
God's impulse and lends it momentum. Still, the reader quickly
learns that this momentum includes a dramatic counter-momentum. The border which the people are destined to pass over is
the border which Israel's leader may not cross. That Moses will
not cross the Jordan River is announced right away, in a divine
speech reported by the prophet: "You also shall not go in there.
Joshua the son of Nun, who stands before you, he shall enter;
encourage him, for he shall cause Israel to inherit it" (Deut
1:37-38). In Deut 3:23-26, after an abortive plea by the prophet,
God declares the question of Moses' entrance into the land a
closed issue: "Enough! Never speak to me of this matter again!"
(3:26). As in 1:37-38, the correlative to the ban placed upon Moses
is the reference to Joshua's mission: "For you shall not go over
this Jordan. But commission Joshua, and encourage and strength-
en him; for he shall go over at the head of the people" (3:27-28).
Moses did not succeed in convincing God to let him enter the
land.[19] The irony is that he is now entrusted not only with the
animating of Joshua (as in 1:38, "encourage him"), but also with
the formal appointing of Joshua as the alternative leader: "Commission Joshua (וצו את יהושע)" (3:28).[20] In giving a detailed account
of the affair, Moses thus leaves no doubt: his act of communication is a valedictory speech, in the full sense of the word. He has
to impart to the audience a sense of momentum toward a land
he will not reach; he has to prepare the people for a future he
will not share. The end, that is, the parting between Moses and
the people, between the speaker and the audience, is present from
the beginning, and has the Jordan River as its symbol.

Moses further tells that his non-crossing means that he will die

---

[19] See the analysis in N. Lohfink, "Die deuteronomistische Darstellung des
Übergangs der Führung Israels von Moses auf Josue: Ein Beitrag zur alttestamentlichen Theologie des Amtes," *Scholastik* 37 (1962) 41, 43.

[20] For the presentation of צוה + a person as direct object as signalling the
appointment of someone to a new function, see Mayes, *Deuteronomy*, 147; see also
N. Lohfink (who speaks of "Rechtsakt"), "Zur Fabel in Dtn 31-32," *Konsequente
Traditionsgeschichte: Festschrift für Klaus Baltzer zum 65. Geburtstag* (OBO 126; ed. R.
Bartelmus and al.; Freiburg: Universitätsverlag; Göttingen: Vandenhoeck &
Ruprecht, 1993) 273 (apropos of the occurrences of the verb in 31:14, 23).

on the eastern bank of the Jordan: כי אנכי מת בארץ הזאת אינני עבר
את הירדן, "For I shall die in this land; I shall not cross the Jordan"
(4:22). Unlike the account for his non-entry into the land, Moses'
disclosure about his death is not presented and conveyed as the
outcome of a divine revelation. Moses' death is a *muerte anuncia-
da* without being, in Moses' discourse, something positively announced by God.[21] Death is on the horizon (how could it not
be?), Moses tells his audience. In Moses' sentence, the link
between death and non-crossing is left unspecified; the two parts
of the sentence are juxtaposed, without even the usual connecting "ו." Will Moses' death take place before the people's crossing—"I shall die in this land *and therefore* I shall not cross the Jordan"? Will Moses die of old age after the people's crossing—"I
shall die in this land *since* I shall not cross the Jordan"? When it
comes to his death, the prophet is unusually stingy with authorized particulars. Regarding this point, more is to come in Deuteronomy, revealing Moses' procrastination about the timing, and
the rationale, of his own death.

Moses' communication, the reader comes to know, unfolds within a unity of time (the day announced in Deut 1:3), and within
a unity of space (Moses is near the Jordan River he will not cross).
On the narrative stage, Moses himself knows that he has reached
the parting point. Speaking, he progressively discloses the necessity that underlies his own speech. This necessity is complex and
results from the combining of two opposite, still divinely driven,
forces: the momentum of the people's entry into the land, and
the counter-momentum of the prophet's destiny outside of the

---

[21] Since Numbers 27, the reader of the Pentateuch knows with Moses (and
with Moses alone, since the prophet does not make the people privy to God's
announcement) that Moses' death will follow his climbing the mountain of
Abarim, "Go up into this mountain of Abarim, and see the land which I have
given to the people of Israel. And when you have seen it, you also shall be gathered to your people" (Num 27:12-13). When giving the same order in Moses'
account in Deuteronomy, YHWH speaks only in terms of non-crossing: "Go up
to the top of Pisgah, and lift up your eyes westward and northward and southward and eastward and behold it with your eyes; for you shall not go over this
Jordan" (Deut 3:27). The theme of death does not occur in Moses' (re)telling,
which, on the other hand, discloses other particulars of YHWH's injunction. Is
the blank about the death motif a datum without any real relevance in Deuteronomy? Or does this blank represent a wishful omission by Moses? Further developments in the speeches and in the narrative, and they alone, may answer these
questions.

land.[22] Moses' recourse to an oral address is in no way supererogatory; his face-to-face relationship with the people of Israel, he
knows, will not be repeated. Oral communication in Deuteronomy thus proceeds from the dramatic necessity into which God has
led his prophet.

3. *Moses' Prophetic Credentials*

In Deut 1:6-7, Moses opens his retelling by bringing his audience
back to a "point of departure" which is itself a commandment to
depart: "YHWH our God said to us in Horeb: 'You have stayed
long enough at this mountain; turn and take your journey.'" Moses
then retraces the journey of the sons of Israel, up to the geographical point where he presently stands and speaks: "So we
remained in the valley opposite Beth-peor" (3:29). "The verse
closes the retrospect which began with 1[6]," Samuel Driver writes,
"and specifies more closely than had been done in 1[5], the spot
which the Israelites had now reached, and at which the discours-
es of Dt. were delivered (cf. 4[46])."[23] Moses and his audience do
not budge an inch during the speech, but the narrative evocation
of the journey sets Israel's future, and Moses' current speech about
this future, within a definite perspective.[24]

In Deuteronomy 4 the two extreme points of the journey, Horeb
and Moab, are connected to each other with full "interface," since
what happens at both places is a communication made of דברים,
"words."[25] In Deuteronomy, the Sinai/Horeb event is reduced to

---

[22] Since Numbers 27:12-13, moreover, the reader of the Pentateuch knows,
with Moses, that the proximity of the mountain overlooking the Jordan draws
Moses' death near. The omission of the theme of Moses' death in Deut 3:27
deceives the prophet's audience—not the prophet and the reader, who are both
in the know. The spatial parameter—the Jordan River—is therefore compound-
ed with a temporal one, the imminence of Moses' death. And so it turns out in
the narrative. Speaking on "this day," it will be revealed, Moses spoke the day of
his death (see in 31:14; 32:48 the progressive announcement, to Moses and to
the reader, of Moses' death "that very day" [32:48]).

[23] Driver, *Deuteronomy*, 61; for the geographical indications, see also Weinfeld,
Deuteronomy, 192.

[24] See Moses' injunction to Joshua in Deut 3:21-22 (echoing his previous injunction to the people in 1:29-31) which draws the moral from the (retold) story:
YHWH will act on the other side of the Jordan as he acted in Transjordan; Joshua
has to act accordingly.

[25] Within Moses' first represented speech, the substantive דברים(ם)/דבר is
attached to YHWH's communication (Deut 4:10, 12, 13, 36) as it is attached to
Moses' (4:2).

its communicational essence, i.e., perceptible "words": "Then YHWH spoke to you out of the midst of the fire; you heard a sound/voice of words (קול דברים), but saw no form" (4:12; see also 4:15).[26] In Exodus 19-20, the theophanic "sound(s)" or "voice(s)" (קול[ו]ת, ק[ו]ל), even when uttered by God (19:19), have definite similarities with the *unarticulated* blast of thunder (see 19:16, 19; 20:18).[27] In Moses' retelling in Deut 4:12, the vocable קול becomes the construct state of the substantive דברים ("the sound of the words"), and is thus associated with the phenomenon of the *articulated* voice: "you heard a 'sound'/'voice' of words (קול דברים), but saw no form; there was only a 'voice' (קול)" (Deut 4:12; see also 4:33, 36). The theophany is accordingly presented as (totally) linguistically articulated. As such, the revelation at Horeb becomes thoroughly compatible with Moses' linguistic reporting in Moab. From one event to the other, no systematic loss whatever is to be expected. Moses' speech act is furthermore the *authorized* conveying of the foundational speech act event. "And now, O Israel," Moses warns, "give heed to the statutes and the ordinances which I *teach* (מלמד) you" (4:1). In so doing, Moses carries out God's command at Horeb: "And YHWH commanded me at that time to *teach* (ללמד) you statutes and ordinances, that you might do them in the land which you are going over to possess" (4:14). In Deuteronomy 4, however, nothing leaks out from the *content* of divine communication. At this stage, Moses lays down the basic relationship between the two speech events and brings to the fore the wonder of divine communication through קול, "voice" and דברים, "words" (see 4:33, 36).

In the second of his represented speeches (that opens in Deut 5:1), Moses for the first time discloses, in direct speech, YHWH's actual stipulations (the "ten words," to start with). The Horeb event is now represented "from within," by the conveying of the "words" once uttered by God "with a loud voice" (5:22). Because of its heading ("*And this is the Torah* which Moses set before the sons of Israel; these are the testimonies, the statutes, and the ordinances, which Moses spoke to the sons of Israel when they came out of Egypt" [4:44-45]), and because of its way of disclosing

---

[26] See Weinfeld, *School*, 207, "Deuteronomy has ... taken care to shift the center of gravity of the theophany from the visual to the aural plane."

[27] See notably the phrase קול השופר, קל שפר, "the voice of a/the horn," in Exod 19:16, 19.

YHWH's teaching, the second Mosaic speech arguably gives access to the Torah referred to in Deut 1:5 as "this Torah." Interestingly enough, the heading "And this is the Torah" is coordinated with a previous narratorial account (Deut 4:41-43) that reports Moses' establishment of the cities of refuge in Transjordan —"Then Moses set apart three cities in the east beyond the Jordan" (4:41). In Deuteronomy, the account of 4:41-43 is the first recording of provisions concerning Israel's future existence. Still, the measures valid for Transjordan are dissociated—by the "And this is the Torah" superscription—from all the following Mosaic provisions and stipulations. A subtle hint is thereby given. The words of the Torah, it seems, have another (material? legal?) destination than the territories "beyond the Jordan" (4:46), that is, in the narrator's parlance, east of the Jordan.

For Moses, to evoke the event of YHWH's utterance at Horeb is to produce his own prophetic credentials. The tremendous experience of God's voice prompted the people's call for a mediator. Addressing Moses, they besought him:

> [25]If we hear the voice of YHWH our God anymore, we shall die. [26]For who is there of all flesh, that has heard the voice of the living God speaking out of the midst of fire, as we have, and has still lived? [27]Go near, and hear all that YHWH our God will say; and speak to us all that YHWH our God will speak to you; and we will hear and do it. (Deut 5:25-27)

God acceded to the people's request, but not without a slight alteration in the petition's wording. In 5:27, the sons of Israel suggest that Moses say (תדבר) whatever YHWH will say (ידבר). In 5:31, God answers by asking Moses to teach (תלמדם) all the "commandments and the statutes and the ordinances" he will tell him (ואדברה). Teaching (למד, Piel) is a modality of communication never linked with God in Deuteronomy.[28] It applies, on the contrary, to Moses' act of communication, and notably at the turning point of 4:1: "And now, O Israel, give heed to the statutes and the ordinances which I teach you (אשר אנכי מלמד אתכם)" (see also 4:5,14; 6:1; 31:22). In that sense, the subtle change introduced by God in the people's request authorizes the legal teaching of Moses in

---

[28] See G. Braulik, "Das Deuteronomium und die Gedächtniskultur Israels: Redaktionsgeschichtliche Beobachtungen zur Verwendung von למד," *Biblische Theologie und gesellschaftlicher Wander: Für Norbert Lohfink SJ* (ed. G. Braulik, W. Gross and S. McEvenue; Freiburg: Herder, 1993) 17.

its actual Deuteronomic form. While speaking, Moses is thus exposing the condition of possibility of his own speech.[29] Far from being any longer the novice who had objected, "I am not eloquent, either heretofore or since you have spoken to your servant; but I am slow of speech and of tongue" (Exod 4:10), or the unconfident prophet in need of external, para-linguistic, signs to confirm what he has to say (see Exodus 4-11), the Deuteronomic Moses now freely and authoritatively produces through speech everything he needs to accomplish his prophetic mission, starting with the narrative of his own prophetic empowerment.

4. Buffer Voice, Surrogate Voice

In their prophetic capacity, Moses' speeches throughout Deuteronomy all proceed from the "foundational scene" retold in Deut 5:23-31. The intervention of Moses' voice is necessitated by the transcendence of YHWH's voice, which stands beyond human common reception. The prophetic mediation is perceptible throughout Deuteronomy, where, as a rule, God's voice is not heard without Moses': God's words appear as a quoted inset within the inset of Moses' words. While citing divine utterances, Moses' voice therefore acts as a buffer voice, shielding his addressees from the lethal encounter with God's *live* voice.

The resumption of the telling by the narrator from Deut 31:1 on creates a new situation. YHWH's voice is heard again without Moses' mediation. This does not mean, however, that the rule established in 5:31 is superseded. In 31:14,16-21; 32:49-52; 34:4, the one whom God immediately addresses is, again, Moses his prophet.[30] On the other hand, Moses does not hesitate to invest his own teaching with the authority of God's voice, in typical prophetic manner: "if you obey *the voice of YHWH* your God, keeping all his commandments which *I* command you this day"

---

[29] This can be seen as a further effect of Deuteronomy's almost pervasive resort to dramatic "showing." As I indicated in the introduction, under such a poetic convention it is incumbent upon the dramatis persona to set up much of the context of his intervention. To a great extent, the pragmatic parameters (who is speaking? To whom? In which capacity? In what kind of speech act? etc.) are provided by the character's speech, since no narrator elaborates upon them. In the act of reading, however, this poetic constraint is registered as a stylistic feature of the character's parlance, and as an indirect portrayal of the character himself.

[30] The only possible exception is the appointment of Joshua in Deut 31:23. In

(13:19). The divine voice, extending beyond the formal citations, thus makes a comeback in Moses' address; it somehow conflates with Moses' teaching in the first person.[31] In some places, God's *I* even makes its way into Moses' own speech. This is the case in 29:4-5, where Moses produces a divine statement in the first person, without any "transformer" signalling the quoted inset: "*I* have led you forty days in the wilderness... . that you may know that *I* am YHWH your God."[32] The voice that could not be heard

---

31:22-23, the MT reads: "So Moses wrote this song the same day, and taught it to the people of Israel. And he commissioned Joshua the son of Nun and said, 'Be strong and of good courage; for you shall bring the children of Israel into the land which I swore to give them: I will be with you.'" The use of "I" in the quote, combined with the theme of past promise and future assistance, makes it clear: YHWH is speaking. This fact leads the Vulgate (in some recensions), and modern translations to anticipate YHWH as the subject of the introductory clause: "And *YHWH/God* commissioned Joshua, ... and said, ..." (see RSV, NEB, NAB, TOB; NJPSV resorts to typography, "And He ...," to imply that God is speaking). However, the LXX presents an interesting alternative reading (the differences are italicized): "And he [*Moses* (in some recensions)] commissioned Jesus the son of Nun and said, 'Be strong and of good courage; for you shall bring the children of Israel into the land which *the Lord* swore [to give] *them; he* will be with you.'" The pros and cons as to the secondary character of either the MT or the LXX are reviewed by L. Laberge, "Le texte de Deutéronome 31 (Dt 31,1-29; 32,44-47)," *Pentateuchal and Deuteronomistic Studies: Papers Read at the XIIIth IOSOT Congress Leuven 1989* (ed. C. Brekelmans and C. Lust; BETL 94; Louvain: Peeters Press/University Press, 1990) 156-57, and by N. Lohfink, "Zur Fabel in Dtn 31-32," 272-73. Laberge concludes in favor of the genuine character of the LXX reading, while Lohfink regards the MT text as primary (Lohfink is followed by F. Nwachukwu, "The Textual Differences Between the MT and the LXX of Deuteronomy 31: A Response to Leo Laberge," *Bundesdokument*, 87-88; see also Dogniez and Harl, *Deutéronome*, 318). Lohfink's main argument is that the summoning in 31:14, "call Joshua, and present yourselves in the tent of meeting, that I may commission him (ואצונו)," is a *totes Motiv* if it is not followed by YHWH's actual commissioning of Joshua (ויצו) in 31:23 (see already Rashi, *ad loc.*). I will construe the verse in the same way; it is likely that the appointment of Joshua as Moses' successor entailed a direct relationship (in speech) between YHWH and the new leader. However, the text preserved in Greek is worth consideration, insofar as it prolongs the Horeb agreement: Moses, and Moses only, is the one who benefits from God's direct address. The Greek rendering of Deut 31:23 may thus represent a correction stemming from a greater, yet ill-inspired, attention to Deuteronomy's narrative consistency. The point is rather methodological: poetic parameters can be relevant in textual criticism.

[31] See also Deut 8:20; 13:5; 15:5; 26:14, 17; 27:10; 28:1, 2, 15, 45, 62; 30:2, 8, 10, 20.

[32] Significantly enough, some Greek manuscripts, the Peshitta and the Vulgate have the opening verb in Deut 29:4 in the third person—"*he* has led you." The codex Vaticanus similarly reads "*He* is the Lord your God" in 29:5. Another unmarked citation of divine speech by Moses is found in MT Deut 11:(13)14-15

becomes paradoxically urgent through Moses' plea; the prophet's buffer voice also acts as a surrogate voice.

In whatever combination, the prophetic voice represents the medium *par excellence* in Deuteronomy's represented world. As announced in Deut 1:1—"These are the words that Moses *spoke*"—oral communication is apparently what Deuteronomy is all about. Is Amsler therefore vindicated in his claim, "Moïse n'écrit rien, il parle"?[33] The following chapter will indicate that another logic, the "logic of writing,"[34] intrudes in Moses' speeches and implicitly prepares Moses' own act of writing.

(with the alternative reading in the third person in the Samaritan Pentateuch, some Greek manuscripts and the Vulgate). The non-unanimity of the versions, I would conclude, pleads in favor of the MT.

[33] Amsler, "Loi orale," 51.

[34] See J. R. Goody, *The Logic of Writing and the Organization of Society* (Cambridge: Cambridge University Press, 1986).

CHAPTER TWO

THE LOGIC OF WRITING IN MOSES' TORAH SPEECH (DEUTERONOMY 5-26)

Write them on the tablet of your heart

Prov 3:3

The paradox of Moses' Torah speech (Deuteronomy 5-28) is that it is haunted by the paradigm of written communication. As I shall show in this and the following chapter, Moses, while speaking, is projecting written communication at the horizon of his ongoing speech act. His addressees, and their descendants in the land, will write; they will transcribe his words—Israel's essential words. In so doing, Moses transfers to "the end" (the reception of his words in the land) what was equally present at the beginning of the Horeb-Moab communication process: commitment to writing. Before Moab (that is, at Horeb) and after Moab (that is, in the land), writing is thus *de rigueur*. A set of passages in Moses' speech retrospectively or prospectively develops the theme of writing, mentioning written records. Their most basic feature is that they use the verbal root כתב, "to write," in narrative accounts (e.g., "he wrote"), in stipulations (e.g., "you shall write"), or in variegated referential phrases (e.g., "written in this 'book'"). The next chapter will deal with references to writing and to written records in Deuteronomy 27-30. The present chapter will focus on Deuteronomy 5-26 and will deal with three references to written communication: God's writing of the tables at Horeb, Moses' injunction requiring the people to transcribe his words on personal and architectural "memorials," and the law providing for the king's writing and reading of a copy of "this Torah." The three themes, however, will be treated in five sections, since the first two themes are duplicated: the tables are rewritten, and the "you shall write" stipulation comes twice in Moses' speech. The analysis will confine itself to the communication aspect of these passages within Moses' speech and within Deuteronomy's overall narrative; other aspects will be broached only incidentally. The objective of the

survey is primarily to record the momentum from and toward written communication that underlies Moses' speech.

1. *"He Wrote Down" (I)—Deuteronomy 5*

In Deut 4:10-14, Moses, for the first time in his speech, recalls
God's revelation at Horeb. The event is summarized, as an act of
communication, in 4:13:

> And he *declared* to you his covenant, which he commanded you to
> perform, that is, the ten words; and he *wrote* them upon two tables
> of stone.

The passage without any transition from oral to written communication—"he declared (ויגד)—he wrote (ויכתבם)"—is found again
in Moses' main retelling of the Horeb event in Deuteronomy 5.
There the reporting of YHWH's declaration of the Decalogue
(5:6-21) is followed right away by the account,

> These words YHWH *spoke* (דבר) to all your assembly at the moun-
> tain out of the midst of the fire, the cloud, and the thick darkness,
> with a loud voice; and he added no more. And he *wrote* (ויכתבם) them
> upon two tables of stone, and gave them to me. (5:22)

The tight sequence "he spoke/declared" ⇒ "he wrote" accounts
for what, in the ensuing speech, is a matter of fact: what is written on the tables is a direct transcription of what YHWH spoke
"on the mountain, out of the midst of the fire, on the day of the
assembly" (9:10; 10:4). This is a basic given that consistently and
forcefully underlies any reference in Deuteronomy to the revelation at Horeb. What Moses makes clear in Deuteronomy, however,
represents a subtle way of getting straight what remains ambiguous in the Sinai narrative in Exodus. The ambiguity in Exodus
stems from the combination of three elements:
   (a) In Exodus' account of the Sinai event, the first writing character to be read about is Moses: "And Moses wrote all the words
of YHWH" (Exod 24:4).[1] The "'book' of the covenant" (Exod
24:7) written by Moses records the stipulations of the Covenant
Code (Exod 20:22-23:19), and arguably the so-called Decalogue

---

[1] Moses' *entrée en scène* as first writing character in the Pentateuch goes back
to Exod 17:14.

(Exod 20:2-17). Only after the making of the Sinai covenant, made on the basis of the "book" in question, do we read about the written tables: "YHWH said to Moses, 'Come up to me on the mountain, and wait there; and I will give you the tables of stone, and the torah, and the commandment I have written for their instruction'" (Exod 24:12). A written record is thus already at God's hand when he calls Moses, but we do not know when its making took place (before or after the theophany? Before or after Moses' own recording activity?).

(b) In Exodus, the content of the tables is not altogether clear. The first mention of the tables, just quoted (Exod 24:12), juxtaposes "the tables of stone, and the torah, and the commandments." The handing on of the tables, reported in 31:18, is not more explicit; the scene occurs, moreover, after God reveals to Moses a further body of Sinaitic stipulations (Exodus 25-31): "And he gave to Moses, when he had made an end of speaking with him upon Mount Sinai, the two tables of the testimony, tables of stone, written with the finger of God." Nothing new—as far as the content of the tables is concerned—is learned from God's intervention at the close of the Golden Calf affair: "Cut two tables of stone like the first; and I will write upon the tables the words that were on the first tables" (34:1). Only in 34:28, when the re-writing of the tables is told, is the content of the tables specified as "the ten words." However, this account follows the revelation to Moses of a further body of ritual stipulations, possibly in decalogal form (Exod 34:14-26), and comes after an introductory statement in 34:27 that does not make anything clear:[2] "And YHWH said to Moses: 'Write these words; in accordance with these words I have made a covenant with you and with Israel.' And he wrote upon the tables the words of the covenant, the ten commandments" (Exod 34:27-28).[3]

---

[2] See Weinfeld, *Deuteronomy*, 205.

[3] In current scholarship, Exodus 34 is increasingly regarded as a post-Deuteronomic interpolation, more precisely, as "a deliberate redactional conflation of prior literary sources (including the Covenant Code, Exodus 13, and Exodus 16) that attempts forcibly to read later legal and textual developments back into the Sinai pericope" (B. Levinson, *Deuteronomy and the Hermeneutics of Legal Innovation* [Oxford: Oxford University Press, forthcoming] 94 [with literature]). One wonders therefore whether the reference to the "ten words" in Exod 34:28 does not represent a redactional strategy, preparing, with deliberate ambiguity, Deuteronomy's rehearsal of the Sinai/Horeb communication process.

(c) The account of the re-writing of the tables in Exod 34:28 seems to imply that it is Moses who wrote down the second edition of the tables: "And he was there with YHWH forty days and forty nights; he neither ate bread nor drank water. And he wrote upon the tables the words of the covenant, the ten commandments." This apparently contradicts God's intention previously communicated to Moses: "YHWH said to Moses: 'Cut two tables of stone like the first; and I will write upon the tables the words that were on the first tables, which you broke'" (Exod 34:1). In order not to compromise God's consistency with his promise, traditional Jewish interpreters (Saadia, Shmuel ben Meir, Ibn Ezra, Nachmanides, Ḥazkuni) discern a referential switch in the last part of the sentence, God being now the subject of the verb, "And [YHWH] wrote." Some modern scholars adopt this line of interpretation (without always mentioning their predecessors).[4] It is nevertheless a fact that the text is opaque, lacking the expected specifics.

Retelling the event in Deuteronomy, Moses sets the record straight. In his account of the story, disentangling the disordered presentation in Exodus, Moses produces what could be called a "fabula," that is, the chronological sequence into which the motifs of a narrative may be reassembled.[5] "And he declared to you his covenant, which he commanded you to perform, that is, the ten words; and he wrote them upon two tables of stone" (4:13): the "words" communicated at Horeb, Moses now authoritatively declares, are the "ten words," and they were directly committed to writing. Is the production of such a "fabula" summary out of Mosaic voice, coming from a speaker who is notable for scrambling the chronological sequence? The production of a "fabula" is rather a further sign of Moses' authority in his retelling. The one who reshuffles the order in which events are presented can do so because he knows the genuine connection of these events. Retelling, Moses tells "after," but he tells what had not been explicitly told before, i.e., that the writing of the "ten words" took place

---

[4] See G. Beer, *Exodus* (HAT; Tübingen: Mohr, 1939) 162; B. S. Childs, *Exodus* (OTL; London: Westminster Press, 1974) 604; R. W. L. Moberly, *At the Mountain of God: Story and Theology in Exodus 32-34* (JSOTSup 22; Sheffield: JSOT Press, 1983) 101-106; 209-10 nn. 197-99; see especially J. Durham, *Exodus* (WBC 3; Waco: Word Books, 1987) 462-63.

[5] See pp. 18-19 above.

after their uttering, with nothing else intervening in the chrono-logical sequence.

In Deut 5:22 Moses adds that YHWH gave him the two tables inscribed with the "ten words": "And he *wrote* them upon two tables of stone, and *gave* them (ויתנם) to me (אלי)." The act of transmission, Moses tells later, actually took place after a signifi-cant delay:

> [9]When I went up the mountain to receive the tables of stone, the tables of the covenant which YHWH made with you, I remained on the mountain forty days and forty nights; I neither ate bread nor drank water. [10]And YHWH *gave* (ויתן) me (אלי) the two tables of stone written (כתבים) with the finger of God; and on them were all the words which YHWH had spoken with you on the mountain out of the midst of the fire on the day of the assembly. [11]And at the end of forty days and forty nights YHWH gave (נתן) me (אלי) the two tables of stone, the tables of the covenant. (9:9-11)

What is depicted in these verses is the handing down of a record, not its writing. No form of ויכתב, "and he wrote," or any equiva-lent, enters the sequence. That the "ten words" were written down before being transmitted is here no truism; it is a narrative datum in keeping with what is known since 4:13 and 5:22: the "ten words" were committed to writing just after being declared.[6] Why, how-ever, did Moses anticipate, in 5:22, the account of the tables' trans-mission, "And he wrote (ויכתבם) them upon two tables of stone, and gave them to me (ויתנם אלי)"? Moses possibly did so in order to give a full picture of the revelation process in his main retelling of the Horeb event. This process includes, beyond the declara-tion of the "ten words" and their commitment to writing, the handing over of the written record. A paradigmatic sequence נתן אל—כתב, "to write"—"to give to," is thus created, extending the first sequence "to declare/speak"—"to write." The sequence "to write"—"to give to," I will show, recurs in significant contexts. The art of telling or retelling is also the art of setting up paradigms.

In Deut 5:22, before mentioning God's writing, Moses inserts a short sentence, ולא יסף, "and he added no more." The phrase echoes an injunction already given by Moses to the people who listen to him, "you shall not add (לא תספו) to the word which I

---

[6] Both Driver, *Deuteronomy*, 87, and Weinfeld, *Deuteronomy*, 323 miss the chrono-logical distinction between the writing and the giving of the tables, introduced by Moses' retelling.

command you or take from it" (4:2).[7] Moshe Weinfeld and
Michael Fishbane showed that this and similar formulations occur
as a motif in Mesopotamian literature.[8] A technical scribal formula, Fishbane further specified, it functions as a colophon and
thus marks the conclusion of literary units.[9] This is notably the
case in the *Erra Epic*, which praises the scribe who committed the
revelation to writing: "He did not leave out a single line, nor did
he add to it" (5:43b-44).[10] In like manner, the short formula of
Deut 5:22 is rhetorically used by Moses as a "canon-formula" to
emphasize the close of the Horeb revelation. "And he added no
more": nothing more, as God's word, is to be expected from this
distinct stage of the revelation. YHWH's immediate writing of the
"ten words" on "two tables of stone" represents a further modality of canonization. What was temporally defined ("He added no
more") is now spatially circumscribed ("on two tables of stone").
In the perspective of Moses' retelling, canonization and commitment to writing call for each other.[11]

While YHWH "added no more," Moses keeps speaking. In
Moses' retelling, the canonizing of the "ten words" is followed by
the conveying of further stipulations, the latter divinely entrusted
to him alone at Horeb. In so doing, Moses the reteller simply
withholds what YHWH did add, beyond the "ten words," in the
Sinai revelation as previously told in Exodus: the so-called Covenant Code (Exod 20:22-23:33).[12] How is Moses' rhetorical manœu-
vre to be understood? Did God speak twice at Sinai/ Horeb,
entrusting Moses with a double set of legal provisions? Does
Moses, in Deuteronomy, keep back the "first" disclosure while dis-

---

[7] See also 13:1; outside of Deuteronomy, see Prov 30:6.

[8] Weinfeld, *School*, 261-64; M. Fishbane, "*Varia Deuteronomica*," *ZAW* 84 (1972)
349-50. See also J. Blenkinsopp, *Prophecy and Canon: A Contribution to the Study of
Jewish Origins* (Notre Dame: University of Notre Dame Press, 1977) 24; E. Reuter,
"Nimm nichts davon und füge nichts hinzu!' Dtn 13,1, seine alttestamentlichen
Parallelen und seine altorientalischen Vorbilder," *BN* 47 (1989) 107-14; Dohmen
and Oeming, *Kanon*, 68-89; and Levinson, *Deuteronomy*, 16-17.

[9] Fishbane, "*Varia*," 350.

[10] Translation in W. G. Lambert, "The Fifth Tablet of the Erra Epic," *Iraq* 24
(1962) 122.

[11] For a consideration of this issue in the history of religions, see W. C. Smith,
"Scripture as Form and Concept: Their Emergence for the Western World,"
Rethinking Scripture: Essays from a Comparative Perspective (ed. M. Levering; Albany:
State University of New York Press, 1989) 29-57.

[12] See Weinfeld, *Deuteronomy*, 323.

playing the "second"? This would amount to awkward revelation procedures, coming from God, and to decided opportunism, coming from Moses. The opposite situation makes sense—it could be epitomized in the psalmist's saying, "Once God has spoken; twice I have heard this" (Ps 62:10). In Exodus, the omniscient narrator reproduces God's speech, and thus gives access to an indisputable source revelation: "And YHWH said to Moses, 'Thus you shall say (כה תאמר) to the people of Israel: . . .'" (Exod 20:22); "Now these are the ordinances which you shall set before them: . . ." (Exod 21:1). In Deuteronomy, the Horeb revelation is thoroughly mediated by, and reflected in, Moses' reporting speech. With the exception of the "ten words," moreover, Moses does not formulate the legal legacy he received at Horeb by quoting God (no stipulation is prefaced with "YHWH said: . . .");[13] Moses, rather, liberally conveys and enforces what God has revealed to him. This conveying has the specific modality of a "teaching," as enjoined upon Moses by God himself: "Now this is the commandment, the statutes and the ordinances which YHWH your God commanded me to teach (ללמד) you" (6:1; see also 4:1, 5, 14; 5:31).[14] The divine command to teach (and not to "say," as proposed by the people in 5:27) accounts for Moses' latitude in his rephrasing of the revelation received "on the mountain." Far from constituting an alternative revelation, the legal corpus in Deuteronomy represents a didactic *reformulation* of God's legal communication at

---

[13] Even in the case of the so-called Decalogue, however, there is a significant difference between the telling of the event in Exodus and its retelling in Deuteronomy. In Exodus, the awkward transition between 19:25 and 20:1 creates a (deliberate?) ambiguity: are the "words" (= the Decalogue) we read in Exod 20:2-17 reported by Moses (see 19:25), or directly uttered by God (see 20:1), and to whom—to Moses or to the people? On this issue, see A. Toeg, *Lawgiving at Sinai* (Hebrew) (Jerusalem: Magnes, 1977) 61-64. In his retelling in Deuteronomy, Moses echoes the ambiguity in question when he places side by side the account of an unmediated revelation (Deut 5:4) and the account of his mediation (Deut 5:5): "YHWH spoke with you face to face at the mountain, out of the midst of the fire; I myself stood between YHWH and you at that time, to declare to you the word of YHWH; for you were afraid because of the fire, and you did not go up into the mountain. He said (לאמר): . . . " By disclosing his active role "at that time," Moses, however, tips the scale in favor of his mediation: it was he who actually conveyed YHWH's "word" to the people. Moses' emphasis on his faithful mediation is, in my view, a subtle way to authorize the rendering of the "ten words" in Deuteronomy: whatever the status of Exodus' recording of the Decalogue, the mediator now straightforwardly reports, as word of God, what he then transmitted.

[14] See pp. 37-38 above.

Sinai/Horeb.[15] The Mosaic "revision" is meant for a new generation that, unlike the generation of the exodus, will cross into the land, and that presumably needs an adapted rehearsal of the covenantal stipulations.

A further aspect of Moses' art of retelling is worth noticing. The retelling of the Horeb event ignores the "'book' of the covenant" that Moses wrote as part of the covenant ritual (see Exod 24:4, 7).[16] Emphasizing God's writing of the tables, Moses drops any mention of his own writing activity at Sinai/Horeb. In Exodus, recording God's "words" in the "'book' of the covenant," Moses intervened as a writing character before any mention of God's own writing. Not so in Moses' retelling in Deuteronomy: Moses establishes God's absolute primacy in the recording process and passes over his own scribal activity in silence. The keeping back of the Horeb "'book' of the covenant," however, has a positive function: it creates room for original developments in Deuteronomy. As I shall show in Chapter Four, the efficiency of Deuteronomy's plot derives to a great extent from the distance created between God's and Moses' respective writings. The former belongs to the foundational revelation event at Horeb; the latter is reported as late as possible, well beyond its point of occurrence in the chronological sequence. The hiatus thus created will turn out to be of prime relevance, narratively speaking. At this point in Moses' speech, however, the point to recall is that the

---

[15] In current scholarship, the legal corpus of Deuteronomy is increasingly approached as the outcome of a process of editorial revision directed on Exodus' Covenant Code. For local revisions, see N. Lohfink, "Zur deuteronomischen Zentralisationsformel," *Bib* 65 (1984) 297-328; M. Fishbane, *Biblical Interpretation in Ancient Israel* (Oxford: Clarendon, 1985) 163-230. For a more comprehensive approach, see B. Levinson, *The Hermeneutics of Innovation: The Impact of Centralization Upon the Structure, Sequence, and Reformulation of Legal Material in Deuteronomy* (Ann Arbor: University Microfilms, 1991) (see also Levinson, *Deuteronomy*, forthcoming); and E. Otto, "Aspects of Legal Reform and Reformulation in Ancient Cuneiform and Israelite Law," *Theory and Method in Biblical and Cuneiform Law: Revision, Interpolation and Development*, (ed. B. Levinson; JSOTSup 181; Sheffield: Sheffield Academic Press, 1994) 160-96. The interesting point in that case is that Moses' claim on stage dramatizes and mirrors the activity of the authors of Deuteronomy's Code. Moses' reformulation of the original provisions (documented in Exodus) parallels the scribes' revision of these stipulations. The narrative provides a rationale (the divine empowerment of Moses in his didactic reformulation) camouflaging the authorial revision of the Covenant Code.

[16] On Deut 5:22 as deliberate polemic against the Covenant Code (in a redactional perspective), see O. Eissfeldt, *The Old Testament: An Introduction* (New York: Harper & Row, 1965) 220-23.

divine writing of the "ten words" is as foundational as their uttering. The Horeb revelation associates Israel from the outset with
the particular economy of written records.

God's recourse to writing, which Moses brings into relief in his
retelling, is a given of considerable import. Weinfeld discerns
"demythologizing" trends in Deuteronomy, favoring, among other
things, a (relatively) abstract conception of the deity.[17] In several
phenomena, Weinfeld specifies, a tendency to eliminate the inher-
ent corporeality of the traditional imagery is to be observed.[18] On
the particular point of divine writing, however, which Weinfeld
does not take into consideration, Deuteronomy sticks to a rather
corporal presentation: the transcendent God, who cannot be seen
in the theophany and manifests himself exclusively through the
immateriality of a voice (see 5:12), engraves his words on stone
tables (5:13). As will be specified in 9:10, the tables in question
are even written "with the finger of God." Is Deuteronomy's reader invited to replace the imagery of the Storm God with that of
a Heavenly Scribe? The link between YHWH and the phenomenon of writing may, however, support a demythologization of its
own. The originality of Deuteronomy's basic assertion—YHWH
did write the ten words on the tables—will stand out when compared with analogical patterns in the ancient Near East.

(a) Moses' retelling that combines in a tight sequence God's
declaring and God's writing of legal provisions (and removes the
mention of any mediator's writing) is particularly meaningful
when compared with ancient Near Eastern presentations of divinely inspired law codes. There the writing process is invariably
incumbent upon the human party, that is, the mediating king.
Lipit-Ishtar was called by the gods to establish justice in the land;
it was up to him to engrave on a stela the laws that are, accord-

---

[17] See Weinfeld, *School*, 190-243; and idem, *Deuteronomy*, 37-44. Weinfeld's thesis has been criticized by J. Milgrom, "The Alleged Demythologization and Secularization in Deuteronomy," *IEJ* 23 (1973) 156-61. Milgrom's review prompted
a response by M. Weinfeld, "On 'Demythologization and Secularization' in Deuteronomy," *IEJ* 23 (1973) 230-33. See also N. Lohfink, "Opfer und Säkularisierung
in Deuteronomy," *Studien zu Opfer und Kult im Alten Testament* (ed. A. Schenker;
Forschungen zum Alten Testament 3; Tübingen: Mohr, 1992) 15-43.

[18] Weinfeld, *School*, 191-209 (or *Deuteronomy*, 37-40) draws attention to the
Deuteronomic concept of the divine abode, to the shift from the visual to the
aural plane in the retelling of the theophany, and to Deuteronomy's conception
of the ark.

ingly, called after his name.[19] Hammurapi was inspired with decisive "truths" by Shamash, the divine custodian of justice;[20] yet, he
repeatedly reminds his future readers that he himself wrote "my
precious words" on "my stela."[21] Beside the publication of legal
codes, one does find, however, a case of handing on of a divinely written document, namely the "tables of the gods" transmitted
by Shamash and Adad to Enmeduranki, the mythical king of Sip-
par.[22] Geo Widengren has called attention to the similarity
between this scene and YHWH's handing over of the written tables
to Moses.[23] Yet, the Mesopotamian "tablets of the gods," or "tablets
of destiny," instrumentally used by the gods to set the fate of every
year,[24] are far from the recorded apodictic stipulations we find in
YHWH's "ten words." By telling how YHWH transmitted to Moses
the nucleus of the Torah on written tables, Exodus and Deuteronomy thus record a communication event that is *sui generis*. Far
from being the secret "tablets of destiny," YHWH's tables record
a publicized ethical revelation. Written by God, the Sinai/Horeb
tables moreover leave no doubt about the source of their authority. In the biblical tradition embodied in Deuteronomy, YHWH is
not merely the dispenser of legal inspiration, "he is," as Moshe
Greenberg points out, "the fountainhead of the law, the law is a
statement of his will."[25] God's immediate writing of the "ten
words," without the mediation of a human lawgiver, is a forceful
expression of his undivided authorship in Israel's basic law.

    (b) Legal revelation at Horeb is a constitutive part of covenant

---

[19] See *ANET*, 161.

[20] See Hammurapi's code, 25b:95 (*ANET*, 178). In Akkadian non-legal literature, a similar phenomenon is observed. Surveying texts such as the *Creation Epic*,
the *Erra Epic*, the *Agushaya Poem* and the *Hymn to Ishtar*, which include mentions
of their genesis, divine approval, composition, authorship or traditing, Foster
points to a "Mesopotamian artistic tradition [tending] to stress the outside [i.e.,
divine] source of inspiration that lent each work its uniqueness" (B. R. Foster,
Before the Muses: An Anthology of Akkadian Literature 1 [Bethesda, MD; CDL, 1993]
19-20). Still, this never implies that a work was written by the (inspiring) deity
itself.

[21] See the epilogue of the Code, passim (*ANET*, 177-78).

[22] See J. C. Craig, *ABRT*, 1 pl. 64.

[23] See G. Widengren, *The Ascension of the Apostle and the Heavenly Book* (UUÅ 7;
Uppsala: Lundequistska, 1950) 24.

[24] See Widengren, *Ascension*, 9-12.

[25] M. Greenberg, "Some Postulates in Biblical Criminal Law," *Yehezqel Kaufmann
Jubilee Volume* (ed. M. Haran; Jerusalem: Magnes, 1960) 11.

making: "YHWH our God made a covenant with us in Horeb" (5:2). In establishing the analogies between the Deuteronomic covenant and ancient Near Eastern oaths and treaties, modern biblical scholarship recovered what was a part of the cultural background of Deuteronomy's implied reader (and thus of Moses' audience). As this readership and audience knew, commitment to writing was a constitutive part of the establishment of these oaths and treaties. "Thus have we spoken [and thus have we writ]ten," the king of KTK and the king of Arpad declare together in the Sefire Treaty (I C 1).[26] Writing down the covenantal stipulations, YHWH unreservedly and sensibly plays the "language game" of covenant making.

When understood against the background of ancient Near Eastern writing practices of both legal drafting and covenant making, Deuteronomy's repeated allusions to God's writing carry a forceful message. Far from being confined to a pre-scriptural world, YHWH, who "let his voice be heard out of heaven" (5:36) is also "on the side" of the written *logos*. Israel's God is not alien to the medium whereby covenantal treaties and legal bodies were brought into existence; covenantal and legal writing belongs to him before belonging to anyone else. Revelations mediated through divine voice have an unsurpassed hierophanic power. Their "*tremendus and fascinans*" side may, however, eclipse the rational quality of what is transmitted.[27] By contrast, a written transmission brings legal revelation into the realm of written rationality. The written tables warrant a continuity between God's revelation and Israel's "literate" thinking. Far from reactivating mythological representations, the reference to a writing God rather highlights the rational discursiveness of God's revelation.

2. *"You Shall Write" (I)—Deut 6:6-9*

Shortly after having reported the commitment of the Horeb "words" to writing, Moses commands Israel to perform a similar

---

[26] Translation in Fitzmyer, *Inscriptions*, 19. The sequence—"we have spoken . . . we have written"—matches closely the sequence in Deut 4:13—"he declared . . . and he wrote."

[27] See the role of the קולת, "sounds/voices," in the account of the Sinai theophany in Exodus 19-20.

recording: "you shall write" (Deut 6:8). The people must do what
God has done. A notable analogy is thereby established between
the giving and the receiving of Israel's covenantal "words." In Deut
6:9 the people are enjoined to cover entrances to both private
and public spaces with דברים, "words." The "words" in question
have been previously referred to as "these words (הדברים האלה)
which I command you this day" (6:6):

> ⁶And these words which I command you this day shall be upon your
> heart; ⁷and you shall teach them diligently to your children, and
> shall recite them when you sit in your house, and when you walk by
> the way, and when you lie down, and when you rise. ⁸And you shall
> bind them as a sign upon your hand, and they shall be as frontlets
> between your eyes. ⁹And you shall write them on the doorposts of
> your houses and on your gates. (Deut 6:6-9)[28]

An ancient interpretation reads in "these words" (6:6) an anapho-
rical reference to the immediately preceding words, that is, "Hear,
O Israel: YHWH your God is one; and you shall love YHWH your
God with all your heart, and with all your soul, and with all your
might" (6:4-5).[29] This traditional reading has long gained scholarly support.[30] An alternative traditional, and now critical, interpretation associates "these words" with the "ten words," that is,
the Decalogue.[31] Some modern scholars, however, discern a far
more comprehensive scope in the "words" referred to by Moses
in Deut 6:6—nothing less than the whole of the Torah to be
taught in Moab.[32] In so doing, these scholars revive Ibn Ezra's

[28] For the translation of ודברת בם, as "and you shall recite them," see G. Fischer
and G. Lohfink, "'Diese Worte sollst du summen': wᵉdibbartā bām—ein verloren-
er Schlüssel zur meditativen Kultur in Israel," ThPh 62 (1987) 59-72.
[29] See the survey of early evidence in O. Keel, "Zeichen der Verbundenheit,"
Mélanges Dominique Barthélemy (ed. P. Casetti, O. Keel and A. Schenker; OBO 38;
Freiburg: Universitätsverlag; Göttingen: Vandenhoeck & Ruprecht, 1981) 166-78.
[30] See the authors listed by F. García López, "Deut. VI et la tradition-rédaction
du Deutéronome," RB 85 (1978) 164 n. 17; The view is adopted by García López,
who is in turn quoted with approval by Keel, "Zeichen," 165.
[31] The identification of "these words" in 6:6 with the Decalogue is largely documented in early Jewish tradition, as well as in Samaritan tradition. See Keel,
"Zeichen," 166-78; as to modern scholarship, see the authors listed by García
López, "Deut. VI," 164 n. 17.
[32] See García López, "Deut. VI," 164 n. 17. See especially Braulik, "Ausdrücke,"
39-66, who is followed on this point by Fischer and Lohfink, "Diese Worte," 60
n. 6; in the article quoted above, Braulik excludes the Decalogue from the "words"
commanded by Moses; in a more recent publication, however, he discerns behind
"these words" "nicht nur der Dekalog (5²²), sondern zumindest das ganze dtn
Gesetz, also 5-26" (G. Braulik, Deuteronomy 1-16,17 [Neue Echter Bibel 15; Würz-

critical insight.[33] I shall indicate how the context of Moses' sentence, as well as the endeavor of his communication, supports this third interpretation. The comprehensiveness of the reference, I shall further point, may well include the "ten words" (see the second interpretation, identifying the "words" to be written with the Decalogue). The first assumption, at the basis of the canonical Jewish šᵉmaʿ prayer and mᵉzûzah practice, proceeds from ambiguities in Moses' phrasing. These ambiguities are actually dispelled by the prophet's ensuing utterances. The interpretation reads in the "words" commanded by Moses a reference to the injunction to love YHWH. In the Mosaic speeches, the call to love YHWH actually never appears as the formal content of a commandment; the love of YHWH is rather identified with the keeping of the commandments (and vice versa). The call to love YHWH is placed side by side with a call to heed, and to keep, his commandments[34]. Analogically, the injunction in 6:5-6 is to be understood as a combination of related calls: "You shall love YHWH your God . . .," that is, you shall keep "on your heart" the words "I command you today." Moreover, the absence of the Deut 6:4-5 heading ("Hear, O Israel . . . and you shall love YHWH") when the injunction is resumed in 11:18-21 is a further sign that the reference to "these words" in Deut 6:6 is to be found elsewhere than in 6:4-5[35].

---

burg: Echter, 1986] 56). See also N. Lohfink, "Der Glaube und die nächste Generation: das Gottesvolk der Bibel als Lerngemeinschaft," *Das Jüdische am Christentum: Die verlorene Dimension* (Freiburg: Herder, 1987) 155-56.

[33] Ibn Ezra, on Deut 4:6: "the liars [= the Karaites] said it refers to the Ten Commandments and concerning them it says 'You shall write them on the doorpost,' the truth is that it refers to all the commandments" (quoted by Weinfeld, *Deuteronomy*, 340).

[34] See for instance Deut 10:12-13, "And now Israel, what does YHWH your God require of you, but to fear YHWH your God, to walk in all his ways, to love him, to serve YHWH your God with all your heart and with all your soul, and to keep the commandments and the statutes of YHWH which I command you this day for your good"; Deut 11:1, "You shall therefore love (ואהבת) YHWH your God, and keep (ושמרת) his charge, his statutes, his ordinances, and his commandments always"; and Deut 11:13; 11:22; 13:4-5; 19:9; 30:16. In Deut 30:20 the phrase "to love YHWH your God" occurs, as an exception, without the parallel reference to the keeping of the commandments.

[35] According to Keel, "Zeichen," 165-66, the antecedent of "these words of mine" in Deut 11:18 is found in the mention of the undivided love of God expressed in 11:13, that partly echoes 6:4-5. In my view, the suggestion is not convincing. First, the sentence of 11:13 is not the most fitting textbase for the operations spelled out in 11:18-20. Second, 11:13 differs from 6:4-5 in its wording. When it comes to the transcription of words, as specified in 6:9 and 11:20, par-

What are the "words" referred to in Deut 6:6? Moses' injunction bears on the words he *commands* (מצוה) Israel. That Moses is in a position to command Israel is precisely made clear in the previous developments. Starting with 5:23, Moses goes back over his installation as YHWH's authorized speaker. The formidable experience of God's voice, Moses says, prompted the people to request a prophetic mediation. YHWH acceded to the people's petition and made Moses privy to the totality of the covenantal stipulations ("all *the commandment* [המצוה] and the statutes and the ordinances") to be taught to the people, and implemented by the people in the land (5:31). This teaching is precisely Moses' endeavor in his speech; it is not, however, a mere conveying of information; it entails an appropriate enforcement:

> ¹Now this is *the commandment* (המצוה), the statutes and the ordinances which *YHWH your God commanded* (צוה) *me to teach you*, that you may do them in the land to which your are going over, to possess it; ²that you may fear YHWH your God, you and your son and your son's son, by keeping all his statutes and *his commandments* (מצותיו), which *I command you* (מצוך), all the days of your life; and that your days may be prolonged. (Deut 6:1-2)

What Moses transmits is presented as *the commandment* (המצוה);[36] Moses' authorized teaching—"YHWH has commanded me to teach you" (6:1)—gives way to an authoritative decreeing—"I command you" (6:2). When in 6:6 Moses refers to "these words I command (מצוך) you today," he thus refers to what YHWH commanded (צוה) him to teach the people, that is, "(all) the commandment (המצוה), the statutes and the ordinances" (6:1; 5:31). The extension of the "words" entrusted to the people's attention and care in 6:6-9 thus is considerable. Nothing tells us whether these "words" include Moses' parenetic comments, beside the expected legal stipulations, which will follow, from 12:1 onward. The phrase "these words, which I command you this day" has, however, in its relative generality, a semantic tendency to encompass all of Moses'

---

tial echoes or thematic variations will not do (it is in my view unlikely that דברים in 6:4 and 11:18 means "things," or "themes," rather than "words").

[36] In the phrases of Deut 5:31 and 6:1, the last two expressions (החקים והמשפטים, "the statutes and the ordinances") apparently refer to individual stipulations (the laws transmitted from Deuteronomy 12 on will indeed be prefaced with the heading "These are the statutes and the ordinances"); the first expression, המצוה, "the commandment," may designate, in a comprehensive way, the nature of Moses' teaching in Moab at God's instigation.

current and authoritative teaching. Nothing explicitly tells us
whether YHWH's "ten words" are included within the "words" in
question. Still, Moses' audience did not attend the Horeb event
(as is indirectly implied in Deut 5:3). This audience gets, in Moses'
teaching "on this day," its authorized access to the Horeb "words."
Concerning the Horeb event, and its disclosure to the Moab audience, Moses' responsibility in transmission is thus all-inclusive.[37]
One may therefore surmise that YHWH's "ten words" are not to
be excluded from what is now committed to the people's future
care.

The "words" entrusted to the people will end up on the doorposts and on the city gates as written text. From the outset, however, they are associated with writing through the metaphor of the
heart, "And these words which I command you this day shall be
upon your heart (על לבבך)" (6:6). Wisdom literature sheds light
on the metaphorical use of "heart" in connection with writing. In
Prov 3:3 and 7:3 (see also 6:21), the disciple is invited to write
his master's instruction "on the tablet of [his] heart (כתבם על לוח
לבך)."[38] Similarly, the use of על, "upon" (your heart) in Deut 6:6,
instead of the more common -ב, "in" (see 30:14; Job 22:22; Ps
37:31; 119:11), most likely hints at a (metaphorical) inscription
"upon the tablet of the heart."[39] Beside this "inscription," actual
writing is implied by the making of the amulets mentioned in v.
8, "And you shall bind them as a sign upon your hand, and they
shall be as frontlets between your eyes." Moses' injunctions aim

---

[37] In the "historical" sequence, the revelation of the Decalogue preceded the
commissioning of Moses; yet, in his retelling, Moses opens his legal teaching in
5:1, before reporting the "ten words": "Hear, O Israel, the statutes and the ordinances which I speak in your hearing this day, and you shall learn them and be
careful to do them." Even the reporting of the "ten words" thus falls within Moses'
legal teaching in Moab.

[38] See also, without the context of learning, Jer 17:1.

[39] See N. Lohfink, "Glaube," 154 n. 20 (pp. 261-62). B. Couroyer suggests a
non-metaphoric reading of על לבבך, "upon your heart" ("La tablette du cœur,"
RB 90 [1983] 416-34). Here, as in 11:18, a reference would be made to a board
hung at the novice's neck (see the breastpiece borne by Aaron על לבו, "upon his
heart" [Exod 28:29; see also 28:30]). Such an engraved pendant would join the
amulets "on the arm" and "between the eyes" to complete the bodily paradigm.
Couroyer's suggestion is most interesting, but would need further textual and
intertextual controls. God's promise to his people in Jer 31:33 to inscribe his
Torah על לבם, "upon their heart," that is בקרבם, "within them," evidences a metaphoric use of the word "heart" in biblical thinking. Without totally excluding
Couroyer's hypothesis, I will not resort to it in these pages.

therefore at an Israel familiar not only with oral tradition ("you shall teach them diligently," "you shall recite them") but also with writing.[40] Does the injunction "you shall write" in 6:9 constitute a hint of widespread literacy in the Israelite society that represents Deuteronomy's implied reader?[41] Or does it simply betray the concern of a class of scribes, responsible for the redaction of Deuteronomy, prescribing their own craft and services to the rest of the people?[42] Such a question cannot be answered on the sole basis of the data found in Deuteronomy. What Deuteronomy does provide is a picture of a covenantal Israel. In the covenantal world projected by Moses' speech, the people is capable of writing, exactly as is YHWH, who has been described in the act of writing. YHWH did not avail himself of the services of a scribe, nor will the people, if we are to go by Moses' speech.

The "words" entrusted to the people in 6:6-8 have the practical identity of a "text," that is, of a determined body of discourse

---

[40] A. Lemaire reads an echo of scholarly practices in the sequence of operations in Deut 6:6-9: "La primauté de l'oral sur l'écrit pour faire retenir quelque chose est clairement indiqué [sic] dans le fameux passage de *Deutéronome VI, 6-9*: pour connaître les commandements par cœur, il faut d'abord les répéter sans arrêt et en toutes circonstances et c'est seulement en dernier lieu qu'on a recours à l'écrit par 'affichage'. L'écriture ne semble conçue que comme une aide à la mémoire après la répétition inlassable qui reste le moyen pédagogique fondamental. Cependant la référence à l''affichage' de textes importants montre que la pédagogie ancienne utilisait aussi les moyens visuels dont elle disposait, ce que nous montre aussi l'emploi des *pithoi* comme des sortes de tableaux à Kuntilat-Ajrud" (*Les écoles et la formation de la Bible dans l'ancien Israël* [OBO 39; Freiburg: Universätsverlag; Göttingen: Vandenhoeck & Ruprecht, 1981] 61-62). Yet, it is not at all evident that 6:6-9 mirrors the sequence of learning practices. Learning is certainly mentioned, but the principle that underlies the organization of the passage is rather the pervasiveness in time and space of divine and Mosaic teaching. Writing on the doorposts and city gates is not the last step in a learning process, but the last mentioned of the symbols and symbolic activities that express the omnipresence of "these words" in Israelite life (and, beside, writing is already implied by the engraved amulets mentioned in 6:6; in Deut 31:22, furthermore, Moses writes down the Song before he teaches it). The search for verisimilitude in ancient Israelite life settings must not lead interpretation away from the purport of the biblical text.

[41] R. de Vaux, *Les Institutions de l'Ancien Testament* (Paris: Cerf, 1958) 83, sees in Deut 6:9; 11:20; 24:1,3 a proof of the diffusion of writing in Israel; see also A. R. Millard, "An Assessment of the Evidence for Writing in Ancient Israel," *Biblical Archaeology Today: Proceedings of the International Congress of Biblical Archaeology, Jerusalem, April 1984* (Jerusalem: Israel Exploration Society, 1985) 308.

[42] See the remarks by M. Haran, "On the Diffusion of Literacy and Schools in Ancient Israel," *Congress Volume: Jerusalem 1986* (ed. J. A. Emerton; Leiden: Brill, 1988) 84-85.

(whatever the medium it implies, oral or written).[43] The use of the term דברים (here, in the specific sense of "words") is meaningful: the Mosaic teaching is not entrusted to the people's care in its formality of "commandment, statutes and ordinances," but in its very wording.[44] As such (in its literality), this teaching lends itself to be learned, taught, repeated and inscribed. The teaching that will pervade Israel's time and space is, moreover, a defined teaching; it is determined as "*these* words" that will be communicated within a unity of time, "this day." What is being communicated "this day" is intended for a specific process of recording (spelled out in 6:6-9), that will take place after the communication process has been completed. The spatial and temporal distance between the uttering of "these words" and their appropriate reception is manifest in the case of the last injunction: the writing down of "these words" on the doorposts and the city-gates will, at any rate, take place only after the settlement in the land. What will be processed in the people's forthcoming tradition is thus a "text," a given body of "words."

Of course the objection may be raised that the extension of the "text" in question does not fit the places listed in 6:8-9, whether bodily (the "words" will be bound "as signs upon your hand and as frontlets between your eyes") or architectural (they will be inscribed "on the doorposts of your house and on your gates"). The smallness of the former locations is particularly obvious. Othmar Keel and Moshe Weinfeld have shown that there is no reason to interpret the injunction in 6:8 as referring to a symbolic "binding," as commonly assumed in modern exegesis.[45] "From various literary and iconographical sources," Weinfeld writes, "we indeed learn that people used to carry on their arms inscribed and uninscribed objects that marked their affiliation to a deity as their protector . . . and similarly there was a widespread custom to carry on the forehead frontlets with sacred signs, which served

---

[43] For the extension of the term "text" to oral compositions, see W. J. Ong, *Orality and Literacy* (London: Routledge, 1982) 13, and W. A. Graham, *Beyond the Written Word: Oral Aspects of Scripture in the History of Religion* (Cambridge: Cambridge University Press, 1987) 21.

[44] See Fischer and Lohfink, "Diese Worte," 60.

[45] See Keel, "Zeichen," 193-215, and Weinfeld, *Deuteronomy*, 341-43 (despite a previous stance in favor of a figurative understanding of the injunction in 6:8 [see Weinfeld, *School*, 301]). Keel, "Zeichen," 179-83, provides reference to the scholarly hypothesis of a symbolic "binding."

as a kind of memorial sign before the deity."[46] As Georg Fischer
and Norbert Lohfink have contended, the written amulets or the
inscriptions on private or public entrances need not be exhaus-
tive in their transcription of "these words."[47] The stipulations in
6:6-9 are meant to catalyze the interiorization of the Mosaic teaching and to foster its pervasiveness throughout time (both personal
and generational) and space (both private and public). This aim
calls for appropriate actions and symbols; it does not require,
either in the singular acts of appropriation and transmission, or
in the individual written tokens, that the totality of the Mosaic
teaching be *de facto* involved. Things may even be explained the
other way around: cultural symbols, expressing religious adhesion
(amulets), or marking off personal and social space (doorposts
and city gates), are a fact; by being inscribed with the "new" teaching, as much as practically allowed, they lend themselves to its
enforcement.[48]

In the covenantal world projected by Moses' speech, God writes,
as well as the people. The content of their respective inscriptions
is identically expressed as הדברים האלה, "these words" (5:22; 6:6),
although differently determined. YHWH wrote down the covenantal stipulations in their foundational extension—the Horeb "ten
words"; the people are enjoined to write the "same" stipulations
in their final extension—Moses' divinely commissioned "words"
in Moab (which include a rehearsal of the Horeb "words"). The
act of writing is associated with the two extremes of the communication process, YHWH as law-giver and the people as subject to
the law. "Le destinataire de la Loi en devient le scripteur."[49] As
far as writing is concerned, Moses the mediator, is, for all we know,
interestingly out of the game.

---

[46] Weinfeld, *Deuteronomy*, 342.
[47] Fischer and Lohfink, "Diese Worte," 60 n. 3.
[48] In the case of the parallel injunction to write (וכתבת, "you will write") given
to the people in Deut 27:3, 8, the opposite principle is at work. There Moses
calls explicitly for the written publication of the totality of the Torah in a single
spot and on a single occasion. In this case, exhaustivity is not only stated, "you
will write *all the words* of this Torah" (27:3, 8), but appropriate means are also
foreseen: "stones" (in the plural), and "large" ones to be sure, will be required
(see also my comments in this chapter on the royal duplicate of the Torah).
[49] Beauchamp, *Testament (2)*, 327.

3. "He Wrote Down" (II)—Deuteronomy 10

With no form to be seen (Deut 4:12), the divine giving of the "ten words" at Horeb, out of the midst of the fire, was an almost immaterial process. And so is Moses' prophetic conveying of the same words in his retelling. The transmitting of the written "words" is, by contrast, eminently material. The following list records the operations (expressed by verbs) attached to the tables; all of the verbs with the exception of two of them ("to write" and "to hew") concern the handling of the *written* tables.

By God:

- כתב (על)	"to write (on)"	4:13; 5:22; 9:10; 10:2, 4.
- נתן (אל)	"to give (to)"	5:22; 9:10, 11; 10:4.

By Moses:

- לקח	"to take"	9:9.
- תפש	"to lay hold of"	9:17.
- שלך, Hiphil	"to cast"	9:17.
- שבר, Piel	"to break"	9:17; 10:2.
- פסל	"to hew"	10:1, 3.
- שים (ב)	"to put (into)"	10:2, 5.

Of the written tables, old and new, it is told four times that YHWH gave (נתן) them to (אל) Moses. As expressed in Moses' remark, "and the two tables of the covenant were in my two hands" (9:15), the tables are essentially geared to handling. In Moses' hands, furthermore, the written word proves to be particularly apt for representation. The handling of the tables, Moses tells his audience, turned dramatic in the Golden Calf episode. The art of the actor joins here the art of the teller: "So I took hold of the two tables, and cast them out of my two hands, and broke them before your eyes" (9:17;[50] cf. 10:2).[51] The written document makes a second-degree language possible—the shattering of the material record

---

[50] As many commentators note, what is in Exod 32:19 a spontaneous reaction of anger ("Moses' anger burned hot, and he threw the tables out of his hands and broke them at the foot of the mountain") becomes in Deut 9:17 a deliberate ("So I took hold of the tables"), and public ("before your eyes"), prophetic act. See for instance von Rad, *Deuteronomy*, 78; Mayes, *Deuteronomy*, 200; and Weinfeld, *Deuteronomy*, 410.

[51] In Deuteronomy the verbe שבר, Piel, "to break into pieces" is otherwise used for the breaking of stelae: see 7:5; 12:3.

being now a sign. The breaking of the tables imparts a message
of its own: breaking a tablet in the ancient Near East invalidated
a document or repudiated an agreement.[52] Moses' deed, performed "before your eyes," has therefore the meaning of "a legal
act, carried out in the presence of witnesses."[53] The prophet
enacts before the people what the people already committed in
their cultic prostitution: the breaking of the covenant sealed in
the written tables (see 9:15).

Words once uttered can be spoken again; words once written
down can be written again. YHWH, the fountainhead of the "ten
words," could easily have repeated the writing down of his genuine revelation. Still the scene depicted in Deut 10:1-5 is not a
scene of "writing again"; it stages the reduplication of a previous
record. So is the case with the physical medium of the inscription, as stated by God in his directive to Moses: "Hew two tables
of stone like the first" (10:1). So is it also for God's writing: "And
I will write on the tables the words that were (אשר היו) on the first
tables which you broke" (10:2); "And he wrote on the tables, as
in the first inscription (כמכתב הראשון), the ten words which YHWH
had spoken to you on the mountain out of the midst of the fire
on the day of the assembly" (10:4). God's act is not an act of copying, and for good reason: the original copy has been shattered.
But neither is it a second "jotting down" of words previously spoken. The inscription is made "as in the first inscription." The "ten
words which YHWH had spoken to you on the mountain out of
the midst of the fire on the day of the assembly" (10:4) are now
modelled on the previous inscription. The principle that guides
God in his writing is the basic principle of written duplication,
from written wording (here, once written) to written wording.[54]
As appears in Moses' speech, YHWH is thus most familiar with
"written thinking."

The telling of the re-writing of the tables in Exod 34:1, 28 was

---

[52] See Weinfeld, *Deuteronomy*, 410, who refers to the Akkadian expression *tup-
pam ḥepû*, "to break a tablet" = "to invalidate a document," "to repudiate an agreement" (see "*ḥepû*," *CAD* 6.171-173).

[53] Mayes, *Deuteronomy*, 200.

[54] See the NJPSV translation for כמכתב הראשון, "the same text as on the first";
see also Dhorme's rendering, "la même inscription que sur la première"; and
Weinfeld, *Deuteronomy*, 418.

rather equivocal as to the identity of the writer. In his re-telling of the scene in Deut 10:1-5, Moses, who is in a position to know, gets the record straight, and excludes any "scribal" participation on his part. "And he [= YHWH] wrote on the tables, as in the first writing, the ten words" (Deut 10:4): God did write, as he wrote the first time. Here, and in the related issue of the ark, Moses makes the most of the art of retelling to complete the picture of a divine foundational writing.

In Deut 10:1-2, summoning Moses to the mountain and enjoining him to prepare tables for a second writing, God associates the future written document with a new reality, the ark:

> [1]At that time (בעת ההוא) YHWH said to me, "Hew two tables of stone like the first, and come up to me on the mountain, and make an ark of wood. [2]And I will write on the tables the words that were on the first tables which you broke, and you shall put them in the ark." (10:1-2)

Scholars have pointed to the specificity of the ark in Deuteronomy.[55] Deuteronomy's ark is shorn of the cultic function and symbolism it has in Exodus: "no mention is made of the Ark's cover (*kprt*) or of the cherubim that endow the Ark with the semblance of a divine chariot or throne."[56] Deuteronomy's ark is equally distinct from the holy war palladium we read about in the book of Numbers, where it serves as "God's seat upon which he journeys forth to disperse his enemies."[57] To go by his retelling in Deuteronomy, Moses apparently confined himself to a wooden framework—"So I made an ark of acacia wood" (Deut 10:3). Deuteronomy's ark is a mere container; its only function is to house the tables of the covenant. In Exod 25:16, this purpose of the ark is mentioned—"And you shall put into the ark the testimony which I shall give you" (see also Exod 39:35; 40:20); in Deuteronomy this comes to the fore as the sole purpose of the acacia 'ărôn.[58]

---

[55] See von Rad, *Studies*, 40; R. E. Clements, "Deuteronomy and the Jerusalem Cult-Tradition," *VT* 15 (1965) 300-12; T. E. Fretheim, "The Ark in Deuteronomy," *CBQ* 30 (1968) 1-14; Mayes, *Deuteronomy*, 203-204; see especially Weinfeld, *School*, 208-209; *Deuteronomy*, 39-40; 417-18.

[56] Weinfeld, *Deuteronomy*, 39.

[57] Weinfeld, *Deuteronomy*, 39. See Num 10:33-36, and compare Deut 1:42-43 with Num 14:42-44; the absence of the ark in the Deuteronomic law of warfare (Deuteronomy 20) is also to be noticed.

[58] See Deut 31:25-26, and my discussion in Chapter Four. Deuteronomy's idea

Deuteronomy's ark, as I shall indicate, has a role of its own in
Deuteronomy's communication issue. Yet, Moses' telling is also
the revisiting of a story already told. The "narrative past" of the
ark renders the Deuteronomic presentation of the same ark quite
problematic. Bearing in mind the authorized depiction of the ark
in Exodus and Numbers, can Deuteronomy's subsequent presentation of the same ark appear likely? How does Deuteronomy cope
with "the proverbial tenacity and enduring influence of first
impressions"?[59] Here too, the answer lies in Moses' art of retelling.
In Deuteronomy, Moses, for the most part, retells a well-known
story. The act of retelling does not prevent him, however, from
telling things never heard before. The Exodus narrative, for
instance, does not speak of any assembling of the ark (or of its
wooden "frame") *before* Moses' third ascent to the mountain. Driver did not miss this point: "In Dt. Moses is instructed to make,
and actually does make, the ark of acacia-wood, *before* ascending
the mount the third time to receive the tables of stone; whereas
in Ex. the command to make the ark is both given to Bezalel, and
executed by him, *after* Moses' return from the mountain (35:30ff.;
36:2; 37:1)."[60] Telling "after," Moses, who is in the best position to know, tells what actually happened before the pretold Exodus.[61] Reporting what happened first, he brings to the fore the
primary function of the ark. This basic finality, somehow akin
to the basic wooden frame built by Moses, does not exclude further functions (such as the ones specified in Exodus and Num-

---

of the ark is found again in 1 Kings 8:9: "There was nothing in the ark, except
the two tables of stone which Moses put there at Horeb."

[59] Sternberg, *Expositional Modes*, 93. The significance of the order of presentation of a message has been intensively studied by psychologists in the last decades.
Their investigations have emphasized the importance of the "primacy effect"—the
decisive influence of information situated at the beginning of a message (see the
survey by Sternberg, *Expositional Modes*, 93-102, and by Perry, "Literary Dynamics," 53-58; both scholars examine the particular effect of this law of perception
in literature).

[60] Driver, *Deuteronomy*, 118.

[61] The absence in Exodus of any scene equivalent to Deut 10:1-3 usually receives
a source-oriented explanation. See for instance Mayes, *Deuteronomy*, 203: "There
probably did originally exist a JE account in a place closely corresponding to the
Deuteronomistic account in Dt. 10:1-3." The former JE account, Weinfeld goes
on, "has apparently been suppressed in Exodus in favor of the priestly account,
according to which the Ark was made by Bezalel after Moses' return from the
mount (Exod 37:1-9) and not before his ascent, as Deuteronomy has it" (*Deuteronomy*, 417). Following J. Wellhausen, *Die Composition des Hexateuchs und der historischen Bücher des Alten Testaments* (4th ed.; Berlin: Reimer, 1963) 93, many schol-

bers);[62] yet, Moses' speech implies that the Deuteronomic role of the ark is the basic one.

What is the purpose of such a presentation of the ark? Deuteronomy's intention on this point is often explained as ideological, namely, as an attempt to reform the Jerusalem cult tradition by demythologizing it.[63] It is, however, my contention that the motif of the ark in Deuteronomy (in Deuteronomy 10 as in Deut 31:25-26, where it reappears) is primarily linked to the issue of communication in Deuteronomy. Although Choon Seow recently contended that in Deuteronomy the ark "appears always to be mentioned incidentally,"[64] a purposeful pattern underlies the references to the ark. In Deuteronomy 10 a paradigm is first set up so as to provide the background for further occurrences of the ark motif.

The institution of the ark, Moses states in his retelling, coincides with God's *rewriting* of the "ten words" ((Deut 10:2; see also

---

ars saw a hint of the alleged JE tradition of the ark in Exod 33:7. The verse says that Moses pitched the tent of meeting לו, "for it/him," that is, in these scholars' view, for the ark (see especially W. Beyerlin, *Origins and History of the Oldest Sinaitic Traditions* [Oxford: Oxford University Press, 1965] 110, 114). A reference to Moses, however, is equally possible, since the tent in question is especially reserved for him (see M. Haran, *Temples and Temple-Service in Ancient Israel* [Oxford: Clarendon, 1978] 263-64). Whatever the genetic reconstruction, and whatever the actual reference of לו in Exod 33:7, the texts of Exodus and Deuteronomy create, in their actual form and sequence, the peculiar chronological effect described in the above paragraph.

[62] Moses thus apparently assembled what became the shell of Bezalel's work of art (see Exod 37:1-16). Such a assumption, however, implies a retrospective reinterpretation of Exod 25:10 and 37:1.

[63] von Rad, *Studies*, 40, speaks of "'demythologising' and rationalising of the old view"; Weinfeld elaborates along the same line; see *School*, 208-209; *Deuteronomy*, 37-44; Clements, "Deuteronomy," 303, discerns in the Deuteronomic presentation of the ark as a mere container a Northern "attempt at reinterpreting the [Jerusalemite] cherubim-throne conception of the ark"; Fretheim, "Ark," 14, sees the reinterpretation of the ark in Deuteronomy as related to "the use made of it by the Jerusalem cult to substantiate the claims to divine election made by the monarchy, as well as the idolatrous practices that had been brought into connection with it at the celebration of the Feast of Tabernacles." Fretheim's postulation of idolatrous practices linked to the ark is largely unsubstantiated. His former conjecture (see p. 12: "The ark was no longer to be used in festival to bolster the claims of the divine election of the monarchy; it was to be used as the container of the covenant law to which the monarchy had to submit itself") will be reassessed in the fifth section of this chapter (apropos of the king's relationship to "this Torah," as specified in Deut 17:18-20), and in Chapter Four (apropos of the relationship of the ark with the Torah "book").

[64] C. L. Seow, "Ark of the Covenant," *ABD* 1.391.

10:5). The ark has therefore a genesis which was not specified in the systematic perspective of Exodus (see Exodus 25; 37; 40). YHWH, who first released unsheathed tables, provided them with their appropriate casing only at the close of the Golden Calf affair. God's institution of the ark is told just after the account of Moses' intercession on behalf of the sinful people (9:18-29), and before God makes his forgiveness explicit (10:10). Placed in such a context, the "invention" of the ark indicates a merciful turn in the people's history, beyond what is now "the sin of the past."[65] Shielded by the portable ark, the "ten words" are now turned into an unalterable record and start a journey which is the people's journey toward the land.

The ancient Near Eastern background of the ark is generally associated with the symbolism and function of the 'ărôn in Israelite holy war and cult.[66] Interesting evidence can be produced, however, highlighting the role of the ark as a container for valuable records. In several ancient Near Eastern contexts, tablets and case relate to each other as parts of the same cultural complex. Stone, clay and wooden boxes were used in Mesopotamia and Egypt to protect original documents in temple precincts and in archive deposits.[67] The burying of written oaths and treaties in special cases under the images of the gods in temples was common in Egypt and the Hittite kingdom—and apparently throughout the ancient Near East.[68] Particularly interesting is the container known in

---

[65] Thus the title given to Deut 9:1-10:11 by Weinfeld, *Deuteronomy*, 398.

[66] For a comparative approach to the relationship between ark and holy war, see F. M. Cross, *Canaanite Myth and Hebrew Epic* (Cambridge: Harvard University Press, 1973) 93-111. For the cultic function of the ark, see R. de Vaux, *Bible et Orient* (*Cogitatio Fidei* 24; Paris: Cerf, 1967) 231-76; M. Haran, *Temple*, 255-59.

[67] See R. S. Ellis, *Foundation Deposits in Ancient Mesopotamia* (New Haven & London: Yale University Press, 1968) 100-106. About the conservation of clay tablets, E. Posner writes, "Boxes were made of wood or clay. Wood seems to have been popular with, and easily available to, the archivists of Knossos on Crete and of Pylos, for bronze hinges and handles found there must have been used on these boxes. Wood probably seemed ideal from the standpoint of physical preservation, because in such receptacles the clay tablets could not rub against material of the same kind, to the possible detriment of the writing on them. . . . For the most part, however, storage boxes were made of clay, and many of them have been excavated" (*Archives in the Ancient World* [Cambridge, Ma: Harvard University Press, 1972] 58-59). In Ancient Egypt, besides the system of niches in temples, "papyrus documents and rolls were stored in wooden chests and jars. Scribes are often represented with their chests lying in front of them, and sometimes wooden boxes containing papyri were found in the tombs" (p. 86).

[68] See de Vaux, *Bible et Orient*, 256-58; Haran, *Temples*, 255 (both with literature).

Sumerian as dub-REC-429, and in Akkadian as *tupšennu*. The latter is found three times in literary texts:[69]
- In the opening of the *Cuthean Legend*:

> Open the *tupšennu* (tablet-box) and read out the *narû* (stone inscription)
> [Which I, Naram-Sin], son of Sargon,
> [Have inscribed and left for] future days.[70]

- In the body of the same legend:

> I have made for you a *tupšennu* (and) inscribed a *narû*-document for you,
> in Cuthah, in the temple Emeslam, in the sanctuary of Nergal,
> I have deposited it for you. (149-51)[71]

- In the prologue of the *Gilgamesh Epic*:

> [Find (?)] the cop[per] *tupšennu*,
> [unfasten] its bro[nze] locks,
> [open] the door to the treasure,
> [take] and read the tablets of lapis-lazuli. (Ii 22-25)[72]

In regard to the occurrence in the *Gilgamesh Epic*, Donald Wiseman was the first to suggest the translation of *tupšennu* as "tablet-box."[73] Probably initially "a type of chest, serving as a treasure-box, which formed part of temple furnishings,"[74] the con-

---

[69] See P. Steinkeller, "Studies in Third Millennium Paleography. 2. Signs ŠEN and ALAL," *Oriens Antiquus* 20 (1981) 243-49. Steinkeller first discusses the Sumerian background of the word, that is, the sign REC-429, which marked a class of metal containers or receptacles, usually made of copper (see pp. 243-45).

[70] Standard Babylonian recension; text and translation in J. G. Westenholz, "Writing for Posterity: Naram-Sin and Enmerkar," *kinattūtu ša dārâti: Raphael Kutscher Memorial Volume* (ed. A. F. Rainey; Tel Aviv: Tel Aviv University, 1993) 206. The incipit is known from the Old Babylonian period onwards; see C. B. F. Walker, "The Second Tablet of *tupšenna pitema*, An Old Babylonian Naram-Sin Legend?" *JCS* 33 (1981) 191-95.

[71] Text and translation in Steinkeller, "Studies," 245.

[72] Standard Babylonian recension; text and translation in Steinkeller, "Studies," 245.

[73] See D. J. Wiseman, "A Gilgamesh Epic Fragment from Nimrud," *Iraq* 37 (1975) 157-59. W. von Soden, "Zu einigen akkadischen Wörtern" *ZA* 67 (1977) 237-39, adopts the same rendering ("Tafelbehälter," "Bauurkundenbehälter"); see also *AHW* 1371b. Wiseman, "Gilgamesh," 158, further connects the *tupšennu*— "tablet-box" with the boxes built into the foundations or walls of Mesopotamian temples, which served as containers for foundation-deposits.

[74] Steinkeller, "Studies," 246; Steinkeller dismisses the foundation-deposit hypothesis, on the basis of the use of dub-REC-429 in the Gudea inscriptions: it is linked to a "chair," it is "brought" into the temple, and there existed an official

tainer in question came to be used as tablet- or *narû*-box, as shown in the literary texts quoted above.[75] Deuteronomy's addressees (and, analogically, Moses' addressees) were not foreign to the cultural data I have just surveyed (suffice it to mention that a fragment of the *Gilgamesh Epic* was found in Megiddo). For such an audience, God's institution of the wooden ark as a chest or case housing the stone tables was therefore, it seems, plausible on cultural grounds.

Tablets provided with their appropriate case were tables deposited, or destined to be deposited, primarily in temples. In the second text of the *Cuthean Legend* quoted above, the making of the container and of the stone inscription is followed by the mention of their deposit in the sanctuary of Nergal. Does this apply to the Horeb tables and ark? The report of the making of the ark in Deut 10:1-5 is followed by one of the narratorial comments that interrupt Moses' speeches (Deut 10:6-9).[76] The narrator's interpolation unfolds in two sections. A first account (vv. 6-7) unfolds along the spatial axis. The account briefly details the people's (future) journey up to and away from the place of Aaron's death (that is, the death of the leader compromised in the Golden Calf affair). A second narratorial note (vv. 8-9) reports an event determined temporally (and not necessarily situated in the journey just described): "At that time (בעת ההוא) YHWH set apart the tribe of Levi to carry the ark of the covenant of YHWH, to stand before YHWH, to minister to him and to bless in his name, to this day" (10:8).[77] That the Levites are entrusted with the *carrying* of the

who was in some way associated with it (see pp. 244-45); in an unpublished paper read in 1980 at the Oriental Institute of the University of Chicago, W. L. Moran equally raised the question whether the "chest" (*tupšennu*) mentioned in the opening of the Epic of Gilgamesh is part of a foundation deposit ("The Epic of Gilgamesh: A Document of Ancient Humanism," quoted by Steinkeller, "Studies," 246).

[75] See Westenholz, "Writing for Posterity," 205-206.

[76] See in Chapter Seven my analysis of Deuteronomy's "frame breaks."

[77] In S. E. Loewenstamm's view, the formula בעת ההוא, "at that time," is an editorial device. It marks instances where redactors supplied historical details passed over in a previous version of Deuteronomy's narrative account ("The Formula *ba'et hahi'* in the Introductory Speeches in Deuteronomy," *From Babylon to Canaan: Studies in the Bible and its Oriental Background* [Jerusalem: Magnes Press, 1992] 42-50). In a forthcoming study I intend to show that the formula functions as a poetic marker, pertaining to Moses', or the narrator's, art of retelling. The fifteen instances (Deut 1:9, 16, 18; 2:34; 3:4, 8, 12, 18, 21, 23; 4:14; 5:5; 9:20; 10:1, 8) signal what could be termed "authoritative secondary disclosures": Moses (or

ark reveals that in Deuteronomy's narrative the ark is properly a vehicle. The ark is thus provided with its own personnel in remote time ("at that time"), and, apparently, at the appropriate time. The narratorial notice is indeed followed, now in Moses' retelling, by God's order of departure: "And YHWH said to me, 'Arise, go on your journey at the head of the people, that they may go in and possess the land which I swore to their fathers to give them'" (10:11). The insertion of the tables within the portable ark (as told by Moses) and the divine institution of the Levites as carriers of the ark (as told by the narrator) thus concur in the same perspective.[78] Moses tells of the relaunching of Israel's journey toward the land, beyond "the sin of the past." Thanks to the narrator's disclosure, we can understand that the people's journey is henceforth a translation journey—the tables and the ark moving now along with the people. Even if no particular place of deposit comes to be mentioned, the land is the journey's explicit destination (10:11).[79]

In terms of communication, the housing of the "ten words" in the ark represents, however, a powerful paradox. When Moses speaks in Moab, the tables have long been secured in the wood container, with no stipulation whatsoever for a periodical or even emergency removal. Rather, we learn from Moses' mouth that YHWH provided for the permanence of the tables' deposit in the ark: "I placed the tables in the ark which I had made; and there they are, as YHWH commanded me" (10:5). In the two Akkadian

---

the narrator in 10:8) reveals what was not told before in the preceding account of Exodus-Numbers, or what has not been told before in the way it is now presented. The formula could be paraphrased "It was at that time that . . .," and signals the filling of gaps in the overall "fabula" of Israel's journey in the desert. In Moses' retelling the formula introduces, for instance, the reference to God's order to "teach" supplementary "statutes and ordinances" (4:14), the account of Moses' actual mediation in the revelation of the "ten words" (5:5), and the disclosure about the first building of the ark (10:1). In the case of 10:8, the narrator is revisiting the accounts of Exod 32:25-29 and Num 1:50; 3:6-8, and establishing what was not told before, notably the relationship of the Levites to the ark. The disclosures in question betray a definite authorial perspective in that they "dramatize" the subtle recasting of Israel's story by Deuteronomy's authors.

[78] Mayes' opinion that 10:8-9 is "out of place" despite its contextual pertinence (ark—carriers of the ark) is therefore disputable (*Deuteronomy*, 205).

[79] The end of the translation of the ark started at Horeb is actually told in 1 Kings 8:1-9: "The priests brought the ark of the covenant of YHWH to its place, in the inner sanctuary of the house, in the most holy place, underneath the wings of the cherubim" (1 Kings 8:6).

texts quoted above, the opposite injunction is found: "Open the
tablet-box and read out the *narû*"; "Find the copper tablet-box,
unfasten its bronze locks, open the door to the treasure, take and
read the tablets of lapis-lazuli!" The "open and read" injunction,
however, bears on tablet cases already deposited in their proper
place, the sanctuary of Nergal and the walls of Uruk. In Deuteronomy, the perspective is reversed: the ark starts its journey (toward
a deposit place?), and no opening of the case is stipulated. As
already said, covenant-makers in the ancient Near East knew the
custom of burying original treaty texts in sanctuaries. The custom
in question entailed the preparation of unsealed copies for state
use.[80] In the case of the "ten words," however, no duplicate was
ever made and put into circulation. The only record of God's revelation is the one deposited in the ark. A hermetic sealing of the
"ten words" within the ark, without any divulging of their content, would be biblical nonsense, a blatant contradiction of the
Hebrew Bible's policy to make "the essentials . . . transparent to
all comers".[81] Such a policy would be deeply contradicted if, within the represented world, and coming to the essential "ten words,"
occultation were the rule. The terms of the Decalogue, to be sure,
have been spelled out orally by Moses (5:6-21), in a rendering
that enabled the sons to hear what their fathers heard. Still,
Moses' oral performance in the plains of Moab occurs as the ultimate rehearsal of the Horeb communication by the authorized
mediator. That the "ten words" are meant for further transmission is more than likely. As I said, they may very well be included within the "words" entrusted to the people's sedulous reception (Deut 6:6-9). An oral transmission, based on Moses' ultimate
rendition, is possible; still, no means for a foolproof transmission
of the "ten words" has thus far been provided for.

---

[80] Weinfeld, *Deuteronomy*, 63-64.

[81] Sternberg, *Poetics*, 55. Sternberg has made a strong case in favor of the
Hebrew Bible's "foolproof composition," "whereby the discourse strives to open
and bring home its essentials to all readers so as to establish a common ground,
a bond instead of a barrier of understanding" (*Poetics*, 50). What is true in the
Bible's transaction between narrator and reader off stage, Sternberg further contends, is true of communication represented on the biblical stage—no essential
is opaque in the characters' interchanges (see "The World from the Addressee's
Viewpoint: Reception as Representation, Dialogue as Monologue," *Style* 20 [1986]
295-317, esp. 303-304, 315-17).

4. *"You Shall Write" (II)—Deut 11:18-21*

In Deut 11:18-21 Moses utters for a second time a set of injunctions relating to the reception of his "words": "You shall therefore
lay up these words of mine in your heart and in your soul. . . .
And you shall write them upon the doorposts of your house and
upon your gates"). The resumption of these reception injunctions
forms an inclusion with the first uttering of these injunctions in
6:6-9, so as to frame a long rhetorical "phrase" interweaving parenetic and historical themes.[82] It is furthermore to be noticed that
the commandment to write in Deuteronomy 11 follows the
account of the divine writing in Deuteronomy 10, just as the "you
will write" injunction in chapter 6 follows the "[YHWH] wrote"
account in chapter 5. The framing device includes therefore an
echoing effect, from God's to the people's writing:

5:22 And he wrote ⇒ 6:9 You shall write

10:4 And he wrote ⇒ 11:20 You shall write

What makes the second parallelism different, in terms of communication, is the theme of the insertion of the written tables in
the ark. In Deuteronomy 5-6, the public display of Moses' "words"
mirrored the written display of God's "words." In Deuteronomy
10-11 a contrast is introduced: the publication of Moses' "words"
("these words of mine" 11:18)[83] now echoes the archiving of God's
"ten words." This contrast is expressed lexically through the verb
שׂים, "to put," which occurs on both sides (and did not occur in
the first parallelism), yet with different prepositions:

---

[82] See Weinfeld, *Deuteronomy*, 448; Braulik, "Gedächtniskultur," 19. For a thorough examination of the differences between the two sets of stipulations, see
Fischer and Lohfink, "Diese Worte," 64-65.

[83] Braulik takes the phrase "these words of mine" (דברי אלה) as a sign that
Moses' words, entrusted to the people in Deut 6:6-9 and 11:18-21, do not include
the "ten words" ("Ausdrücke," 21). The latter, Braulik contends, are exclusively
designated as God's דברים, "words" (Braulik overlooks the fact that God does once
call the Horeb revelation דברי, "my words" [4:10]). It seems difficult, however, to
oppose God's words to Moses' on the ground of "authorship," since both the
Horeb and the Moab revelations proceed from the same divine lawgiver. The criterion, in my view, is rather pragmatic: God calls "my words" what he utters, and
so does Moses when he conveys the divine revelation.

Deut 10:2   Deut 11:18

ושמתם בארון   ושמתם את דברי אלה על לבבכם ועל
                                                                                נפשכם

And you shall *put* them [the   You shall *put* these words of mine
written tables] into the ark   upon your heart and upon your
                                                         soul

Deut 10:5

ואשם את הלחת בארון

And I *put* the tables into the ark

The first injunction in 11:18 is immediately followed by the reference to the written amulets—"You shall put these words of mine
upon (על) your heart and upon (על) your soul; and you shall bind
them as a sign upon (על) your hand, and they shall be as frontlets
between your eyes" (11:18)—so as to group together the bodily,
that is, individual, "laying up" of the transmitted "words." Whereas God's "words" were put into the ark, Moses' are to be put upon
(metaphorical or literal) parts of the body. As in 6:9, the individual "laying up" leads to the public inscription, "on the doorposts and the city gates" (11:20). Moses' injunction thus makes
clear that the final purpose of his words—his current teaching—is
to be brought to the fore, to be transmitted and displayed in the
promised land. Publication, and not archiving, is the last word.

    At the close of Deuteronomy 5-11, and when it comes to Deute-
ronomy's communication process, two things stand out:
    (i) God's revelation, in its foundational and divine form, is
    heading *toward* the land, written down, yet sealed in a wood-
    en box;
    (ii) God's revelation, in its final and Mosaic form, has to be
    learned, taught and written down *in* the land.
A momentum has thus been created that directs everything toward
home, i.e., into the land. Yet, things do not concur in coordinated
fashion within this momentum. The vehicle of God's communication from Horeb and toward the land, the mobile ark, is unre-
lated to Moses' teaching in Moab, which similarly calls for a "translation" into the land. No foolproof conveyance of Moses' Torah
into the land, and publication of the same Torah in the land, has
been provided for so far (oral tradition, however faithful, is not
foolproof). Yet a foolproof transportation of God's "ten words"
has been established—the written tables, housed in the ark. Paradoxically, the institution of the ark involves the removal of God's

written words from publication. Moses' communication thus seems to require further ways and means, so that things may be properly brought home.

5. *"He Shall Write a Copy of this Torah"—Deut 17:18-20*

The references to writing thus far reviewed (the double account of God's writing at Horeb; the injunctions for the people to write in the land) belonged to the introduction of Moses' second speech. In the core section of this speech, which conveys individual stipulations, a further reference to writing is found, in the framework of the "royal law" (Deut 17:14-20). The "royal law" is part of a larger complex of legal provisions concerning public offices (Deut 16:18-18:22). As Lohfink has indicated, these laws provide for the distribution and regulation of the functions of power in "landed" Israel, around a Torah which, in the new society, has pride of place.[84] Because of its particular features, the law concerning the king has, moreover, a unique value for Moses' audience and regarding Moses' act of communication. The "royal law" casts the king as the model Israelite,[85] and it does so by turning him into the Torah's arch-reader. In the "royal law," as I shall show, Moses' speech indirectly prophesies about its own reception as written Torah.

The law concerning the king presupposes that Israel, having completed the occupation of the land, will want to set a king over itself, like all the surrounding nations (17:14). The legal provision first determines that the king must be chosen by YHWH and that he must be a native Israelite, "one among your brothers" (17:15). A portrait of the ideal king follows, in two stages. A triple prohibition—the king is not to multiply (לא ירבה לו) horses, or wives, or riches (17:16-17)—gives way to a positive stipulation, which specifies the king's relationship to the Mosaic Torah (17:18-20).[86]

---

[84] N. Lohfink, "Die Sicherung der Wirksamkeit des Gotteswortes durch das Prinzip der Schriftlichkeit der Tora und durch das Prinzip der Gewaltenteilung nach den Ämtergesetzen des Buches Deuteronomium (Dt 16,18-18,22)," *Testimonium Veritati: Festchrift Wilhelm Kempf* (ed. H. Wolter; Frankfurt: Knecht, 1971) 143-55.

[85] See Lohfink, "Sicherung," 150.

[86] In modern genetic approaches, the stipulation in Deut 17:18-20 is usually

[18]And when he sits on the throne of his kingdom, he shall write for himself a copy of this Torah in a "book" (rps), from that which is in charge of the Levitical priests; [19]and it shall be with him, and he shall read in it all the days of his life, that he may learn to fear YHWH his God, by keeping all the words of this law and these statutes, and doing them; [20]that his heart may not be lifted up above his brethren, and that he may not turn aside from the commandment, either to the right hand or to the left; so that he may continue long in his kingdom, he and his sons, in Israel.

a. *"He Shall Write for Himself"*

Writing is often associated with royal figures in the ancient Near East. That the material inscriptions were probably in most cases produced by court scribes is in this matter less relevant than the formal attribution of writing to kings in literary sources.[87] In *Enmerkar and the Lord of Aratta*, Enmerkar, the king of Uruk, is even credited with the invention of writing on clay.[88] Inscriptions

---

regarded as a secondary interpolation; see the *status quaestionis* in F. García López, "Le roi d'Israël: Dt 17,14-20," *Das Deuteronomium: Entstehung, Gestalt und Botschaft* (ed. N. Lohfink; BETL 68; Louvain: University Press, 1985) 277-97, especially 278. U. Rütersworden, for instance, claims that the mention of a Torah book, here (v. 18) as elsewhere in Deuteronomy, is sufficient to determine the late character of the passage (*Von der politischen Gemeinschaft zur Gemeinde: Studien zu Dt 16,18-18,22* [BBB 65; Frankfurt: Athenäum, 1987] 63). F. Crüsemann answers that, to go by Jer 8:8, the concept of written Torah is already known in Jerusalem in pre-exilic times; a late dating is therefore not necessary (*Tora*, 277); Crüsemann, however, contends that the *reflexive* character of the reference to the Deuteronomic Torah in 17:18-20 is foreign to the original Deuteronomy (p. 275). Whatever the redactional genesis of the passage, it is to be noted that semantic, syntactic, and echoing features promote the cohesion of the entire passage. The triple prohibition, לא ירבה לו, "He will not multiply for himself," is for instance echoed in the stipulation, וכתב לו, "he shall write for himself." The syntactic construction verb + preposition + ו recurs further: והיתה עמו, "it (= the Torah, fem.) shall be with him"; וקרא בו, "and he shall read in it (the "book," masc.)." C. Schäfer-Lichtenberger has recently contended that "die semantische Struktur des Textes ist durch ein Netz von stichwortartigen Beziehungen bestimmt," and has carefully established this network of structural correspondences (*Josua und Salomo: Eine Studie zu Autorität und Legitimität des Nachfolgers im Alten Testament* [VTSup 55; Leiden: Brill, 1995] 84-85).

[87] It is worth noticing, however, that Assurbanipal (at least the Assurbanipal portrayed in the so-called Rassam Cylinder) boasts of having "penetrated into all (the intricacies) of the art of writing" (*AR* 2.292 [§ 767]).

[88] See Westenholz, "Writing for Posterity," 207 (see n. 3 for literature), 214. The same Enmerkar is accused by Naram-Sin in the *Cuthean Legend* of not leaving his memoirs on a *narû* inscription for Naram-Sin to read it out and bless its owner (see Westenholz, "Writing for Posterity," 205-207, 214-18). On the Meso-

were one of the means by which rulers hoped to perpetuate their names and also to receive the blessing of future generations. Thus the autobiographical inscription of Idrimi, king of Alalakh in the 15th century BCE, ends: "I wrote my achievements on my statue. Let people [read it] and ble[ss me]."[89] The recourse to writing by royal rulers reportedly extended to the publication or recording of legal stipulations, as in Hammurapi's Code; "I wrote my precious words on my stela," the king five times boasts in the epilogue to the code.[90] Kings also are presented as writers in treaty-making, as in the Sefire inscriptions, "Thus have we spoken [and thus have we writ]ten. What I, [Matî'̔]el, have written (is to act) as a reminder for my son [and] my [grand]son who will come a[fter] me" (I C 1-4).[91] Against this cultural and literary background, the peculiar character of the royal writing in Deut 17:18 stands out, in being a stipulation enjoined *upon* the king, "he shall write."[92] The act of writing does not come at the king's initiative, as in the examples cited above (sometimes under divine inspiration, as in the case of Hammurapi)[93]; it is the king's first duty, "when he sits on the throne of his kingdom" (17:18).

While speaking, Moses has shifted his audience into its future in the land: "When you come to the land" (17:14). From this perspective, he anticipates the completion of his communication.

---

potamian traditions about the divine transmission of the secret of writing to antediluvian kings, see P. Grelot, "La légende d'Hénoch dans les Apocryphes et dans la Bible," *RSR* 46 (1958) 7-9.

[89] *ANET*, 558. So did Naram-Sin, king of Akkad (see the standard Babylonian recension of the *Cuthean Legend*, l. 1-3; 175-76; text and translation in Westenholz, "Writing for Posterity," 206), and Gilgamesh, king of Uruk, according to the epic that bears his name (1:8; *ANET*, 73).

[90] See the code's epilogue, *ANET*, 178.

[91] Translation in Fitzmyer, *Aramaic Inscriptions*, 19.

[92] As I indicated above, it is my view that the injunction is to be taken at face value insofar as it represents an element of Deuteronomy's proposition; like YHWH and the people, the king is presented as a writing character, i.e., as the subject of the verb כתב, "to write." In that sense, a translation such as the *Einheitsübersetzung*'s, "soll er von dieser Weisung . . . eine Zweitschrift anfertigen lassen," underreads the text's claim, and overshadows the link created between Israel's future king with other writing figures in Deuteronomy. The historical reality behind Deuteronomy's proposition can be reconstructed in various ways. Schäfer-Lichtenberger, *Josua und Salomo*, 81 n. 286, believes that "schriftkundigkeit des Königs muß nicht vorausgesetzt werden. Denkbar ist, daß hinter dieser Formulierung das Postulat steht, der König solle schrift- und lesekundig sein."

[93] *See Hammurapi's Code*, 25b:95: "I am Hammurapi, the just king, to whom Shamash has granted truths"; for this translation, see Greenberg, "Postulates," 286.

"Ces versets," Caquot writes, "semblent supposer que la loi deuté-
ronomique ('cette loi') est un tout formé alors que l'énoncé n'en
est pas achevé."[94] Since Moses started to convey the particular stipulations (in Deut 12:1), and up to the present provisions about
the king, never have the people heard (and the reader read)
about the Torah as a comprehensive legal corpus.[95] The linkage
of the king with the "total Torah" points to a kind of exemplary
status, which will be specified below. Moses associates the king
with a written corpus, which is itself produced on the basis of an
implied (preexisting) written Torah: "he shall write for himself a
copy (משנה) of this Torah." The "duplicate" (the word משנה derives
from the root שנה, "to repeat, to do again") implicitly requires a
standard copy, an *editio princeps*, from which the transcript is to
be made.[96] The end of the verse, the phrase מלפני הכהנים הלוים,
makes sense in the context of such a transcription. In some contexts, Drivers points out, לפני "might signify 'under the eyes of, in
the keeping of'."[97] The use of the compound preposition מלפני
can then imply that the duplicate was made "(from) under the
supervision of," or, in a brachyology, "from [the standard copy
which is] in charge of" the Levitical priests.[98] At any rate, the
preposition מלפני does not mean, as sometimes understood, "at the
dictation of"[99] or "by," as if the transcription was achieved by the
Levites.[100] No oral transmission by the Levites or instrumental
mediation of the Levites in the act of copying is brought into play.
The Levites rather appear as the ones from whom the standard

---

[94] A. Caquot, "Remarques sur la 'loi royale' du *Deutéronome* (17/14-20)," *Sem*
9 (1959) 30.

[95] As Braulik points out, the occurrence of "torah" in Deut 17:11 refers to the
limited legal teaching by the Levites, and not to the Mosaic teaching as a comprehensive body ("Ausdrücke," 36 n. 115).

[96] What is implied in Deut 17:18 is made explicit in Josh 8:32, "[Joshua] wrote
upon the stones a copy (משנה) of the Torah of Moses, *which he* [Moses] *had written* (אשר כתב) before the eyes of the sons of Israel."

[97] Driver, *Deuteronomy*, 212 n. 18; Driver notably refers to 1 Sam 3:1; see RSV,
"Now the boy Samuel was ministering to YHWH under (לפני) Eli" (see also NJPSV).

[98] See P. Buis, *Le Deutéronome* (VS Ancien Testament 4; Paris: Beauchesne,
1969) 17: "d'après [le texte conservé par] les prêtres lévites"; the *Einheitsübersetzung*: "von dieser Weisung, die die levitischen Priester aufbewahren"; see also
Fischer and Lohfink, "Diese Worte," 68, and Crüsemann, *Tora*, 318.

[99] See NEB, which apparently presupposes מפי, "from the mouth of," instead
of מלפני, cf. Jer 36:18.

[100] See NJPSV, "he shall have a copy of this Teaching written for him on a
scroll by the levitical priests."

copy emanates, the ones in charge of the *Urschrift*. This is in keeping with what is known up to now from the role of the Levites, divinely appointed as custodians of the *written* tablets in the ark (see Deut 10:8).[101]

From the original copy, the Torah is to be transcribed on a ספר. In Deuteronomy the word ספר occurs with variegated meanings. The particular ספר forming the royal copy of the Torah is characterized as a transportable item ("it shall be with [the king]"), lending itself to personal reading ("[the king] shall read in it"); it has therefore most probably the form of a book scroll.[102] The injunction to the king—"he shall write"—echoes the command to the people in Deut 6:4-9 and 11:18-21—"you shall write."[103] In both cases the allegiance to the covenantal stipulations implies their transcription (see the use of כתב, "to write," in 6:9; 11:20 and 17:18), in order to let them permeate one's space and time. The people were required to don inscribed amulets and to surround themselves with architectural inscriptions displaying Moses' "words." Yet, the most appropriate medium for the "words" in question only appears in association with the king. The written ספר, "book scroll," that the king produces for himself not only holds the whole of "this Torah," it also enables the "total Torah" to pervade the space of the king's life ("[this Torah] shall be with him" [17:19]), and time ("He shall read in [the Torah book] all the days of his life" [17:19]). The making of duplicates is constitutive of written cultures, as evidenced by the duplicated tablets that pervaded Mesopotamia, and the related phenomenon of scribal colophons.[104] The integral reproducibility of inscriptions and written records is, in itself, an amazing phenomenon. The making of a duplicate results in another token of the same totality (oral repetition can faithfully reproduce a linguistic or literary

---

[101] See Weinfeld, *School*, 53.

[102] See Lohfink, "Sicherung," 67; see also the technical considerations by M. Haran, "Book-Scrolls in Israel in Pre-exilic Times," *JJS* 33 (1982) 166-67.

[103] See Caquot, "Remarques," 31; Fischer and Lohfink, "'Diese Worte'," 68-69; G. Braulik, *Deuteronomium II* (Neue Echter Bibel 28; Würzburg: Echter) 129-30.

[104] See A. L. Oppenheim, *Ancient Mesopotamia: Portrait of a Dead Civilization* (Rev. ed.; Chicago: University of Chicago Press, 1977) 150, 240-41; E. Leichty, "The Colophon," *Studies Presented to A. Leo Oppenheim* (ed. R. D. Biggs and J. A. Brinkman; Chicago: Chicago University Press, 1964) 147-54. See especially the phrase commonly included in the Mesopotamian colophons: "according to its original, written, checked, and copied" (see Leichty, "Colophon," 150).

whole; yet, it cannot synchronically present the whole as such).[105]
Thanks to the duplicate on a book scroll, the totality of the Torah
is "attached" to the king ("and [the Torah] shall be with him"),
in a manner similar to the intimate proximity of the written
amulets (to be) carried by the people.[106] A written copy gives a
message, however conceptual, a physical presence. Ascending the
throne, the king will not be alone; "with him" will be the Torah
scroll. Thanks to the mediation of a written duplicate, the whole
of the Horeb-Moab revelation will thus be attached to Israel's king,
in another time and place.[107]

The mediation of the Torah book warrants the presence of the
totality of the covenantal regulations next to the king; the same
mediation also enables the king to have permanent access to this
totality, as is required from him: וקרא בו כל ימי חייו, "and he shall
read in it all the days of his life" (17:19). This injunction features,
in Moses' speeches (as in Deuteronomy), the first occurrence of
the verb קרא, "to call," in its specific meaning of "to read."[108] The

---

[105] It has been said that Deuteronomy is the book that effects the passage from
the (many) תורות, "prescriptive teachings," to the single Torah (see P. Beauchamp,
L'un et l'autre Testament: Essai de lecture [Paris: Seuil, 1976] 59-60; 153-54). The
role of writing in the creation and the perception of the unity of the Torah is
not inconsiderable. In his *Logic of Writing*, Goody highlights the particular economy of written records, especially Holy Writs and written law, in society. "The
construction of the text," Goody writes, "which is in any case something other
than the transcription of discourse, can lead *to its contemplation*, to the development of thoughts about thoughts, to a metaphysic that may require its own meta-
language" (p. 38, my italics). In Deuteronomy 17, through the "scene" of royal
writing and reading, Moses prompts his audience to anticipate the "contemplation" of the Torah in its written integrity, and thus in its unity.

[106] In a Mesopotamian text, the mythical king Enmeduranki receives, in what
seems to be his enthronement, "the tablets of the gods, the bag with the mystery
of heaven and earth" (*ABRT* 1.64). Widengren sees in this mention a reference
to tablets contained in a kind of pouch and attached to the god's or king's breast
(*Heavenly Book*, 11-12). Is this a remote analogy of the Torah destined to be "with"
the king?

[107] See the divine injunction to Moses' successor (not yet a king) in Israel's
leadership, Joshua, "This book of the Torah shall not depart out of your mouth,
but you shall meditate on it day and night" (Josh 1:8).

[108] In the Pentateuch so far, only Moses has been described in the act of reading (Exod 24:7). Israel's future king is therefore the first Israelite beside Moses
to be associated with reading. In the ancient Near East, kings are most often associated with writing (see above, pp. 72-73). References to reading are less frequent.
The Hittite treaty with Mittani provides for a periodic reading of the treaty "before
the king of Mittani and before the men of the land of Ḫurri" (see Weinfeld,
School, 64 n. 3). The Hittite king Telipinus is linked with reading in an injunction of the instruction that bears his name: "Sieh nach in der Tafel" (*TUAT*
1.469).

phrase וּקָרָא בּוֹ, "and he shall 'call' (= read) in it," echoes syntactically the phrases linked to the people's reception of the "words" in 6:7 and 11:19, דִּבַּרְתָּ בָּם, "you shall 'talk in them' (= recite them)", and לְדַבֵּר בָּם, "to 'talk in them' (= recite them)," but shifts the reception process to the context of written communication. As is often pointed out, the reception of a written message in ancient times included a fair part of orality, since the record was read aloud. "One normally 'mouthed' the words of the text and preferably voiced them aloud, not only in reading them but even in composing or copying them into writing."[109] Reading was somehow resurrecting the "voice of the words." Still, the idiom קָרָא בּ- definitely implies a written medium, of which a part only is "activated" by the reader.[110] By associating the two verbs כָּתַב and קָרָא with the figure of the king, and by linking these verbs with the (re)production and the reception of a Torah "book" (סֵפֶר), Moses sets up a full paradigm.

The royal duty to write down "a copy of this Torah" bears on a comprehensive Torah that includes the provisions in Deut 17:14-20 about the exercise of kingship (and thus the "he shall write" command).[111] This reflexive logic is remarkable. Ancient Near Eastern kingships were far from being constitutional monarchies. The authority of the Hittite kings is known, however, to

---

[109] Graham, *Oral Aspects*, 33; on this topic, see the studies by J. Balogh, "'*Voces paginarum*': Beiträge zur Geschichte des lauten Lesens und Schreibens," *Philologus* 82 (1926-27) 83-109, 202-40; G. L. Hendrickson, "Ancient Reading," *The Classical Journal* 25 (1929) 182-96. More specifically about קרא, see C. J. Labuschagne, "קרא, qr', rufen," *THAT* 2.672; F. L. Hossfeld and H. Lamberty-Zielinski, "קרא, qārā'," *TWAT* 7.133-35; see also the remarks by H. Mechonnic, *Le signe et le poème* (Paris: Gallimard, 1975) 536, which are echoed by D. Boyarin, "Placing Reading: Ancient Israel and Medieval Europe," *The Ethnography of Reading* (J. Boyarin ed.; Berkeley: University of California Press, 1993) 10-37. Was the act of reading enjoined upon the king in Deut 17:19 a "reading aloud to someone," as Boyarin contends, who explains Deut 17:19 by the various scenes of reading staged in 2 Kings 22-23 (see pp. 13-14)? Boyarin, it seems, overlooks what can be gathered from Josh 1:8, "This 'book' of the Torah," God enjoins Joshua, "shall not depart out of your mouth, but you shall recite it (וְהָגִיתָ בּוֹ) it day and night" (see also Ps 1:2). In conjunction with a reference to the Torah "book" in Josh 1:8, the idiom הגה בּ- expresses a kind of meditative "(low)-voiced" recitation, and betokens the Hebrew Bible's familiarity with soliloquy reading (on this topic, see Fischer and Lohfink, "Diese Worte," 70-72).

[110] See Jer 36:6, 8, 13, 14; Hab 2:2; Neh 8:3, 8, 18; 9,3; 2 Chr 34:18.

[111] Weinfeld, *Deuteronomy*, 4, presents Deuteronomy as "a kind of manual for the future king of Israel."

have been carefully circumscribed by law.[112] The piece of omen
literature known as the *Advice to a Prince*, found in the library of
Ashurbanipal, represents a Mesopotamian attempt to remind the
ruler of some basic duties related to the implementation of justice.[113] But nowhere do we find in the ancient Near East the situation where a ruler is enjoined to write "for himself" the laws that,
among other stipulations, regulate his own exercise of power.[114]
The Deuteronomic law that "dissociates" the royal ruler from his
Israelite fellows aims to ensure the king's non-dissociation from
the people, "that his heart may not be lifted up above his
brethren" (17:20), among whom he has been chosen (17:15). This
will be ensured by the king's adherence to the Torah "book." For
Moses' audience, which has been defined as a community of
"brothers" (see 15:1-18),[115] and to which "this Torah" is addressed,
a powerful paradigm is thus given in the presentation of the king
as the Torah "book"'s arch-reader.

b. *The Royal Reading as* Mise en Abyme *of the People's Reception*

The specific relevance, for Moses' audience, of the injunctions
revolving around the royal writing and reading of "this Torah"
deserves closer analysis. The reception injunctions in Deut 6:4-9
and 11:18-21 were aimed at Moses' present audience and were
accordingly formulated in the second person. The "royal law" aims
at a figure that belongs to Israel's future ("When you come in the
land . . . and you possess it . . . and then say: 'I will set a king
over me'" [17:14]). Although in kinship continuity with Moses'
audience, the royal character belongs to another time and place

---

[112] See O. R. Gurney, *The Hittites* (Baltimore: Peguin, 1952) 25; Gurney is referring to the legislation established by Telepinus, whose laws seem to have been
observed down to the last days of the Hittite Empire.

[113] Text and translation in *BWL*, 113-15.

[114] N. Lohfink, "Sicherung," 68, sees in the "commandment" in 17:20 (מצוה,
"commandment," in the singular as against "the words" and the statutes" in the
plural in 17:19) a reference to the *Königsgesetz*; Braulik, "Ausdrücke," 53, sees
rather in "these statutes" (החקים האלה) in 17:19 the element that "weist zurück auf
die Bestimmungen des Königsgesetzes 17,14ff."

[115] See G. Braulik, "Das Deuteronomium und die Menschenrechte," *TQ* 166
(1986) 22-23; L. Perlitt, "Ein einzig Volk von Brüdern: zur deuteronomischen
Herkunft der biblischen Bezeichnung 'Bruder'," *Kirche* (FS. G. Bornkamm; ed.
D. Lührmann and G. Strecker; Tübingen: Mohr, 1980) 27-52.

of Israel's destiny, and as such, he falls beyond the reach of Moses' present address. This combination of continuity and discontinuity is further observed in the object of the king's care. The Torah he will transcribe and peruse is unquestionably "this Torah" (see 17:18,19). What the king will read is, without any addition, what the people are currently hearing. In that measure, Moses' speech is in full agreement with the Hebrew Bible's policy of disclosure. Still, the continuity in content goes along with a variation in medium. What the king will be perusing is *a duplicate of a written record* of "this Torah." In the king's reading, Moses' audience is presented with a prophetic scenario, which both prolongs the ongoing communication ("this Torah"), and transposes it in a kind of ideality ("[the king] will read").

In casting the king's reception of (a copy of) "this Torah," Moses' speech projects its own reception—via the representativity of an exceptional reader. The producing and reading by the king of the Torah's duplicate (משנה) in a particular 'book' (ספר) therefore functions as what has been called in modern literary theory a *mise en abyme*[116] or "duplication intérieure,"[117] that is, the embedding in a work of a representation of this work.[118] The royal duplicate on a particular scroll book is, within Moses' Torah speech, an embedded representation of "this Torah" (in its future written form).[119] The integrality of "this Torah" is thus anticipat-

---

[116] The expression goes back to A. Gide's journal (*Journal 1889-1939* [Paris: Gallimard, 1948] 41): "J'aime assez qu'en une œuvre d'art on retrouve ainsi transposé, à l'échelle des personnages, le sujet même de cette œuvre. Rien ne l'éclaire mieux et n'établit plus sûrement toutes les proportions de l'ensemble." This phenomenon is assimilated by Gide to a device in heraldry, "[le] procédé du blason qui consiste, dans le premier, à en mettre un second 'en abyme'."

[117] B. Morrisette, "Un héritage d'André Gide: la duplication intérieure," *Comparative Literature Studies* 8 (1971) 125-42.

[118] For a typology of the *mise en abyme*, see L. Dällenbach, *Le récit spéculaire: essai sur la mise en abyme* (Paris: Seuil, 1977). Dällenbach's theoretical frame is discussed by M. Bal, *Femmes imaginaires. L'ancien testament au risque d'une narratologie critique* (Utrecht: Hes; Paris: Nizet, 1986) 166-80; in the Hebrew Bible, see J.-P. Sonnet, "Le Sinaï dans l'événement de sa lecture: la dimension pragmatique de Exode 19-24," *NRT* 111 (1989) 338-43, and the survey by J.-L. Ska, *'Our Fathers Have Tolds Us': Introduction to the Analysis of Hebrew Narratives* (Subsidia Biblica 13; Roma: Pontifico Istituto Biblico, 1990) 47-53.

[119] It goes without saying that the motif of the king's reading of the Torah "book" has a further relevance as to the reading process of the (framing) Book of Deuteronomy. This relevance goes beyond Deuteronomy's represented world, and bears on Deuteronomy as representing medium. Yet this further pertinence is indirect (it is not the "Book of Deuteronomy" which is in the hands of the

ed and represented to the audience. "A condensed image of the overall design,"[120] the *mise en abyme* is somehow chronologically disturbing, since it totalizes at one point what the linguistic message spells out discursively. The "duplication intérieure," however, catalyzes the addressee's hermeneutic task in varied ways according to its place within the whole that it mirrors.[121] In the projected "duplicate" of Deut 17:18, the audience (and, behind it, the reader) learns that Moses' communication will eventuate in a written corpus, the standard copy that underlies the royal duplicate. The operations enjoined on the people in Deut 6:4-9 and 11:18-21 now have the background of a future, though not yet explicit, *Urschrift*.

As pointed out by Lucien Dällenbach, the *mise en abyme* can specifically stage the production or the reception of the embedding work.[122] In the case of the royal copy of the Torah, the representation of the production process is at best a second degree representation—the mention of the making of a duplicate. The injunction "he shall write" implies, as said above, that the standard copy itself will be written; the root כתב, "to write," is thereby attached to the future of Moses' Torah. In Deut 17:18-20, the *mise en abyme* is, however, primarily oriented toward the reception process. In the king's relationship to the Torah book, Moses' audience can infer its own relationship, in another time and place, to Moses' Torah. What is expected from the king's reading is presumably pertinent to the people's reception ethics. This is (retrospectively) confirmed by the fact that the expected outcomes of the king's reading all echo attitudes attached to the people's reception of the Horeb-Moab revelation. The finality of the royal reading is expressed in a complex final sentence (vv. 19b-20), introduced by the conjunction למען, "to the end that." In the following paragraphs, I will indicate the echoing effects that relate the king's reception of the Torah 'book' to the people's overall reception of YHWH's revelation through Moses.

(i) The first function expressed is the king's learning the fear of God: "that he may learn to fear (ילמד ליראה) YHWH his God"

---

king, but "this Torah") and is built upon a primary pertinence within Deuteronomy's represented world.

[120] Jefferson, "*Mise en abyme*," 197.
[121] See Dällenbach, *Récit spéculaire*, 82-89.
[122] See Dällenbach, *Récit spéculaire*, 100-22.

(17:19). As has been pointed out by Fischer and Lohfink, the motif of the fear of God is not explicitly mentioned in the "you shall write" passages in Deuteronomy 6 and 11 (yet it is "in the air," these scholars contend)[123]; the motif, however, explicitly appears, as a kind of *Leitmotiv*, in Moses' retelling of the Horeb event.[124] The purpose of the king's exposure to the Torah "book" in that sense literally echoes the purpose of the revelation of God's words at Horeb, as stated by God himself: "Gather the people to me, that I may let them hear my words, so that they may learn to fear (ילמדון ליראה) me all the days that they live upon the earth, and that they may teach (ילמדון) their children to do so" (see also the motif of the fear of God in 5:29 and 6:2 in connection with Moses' further revelation, obtained at Horeb and divulged in Moab).[125] The mediation of the Torah book, written and intensively read, thus achieves, in further time and space, what was in God's view at Horeb "on the day" the people stood before him (see 4:10).

(ii) The final sentence goes on: "by keeping (לשמר) all the words of this Torah and these statutes, and doing them (לעשתם)." The verb שמר, "to keep," is, in various combinations, and especially in tandem with the verb עשה, "to do," one of the key words of Moses' parenesis aiming at the reception of the Horeb-Moab Torah.[126] What is expected from the king thus mirrors the responsibility of the audience.

(iii) As noted above, the paradox of the law that singles out the king's duties is that it aims at preventing the king from singling himself out above his fellow Israelites: "that his heart may not be lifted up (רום לבבו) above his brethren." The warning echoes a previous warning, meant for the entire people: "then your heart be lifted up (ורם לבבכם), and you forget YHWH your God" (8:14). Giving way to pride, the king would repeat in himself, and in the midst of the people, the depravity that threatens the people itself. In both cases, the warning against pride follows a triple reference to the multiplication of possessions. The triple mention in

[123] See Fischer and Lohfink, "Diese Worte," 68.
[124] See Fischer and Lohfink, "Diese Worte," 68-69.
[125] In Deut 4:10, 5:29, and 6:2, the motif of the fear of God is associated with the perspective of the generations to come; the similar perspective is present in 17:20, "he and his sons."
[126] See 4:2, 6, 40; 5:1, 29, 32; 6:2, 3, 17, 25; 7:11, 12; 8:1, 6, 11; 10:13; 11:1, 8, 22, 32; 12:1, 28; 13:1, 5, 19; 15:5; 16:12; 17:10.

8:13—"And when your herds and flocks multiply (ירבין), and your silver and gold is multiplied (ירבה), and all that you have is multiplied (ירבה)"—is echoed in the triple ban imposed on the king (featuring a triple ירבה in 17:16-17, and the recurrence of the "silver and gold" motif in 17:17).

(iv) A further echoing takes place in what comes next in the "royal law": לבלתי סור מן המצוה ימין ושמאול, "and that he may not turn aside from the commandment either to the right hand or the left" (17:20). In 5:32, introducing the teaching he is about to deliver, Moses gives the people a similar warning: "You shall be careful to do therefore as YHWH your God has commanded you; you shall not turn aside to the right hand or to the left (לא תסרו ימין ושמאל)."[127]

(v) "To the end that he may prolong his days (למען יאריך ימים) in his kingdom, he and his sons, in the midst of Israel." The final part of the complex sentence echoes, *mutatis mutandis*, the promise of a long life in the land repeatedly formulated for the audience's sake (see 4:40; 5:16, 33; 6:2; 11:9,21). The reference to the sons probably has a dynastic relevance.[128] Yet the mention of the generation(s) to come echoes Moses' wish for the entire people (see 4:40; 5:29; 6:2; 11:21; 12:28). The perspective of multiplied days in the land in 11:21 is a particularly telling parallel since it represents, as in the "royal law," the *telos* of the appropriate reception of Moses' communication.

Scattered reception injunctions meant for the entire people come to be woven together in the king's relationship to the Torah "book." What originally related to the reception of the Horeb-Moab *oral* revelation is, so to speak, unified and intensified, as under a magnifying glass, in the king's relationship to the *written* Torah. While projecting the king as the Torah's arch-reader, the "royal law" fills in some gaps about previous reception injunctions and creates defined expectations as to the outcome of Moses' oral communication. More than ever, the logic of writing permeates Moses' speech.

Moses' Torah speech (Deuteronomy 5-28) features further references to writing (in Deuteronomy 27-28). As opposed to the instances reviewed in this chapter, which dealt with writing at the

---

[127] See also the use of the verbal root סור, "to turn aside," in Deut 9:12, 16 and 11:16.
[128] See Caquot, "Remarques," 32-33.

extreme points of Moses' communicational perspective (at Horeb, in the land), the references to writing in Deuteronomy 27-28 pertain to the entry of the people into the land. Writing therefore will also figure "in between," that is, between the past in the desert and the future in the land. Yet the part of the speech thus far reviewed made it clear: Moses' Torah has a close affinity with the "logic of writing." The Torah is conveyed thoroughly by "word of mouth," but it is haunted by textualization—in God's foundational revelation, and in the people's future reception. Strangely enough, Moses himself, the mediator, has himself no active part in written communication.

Excursus: The Writing of the Bill of Divorce in Deut 24:1-4

The references to writing surveyed in this second chapter all pertained to the communication, or reception, of the Horeb-Moab revelation. This is not the case with the two mentions of the writing of a divorce bill by the Israelite husband in Deut 24:1, 3 (וכתב לה ספר כריתת), "and he writes her a bill of divorce").[129] In these instances, the content and wording of the writ is foreign to Moses' "words" (and is moreover left unspecified). The difference from the references to writing so far surveyed (and meant for Moses' audience) further appears in that the writing of the divorce bill is not the object of a stipulation. The bill in question is twice mentioned in the protasis of a legal provision (that forbids the remarriage of a divorced woman by her former husband); thus mentioned, the writing of the bill is apparently referred to as a practice taken for granted. A further contrast is to be noticed. In the reception injunctions so far, writing was a way to surround

---

[129] Does the ספר כריתת, the "writ of cutting off," as Driver translates (*Deuteronomy*, 271), echo the phrase כרת ברית, "to cut [i.e., establish] a covenant"? (The phrase כרת ברית occurs eleven times in Deuteronomy, and five times before Deut 24 [4:23; 5:2, 3; 7:2; 9:9].) The bill (ספר) of divorce would then be the (inverting) mirror of the embedding covenantal ספר. In Deuteronomy, however, Israel's covenantal relationship to YHWH is never expressed through conjugal metaphors (see Weinfeld, *School*, 81-82 n.6), with the sole exception of Israel's prophesied "prostitution" (זנה) in Deut 31:16. It thus seems far-fetched to see in the bill of divorce of Deut 24 an inverted allegory of Israel's covenantal "bill." Interestingly enough, Jer 3:1 hints at the legislation spelled out in Deut 24:1-4 while exposing Israel's religious prostitution. The development of the theme of conjugal love between God and Israel definitely belongs to the prophetic vein.

oneself with specific words, or to keep them as close as possible. Not so with the bill, which is to be handed to the divorced wife, who is herself to be sent out of the house (see 24:1, 2). The reference to writing in Deuteronomy 24 therefore falls out of the communication paradigm progressively worked out in Moses' speech.[130] It bears further witness, however, to the presence of the logic of writing within Deuteronomy's represented world.[131]

The reference of the word ספר in 24:1,3, as differentiated from the use of the same word in Deut 17:18, reminds us of the non-univocality of the term ספר when it comes to written records. The difference not only lies in the size of the record (a bill of divorce is not a legal corpus), but also in its function.[132] As a written record being handed on, the ספר of Deuteronomy 24 (and of Is 50:1 and Jer 3:8) comes close to the meaning of ספר as (dispatched) "letter";[133] the closest semantic parallel, however, is found in the "deed of purchase" documented in Jeremiah 32.[134] In Deuteronomy 24, as in these latter instances, the ספר formally represents or records a legal act.[135] In Deut 17:18, the same word, ספר, apparently referred only to the physical medium (arguably a scroll book) of the royal copy of the Torah. Other occurrences of ספר in Deuteronomy will further document the range of uses of this crucial word.

---

[130] The sequence נתן—כתב, "to write"—"to give" in 24:1, 3 echoes, to be sure, the similar sequence in 5:19; 9:10 (inverse order) and 10:4, about the transmission of the tablets by God to Moses. Yet the communication paradigm that underlies the book of Deuteronomy is rather built on the sequence נתן—אל-כתב, "to write"—"to give *to*" (5:19; 9:10; 10:4; 31:9). In Deut 24:1, 3, the verb נתן is twice followed by בידה, "in her hand";

[131] No specific legal procedure stipulated so far in the Pentateuch included a reference to writing by lay individuals (the commitment to writing included in the ordeal of Num 5:23 is performed by the priest).

[132] See Hossfeld and Reuter, "ספר *sepær*," 933-34.

[133] See 2 Sam 11:14, 15; 1 Kgs 21:8, 9, 11; 2 Kgs 5:5, 6, 7; 10:1, 2, 6, 7; 19:14; 20:12; 2 Chr 32:17; Is 37:14; 39:1; Jer 29:1, 25, 29; Esth 1:22; 3:13; 8:5, 10; 9:20, 25, 30; see also the Lachish Ostraca 3; 5; 6 (*ANET*, 322).

[134] See Jer 32:10, 11, 12, 14, 16, 44.

[135] As such the reference to writing attached to the "bill of divorce" documents one of the most archaic uses of writing. See Goody, *Logic of Writing* 134: "In many early systems of law, writing was . . . extensively used for the transfers involved in marriages, sale, debts and testaments." In the ancient Near East, see for instance the Nuzi tablet containing the statement by a husband: "I married PN; and now on this day I have divorced my wife PN . . ." (text and translation in C. J. Gadd, "Tablets from Kirkuk," *RA* 23 [1926] 111), and the written divorce settlements in *ANET*, 217 (in new Sumerian) and *ANET*, 218 (in old Assyrian).

CHAPTER THREE

THE METAMORPHOSES OF THE *SĒPER*
(DEUTERONOMY 27-28; 29-30)

> Oh that my words were written down!
> Oh that they were inscribed in a record (ספר)!
> Oh that with an iron pen and lead
> they were graven in the rock for ever!
>
> Job 19:23

> Then I took the sealed deed (ספר) of purchase
> ... and the open [copy].
>
> Jer 32:11

Starting with Deuteronomy 27, the theme of written communication turns particularly insistent in Moses' speech. Between Deuteronomy 27 and 30, the verb כתב, "to write," occurs eight times
(27:3, 8; 28:58, 61; 29:19, 20, 26; 30:10). In the last six instances,
the passive participle כתוב, "written," is invariably determined with
the expression (הזה) בספר, "in the (this) *sēper*." The present chapter will review these eight occurrences in their respective contexts.
Thus far in Moses' speech, writing has been either past action,
before Moses' act of communication, or future action, commanded by Moses for across the Jordan. Is writing now, for the
first time, on hand? The meaning and reference of the word ספר,
usually translated as "book" or "scroll," will constitute a decisive
issue in the inquiry. (Pending the appropriate semantic clarifica-
tion, the transliteration *sēper* will be used in the following pages.)
The overall division of Deuteronomy—marked off by the four
headings—will also be of special importance in this matter.[1] The
idiom (הזה) בספר, "in (this) *sēper*," is found in both the second

---

[1] Lohfink has recently contended that the sequence of the four Mosaic speeches in Deuteronomy's text does not mirror their sequence as events ("Fabel,"
65-78). In his view, Deuteronomy's central speeches (Deuteronomy 5-28, 29-30)
did not follow each other; the second speech (5-28) took rather place during the
third one (29-30). For a discussion and a dismissal of this hypothesis, see the
excursus at the end of the present chapter, pp. 112-16.

speech of Moses (Deut 4:44, "And this is the Torah") and in his
third speech (29:69, "These are the words of the covenant"). The
lexical consistency apparently expresses invariance in the semantic and referential use of the term. Yet, the lexical bid for continuity will be overridden by the pragmatic situation of each one
of the speeches. Deuteronomy, in its dramatic shaping, is irreducible to a combinatory system of invariable lexical elements.
The meaning and reference of the same word can vary considerably according to the context of its rhetorical use. By retracing
the metamorphoses of the *sēper* between Deuteronomy 27 and 30,
this chapter will review the new turns of Deuteronomy's dialectic
of oral and written communication.

1. *Writing "beyond the Jordan"—Deut 27:1-8*

By recording in Deut 26:16-19 YHWH's and Israel's mutual
covenant declarations, predicated on the basis of the stipulations
so far conveyed, Moses apparently rounds out an important part
of his speech. In Deuteronomy 27:1, an exceptional intrusion of
the narrator—"Now Moses and the elders of Israel commanded
the people, saying"—emphasizes the new beginning in Moses'
communication act. Starting with Deut 27:2, a new set of regulations is introduced, which shifts the scene to a specific time and
place:

> [2]And on the day you pass over the Jordan to the land which YHWH
> your God gives you, you shall set up large stones, and plaster them
> with plaster; [3]and you shall write upon them all the words of this
> Torah, when you pass over to enter the land which YHWH your God
> gives you, a land flowing with milk and honey, as YHWH, the God
> of your fathers, has promised you. [4]And when you have passed over
> the Jordan, you shall set up the stones, concerning which I com-
> mand you this day, on Mount Ebal, and you shall plaster them with
> plaster. [5]And there you shall build an altar to YHWH your God, an
> altar of stones; you shall lift up no iron tool upon them. [6]You shall
> build an altar to YHWH your God of unhewn stones; and you shall
> offer burnt offerings on it to YHWH your God; [7]and you shall sac-
> rifice peace offerings, and shall eat there; and you shall rejoice
> before YHWH your God. [8]And you shall write upon the stones all
> the words of this Torah very plainly. (27:2-8)

The stipulation is complex, combining in repetitious sentences
the reference to the erection of two stone monuments. The stipulation is not altogether clear as to the spatial and temporal parameters of its execution.[2] A framing inclusion, however, emphasizes the injunction to write "all the words of this Torah" upon
stones in the open (vv. 2-3; 8). Against the background of Moses'
previous injunctions concerning the reception of the "words" of
the Torah, the injunction in Deuteronomy 27 brings out a most
original stipulation (see the precedents in Deut 6:4-9; 11:18-21
and 17:18-20).[3] Moses' Torah words are not only meant for written duplication by the people and by the king in the land, once
settled; they are also destined to lead the entry of the people into
the land. In the following paragraphs I will describe the implications of the "beyond the Jordan" scenario in Deuteronomy's communicational perspective.

a. *Beyond the Jordan*

In Deut 27:2-8, as in the previously formulated reception injunctions, Moses projects the words of his ongoing act of communication into another time and place. In Deut 27:2 he emphasizes
the temporal parameter: "*On the day* you pass over the Jordan to
the land which YHWH gives you, you shall set up large stones";[4]
in 27:4 he spells out the place, "Upon crossing the Jordan, you
shall set up these stones, concerning which I command you this
day, *on Mount Ebal.*" How are the two parameters to be combined?
Is the temporal immediacy ("On the day you pass over the Jordan") reconcilable with the apparently remote spatial determina-

---

[2] The complexity and repetitiousness of the passage have given rise to several
hypotheses as to its genesis; see for instance M. Anbar, "The Story about the
Building of an Altar on Mount Ebal: The History of Its Composition and the
Question of Centralization of the Cult," *Das Deuteronomium: Entstehung, Gestalt und
Botschaft* (ed. N. Lohfink; BETL 68; Louvain: University Press, 1985) 305-308 (with
literature).

[3] See A. Dillmann, *Numeri, Deuteronomium und Josua* (Leipzig: Hirzel, 1886)
270-71, who establishes a connection between the reception injunctions in
Deuteronomy 6, 11 and Deuteronomy 27.

[4] As Driver, *Deuteronomy*, 295, points out, the "day" in question hardly means
"in the time when"; "אֲשֶׁר בְּיוֹם is not quite the same as בְּיוֹם"; (for the latter, see
Gen 2:4 and Num 3:1); where the former occurs (2 Sam 19:20; Esth 9:1), the
idiom denotes a literal "day."

tion ("on Mount Ebal")?[5] L'Hour suggests with perspicacity to
read Deut 27:2-8 in the light of Deut 11:29-30, a text which significantly aligns Jordan, Gilgal and Ebal-Gerizim:[6]

> [29]And when YHWH your God brings you into the land which you
> are entering to take possession of it, you shall set the blessing on
> Mount Gerizim and the curse on Mount Ebal. [30]Are they not beyond
> (בעבר) the Jordan, west of the road, toward the going down of the
> sun, in the land of the Canaanites who live in the Arabah, over
> against (מול) Gilgal, beside the oak of Moreh?

The effect achieved is the collapsing of the distance between the
two extreme points (Ebal and Gerizim, on the one hand, and the
Jordan river, on the other). As Driver puts it, "in 11:30, ʿEbal
seems to be represented as nearer to Jordan than it actually is."[7]
The direction is westward; the distance, the rhetorical question
emphasizes, is just "prepositional": "beyond," "toward," "in," "over
against," "beside." No reference is made to the length of the journey (cf. Deut 1:2 "It is an eleven day's journey from Horeb by the
way of Mount Seir to Kadesh Barnea"). The stratagem, L'Hour
goes on, has been successful to the point that many mistakenly
imagined Ebal and Gerizim close to Jericho.[8] What is achieved in
a similar way in Deut 27:3-8, is the presentation of the inscription
on the large stones as a ritual act attached to the entry into the
land, marking out the temporal *as well as* the spatial "beyond the
Jordan."

b. *The Liminal Character of the Stone Inscription*[9]

The previous reception injunctions meant for the people presupposed a settled Israel, and even an urban environment (see

---

[5] The book of Joshua, as is known, has its way of solving the problem. It duplicates the stone memorials. The twelve stones erected at Gilgal (Joshua 4), on the
very day of the crossing, fit the command as expressed in Deut 27:2 ("on the day
you pass over the Jordan"); the inscription of the words of the Torah on the
stones of the altar on Mount Ebal (8:30-35) is an interpretation of the command
as read in Deut 27:4 ("on Mount Ebal").

[6] See J. L'Hour, "L'Alliance de Sichem," *RB* 69 (1962) 168.

[7] Driver, *Deuteronomy*, 295.

[8] L'Hour, "Alliance," 168; see his references in n. 187 to the ancient tradition
of interpretation.

[9] The concept of liminality goes back to the French anthropologist A. van Gen-

Deut 6:9 and 11:20), providing architectural surfaces for the transcription of the Horeb-Moab words (the doorpost, the city gate). The setting of the Deut 27:2-8 stipulation has natural parameters (the river, the mountain), and requires the erection of an appropriate support amidst nature. Moses' injunction to resort to erected stones (והקמת לך אבנים גדלות, "you will set up for you large stones"), however, seems to clash with a regulation previously uttered. Moses' audience has heard the strong prohibition: "And you shall not set up (תקים) a pillar (מצבה), which YHWH your God hates" (Deut 16:21-22).[10] The inconsistency of Moses' request in 27:2,4 is apparently reinforced by Moses' further command to build a sacrificial altar next to the steles (27:5-7). Doesn't such an altar contradict one of Deuteronomy's central requirements, that is, the centralization of the sacrificial cult in Jerusalem (see Deuteronomy 12)? These tensions call for closer attention to the temporal and spatial determinations of Moses' commands.

(i) The Sacrificial Altar. The stipulations in Deuteronomy 12 about the cult centralization, it is important to notice, come within a temporal perspective:

> [10]But when you go over (ועברתם) the Jordan, and live in the land which YHWH your God gives you to inherit, and when he gives you rest from all your enemies round about, so that you live in safety, [11]then to the place which YHWH your God will choose, to establish his name, thither you shall bring all that I command you: your burnt offerings (עולתיכם) and your sacrifices, your tithes and the offering that you present, and all your votive offerings which you vow to YHWH. (12:10-11).

In other words, the crossing of the Jordan and the entering into the land do not imply the immediate enforcement of cult centralization. The latter will take place at the end of a settlement

---

nep (1837-1957), who examined the ceremonial sequence accompanying a change of status for an individual or a group in various societies (see especially *The Rites of Passage* [Chicago: University of Chicago Press, 1960]). In this sequence, the liminal stage follows the stage of separation from normal life and from the community, and is followed by the stage of reintegration. During the liminal stage, the person or the group undergoing the ritual process enjoys a special sacredness, but is also particularly vulnerable to specific dangers.

[10] See also Moses' command to destroy the nations' erected monuments (Deut 7:5; see also 12:3); from Moses' condemnation of pagan cultic monuments, it does not directly follow, however, that the Israelite cult is to be denied such monuments.

process, which leaves room for intermediate stipulations.[11] The sacrificial altar of Mount Ebal, which is related to a single sacrificial performance, therefore belongs to Moses' code in Deuteronomy as much as the future single altar in Jerusalem.[12] Even if the altar in question is a long-lasting monument, it has no further *raison d'être* than the rite of passage stipulated in Deuteronomy 27. The stipulation in Deut 27:2-8 has no bearing beyond ביום כאשר, the single day of the crossing. It provides for a liminal cultic action, marking off the passage into the promised land.

(ii) The Steles. The steles to be set up upon crossing the Jordan have a liminal character as well. By covering them with the "words of this Torah," the people publicize the terms of their entry into and their inheritance of the promised land:

> [2]You shall set up large stones, and plaster them with plaster, [3]and you shall write upon them all the words of this Torah upon crossing (בעברך), *in order that you may enter the land* (למען אשר תבא אל הארץ) which YHWH your God gives you, a land flowing with milk and honey, as YHWH, the God of your fathers, has promised you. (Deut 27:2-3)

In modern translations the final clause introduced by למען אשר ("in order that") is often linked to the infinitive construct that immediately precedes it (בעברך): "when you pass over *to* enter the land."[13] It seems preferable to follow the Massoretic scansion: the *'Atnāḥ* caesura falls between בעברך and למען אשר תבא אל הארץ, and the Massoretic text therefore construes the final clause as determining the main verbs, "you shall set up," "you shall write" (see my translation above) In such a reading the publication of the Torah words "upon crossing" aims at the people's effective entry into the land.[14] In like manner Moses, in his exhortations, sever-

---

[11] Contra Mayes, *Deuteronomy*, 342, for whom the real concern in Deuteronomy "is focused ... on the idea of Israel's subjection to the law on the point of entry into the land."

[12] The lawfulness of the altar to be built on Mount Ebal is enhanced by the stipulations about its building, which stem from the Covenant Code in Exod 20:25. Interestingly enough, these stipulations provide for altars to be built בכל המקום, "in every place" (Exod 20:24).

[13] RSV; see also *Einheitsübersetzung*, NJPSV, BJ.

[14] See Jerome's Vulgate, and Ibn Ezra, on Deut 27:3; among modern versions, see Dhorme, TOB, and the correction to the *Einheitsübersetzung* suggested by Braulik, *Deuteronomium II*, 200.

al times subordinated the entry (בא) into the land and the possession (ירש) of the land to the obedience of the Torah stipulations (see Deut 6:18-19; 8:1; 11:8, 22-25).[15] The symbolic actions
related to the *crossing* are therefore a prelude to the actual *entry*.[16]
Fulfilling Moses' commands on the very day of the crossing, the
people will perform liminal rites and provide their journey into
the land with, so to speak, its proper gate.[17] That the inscription
is not to be engraved but to be made on plastered slabs may be
explained by the delay of execution (it is to be completed within the hectic day of the crossing) and/or by readability requirements (see 27:8, "you shall write ... very plainly"). The primary
purpose of the inscription is its use in the covenantal pledge at
Ebal-Gerizim.[18] What is needed is an *ad hoc* display of the Torah
words.

In their liminal character, the "large stones" to be erected upon
crossing the Jordan are therefore temporally and spatially distinct
from the stele prohibited in Deut 16:22.[19] Any lingering suspicion
of the orthodox character of the "large stones" is dispelled, more-

---

[15] See Braulik, *Deuteronomium II*, 200, who refers to Deut 6:18-19; 8:1; 11:8,
22-25, where the entry (בא) and the possession (ירש) of the land follow the actual obedience to the Mosaic Torah.

[16] Commenting on the sentence introduced by למען אשר, Driver points out: "The
words seem clearly to contemplate the occupation of Canaan as still future"
(*Deuteronomy*, 297); see also pp. 295-96.

[17] The metaphor of the gate makes sense against the background of the future
inscription of the Mosaic "words" on the doorposts of the family houses and on
the city gate. The temporal liminality of the inscription has been illustrated in
the "royal law," which provides for the making of the duplicate by the king "when
he sits on the throne of his kingdom" (Deut 17:18).

[18] That the inscription is to be made on plastered slabs entails its non-lasting
character: "writing on plaster in the open," Anbar points out, "would not survive
weathering." "Examples of writing on plaster have been found at Deir Alla and
Kuntillet Ajrud," Anbar goes on, yet "both [are] inside buildings" ("Story," 305
n. 8). Driver, *Deuteronomy*, 296, refers to Egyptian analogues and adds that "figures, or characters, inscribed by this method were very permanent." Concerning
the inscription stipulated in Deut 27:2-8, Driver accordingly thinks that "the laws
inscribed upon the slabs remain as a *permanent* record of the fact" (pp. 296-297,
my italics). Yet, as Emile Puech reminded me in a private conversation, Egypt
and Samaria enjoy different weathering régime. It is my view, moreover, that the
inscription of the Torah "on the large stones" is primarily meant for the single
day of the Ebal-Gerizim ceremony (see P. C. Craigie, *The Book of Deuteronomy*
[NICOT; Grand Rapids: Eerdmans, 1976] 29).

[19] The distinction is also lexical. As is often pointed out, Deut 27:2, 4, 8 sensibly avoids the technical term of מצבה ("stela") and resorts to the more neutral
אבנים (גדלות) "(large) stones."

over, by the content of the future inscription: "all the words of
this Torah." The paradox is that the prohibition against the steles in the future centralized cult will be displayed on a stele-like
stone monument.

c. *Analogues in the Pentateuch and in the Ancient Near East*

What is, however, the positive need for such a determined medium—a (liminal) stone inscription? In the Pentateuch so far, steles mainly evoked the figures of Jacob and Moses; yet the steles
Jacob and Moses set up were mute monuments. In the ancient
Near East, on the other hand, inscribed "field" monuments served
specific purposes. These analogues will indirectly shed light on
the originality of Moses' stipulation in Deuteronomy 27.

In the book of Genesis, Jacob's relationship to the land, especially in his going out and coming in, is expressed in the erection of steles (see Gen 28:18 (אבן),22; 35:14,20; see also the altars
in 33:20 [in Shechem] and 35:7).[20] None of the steles Jacob set
up is inscribed. In Deuteronomy 27 Moses, on the contrary, makes
provision for liminal stones covered with "all the words of this
Torah." The originality of Moses' initiative stands out against the
background of a similar initiative at Sinai (as told in Exodus 24).
After having forbidden steles, that is, the Canaanites' and other
pagan nations' erected monuments (Exod 23:24), Moses sets up
(uninscribed) steles: ויבן . . . ושתים עשרה מצבה, "And he built ... and
twelve pillars" (Exod 24:4). What is an integral part of the
covenant ceremony in Exodus 24 is projected on another time
and place in Deuteronomy 27. What was performed by the mediator ("Moses set up") is entrusted to the people themselves ("you
shall set up"). What was a mute monument abutting on a written
document becomes an inscribed monument ("you shall write
upon [the stones]").

Engraved steles are an exception in biblical *Eretz Israel*: "plain
stones predominate by far in Palestine in the Bronze and Iron
ages. The few inscribed stones found in Palestine are virtually all

---

[20] In Gen 31:45-52, Jacob and Laban set up a stele (מצבה) as well as a cairn
(גל) at the border of Aram and Gilead on the occasion of a treaty. The stones
bear witness to the contract and mark the border between Aram and Israel. On
the relationship between land and steles, see A. Cooper and B. R. Goldstein, "The
Cult of the Dead and the Theme of Entry into the Land," *BibInt* 1 (1993) 285-303.

of demonstrably foreign influence or origin."[21] Analogues to the Deuteronomy 27 written stones are not lacking in Israel's neighboring cultures. I already pointed to textual analogies between Deuteronomy and the 8th century Aramaean steles found at Sefire, which contain a lengthy text of a treaty between KTK and Arpad. The three standing stones of Sefire match the "large stones" of Deuteronomy 27 in their function as well. In both cases, the witness function usually attached to plain stones is made explicit by the inscription of the terms of the covenant.[22] The recording of a legal body on an erected stone has its paradigm and masterpiece in the diorite stela that bears the 18th century Code of Hammurapi. Other analogues match the setting of the "beyond the Jordan" written stones. Weinfeld has called attention to the affinity between the stones of Deuteronomy 27 and stone monuments erected by Greek settlers at the conclusion of their journey.[23] Some of these steles bore legal inscriptions: "In Cyrene, besides the stele of the founders, which concerned the obligations connected with settlement, there was another stele containing sacred laws, which the god Apollo commanded the settlers to observe on their arrival in the land of Libya."[24] Another analogue is provided by the so-called boundary stones, found throughout Mesopotamia from the Third Millennium down to the first half

---

[21] C. F. Graesser, "Standing Stones in Ancient Palestine," *BA* 35 (1972) 35.

[22] See D. J. McCarthy, *Treaty and Covenant* (AnBib 21a; Rome Biblical Institute Press, 1981) 196-97, "Thus, a stone or stones function as witnesses of a covenant in Gen 31:48.52, Jos 24,27 and Is 19,19-20; there are stelae connected with the covenant rites in Ex 24,4, and while the function is undefined, surely this is a reflex of the idea of stela as witness. In these cases the stone itself functions as witness and there is no mention of its being inscribed. On the other hand, in Dt 27 the witness idea has fallen into the background and the stones serve to record the document... . First of all, there is the concern for the written record shown in some of the Hittite treaties and the vassal treaty of Esarhaddon. It is easy to conceive this concern's being developed in the direction of a monumental record, more impressive, more enduring and endowed with numinous qualities. Nor is this just speculation. That is exactly what we have at Sefire. The stela records the treaty, but is also considered to be something active which by its own power proclaims the treaty (Stela I, B, 8). Thus the apparent change in function of the stones is simply a making explicit of the witness idea. The treaty tradition emphasizing writing has made the monument a more powerful witness in Israel as in Syria."

[23] See M. Weinfeld, "The Pattern of the Israelite Settlement in Canaan," *Congress Volume: Jerusalem 1986* (ed. J. A. Emerton; VTSup 40; Brill: Leiden, 1988) 280-82.

[24] Weinfeld, "Pattern," 281 (Weinfeld produces no further example of inscribed standing stone).

of the seventh century.[25] In Akkadian they were called *narû*
("stele," or "stone monument"), *abnu* ("stone," see the אבנים in
Deut 27:2,4,8), *asumittu* ("stele"), or more rarely *kudurru* ("boundary," "boundary marker"), the name which has won acceptance as
their modern designation. Shaped like oval boulders, they recorded legal acts (mainly royal grants of land), curses on any who
might contravene the legal act or defile the stone (see Deut 19:14;
27:17), reliefs depicting the ceremony of the king's grant, and
symbols of the gods. The *kudurru* was not in itself a legal document, which usually required witnesses, sealing, and a precise
date. The narrative portion (the description of the legally binding act and its background) had to be based on a sealed legal
document written on clay—the formal legal proof or registration
of the transaction. The *kudurru*, on the other hand, was a docu-
mentary monument intended to strengthen or confirm the efficacy of the legal action; it was essentially for display. It is not precisely known whether *kudurrus* were ever placed on fields either
as boundary marker or simply as signs of ownership. The inscribed
stones of Deuteronomy 27 are therefore not unprecedented in
the ancient Near East, in their covenantal aspect (see Sefire), their
legal content (see Hammurapi), or in their relationship to a granted land (see the Mesopotamian *kudurrus*). Whatever the specific
function of each one of these stone monuments, public display
of texts which have force of law is, in any case, intended. In all
the cases listed above, the inscription was made by engraving and
was meant as a long-lasting record. The use of plastered slabs in
the case of the Torah inscription in Deuteronomy 27 apparently
contradicts this latter purpose. The inscription in question, however, is actually meant for a single ritual occasion. Public communication through non-lasting writing media was not unknown
in the ancient world. Classical Greece, for instance, made extensive use of the so-called λευκώματα, boards or tablets covered with
white plaster that were used to bring official issuances to the attention of the citizens.[26] In its specific purport, Moses' command in
Deut 27:2-8 eludes, however, comparative analysis. A better grasp
of such a purport requires a closer understanding of Moses' communication design.

---

[25] See J. A. Brinkman, "Kudurru," *RLA* 6.267-74, which I summarize.
[26] See Posner, *Archives*, 97-99.

d. *A Communicational Diptych*

What makes the Deut 27:1-8 reception injunction different from the previous ones is primarily the dramatic character of its setting. Up to now Moses referred to reception operations to be performed within the land, once settled, that is, in relatively distant time and place. In Deut 27:1-8, Moses, who faces the Jordan River, stipulates about what will take place beyond the river, on the day of its crossing. The "beyond the Jordan" stipulation calls for an execution close in time and place (according to Moses' perspective) to the time and place of its uttering.[27] Yet the Jordan River, which separates the stipulation's enunciation from its execution, is also the parting point between the speaker and his audience: "for you shall not go over this Jordan" (3:27). Unlike Jacob, Moses will not enter the land. Yet he will reach it symbolically through the command he gives to erect "large stones" upon the crossing and to write down on these stones "all the words of this Torah." The orality of Moses' Moab speech could have meant the vanishing of his words, tied to the limits of his communication act, symbolically expressed in "this Jordan." Moses' command "you shall write" is an ingenious way of transcending the limitations of time and space. Extending the range of his act of communication, he makes sure "the words of this Torah" will be set up in the land as a gate to the land. Projecting his words beyond the Jordan, Moses projects them also beyond his death, linked to his non-crossing of the Jordan River. In Deut 27:2-8, Moses therefore provides for symbolic actions to be performed with his own words, yet without his presence.

The actions projected beyond the Jordan bear interesting resemblance to Moses' foundational actions in the covenant-making at Sinai (in Exodus 24). There Moses had a triple initiative: "And Moses wrote all the words of YHWH [on a *sēper*] ... and built an altar at the foot of the mountain, and twelve steles (מצבה), according to the twelve tribes of Israel" (Exod 24:4). Retelling the Horeb covenant in Deuteronomy 5, Moses passes over these ritual actions in silence. Yet Moses provides for corresponding actions in Deuteronomy 27, in the frame of the Moab covenant. A part

---

[27] The narrowing effect is mirrored in the structure of the discourse: the Deut 27:2-8 injunction, which comes last in the order of presentation, is the one that will come first in the order of execution.

of the covenant ritual (as set up in the Sinaitic paradigm) is thus
projected by Moses beyond the Jordan and entrusted to other
agents.[28] The making of the Moab covenant is accordingly a two
step process. A first act takes place in Moab, in the presence of
the mediator (see already the mutual declaration in 26:1-19, conveyed by Moses); a second act will take place beyond the Jordan,
without the mediator. In the latter step the people become, so to
speak, the Mosaic agent. In the writing and the displaying of the
terms of the covenant on the threshold of the land, the people
will then perform a most meaningful act, opening "a ceremony
tying people, Land and Law."[29]

The continuity of the covenant from one bank of the Jordan
River to the other is assured in "all the words of this Torah." Still,
how will the words in question be handed over from one place
to the other? No foolproof transmission of the Torah has been
provided for so far. In Deut 17:18, to be sure, a hint was given as
to a written mediation (since the king had to make a copy of what
was apparently an *Urschrift*). No equivalent clue is found in Moses'
stipulation in Deut 27:2-8. Does the command rely on oral techniques of memorization? Those were explicitly mentioned in Deut
6:6-7 and 11:18-19. Yet, however faithful, these techniques are not
foolproof, whereas the issue at stake is, precisely, the transmission
and inscription of "*all* the words of this Torah." On the other
hand, one thing is certain from now on: whatever follows and
takes places in Moab, *before* the crossing of the Jordan, will fall "in
between," i.e., between the command of Deut 27:2-8 and its implementation. The temporal and spatial slot for a resolution of the
communication riddle has been narrowed down by Moses' speech
itself.

---

[28] The "you" upon which the ritual actions "beyond the Jordan" are incumbent is the people. Starting with Deut 27:1, Moses, however, associates to himself
other speakers—the elders in 27:1, the Levites in 27:9—who will have a role in
the enforcement of the Torah "beyond the Jordan." This procedure, which con-
fers considerable authority on these co-speakers, may be another way to insure
east of the Jordan what will be implemented west of the Jordan. See Craigie,
Deuteronomy, 327; and cf. Lohfink, "Ältesten," 29-30.
[29] McCarthy, *Treaty*, 199.

2. *sēper in Deuteronomy 28*

The theme of written communication reappears in Deut 28:58, 61 in a double mention combining the passive participle כתוב, "written," and the substantive ספר, *sēper*:

> [58]If you are not careful to do all the words of this Torah which are written in this *sēper* ... [59]then YHWH will bring on you and your off- spring extraordinary afflictions . . [61]Every sickness also, and every affliction which is not written in the *sēper* of this law, YHWH will bring upon you, until you are destroyed. (28:58-61)

The elucidation of the meaning and reference of the two ספר men- tions requires that Deut 28:58-61 be related to its pragmatic con- text: Who is speaking in Deuteronomy 28? To whom? Where, and on what occasion? In Deuteronomy 27, the stipulation concern- ing the inscription "beyond the Jordan" gives way to the formu- lation by Moses of the admonition to be uttered by the Levites at Ebal-Gerizim, that is, at the place of the stone inscription:

> [11]And Moses charged the people the same day, saying, [12]"When you have passed over the Jordan, these shall stand upon Mount Geriz- im to bless the people ... [13]And these shall stand upon Mount Ebal for the curse ... [14]And the Levites shall declare to all the men of Israel with a loud voice: ... [*the spelling out of the curses follows*]." (27:11-14)

Yet, what about the speech recorded in Deuteronomy 28? As Lohfink has recently indicated in an article entitled "Moab oder Sichem—wo wurde Dtn 28 nach der Fabel des Deuteronomiums proklamiert?," the discursive situation of Deuteronomy 28 is ambiguous.[30] The indeterminacy mainly stems from the ambiguity of the transition between 27:12-26 (the maledictions to be uttered by the Levites at Ebal-Gerizim) and 28:1-68. Formally speaking, both 27:12-26 and 28:1-68 hang upon the introduction in 27:11, "And Moses charged the people the same day, saying ..." In 27:12-26 one reads the dispositions related to the Ebal-Ger-

---

[30] N. Lohfink, "Moab oder Sichem—wo wurde Dtn 28 nach der Fabel des Deuteronomiums proklamiert?" *Studies in Deuteronomy in Honour of C. J. Labu- schagne on the Occasion of his 65th Birthday* (ed. F. García Martínez et al.; Leiden: Brill, 1994) 139-53.

izim speech and the curses to be pronounced over there by the Levites (27:14, "And the Levites shall declare to all the men of Israel with a loud voice: ..."). At the beginning of chapter 28, no textual element explicitly says that the anticipation of the Ebal-Gerizim speech is over; no textual element establishes that Moses is now speaking *sans plus* to the sons of Israel listening to him in the plains of Moab.[31] Most important of all, 27:12-26 does not include the blessings announced (in 27:12) for the ceremony at Ebal-Gerizim, while blessings are read in 28:3-14. The disposition of the people on Mount Ebal and Mount Gerizim remains a *totes Motiv* if the matching piece of the maledictions (that is, the benedictions) is not included as well in the words to be pronounced on the twin mountains. The solution Lohfink advocates (as a preference, not as a critical certainty) stands half-way between the two possibilities.[32] In Lohfink's view, Moses communicates to the people gathered in Moab specific words—benedictions and maledictions—intended to be formally proclaimed by the Levites in the forthcoming ceremony at Ebal-Gerizim.[33] Why such a deferment of a significant part of the verbal making of the covenant? In the conclusion of his article Lohfink puts forward a possible answer.[34] The benedictions and maledictions are deeply linked to the existence in the land and to the possibility of losing the land. It is possibly only in the land that the benedictions and maledictions can be pronounced with full strength. Furthermore, as I suggested above, the conclusive and most (self-)committing part of the covenant making will thus be performed by those, and only those (Moses being now out of the picture), who will have to live in the land according to the Torah. The solution suggested by Lohfink—in Deuteronomy 28 Moses communicates what

---

[31] Does the reappearance of an "I" locutor in Deut 28:1 (and of the "you" of the people) signal the end of the quote, as it is generally supposed? Lohfink, "Moab oder Sichem," 142, points out that there are other passages in Deuteronomy where a speech attributed to a plurality of speakers (like the Levites in this case, see 27:14) is brought into play in the first person of the singular (see 26:13-15; 27:1b, 10).

[32] See Lohfink, "Moab oder Sichem," 150.

[33] Lohfink, "Moab oder Sichem," 145. About Deuteronomy 28 as performed at Sichem, see also Braulik, *Deuteronomium II*, 199, "dieser Text ist nicht eigentlich Mosetora aus Moab, sondern nur ein in der Mosetora angeordneter liturgischer Text für eine einmalige Zeremonie nach der Landnahme, von Leviten vorzutragen."

[34] See Lohfink, "Moab oder Sichem," 151-52.

the Levites will formally proclaim at Ebal-Gerizim— provides in my view the adequate framework for the elucidation of the sense and the reference of the word *sēper* in Deut 28:58,61. The pragmatic context of the speech (in its performance at Ebal-Gerizim), the possible meaning of *sēper* as "inscription" (engraved on stone), and Moses' description of the content of the record in question, as I shall now indicate, argue in favor of the equation of the *sēper* mentioned in Deuteronomy 28 with the inscription on the "large stones" referred to in Deuteronomy 27.

The first mention of the *sēper* occurs in Deut 28:58 after the spelling out of the maledictions (קללות) that threaten the people (28:15-57), "if you will not obey the voice of YHWH your God or be careful to do all his commandments and his statutes" (28:15). A second mention follows closely (28:61), in a rhetorical overbid: not only the afflictions recorded in the *sēper* will rain on the rebellious people, but even all the un-recorded ones. Extra-biblical treaty literature from the Neo-Assyrian period are characterized by an expansion of the curse component (as against blessings) that strives for a kind of exhaustiveness.[35] The same tendency is found in Deuteronomy 28, either in its way of listing the calamities or by the rhetorical reference to (even) un-listed afflictions.

> [58]If you are not careful to do all the words of this Torah which are written in this *sēper*, that you may fear this glorious and awful name, YHWH your God, [59]then YHWH will bring on you and your offspring extraordinary afflictions, afflictions severe and lasting, and sicknesses grievous and lasting. [60]And he will bring upon you again all the diseases of Egypt, which you were afraid of; and they shall cleave to you. [61]Every sickness also, and every affliction which is not written in the *sēper* of this law, YHWH will bring upon you, until you are destroyed. (28:58-61)

What is the *sēper* twice mentioned? Not enough attention has been paid to the fact that the mentions of the *sēper* in Deuteronomy 28 occur after the reference to the writing upon the "large stones" in Deuteronomy 27. In 27:3, 8, Moses twice enjoins the people to

---

[35] See McCarthy, *Treaty*, 150-51; for a study of the Deuteronomy 28 curses on comparative grounds, see Weinfeld, *School*, 116-29 (and the reference to previous studies). Most recently, see H. U. Steymans, "Eine assyrische Vorlage für Deuteronomium 28,20-44," *Bundesdokument und Gesetz: Studien zum Deuteronomium* (ed. G. Braulik; Herders Biblische Studien 4; Freiburg: Herder, 1995) 119-41.

write ("you shall write," וכתבת). In what follows, Moses (or the Levites he is quoting) refers to what is "written" ([ה]כתוב[ים]; Deut 28:58, 61). When it first occurs in Moses' speech, in 28:58, the *sēper* literally resumes the content of the inscription on the "large stones" of 27:3, 8:

Deut 27:3, 8   Deut 28:58

וכתבת עליהן את כל דברי התורה הזאת   את כל דברי התורה הזאת הכתובים בספר
                                                                              הזה

And you shall *write* upon [the stones]   *All the words of this Torah*
all the words of this Torah   *written* on this *sēper*

The identity in content raises the question of the medium: is there any possible affinity between the future inscription on the "large stones" (as a result of the imperative "you shall write" in Deut 27:3, 8), and the *sēper* mentioned in 28:58? Aramaean and Phoenician documents are of interest here, especially the Sefire treaties.[36] In Sefire, the recurring phrase עדיא זי בספרא זנה is translated by Joseph Fitzmyer, "the treaty which is in this inscription."[37] He comments: "*spr* denotes here the text of the inscription engraved on stone; there is no reason to suppose that it was written at first on some soft material. In Sf I C 17 we find *mly spr' zy bnṣb' znh*, 'the words of the inscription which (is) on this stele.'"[38] The word ספר also means "inscription" in the inscriptions of Kilamuwa and Aḥiram.[39] Surveying the use made of *sēper* in western-Semitic epigraphic texts of the first half of the first millennium or shortly thereafter, Alberto Soggin points out that the meaning of "book" hardly ever appears. Only "inscription" and "letter" are firmly attested.[40] Concerning the occurrences of ספר

---

[36] The three Sefire inscriptions are to be dated around 754, see Fitzmyer, *Aramaic Inscriptions*, 2-3.

[37] See I B 33; II B 9,18; II C 13; III 4, 14, 17, 23; see also I A 6, "the st[ele with t]his [inscription]"; I B 6, "the words of thi[s] inscription"; I C 17, "the words of the inscription which is on this stele"; II C 2, 4, 6, 9, "these inscriptions" (ספריא).

[38] Fitzmyer, *Aramaic Inscriptions*, 65. Fitzmyer lists Deut 27:2-8 among the biblical passages which, in his view, are to be reconsidered under the light of such a use of the word ספר (see p. 66).

[39] The Aḥirām sarcophagus (*ca.* 1000) bears: ימח ספרא (*KAI* no. 1, l. 2), "(so) soll seine Inschrift ausgelöscht werden" (*KAI* 2.2); the Kilamuwa (Zincirli) inscription (*ca.* 825) reads: ומי ישחת הספר (*KAI* no. 24, l. 15; see also l. 14): "Und wer diese Inschrift verdirbt" (*KAI* 2.31).

[40] J. A. Soggin, *Old Testament and Oriental Studies* (BibOr 29; Rome: Biblical

in Deuteronomy and in the Deuteronomistic history, Soggin concludes: "we must seriously ask ourselves if the 'book' referred to is not in reality the 'document', the 'inscription' on which the text of the 'Covenant' was transcribed and conserved, especially since, in some of these passages, the erection of a stele, just as in Sefire e.g. is explicitly mentioned."[41] It therefore appears that the semantic field of the word ספר comprehends the notion of "inscription," including the possible sense of "inscription on a stele."[42] Between the inscription on stone anticipated in Deuteronomy 27 and the double mention of the ספר in Deuteronomy 28, a continuity is thus more than possible.

It is my contention that Deuteronomy 27-28 is built upon such a continuity. Referring to "the words of this Torah written in this inscription" (28:58), the Levites will refer to the inscription of the Torah on the "large stones." Speaking after the crossing of the Jordan river, and speaking at Ebal-Gerizim, they will then have the record in question "before the eyes," as an object they can point at: "all the words of this Torah written in this inscription (ספר)." The making of the inscription "beyond the Jordan" will

---

Institute Press, 1975) 184-86; see also *DISO*, 196-97, which under the entry ספר III lists the meanings "inscription," "lettre, missive," "document, contrat, acte." In the biblical context, it is worth noticing that Isa 30:8 ועל ספר חקה ("And inscribe it in a record" [NJPSV]) and Job 19:23-24 בצור יחצבון . . . בספר ויחקו ("would they were inscribed in a record ... incised on a rock" [NJPSV]) exclude, when it comes to the *sēper*, the use of a soft material. It has been suggested that the occurrences of *sēper* in Isa 30:8 and Job 19:23 are derivatives from the Akkadian *siparru*, "bronze", (see Judg 5:14) (see H. Zimmern, *Akkadische Fremdwörter als Beweis für Babylonischen Kultureinfluß* [2d ed.; Leipzig: Hinrichs, 1917] 59). The ספר II (= "bronze") hypothesis has been characterized by *HALAT*, 3.724, as a "überholte Herleitung aus akk *siparru*." See however M. Dietrich - O. Loretz, "Akkadische *siparru* "Bronze", Ugaritisch *spr*, *ġprt* und Hebräisch *spr*, *ʿprt*," *UF* 17 (1986) 401.

[41] Soggin, *Old Testament*, 185-86. In Deut 27:2,4, Moses gives the order to "plaster [the large stones] with plaster" before carrying on with the inscription. The technique of inscription on plastered stone is known to us from some wall inscriptions going back to the 8th century BCE, especially the inscriptions of Kuntillet Ajrud and of Deir ʿAlla. It is worth noticing that the text inscribed on plaster at Deir ʿAlla opens with the word ספ[ר] which Caquot and Lemaire translate as "inscription" ("[Ins]cription de [Balaa]m [fils de Be]or, l'homme qui voyait les dieux)" (see A. Caquot et A. Lemaire, "Les textes araméens de Deir ʿAlla", *Syria* 54 [1977] 194). In their commentary, "inscription" is understood as "écrit (traitant) de," or, what is quite different, "histoire de" (p. 194). Lemaire has recently expressed another view, and sees in the text of Deir ʿAlla "probably a copy of an Aramaic *book* about the seer Balaam son of Beori" (A. Lemaire, "Writing and Writing Materials," *ABD* 6. 1001; my italics).

[42] See the remarks by Lohfink, "Bundesschluß," 39 n. 4.

thus lead up to the Ebal-Gerizim supplementary covenant ceremony. The solemnity of this ceremony will be enhanced by the
written display of the terms of the covenant, especially of its
appended curses.[43] Curses, it seems, enjoyed a special efficacy
when written. Commenting upon a reference by Ashurbanipal to
the efficacy of the curses *written* in oath texts,[44] McCarthy concludes that "writing was an added assurance of power."[45] A
micro-system is thus formed by Moses' instruction in 27:3, 8 to
inscribe the Torah words, and by the reference in 28:58 to the
inscription (ספר) of the same Torah words. So much for the future
of Moses' Torah on the western bank of the Jordan; in 28:69, the
third heading of Deuteronomy brings the focus back to what takes
place on the eastern bank of the Jordan, i.e., in Moab: "These are
the words of the covenant which YHWH commanded Moses to
make with the people of Israel in the land of Moab, besides the
covenant which he had made with them at Horeb."[46] To the ulti-

---

[43] The inscription stipulated in Deut 27:3,8 includes "all the words of this
Torah," and so does the *sēper* in 28:58. Yet, are the benedictions and maledictions meant for Ebal-Gerizim included in such a "Torah"? An indirect answer is
given in 28:61: "Also (גם) every sickness, and every affliction which is not recorded in the *sēper* of this Torah, YHWH will bring upon you." In other words: these
unrecorded afflictions supplement the ones recorded "in the *sēper* of this Torah."
Lohfink, "Moab oder Sichem," 145, argues that 28:61 is self-referential: there are
recorded maledictions, and these are part of the very text (הספר הזה) which is now
communicated. Such a referential logic is actually possible only if the Ebal-Gerizim speech of Deuteronomy 27-28 is communicated right away by Moses (who
reads it) as a written *text* to be read by the Levites. This is indeed Lohfink's
assumption: "Mose teilt Dtn 28 in Moab dem Volk Israel zwar als Text mit, da er
den Wortlaut des sichemitischen Segens und Fluches ja öffentlich vorschreibt.
Aber diesen Text proklamiert Mose in diesem Augenblick nicht formell über
Israel. Mose befiehlt nur die Proklamation dieses Textes für eine spätere Zeremonie in Sichem" (p. 145). However, there is no sign of an act of reading either
in Deut 27:11 ("And Moses charged the people the same day, saying") or in 27:14
("And the Levites shall declare [ואמרו . . . וענו] to all the men of Israel with a loud
voice"). Rather than self-referential, the mention of the *sēper* is plainly referential: while declaring what they have to declare, the Levites will point at the inscription on the large stones.

[44] See *AR* 2.367 (§ 949), "Every curse, written down in the oath they took, in
my name, and that of the gods, thy sons, - instantly didst thou visit upon them
an evil fate."

[45] McCarthy, *Treaty*, 117.

[46] About Deut 28:69 as superscript, see especially Lohfink, "Bundesschluß,"
32-35; idem, "Überschrift oder Kolophon?," 40-52. The view that Deut 28:69 is a
subscript to what precedes it has notably been defended by Driver, *Deuteronomy*,
319, and van Rooy, "Superscript or Subscript?," 215-22. Lenchak, *"Choose Life!"*,
172-73, summarizes the discussion and concludes: "a good case can be made that

mate *peripeteia* of Moses' communication in Moab I shall now turn.

3. *sēper in Deuteronomy 29-30*

The Deut 28:69 heading, "These are the words of the covenant," leads into a Mosaic speech that indeed sets the stage for an imminent covenantal procedure: "You stand this day all of you before YHWH your God ... that you may enter into the sworn covenant of YHWH your God (בברית יהוה אלהיך ובאלתו), which YHWH your God makes with you this day" (30:10-12). In this speech Moses refers four times to covenant regulations "written in this *sēper*" (29:19,26), or "in the *sēper* of this Torah" (29:20; 30:10).[47] Written communication that has thus far been a fact of the past or an injunction to be implemented suddenly comes close, to the point of being on hand for Moses, under the form of "this *sēper*." Moses' pointing to a specific ספר within Deuteronomy's represented world is meant for an audience in a position to grasp the act of reference. This is not true for the reader, who does not see what the audience supposedly sees, and whose way of making sense of Moses' reference is necessarily a process of trial and error.

a. *The Interpretative Frame*

The first occurrence of *sēper* in Moses' "words of the covenant" appears in the terse combination: בספר הזה, "the imprecations written *in this sēper* will settle upon him" (Deut 29:19). How is the reader to handle this lack of explicitness? It is important to remember that the phrase "in this *sēper*" belongs to the reader's *déjà lu*. In his previous speech, Moses referred to "the words of the Torah which are written *in this sēper*" (28:58). Since in Deuteronomy's world no less than in the metaphysician's *non sunt multiplicanda entia sine necessitate*, the identity of the *sēper* in question with the Ebal-Gerizim "inscription" may be surmised at first. Yet

---

the verse is one of a series of superscripts found in Dt and has greater literary and terminological contacts with what follows. The dissociation between the covenant of Horeb and that made at Moab also tends to link the verse with what follows rather than what precedes it" (p. 172).

[47] In Deut 29:26, as I shall indicate, Moses is actually quoting a future speech by a collective speaker.

the narrative and rhetorical context of Deut 29:19 work against such a guess. In Deuteronomy 28, the Mosaic speech anticipated the Levitical admonition to be delivered at Ebal-Gerizim. In this context, the *sēper* referred to the inscription of the Torah on the "large stones." In Deuteronomy 29-30, Moses speech focuses on the "here and now" of the covenant-making in the plains of Moab. To go by Moses' discourse, the covenantal procedure involves the presence of a determined document—"this *sēper*." It is most unlikely that the Moab ספר (29:19, "this *sēper*") is materially identical with the "beyond the Jordan" ספר, the future inscription on the "large stones" (28:58, "this *sēper*"). Yet a formal resemblance has been created beyond the material difference: on both sides it is a question of "this *sēper*." This formal analogy gives rise to further guessing: does the formal resemblance imply a resemblance in content as well? Since Moses' injunction in Deut 27:2-8, the written embodiment of the Torah belongs to the people's near future; has it been somehow anticipated, so as to be "very near" to Moses and his audience?

The affinity in content of the Ebal inscription (mentioned in Deuteronomy 27-28) and the Moab written record (mentioned in Deuteronomy 29-30) is perceptible in all four mentions of the *sēper* in Deuteronomy 29-30. The three phrases, "every imprecation (אלה) written in this *sēper*" (29:19), "in accordance with all the imprecations of the covenant (אלות הברית) written in this *sēper* of the Torah" (29:20), and "every malediction (קללה) written in this *sēper*" (29:26) refer to curses, which were indeed spelled out in 27:15-26 and 28:15-68.[48] In true ancient Near Eastern fashion, these curses were expressed after the legal stipulations, in the section to be proclaimed by the Levites at Ebal-Gerizim (see 27:13 [הקללה, "the malediction"]; 28:15, 45), and to be recorded in the *sēper*-inscription of Mount Ebal (see 28:61). According to Moses' fourth and last mention of the *sēper* (in Deut 30:10), the document in Moab also features legal stipulations—"[YHWH's] commandments and his statutes, which are written in this *sēper* of the Torah." The legal body of the Torah, equally to be displayed on the "large stones" (see 27:3, 8; 28:58), is thereby recalled. The two records—the future inscription beyond the Jordan, and the

---

[48] See the remark by Lenchak, *"Choose Life!,"* 116.

document on hand in Moab—thus overlap in content while they differ in material form. The integral reproducibility of a written message, and the possibility for a text to have concomitantly two or more spatial embodiments are not a minor aspect of the revolution of writing. Moses brings this remarkable phenomenon into play in the case of the royal duplicate (משנה) (Deut 17:18). Deuteronomy plays on the same law of written communication in the transition between Moses' Torah speech and his "words of the covenant."

b. *In Medias Res*

Nothing is properly *told* about the *sēper* on hand in the course of the Moab covenant. Moses refers his audience to an existing written record that the narrator had not told his reader about in advance. In letting his *dramatis persona* catch the reader unawares, Deuteronomy's narrator is faithful to his dramatic manner: in Deuteronomy's unfolding, things are primarily shown (by the character's speeches), not told (by the narrator). Contrary to the plasticity of the omniscient narrator's telling (the narrator can be at any temporal or spatial point of the represented world), characters' speeches are by necessity located *in medias res*. They are inserted between what precedes and what follows them, and they generally project a state of affairs in the represented world. In most cases characters do not specify the context of their current speech intervention: the narrative context (previous speech acts, the state of affairs in the represented world) assures such a pragmatic background. In his terse introduction in Deut 28:69, "These are the words of the covenant ...", the narrator chose not to make the reader privy to what happened in the world prior to the uttering of the words in question. The opposite policy is observable in Exod 24:3-8, which *tells* all the preliminaries to the people's oath (the writing of the covenant *sēper*, the building of the altar, the setting up of steles, etc.). Deuteronomy's narrator, here as elsewhere, opts for conveying almost right away the *dramatis persona*'s speech.

Deuteronomy's way of presentation requires the reader's competence and imaginative participation. What are the reader's expectations in a context such as the covenant-making of Deuteronomy 29-30? The paradigm behind such expectations is

arguably provided by the "covenant at Horeb" (see 28:69: "besides
the covenant which [YHWH] had made with them at Horeb"),
which the covenant in Moab supplements.[49] In Exodus 24 the formal making of the covenant presupposed the writing and the reading of the covenant *sēper* (24:4, 7).[50] The Sinai paradigm tallies,
moreover, with the ancient Near Eastern covenant procedures:
"Der allgemeinen Aufassung des alten Orients entspricht es," V.
Korošec points out, "daß für den Vertragsabschluß die schriftliche
Ausfertigung wesentlich ist."[51] A similar procedure indeed accom-
panies the supplementary covenant in Moab: a document (*sēper*)
recording all of the stipulations underlying the covenant (benedictions and maledictions included) is on hand in the Moab
covenant ceremony.

Yet reference is repeatedly made in Deuteronomy 29-30 to a
written document without any hint at the reading of the document in question. This significant feature is actually consistent
with the communication process in Deuteronomy. Everything
recorded in the written Torah has been *heard* beforehand by
Moses' audience. The covenant in Moab is therefore made with
full knowledge of the terms, maledictions included.[52] This ideol-
ogy of overt communication is somehow epitomized in Deut 29:28:
"The secret things [הנסתרת] belong to YHWH our God; but the
things that are revealed [והנגלת] belong to us and to our children
for ever, that we may do all the words of this Torah." Thus none

---

[49] See Lohfink, "Fabel," 72-74; and idem "Bund," 231-32. See also p. 114 n. 66
below.

[50] In 2 Kings 23:1-3, similarly, the covenant is made on the basis of the *sēper*
solemnly read to all the people of Judah and Jerusalem. In Josh 24:25-26, however, the sequence is apparently in the reverse order, but the sequence of events
does not necessarily mirror the sequence of sentences (*wayyiqtol* forms can express
perfect or pluperfect actions).

[51] V. Korošec, *Hethitische Staatsverträge: ein Beitrag zu ihrer juristischen Wertung*
(Leipziger Rechtwissenschaftliche Studien 60; Leipzig: Weicher, 1931) 26; Korošec goes on: "Die Vertragsurkunde ist nicht bloß ein Beweismittel für den etwa
durch Übereinstimmung beider Parteien zustande gekommenen Vertrag, sondern
der Vertrag entsteht erst durch die Errichtung der Urkunde ... Die Vertragsurkunde gehört somit zu den Dispositivurkunden." See also N. Lohfink, "Zur
Fabel in Dtn 31-32," *Konsequente Traditionsgeschichte: Festschrift für Klaus Baltzer zum
65. Geburtstag* (ed. R. Bartelmus, Th. Krüger and H. Utzschneider; OBO 126;
Freiburg: Universitätsverlag; Göttingen: Vandenhoeck & Ruprecht, 1993) 268.

[52] A final "chapter" will be added in the last minute (the song האזינו), due to
further divine revelation, but not without appropriate communication (Deut
31:22: "So Moses wrote this song the same day, and taught it to the people of
Israel").

of the essentials is opaque to the audience or to the reader. The overlapping in content, as far as the essentials are concerned, between Moses' speech in Deuteronomy 5-28 and the ספר-record in Deuteronomy 29-30 echoes another equation: the identity in content between Moses' Torah speech and the future inscription "beyond the Jordan." The two written embodiments of the Torah, on the two banks of the Jordan River, accordingly match each other. Deuteronomy's policy of disclosure and the "miracle" of written duplication are tightly connected.

c. *The Purposeful Reference to the sēper*

The repeated mention of the written document in Deuteronomy 29-30 raises a further question: are the references to "this *sēper*" casual references to what lies on hand, or do these mentions serve any purpose? Reference is made to the *sēper* (or "document," "record") in three consecutive passages:

(i) In Deut 29:17-20, Moses rules out any double standard regarding the covenant commitment. He attacks the behavior of the individual who, in the secret of his conscience (בלבבו, "in his heart"), endeavors to go against the public commitment: "I shall be safe, though I walk in the stubbornness of my heart" (29:19). In no way, Moses goes on, will this individual escape God's anger and elude the curses attached to the communal self-imprecation:

> [19]The imprecation (אלה) written in this record (ספר) would settle upon him, and YHWH would blot his name from under heaven. [20]And YHWH will single him out from all the tribes of Israel for calamity, in accordance with all the imprecations (אלות) of the covenant written in this record (ספר) of the Torah." (29:19-20)

The publicity of the written *sēper* is no incentive for private and secret infringing thoughts. It is rather the transgressor's name that will be deleted from the written condition, by being blotted out "from under heaven." The written imprecation has a strategy of its own, as the metaphor indicates: "the imprecation (אלה) written in this record would settle (רבצה) upon him" (רבץ is said of animals lying down).[53] The written אלה, so to speak, watches what

---

[53] See Gen 49:9, 14; Exod 23:5; Num 22:27, etc.; see also the metaphorical use of the verb in Gen 4:7 (about sin).

is secretly conceived against it.[54] Private plans of transgression,
Moses warns, do not outsmart the divine design embedded in the
written *sēper*.

(ii) In Deut 29:22-27 the perspective inverts itself. The previous development dealt with the prospect of an individual mem-
ber of the people; the view is now retrospective, from future to
past, and contemplates collective realities. Along with foreigners,
future generations of Israelites will inquire about the calamities
brought upon the land: "And the generation to come, your children who rise up after you and the foreigner who comes from a
far land, would say, when they see the afflictions of that land
..." (29:22).[55] In 29:19-20 the curses-imprecations of the written
sēper will surround the individual as deterrent threats; in the scenario of vv. 22-28 the same menaces are considered as carried out.
The covenant and its record encompass Israel's future and provide a rational framework within which questions ("Why has
YHWH done thus to the land?") find answers: "It is because they
forsook the covenant of YHWH ... Therefore the anger of YHWH
was kindled against this land, bringing upon it every curse (קללה)
written in this record (ספר)" (29:26). The *sēper* becomes the touchstone of God's consistent behavior in the future. Written curses
are not only deterrents aiming at secret thoughts, they are also
carried out in history, before the eyes of foreigners and future
generations. But there is more: the phrase "this record" in 29:26
occurs in a context other than Moses' covenant speech in Moab.
The expression is part of the quoted words introduced by ואמרו in
29:24, "And they will say." The anonymous people who will answer
the nations' question[56] about the desolation of the land will point

---

[54] See the remark by Lohfink, "Bundesschluß," 39.

[55] About the literary genre of the question addressed to Israel by foreigners
or future generations, and about ancient Near Eastern parallels, see W. L. Moran,
"The Ancient Near Eastern Background of the Love of God in Deuteronomy,"
CBQ 25 (1963) 83-84; D. R. Hillers, *Treaty-Curses and the Old Testament Prophets*
(BibOr 16; Rome: Pontifical Biblical Institute, 1964) 65 n. 60; D. E. Skweres, "Das
Motiv der Strafgrunderfragung in biblischen und neuassyrischen Texten," *BZ* 14
(1970) 181-97; B. O. Long, "Two Question and Answer Schemata in the Prophets,"
JBL 90 (1971) 129-39; Weinfeld, *School*, 115 n. 1; W. Vogels, "The Literary Form
of 'The Question of the Nations,'" *EgT* 11 (1980) 159-76.

[56] The verb אמר occurs three times in Deut 29:21-24 with three different sub-
jects: the future Israelite generation and the foreigner in v. 21; "all the nations"
in the question of v. 23; and an unspecified (and implicit) "they" in the answer
of v. 24. According to Weinfeld, *School*, 115 n. 1, "all the nations" in v. 23 resumes

to "this record": "Therefore the anger of YHWH was kindled against this land, bringing upon it all the curses written in this record" (29:27). The formulation בספר הזה, "in this record," identical to that in 29:19 (where Moses refers to a document on hand)[57] must not put anyone off the track. The written document referred to in 29:17 belongs to a different context, both temporally (29:22, "after you") and spatially (the scene takes place in the land). But this is no surprise: it is a property of written records to transcend the *hic et nunc* of the context of their origin. In so doing, they can provide valuable points of reference for third parties (future generations, foreign nations).[58] The maledictions recorded in the *sēper* will indeed enable people foreign to the Moab ceremony to verify that YHWH is not arbitrary in his behavior toward the idolatrous people.

(iii) The whole section of Deut 30:1-10 is to be read as a "subsequent future," prophesying a return from exile, beyond the (future) calamity alluded to in the previous development. The *sēper* is no longer presented as a record of imprecations or curses, but of stipulations: "since you will be heeding the voice of YHWH your God and keeping his commandments and his statutes which are written in this record of the Torah" (30:10). Such a prophecy has already been uttered by Moses to the sons of Israel gathered in the plains of Moab (in 4:29-31).[59] After their being scattered, and after their idolatrous worship among the nations, the people would "return to YHWH your God and heed his voice" (4:30). At that point of his communication Moses had still to "set" the Torah "before the sons of Israel" (4:44). Revisiting the same

---

the subject of אמר in v. 21, "so that at the end the question is asked by the Israelites, the foreigners, and all the nations together and answered by them too. This goes well with [an] Assyrian parallel text [see *AR* 368 (§ 949)] where the vassals ask themselves and answer for themselves."

[57] Let alone the previous reference in Deut 28:58, in the context of the Mosaic speech meant for the Levites at Ebal-Gerizim.

[58] Such is the avowed purpose of Hammurapi's code: "Let any oppressed man who has a cause ... read carefully my inscribed stela and give heed to my precious words, and my stela make the case clear to him; may he understand his cause; may he set his mind at ease!" (Deut 25:3-19; *ANET*, 178).

[59] The thematic and textual affinity between Deuteronomy 4 and Deuteronomy 30 has been highlighted by studies on Deuteronomy's redactional history. See for instance, A. D. H. Mayes, "Deuteronomy 4 and the Literary Criticism of Deuteronomy," *JBL* 100 (1981) 23-51; D. Knapp, *Deuteronomium 4: Literarische Analyse und theologische Interpretation* (GTA 35; Göttingen: Vandenhoeck & Ruprecht, 1987); Weinfeld, *Deuteronomy*, 215-16.

prophecy after the conveying of the Torah, Moses now significantly combines the heeding to YHWH's voice with the keeping
of the stipulations written in "this *sēper*." In Deuteronomy the relationship to YHWH's voice is increasingly presented as mediated
by the relationship to the commandments Moses is conveying:
"and obey his voice in all that I command you this day" (30:2).[60]
In the perspective opened in 30:10, Moses' oral mediation gives
way to the written document's: "since you will be heeding the
voice of YHWH your God and keeping his commandments and
his statutes which are written in this record of the Torah." The
concept of obedience includes now the reference to the divine
voice as well as the reference to the written record. God's voice
that could not be heard except through Moses' is now mediated
by the written stipulations of "this record of the Torah." In that
sense Deut 30:10 epitomizes Deuteronomy's overall communication process.

The references to the *sēper* in Deut 29-30 therefore seem not
to have been made at random. In all three passages the specific
economy of written records has a significant role. Whether in the
dialectic of publicity and secrecy (29:16-21), in the possibility of
interpreting history according to non-arbitrary criteria (30:22-28),
or in the mediating of voices (the inaccessible divine voice and
the transient prophetic voice), the written condition has a relevance of its own.

d. *Curiosity and Suspense*

In Deuteronomy 27-28 Moses twice alludes to a future record of
the Torah—the first time by stipulating its making (Deut 27:2-8),
and the second time by having the Levites refer to it in their
future speech at Ebal-Gerizim (Deut 28:58-61). In both cases
Moses is dealing with a future record, located "beyond the Jordan." The mentions of the *sēper* in Deuteronomy 29-30, by contrast, point to a document on hand in the making of the Moab
covenant (Deut 29:19, 20, 26; 30:10). Various hints, however, give
away the overlapping in the content of the two written records.
What will be "beyond the Jordan" seems therefore to be very close
as well. This situation raises an interesting play of questions, relat-

---

[60] See also Deut 13:19; 15:5; 27:10; 28:1, 2, 15; 30:2.

ed to curiosity and suspense. "Both [curiosity and suspense],"
Sternberg writes, "are interests that derive from a felt lack of information about the world, give rise to a play of hypotheses framed
to supply the missing link, and generate expectations of stable
closure."[61]

The fourfold mention of the *sēper* in Deuteronomy 29-30 primarily raises a question of curiosity, that is, a question relating
"to an accomplished fact in the world: an incident, relationship,
motive, character trait, plot logic, which has already played some
part in determining the narrative present."[62] Faced with repeated
reference to a written record, the reader cannot fail to wonder:
what is the genesis of the document in question? The act of writing belongs to the future of the sons of Israel (וכתבת, "you shall
write," 27:3,8); was it anticipated? By whom? Is it by Moses, who
delivered orally what is now written (29:20; 30:10, "This Torah
sēper"), and whom the use of the deictic זו, "this [*sēper*]," somehow ties to the record in question? The command to write in
Deuteronomy 27 was linked to "large stones"; what is the nature
of the *sēper* Moses is dealing with in the plain of Moab? As I indicated, the act of copying (17:18) or writing down (6:9; 11:20) is
one of the basic operations Moses enjoins on his audience; in
Deut 29-30, do we encounter a further משנה, "copy" (see 17:18) of
the Torah words? Yet, the *sēper* referred to by Moses in Moab
arguably antedates all of the future transcriptions (they all belong
to Israel's existence "after Moab," either in its crossing of the Jordan or its dwelling in the land). The record that is present on
stage in Deuteronomy 29-30 chronologically and spatially precedes
whatever writing operation Moses has stipulated in his speeches.
Curiosity therefore sharpens: do we encounter in Deuteronomy
29-30 the *editio princeps* of the recording of the Torah words? Does
Moses' *sēper* in Moab represent the condition of possibility for all
further commitment to writing?

The curiosity question arouses a suspense question as well. "In
art as in life," Sternberg writes, "suspense derives from incomplete
knowledge about a conflict (or some other contingency) looming
in the future."[63] Enjoining Israel to write down beyond the Jor-

---

[61] Sternberg, *Poetics*, 283.
[62] Sternberg, *Poetics*, 283.
[63] Sternberg, *Poetics*, 264.

dan all the words of the Torah, Moses is not sparing of details as
to the place and the manner of the inscription. Nothing is said,
however, about the actual transmission of "all the words" to be
written down. Here as elsewhere in Deuteronomy, the writing
operations enjoined by Moses may be thought of as based on
memory—the proverbial memory of ancient man. Still, the order
conveyed to the king in Deut 17:18—"he shall write for himself
in a *sēper* a copy (משנה) of this Torah"—has rather directed the
reader's imagination and expectation toward the act of copying,
that is, toward the transcription from record to record, from *sēper*
to *sēper*. Is such an expectation appropriate when it comes to the
future inscription on the "large stones"? Having reached Moses'
speech in Deuteronomy 29-30, the reader is caught between two
written realizations of the Torah (and two embodiments of the
sēper): the stone "inscription" at Ebal and the covenant record in
Moab. After having referred to an "over the Jordan" writing down
of the Torah, Moses set out before the people a written record
of the same Torah. The question that arises is therefore the question of a possible link, in the represented world, between the two
written instances of the Torah. However likely in a pure logic of
communication, such a link is problematic in Deuteronomy's plot
insofar as Moses is concerned. Moses is closer than anyone else
to the *sēper* (he is the one who says "this record"); still, the same
Moses is the only character on stage who will not reach the other
side of the Jordan, that is, the site of the inscription. Moses, the
reader knows, is about to depart from the rest of the people, that
is from the "you" upon whom the commandment to write is
incumbent. No less than curiosity (what is the genesis of the *sēper*
displayed by Moses in Moab?), suspense (are both written transcriptions of the Torah meant to coalesce, and how, beyond
Moses' death?) defines the reader's state of mind at the turn of
Deuteronomy 31.

*Excursus: The Sequence in "Fabula" of Deuteronomy's Middle Speech
Units (Deuteronomy 5-28 and 29-30). A Discussion of Lohfink's
Reconstruction*

The sequence of Deuteronomy's middle speech units (Deuteronomy 5-28; 29-30) has a decisive bearing in the present inquiry. It

is my view that the sequence of events in Deuteronomy's "fabula" parallels the textual sequence (or "sujet") of Deuteronomy's four speech units. In other words, it is my view that Moses delivered the Torah speech (Deuteronomy 5-28) before he uttered the "words of the covenant" (Deuteronomy 29-30). This would seem self-evident, except that Lohfink has recently proposed a reconstruction of Deuteronomy's "fabula" that features a non-sequential combination of Deuteronomy's central units (Deuteronomy 5-28, 29-30).[64] In Lohfink's opinion, Moses conveyed the Torah (Deuteronomy 5-28) *during* the ritual of the covenant referred to in his speech in Deuteronomy 29-30, and he did so by *reading* aloud to the assembled people a Torah already committed to writing (in a "Bundesdokument" [ספר]). Lohfink's argument can be summarized as follows. The double convocation of the people by Moses in 5:1 and 29:1 ("And Moses summoned all Israel and said to them") does not mean that two assemblies were held in succession; rather, the same solemn gathering is narrated twice, from two different perspectives. The overlapping of the two scenes is implied by performative utterances in Deuteronomy 26-27 that signal the establishment of the covenantal bond. These performative utterances are essentially YHWH's and Israel's oath of mutual commitment recorded by Moses in Deut 26:16-19, the declarations by Moses and the elders in 27:1, and by Moses and the Levitical priests in 27:9.[65] These statements have their logical place in the course of the covenantal ritual alluded to by Moses in Deuteronomy 29-30; they cannot have taken place before this ritual. Coming toward the end of Moses' second speech (Deuteronomy 5-28), these declarations are one piece with the Torah unit they conclude. The whole Torah was thus delivered during the ritual of the covenant in Deuteronomy 29-30. It is possible to further reconstruct the "fabula" and to determine the exact location of the conveying of the Torah during Moses' "words of the covenant." Moses' speech in 29:1-14 presents the "passage into the covenant" as still impending (see 29:9-11, "You stand this day all of you ... that you may pass into the covenant"). The Torah, with its conclusive declarations of covenantal commitment, cannot

---

[64] See Lohfink, "Fabel," 65-78; idem, "Bund," 228-33.

[65] On this specific issue, see Lohfink, "Bund," 233-37; see also idem, "Die Ältesten Israels und der Bund: Zur Zusammenhang von Dtn 5,23; 26,17-19; 27,1.9f und 31,9," *BN* 67 (1993) 26-42, esp. 31-35.

have been transmitted before this introductory statement. Yet it must immediately follow it. In 29:19, 20, for the first time in the covenantal ritual, Moses refers to the ספר-"document" (29:19, "this 'document'"; 29:20, "this 'document' of the Torah"). This implies that Moses conveyed the Torah beforehand, and that he did so by reading the "document" in question. The double mention of the ספר-"document" is contained in a rhetorical section that opens in 29:15. Lohfink therefore concludes: "Das zusammen legt nah, die Verlesung des Bundesdokuments mitsamt den nach Dtn 26,16 - 27,10 dabei erfolgenden formellen Bundesschlußdeklarationen eher vor dem Vortrag dieses Abschnitts, also zwischen 29,14 und 29,15 anzusetzen."[66] The "fabula" reconstructed by Lohfink thus presents the following sequence:

$$[\; 5 \; \text{————————} \; 26 \; (-28) \;]$$
$$\Downarrow$$
$$[\; 1–4 \;] \quad [\; 29–29:14 \quad 29:15 - 30 \;] \quad [\; 31–34 \;]$$

In my view Lohfink's hypothesis unnecessarily complicates Deuteronomy's "fabula" and presupposes sophisticated interpretative operations that the reader will most likely not be able to carry out.[67] The succession of Deuteronomy 5-28 and 29-30 can be understood as the representation of two distinct and successive covenantal procedures: an oral transaction in Deuteronomy 5-28, and a ritual "crossing into the covenant" in Deuteronomy 29-30. The former, entirely verbal procedure is concluded by the mutual oath recorded in Deut 26:16-19, and by the declarations in Deut 27:1, 9. Moses, interestingly enough, introduces the content of his speech in 4:45 as עדת, a term that has been compared to the Aramaic עדן (plural) and to the Akkadian *adê*, "oath."[68] The Torah

[66] Lohfink, "Bund," 233. In Lohfink's view, the account of Exod 24:3-8 represents the "Informationsquelle für die Erwartungsstrukturen" of Deuteronomy's implied reader ("Fabel," 72; see also "Bund," 231-32). Exodus 24 tells of a twofold covenantal procedure: an oral communication of the stipulations of the covenant, followed by the people's commitment (24:3); a covenantal ritual on the next day, that includes the reading of the same stipulations in the "'record' (ספר) of the covenant," and a second commitment of the people (24:4-8). The sequence of events in Deuteronomy, Lohfink avers, mirrors the ritual of the second day in the Sinai covenant.
[67] See pp. 19-20 above for my reservations concerning Lohfink's view of the non-sequential character of Deuteronomy's speech units.
[68] See especially A. Lemaire and J.-M. Durand, "Un problème d'équivalence

speech thus arguably mirrors the oath section in the making of the covenantal bond. In the latter procedure, projected by Moses' speech in Deuteronomy 29-30, what is required from the people is a "passage": "that you may pass (לעברך) into the sworn covenant."[69] The phrase עבר בברית / באלה, "to pass into the covenant / the adjuration," may represent a (frozen) technical formula for "entering the covenantal bond," as in the parallel expression בוא בברית / באלה, "to come into the covenant / the adjuration" (see 1 Sam 20:8; Jer 34:10; Ez 16:8; 17:3; Neh 10:30; 2 Chr 15:12).[70] The phrase in Deut 29:11 (featuring the verb עבר, "to pass"), however, is an hapax in the Hebrew Bible and possibly has an idiosyncratic value. In two references to covenant making, in Gen 15:17 and Jer 34:18-19, the verb עבר refers to a literal "passage," that is, a ritual crossing. In Jeremiah 34, moreover, the phrase "to come into the covenant (בוא בברית)" (34:10) is particularized as "to pass (עבר) between the parts of the calf" (34:18, 19). In my view, the use of עבר, "to pass," in Deut 29:11, similarly refers to a ritual crossing. The point is that the people's commitment is now expressed by a non-verbal action—a ritual step. This step amounts to a ratification of the covenantal bond first created orally.[71] The

---

sémantique assyro-araméo-hébraïque: adê - ʿdn / ʿdyʾ / ʿdy - ʿēdūt / ʿēdwōt / ʿēdōt," Les inscriptions araméennes de Sfiré et l'Assyrie de Shamshi-Ilu (Ecole Pratique des Hautes Etudes 20; Genève and Paris: Droz, 1984) 91-106. See also N. Lohfink, "ʿd(w)t im Deuteronomium und in den Königsbüchern," BZ 35 (1991) 86-93. Lohfink, pp. 90-93, examines what he considers to be the two possible semantic values of the word in the Hebrew Bible, that is, "oath, contract" and "teaching" (for the latter, see B. Couroyer, "ʿēdūt: Stipulation de traité ou enseignement?," RB 95 [1988] 321-31). Lohfink concludes that both possibilities have strong and weak points, and that the context alone can help decide. In the case of עדה in Deut 4:45, it seems to me that the reference to a convenantal commitment through oath in the same unit (in 26:16-19 notably) tips the scale in favor of the meaning of עדה as "oath."

[69] The two terms ברית . . . אלה, "covenant ... adjuration," translated as a hendiadys, "sworn covenant," appears also in Deut 29:13; see also the occurrence of ברית in 29:8, "Be careful to do the words of this covenant (דברי הברית הזאת)," and those of אלה in 29:18 and 30:7.

[70] In this discussion on the meaning and reference of the phrase לעברך בברית in Deut 29:11, I follow and summarize Lohfink, "Bund," 226-27.

[71] In a careful analysis of Jeremiah 34 and Genesis 15, Å. Viberg concludes that "both in Gen 15 and Jer 34 the legal symbolic act of walking through a divided animal, or animals, has been found to have the legal function of ratifying a covenant that has been made" (Symbols of Law: A Contextual Analysis of Legal Symbolic Acts in the Old Testament [CB 34; Stockholm: Almqvist & Wiksell International, 1992] 68). It is worth noticing that in Gen 15:13, God's spoken promise comes before the symbolic crossing (15:17) which assures Abraham that God will stand

ספר-record of the Torah, to which Moses refers in his speech
(29:19, 20, 27; 30:10), constitutes the written "precipitate" of the
prior, verbal transaction, and represents the terms of the people's
ritual commitment. This document is not read, but this is no surprise: the people have just heard beforehand the words of the
Torah.[72] It is important to notice that no hint whatsoever of an
act of reading can be found in the introduction of the Torah unit
(see 5:1, ויאמר, "he said") or in Moses' "words of the covenant,"
let alone between 29:14-15.[73] The sequence of Deuteronomy's
speech units is thus, *pace* Lohfink, not contradicted by their
sequence in Deuteronomy's "fabula." The successive headings provide the reader with a straightforward guideline in Moses' last—
and quite full—day.[74]

---

by his promise. It is, moreover, Viberg's opinion that none of the alleged
extra-biblical parallels to Genesis 15:17 and Jeremiah 34:18-19 (from Mari, Sefire
and Assyria) portray the same act as in Genesis 15 and Jeremiah 34: "None of
them presents either a divided animal or someone partaking in the covenant by
walking through the parts" (p. 56). These texts document a different performance
(the killing of an animal, or animals), yet they may perform a similar legal function—the sanctioning of a treaty (see pp. 53-55). Viberg finally indicates that no
explicit self-imprecatory or sacrificial aspect (as usually contended) is found in
either the biblical or extra-biblical texts. The texts identifying the fate of the party who transgresses the covenant with the fate of the killed animals are not part
of self-commitments; they are voiced by the other party as a curse. See Viberg's
analysis of the treaty between Ashurnirari VI of Assyria and Mati'ilu of Arpad (I
10-17), the Sefire Treaty (I A 39-40), and the vassal treaty of Esarhaddon (ll.
547-54) (pp. 54-55). It is, however, my view that a *non-verbalized* self-imprecation
may be implied by a ritual like the one documented in Jeremiah 34.

[72] The reconstruction I suggest equally tallies with the reader's expectations
delineated by the account in Exod 24:3-8. The oral transaction of Deuteronomy
5-28, on the one hand, arguably mirrors the oral commitment in Exod 24:3,
"Moses came and told the people all the words of YHWH and all the ordinances;
and all the people answered with one voice, and said, 'All the words which YHWH
has spoken we will do'." Deuteronomy 29-30, on the other hand, is equivalent to
the ritual of Exod 24:4-8. In Exodus 24 the covenantal ritual is distributed over
two days; the reading of the "'book' of the covenant" on the second day, before
the people's final commitment, therefore makes (practical) sense. Deuteronomy's
unity of time does not necessitate such a rehearsal: the people have just heard
what they ratify in their ritual "crossing."

[73] In the Hebrew Bible the act of reading is described in a typical way, that
basically associates the verb קרא, with the meaning of "to read (out)," and the
object of the reading. See the survey in Hossfeld and Lamberty-Zielinski, "קָרָא
qārā'," 133-36.

[74] The relocation of Deuteronomy 5-28 as an independent unit within Moses'
"words of the covenant" (between Deut 29:14-15) is all the more unlikely in my
view, since the Torah speech is narratively coordinated with the narratorial
account in Deut 4:41-43 ("Then [אז] Moses set apart three cities in the east beyond
the Jordan ... *And* this is the Torah which Moses set before the sons of Israel"
[4:41-44]). See my remarks p. 18 n. 42 and p. 37 above.

CHAPTER FOUR

WRITING THE "BOOK," WRITING THE SONG
(DEUT 31:1-32:47)

> Enfin cette idée du Temps avait un dernier prix pour
> moi, elle était un aiguillon, elle me disait qu'il était
> temps de commencer . . . . Que celui qui pourrait
> écrire un tel livre serait heureux, pensais-je, quel
> labeur devant lui!

> Marcel Proust, *Le Temps retrouvé*

In Deut 31:1-32:47, in the wake of the דברי הברית, "words of the covenant" he has just uttered (see 28:69), Moses makes arrangements for his succession and for the "landed" future of the new-born covenant. In so doing, he endows the covenant in Moab with its full import. The issue of communication is intimately connected with Moses' final instructions. Deuteronomy 31 will progressively answer the questions of curiosity and suspense generated by the previous chapters; YHWH's theophany (Deut 31:14-23), the turning point in the recorded story, will also bring about sudden developments in Deuteronomy's theme of communication. As Olson points out, the process recorded in Deuteronomy 31 eventuates in a rather complex system of succession, for Moses "will be replaced not just by another human leader but by a combination of a human leader (Joshua in addition to all the elders, Levites ...), a written normative text ('the book of the *torah*'), and a song (the Song of Moses)."[1] The first section in this chapter will deal with different approaches generated by the complexity of Deuteronomy 31; two further sections will comment on the two stages of the text, marked off by God's intervention in 31:14. What will emerge is the dramatic narrative of the Torah "book's" genesis.

---

[1] Olson, *Deuteronomy*, 21 (see also pp. 134, 180-181).

1. *Two Approaches to the Art of Telling in Deuteronomy 31*

Deuteronomy 31 has long been known as a *pièce de résistance* for genetic approaches. An apparent patchwork of variegated "sources,"[2] the chapter seems to have undergone a thorough redactional reshaping that makes it difficult "für die vorherge-hende Entwicklungsstufen des Textes genauere Angaben zu machen."[3] The situation is allegedly not brighter when it comes to the text's narrative dynamic: "in fact," Gerhard von Rad writes, "the whole chapter contains debris of traditions rather than a real advance in the narrative."[4] Von Rad's severe diagnosis is echoed in Lohfink's statement that in Deuteronomy 31 both the narra-tive situation and the sequence of actions are "eigentümlich ver-wirrt, zusammenhanglos und unwirklich."[5] Having premised this, however, Lohfink tries to figure out the specific art of telling embodied in Deuteronomy 31. In two investigations, separated by thirty years, Lohfink proceeds according to two distinct approach-es. In a 1962 article, "Der Bundesschluß im Land Moab," he focus-es on what is actually the "sujet" of Deuteronomy 31—the actual disposition and articulation of the motifs in the text, as encoun-tered by the reader.[6] In a 1993 study, "Zur Fabel in Dtn 31-32,"[7]

[2] See the *status quaestionis* by Lohfink, "Bundesschluß," 45-46 (reviewing the contributions by A. Klostermann, R. Smend, M. Noth), and in C. J. Labuschagne, "The Song of Moses: Its Framework and Structure," *De Fructu Oris Sui: Essays in Honor of Adrianus van Selms* (ed. I. H. Eybers et al.; Leiden: Brill, 1971) 86-90 (discussing the genesis of Deut 31-32 as reconstructed by M. Noth, G. Fohrer, and O. Eissfeldt). See also J. Blenkinsopp, *Prophecy and Canon*, 82-83. Recent devel-opments are found in M. Rose, "Empoigner le Pentateuque par sa fin! L'investi-ture de Josué et la mort de Moïse," *Le Pentateuque en question* (ed. A. de Pury; Geneva: Labor et Fides, 1989) 129-47, and in Blum, *Komposition*, 85-88.
[3] Lohfink, "Bundesschluß," 51.
[4] Von Rad, *Deuteronomy*, 190.
[5] Lohfink, "Bundesschluß," 49. The narrative complexity of Deuteronomy 31 prompted A. Rofé to surmise an accidental inversion of columns in the process of textual transmission (*Introduction to Deuteronomy: Part I and Further Chapters* [Jerusalem: Akademon, 1988] 199-207 [Hebrew]). What is not uncommon in a codex is, however, hard to imagine in a scroll. More is to be gained by scruti-nizing the narrative logic of the chapter's actual sequence.
[6] N. Lohfink, "Der Bundesschluß im Land Moab," *BZ* 6 (1962) 32-56, esp. 48-51.
[7] N. Lohfink, "Zur Fabel in Dtn 31-32," *Konsequente Traditionsgeschichte: Festschrift für Klaus Baltzer zum 65. Geburtstag* (ed. R. Bartelmus, Th. Krüger and H. Utz-schneider; OBO 126; Freiburg: Universitätsverlag; Göttingen: Vandenhoeck & Ruprecht, 1993) 255-79; see also Lohfink's extension of the inquiry to Deuteron-omy's overall "fabula" in "Fabel," 65-78.

Lohfink addresses the same text from the point of view of its "fabula." The investigation now aims to reestablish the *Ereignisfolge* (order of events), or *Fabel*, as distinct from the *Erzählfolge* (order of narration).[8]

a. An "Esthetic and Systematic" Organization?

The primary aim of Lohfink's 1962 article is to show that the textual domain of the superscription in Deut 28:69—"These are the words of the covenant ... in the land of Moab"—stretches as far as 32:47. Besides the long speech of Deuteronomy 29-30, the motifs of Deuteronomy 31-32—the speech to the people and to Joshua, the writing down of the Torah, the theophany and the revelation of the Song *ha'ǎzînû*, the completion of the Torah "book," the communication of the Song—all constitutively belong to the economy of the new Moab covenant. When it comes to Deuteronomy 31, Lohfink's additional purpose is to show that there is no "stylistic" interruption between this chapter and what precedes it in Deuteronomy, in particular the speeches of Deuteronomy 29-30. Deuteronomy 31, Lohfink contends, cannot be contrasted as a *narrative* piece with the preceding (and subsequent) long speeches. The redactor of Deuteronomy 31 "wollte nicht erzählen sondern—genau wie das bisherige Dt es tut— 'Reden' zusammenstellen."[9] Lohfink accordingly views Deuteronomy 31 as a "Redenmontage" organized according to "systematisch-ästhetisch" principles.[10] The esthetic principle is found in the alternation of short and long speeches throughout the chapter[11]:

I	2-6	(5 verses)	long
II	7-8	(2 verses)	short
III	10-13	(4 verses)	long
IV	14	(1 verse)	short
V	16-21	(6 verses)	long

---

[8] See Lohfink, "Fabel," 65; cf. idem, "Fabel in Dtn 31-32," 255.
[9] Lohfink, "Bundesschluß," 49.
[10] See also the summary in Lohfink, "Fabel in Dtn 31-32," 261-63.
[11] The following charts are found in Lohfink, "Bundesschluß," 74-75 (my translation). Lohfink does not take Deut 31:30, and therefore the following Song, into account.

VI	23	(1 verse)	short
VII	26-29	(4 verses)	long

The three short pieces (II, IV, VI) have in common the theme of
Joshua's installation as Moses' successor; the middle speech (IV)
is linked to the theophany, which Lohfink sees as the center of
the speech system as well as of the whole chapter:

Part II	Moses installs Joshua
Part IV	YHWH discloses Joshua's installation; theophany
Part VI	YHWH installs Joshua

The long pieces (I, III, V, VII) fit into another system in which
bright future ("Helle Zukunft") and dark future ("Dunkle Zukunft") succeed each other; in each one of these regimes the
Torah plays a specific role:

Part I	Bright future
Part III	Role of the Torah in the bright future
Part V	Dark future
Part VII	Role of the Torah in the dark future

The whole picture thus combines salvation ("Heil") speeches (I,
II, III) and subsequent judgment ("Unheil") speeches (V, VI, VII)
around a "Kompositionszentrum," the theophany (IV).[12]

Expounding Deut 31:1-32:47 in the next sections, I will look
again at, and confirm, some of the suggestions presented by
Lohfink in his 1962 essay. Yet, instead of privileging esthetic principles (such as the alleged alternation of short and long speeches), I will focus on the narrative logic that underlies the sequence
of scenes in Deuteronomy 31:1-32:47. For what is read in these
chapters is, *pace* Lohfink, properly a narrative. "Echt deuterono-
misch," Lohfink writes about the redactor of Deuteronomy 31,
"vermeidet er die Erzählung."[13] In Lohfink's view, Deuteronomy
31 thereby mirrors the whole of Deuteronomy: "Auch Dtn 31 will
nicht 'Erzählung', sondern, wie fast alles im Dtn, 'Zusammen-

---

[12] It should be noticed, however, that the so-called theophany includes at least
two speeches (IV = v. 14, and V = vv. 16-21), and very likely a third one as well
(VI = v. 23). This weakens the identification of part IV, both with the theophany
and with the fulcrum of the composition; it is, nevertheless, a fact that the theophanic event represents a turning point in the whole picture.
[13] Lohfink, "Bundesschluß," 55.

stellung von Reden' sein."[14] Yet the reproduction of speeches can be a distinctly *narrative* mode. As I indicated in the introduction in a reference to both Alter and Sternberg, biblical narrative is poised between "narration and dialogue," in other words, between the "telling" and the "showing" modes of the narrative genre.[15] The difference between Deuteronomy 31 and the previous chapters of the book, as well as the difference between Deuteronomy as a whole and the rest of the narrative corpus of the Hebrew Bible, is at best a question of degree. Deuteronomy, especially in its long speeches, makes the most of the "showing" mode which is found in all biblical narratives. Therefore, the quality of narrative in Deuteronomy 31 cannot be denied, no more than it can be rejected for the previous parts of Deuteronomy.

There is, however, a narrative difference between Deuteronomy 31 and the previous chapters of the book. Before chapter 31 it was Moses who conducted the telling. But he did so as secondary locutor, to whom the primary locutor, the omniscient narrator, had delegated the bulk of the task. In Deuteronomy 31 the primary locutor perceptibly becomes the conductor of the narration. In Deut 29:9, for instance, it is Moses who sets the stage for the covenant ceremony, "You stand (נצבים) this day all of you before YHWH." In 31:14 it is now the omniscient narrator who fulfills the same narrating function: "And Moses and Joshua went and presented themselves (ויתיצבו) in the Tent of meeting." As I will indicate in my last chapter, there is a specific reason for such a narrative change. Deuteronomy 31:1-32:47, it could be said, records Moses' ultimate education, linked to his becoming a writing prophet, and to the completion of his mission as a prophet. The narrative brings to the fore issues related to Moses' authority, which require a "further" level of narration, that is, of authority—the authority of Deuteronomy's omniscient narrator.

---

[14] Lohfink, "Bundesschluß," 49.

[15] In a recent study, "Bund als Vertrag im Deuteronomium," *ZAW* 106 (1995) 218-21, however, Lohfink adopts the distinction "telling"—"showing" (which pertains to the science of *narrative*) as a conceptual tool particularly fitting for Deuteronomy's poetics.

b. *Temporal Deformations: Up to What Point?*

In his 1993 study Lohfink analyzes the narrative content of
Deuteronomy 31-32 from the point of view of its *Fabel*. The inquiry
therefore strives to uncover "was … als Geschehenfolge dem Text
unterliegt."[16] The distinction echoes discussions among Jewish
medieval commentators. Ibn Ezra, for instance, makes use of the
rabbinic interpretative guideline אין מוקדם ומאוחר בתורה ("there is
no earlier and later in the Torah") to reestablish an order of
events behind the given order of narration,[17] whereas Nachmanides endeavors to demonstrate the consistency of the order
of narration in question, והנה הכל כסדר האמור בתורה, "and [in this
way] everything fits with the order told in the Torah."[18] The following paragraphs present Lohfink's reconstruction of the
sequence of events that allegedly underlie Deuteronomy 31-32.[19]
The superscribed letters in parentheses ([a,b,c, etc.]) refer to my ensuing comments on specific points. I will further discuss some of
Lohfink's views in my own presentation of Deuteronomy 31.

> (1) (in undetermined time:) Writing down of the Torah by Moses
> (31:9, 24).[a]
>
> (2) General assembly of the people (I), in which Moses concludes
> the Moab covenant (Deuteronomy 29-30), directs all Israel toward
> the impending conquest of the land west of the Jordan (31:1-6), and
> installs Joshua as military leader (*Feldherr*) and allotter of the land
> (*Landverteiler*) (31:7f.).
>
> (3) Theophany to Moses and Joshua, which comprises the revela-
> tion of the Song of Moses and the installation of Joshua as military
> leader by YHWH (31:14-23).[b]
>
> (4) Convocation of the Levites by Moses and transmission to them
> of the written Torah (31:24-27; see 31:9).[c]
>
> (5) Convocation of the elders by the Levites, and oral transmission
> of the Song to them (see 31:28-30).[d]
>
> (6) Directions given to both groups for implementing the procla-
> mation of the Law every seven years (31:10-13).[e]

---

[16] Lohfink, "Fabel in Dtn 31-32," 256.
[17] See Ibn Ezra's comment on Deut 31:16.
[18] In his comment on Deut 31:24-26.
[19] See N. Lofhink, "Fabel in Dtn 31-32," 270 (my translation); the reconstructed
scenario has been adopted by G. Braulik, *Deuteronomium II*, 222.

(7) General assembly of the people (II), in which Moses, together with Joshua, teaches the Song to the entire people (32:44).[(f)]

(8) Moses' last words to all Israel (32:45-47).

[(a)] In accordance with the mentions of the (written) ספר in Deut 29:19, 20, 26 and 30:10, Lohfink deems the writing down of the Torah prior to the (first) general assembly (Deut 29:1-31:8).[20]

[(b)] What is told in Deut 31:9-13 (with the exception of the statement of Moses' writing down of the Torah) is understood by Lohfink as a prolepsis, referring to stages (4) and (6) in the *Ereignisfolge*. The reason lies in Lohfink's claim that the allusions to Moses' writing (in 31:9, 24) refer to one and the same act,[21]

[(c)] and that the mention of Moses' dealings with the Levites in Deut 31:9 and 31:25 equally belong to a single convocation of the "carriers of the ark."[22]

[(d)(e)] The fact that in Deut 31:28 the Levites are requested by Moses to convene the elders (in order that he may teach the Song to both groups) indicates that, in Lohfink's view, Moses' address to both groups (Levites + elders, see 31:9) in 31:10 takes place after the convocation of the elders.

[(f)] Stages (4) and (5) are understood by Lohfink as Moses' address to כל קהל ישראל (see Deut 31:30), which Lohfink regards as a "Notabeln-versammlung," distinguished from the congregation of "all Israel," כל ישראל.[23] Moses' teaching (together with Hoshea-Joshua) of the Song mentioned in 32:44 implies therefore a second general assembly of the people.[24]

Lohfink's reconstruction of the "fabula" of Deuteronomy 31-32 goes with a substantial reshuffling of the motifs presented sequentially in the two chapters. The theophany (31:14-23) takes place before the "first" mention of a transmission of the written Torah to the Levites (and elders) (31:9-13); the two mentions of the transmission of the written Torah (31:9, 24-26) refer to a single

---

[20] Lohfink, "Fabel in Dtn 31-32," 268. Lohfink's construing of Deut 31:9 makes sense: ויכתב משה can legitimately be read as "Moses *had* written" (see my comments pp. 168-73 below); it is difficult, however, to find an equivalent pluperfect *way-yiqtol* in Deut 31:24-25: the ויהי form signals the event of the transmission of the Torah "book" to the Levites (which Lohfink does not situate in "anterior" past), and not the writing or the completion of the writing of the Torah "book."

[21] See Lohfink, "Fabel in Dtn 31-32," 263-64. See, however, p. 270 for an alternative construing (the "writing up to the end" of 31:24 as "Ergänzung" of the written Torah).

[22] Lohfink, "Fabel in Dtn 31-32," 264.

[23] See Lohfink, "Fabel in Dtn 31-32," 264-65, 275-78 ("Anhang II: Zum Terminus כל קהל ישראל"). See my comment pp. 215-17 below.

[24] See Lohfink, "Fabel in Dtn 31-32," 266-67.

event;[25] the Song is transmitted to the Levites and the elders
(31:28-30) before they are instructed about the future reading of
the Torah (31:10-13), etc. In Lohfink's view what legitimates the
perception of such a difference between narrative order and order
of events is the presence of a similar phenomenon earlier in the
book, "Wenn man bedenkt, wie elegant in Dtn 1-3, Dtn 5 und
Dtn9f durch ein mehrfach gestaffeltes System von Rückblenden
Fabel und Erzählstruktur gerade im Auseinanderklaffen bezie-
hungsreichen neuen Sinn produzieren ..."[26] It can be objected
that the narrative situations in Deuteronomy's first chapters and
in Deuteronomy 31-32 differ noticeably, especially in relation to
the reader's hermeneutical task. Dealing with Moses' narration in
chapters 1-3, 5, or 9-10, the reader is confronted with events he
has already been told about, in their genuine chronological connection. In these chapters, as Sternberg writes, Moses "does not
so much tell as retell. Given the sequence of the Bible's narrative
canon, by the time we reach Deuteronomy the historical path
Moses erratically retraces is as familiar to ourselves as to his dramatic audience, and as followable, hence foolproof; the matter is
not essentially new, only the manner."[27] The same cannot be said
of Deuteronomy 31-32. In these chapters the narrator's disclosure
is a firsthand narration that does not rely on any previous historical knowledge. As elsewhere in biblical narrative, this telling
may include a certain amount of chronological deformation, but
never at the expense of the intelligibility of the story-line. In my
view, Lohfink's reconstruction of the "fabula" is over-sophisticat-
ed, and exceeds any (real or implied) reader's competence. Such
a fundamental reshuffling of the narrative data overlooks textual
hints that keep the order of events fairly close to the order of
presentation (without excluding temporal deformation), and con-
fer on the text a dramatic quality that escaped Lohfink. Some of
these hints, as I shall indicate in the next sections, are phenomena of inter-textuality within Deuteronomy's narrative world.
Faced with Deuteronomy 31-32, the reader cannot make use of

---

[25] The idea of a commissioning of the Levites in two stages (Deut 31:9-13 and
31:24-29) is also excluded by von Rad, *Deuteronomy*, 190, but on non-narrative
grounds; in his view the two speeches represent doublets, which he calls "débris
of traditions."

[26] Lohfink, "Fabel in Dtn 31-32," 261.

[27] Sternberg, "Grand Chronology," 138.

previous knowledge of historical events; yet he can take advantage of the narrative knowledge imparted to him throughout his reading (literary paradigms, narrative patterns, consistency in the represented world, etc.).

c. *Addresses in Sequence*

My expounding of Deuteronomy 31 will fall in two parts, corresponding to the two panels of the narrative, on either side of v. 14, which records Moses' and Joshua's convocation in the Tent of Meeting. Instead of conflating the two references to the transmission of the written Torah to the Levites (31:9-13 and 31:25-26) into a single event, as Lohfink suggests,[28] I will show that a double entrusting of the written Torah to the Levites, before and after the theophany, makes sense in Deuteronomy's narrative logic. As Dillmann has already pointed out,[29] Moses' provisions for the future of the written Torah are organized in two stages: the arrangements for the future *reading* of the written Torah (in 31:9-13), on the one hand; and the dispositions concerning the *conservation* of the Torah "book" as witness confronting Israel (31:24-26), on the other.[30] A further point will support my reading. In Deuteronomy 31 direct addresses to groups or individuals form a significant pattern that bears upon Deuteronomy's theme of communication.

As Polzin points out, Deuteronomy 31 features the first divine speech directly quoted by Deuteronomy's narrator, i.e., the first divine speech not reported by Moses.[31] The recipient of the *theologoumenon* is Moses himself (see 31:14, 16); but Joshua, summoned in turn to the Tent of meeting (31:14), becomes the first individual besides Moses to be addressed directly by God (see 31:23).[32] Apparently nothing less than a theophany was required

---

[28] Lohfink's "fabula" also uncouples what the text presents sequentially: the address to Joshua and the commissioning of the Levites and the elders by Moses in Deut 31:7-8 and 31:9.

[29] Dillmann, *Deuteronomium*, 387.

[30] As I shall indicate, these two stages correspond, in ancient Near Eastern treaty literature, to the dispositions of the *periodical reading* of the document and to the provisions for its *deposition*.

[31] See Polzin, *Moses*, 25; but see already Lohfink, "Bundesschluß," 49. In the wake of his speech in the theophany (Deut 31:14, 16-21, 23), YHWH intervenes two further times as a speaking character, in 32:49-52 and 34:4.

[32] I will justify the attribution of the speech in Deut 31:23 to YHWH in the

in order to override the communication rules established in Deut
5:23-33 (Moses as sole Israelite exposed to God's voice). Deuteronomy 31 also records Moses' first addresses to individual or particular characters, directly quoted by the narrator. Thus far, and
since 1:1, Moses has spoken exclusively to "all Israel" (see also 5:1;
27:1 ["the people"]; 27:9; 29:1). In a speech meant for all, Moses
has occasionally reported words he spoke to individuals (e.g. 3:21,
"And I commanded Joshua at that time, 'Your eyes have seen ...'")
or to particular groups (e.g., 1:16, "And I commanded your judges
at that time, 'Hear the cases ...'"). In Deuteronomy 31, besides
further words by Moses meant for "all Israel" (31:1 and 31:30, "all
the assembly of Israel"), the reader encounters for the first time
Moses' direct address to an individual, Joshua (see 31:7), and to
particular groups, the elders (see 31:10) and the Levites (see
31:10, 25).

The direct addresses by God or by Moses in Deuteronomy 31
to groups or individuals present an interesting pattern. On two
occasions, before and after God's direct speech to Moses (vv.
14-21), an address to Joshua is immediately followed by an address
to the Levites. In other words, the reader runs twice into the
sequence Joshua-Levites as recipients of direct speeches:

To the people (2-6)	By Moses
To *Joshua* (7-8)	By Moses
To the *Levites* and the elders (10-13)	By Moses
To Moses (14)	By YHWH
To Moses (16-21)	By YHWH
To *Joshua* (23)	By YHWH
To the *Levites* (26-28)	By Moses
To the people (32:1-43)	By Moses

Joshua's leadership emerges as a decisive factor in the interventions that form the core of Deuteronomy 31 (in a sense, the scenes
in question constitute the narrative fulcrum of the whole book,
combining the establishment of a new leader with the establishment of a further covenant).[33] Moses' encouragement of Joshua
as new leader (31:7-8) is followed by Joshua's being called to the

---

third section of the present chapter; see p. 153-54 below. See also my remarks
p. 39 n. 30 above.

[33] On this point, see K. Baltzer, *Das Bundesformular* (WMANT4; Neukirchen-Vluyn: Neukirchener Verlag, 1960) 76-79; see also Lohfink, "Bundesschluß,"
71, and "Fabel in Dtn 31-32," 271-72.

Tent of Meeting (31:14), and by his appointment, in direct
address, by God himself. The interesting point is that each of the
speeches to Joshua (as the one who will enter the land) leads to
a subsequent address to the Levites as carriers of the ark (in
31:10-13 along with the elders). In both cases, Moses' injunction
to the Levites bears on the future of the Torah's written record.
The two speeches to Joshua echo each other, but so also do the
two introductions to the instructions to the Levites:

Deut 31:7-9

חזק ואמץ כי אתה תבוא את העם הזה אל
הארץ אשר נשבע יהוה לאבותם לתת להם
הוא יהיה עמך ...
ויכתב משה את התורה הזאת ויתנה אל
הכהנים בני לוי הנשאים את ארון ברית
יהוה

*Be strong and of good courage; for
you shall go with this people into the
land which YHWH has sworn to their
fathers to give them ... [YHWH]
will be with you ... And Moses
wrote this Torah, and gave it to the
priests the sons of Levi, who carried
the ark of the covenant of YHWH*

Deut 31:23-25

חזק ואמץ כי אתה תביא את בני ישראל
אל הארץ אשר נשבעתי להם
ואנכי אהיה עמך
ויהי ככלות משה לכתב את דברי התורה
הזאת על ספר עד תמם ויצו משה את
הלוים נשאי ארון ברית יהוה

*Be strong and of good courage; for
you shall bring the sons of Israel
into the land which I swore to them:
I will be with you. When Moses had
finished writing the words of this
Torah in a "book," to the very end,
Moses commanded the Levites who
carried the ark of the covenant of
YHWH*

In my view the double set of addresses, to Joshua and to the
Levites, before and after the revelation to Moses in the Tent of
Meeting, indicates a meaningful link in Deuteronomy's overall
plot. The double narrative sequence combines the issue of Moses'
succession with the issue of Moses' communication, now committed to writing. More precisely, it combines the dynamism of
Joshua as crossing leader (as opposed to the blocked Moses) and
the pervasive dynamism of written communication now entrusted
to its appropriate bearers, the Levites, "who carried the ark of the
covenant of YHWH."

2. Before the Theophany—Deut 31:1-13

In this section I will examine the first part of Deuteronomy 31,
up to the convocation of Moses and Joshua in the Tent of Meet-

ing (31:14). More specifically, I will focus on the link created between the first address to Joshua (vv. 7-8) and the first address to the Levites (here associated with the elders) (vv. 9-13). Both figures, I will indicate, are "dynamic" and are interrelated in their respective missions. The written Torah exploits their combined dynamism. A Torah-beyond-Moses, the "book" of the Torah will perpetuate the Horeb experience when it is read in the land.

a. *Joshua as the Crossing Character—Deut 31:1-8*

Moses' address to "all Israel" in Deut 31:2-6 deftly introduces the theme of Joshua's mission. "I am a hundred and twenty years old this day; I am no longer able to go out and to come in. YHWH has said to me, 'You shall not go over this Jordan'" (31:2). Although dealing with the issue of succession, Moses, interestingly enough, avoids any reference to his own death. He apparently makes the most of the cryptic prophecy made in 4:22, "For I shall die in this land; I shall not cross the Jordan." As the wordless coordination of the two clauses indicates, Moses avoided making any explicit link between his dying in Moab and his non-crossing of the Jordan.[34] Yet Moses knows—and the reader of the Pentateuch has known with him since Num 27:12-13—that he will not cross the Jordan *because* he will have died for his sin (after having climbed the mountain of Abarim) *before* the people's crossing. In Deut 31:2 Moses rather puts forward his old age and his present incapacity to "go out and come in,"[35] as well as YHWH's literal order, "You shall not go over this Jordan" (31:2). Is Moses still unreconciled, as in his first speech, with God's decree about his death? Is it still too much for him to bring his forthcoming demise to expression? On the other hand, Moses makes a forceful point by presenting his personal condition as a situation that

---

[34] See my comment, p. 34 above.

[35] Confronted with the statement by the narrator in Deut 34:7, "Moses was a hundred and twenty years old when he died; his eye was not dim, nor his natural force abated," the reader must assess retrospectively Moses' claim; see my comments in Chapters Five and Six. In his exposition of 31:2-3, Nachmanides points out the discrepancy between the text here and the Scripture's (הכתוב) testimony about Moses' health in 34:7, and daringly suggests that Moses said what he said לנחם, "in order to console" the people of Israel about his non-crossing. The medieval commentator does not deny Moses the recourse to rhetorical arguments at the expense of truth.

calls for military succession. The expression "to go out and to come in," as Ibn Ezra has already pointed out, pertains to waging war.[36]. The encouraging of Joshua as military commander, reported in 31:7-8, is therefore highly motivated.

The address in Deut 31:2-6 is a word of encouragement meant for כל ישראל, "all Israel," which intends to leave no doubt that YHWH will help the people win possession of the land. The God who bars Moses from entering into the land (31:2, "YHWH has said to me, 'You shall not go over this Jordan'") will ensure for the crossing of the Jordan River (31:3 "YHWH your God will himself [הוא] go over before you") as well as the conquest of the land ("he will himself [הוא] destroy these nations before you, so that you will dispossess them"). He will do so by providing a new leader, Joshua ("Joshua himself [הוא] will go over at your head, as YHWH has spoken"). God will act, Moses assures the people, just as he has thus far on behalf of the people's passage through hostile land (31:4). The assurance that YHWH will bring the people "home" means that the people will have to implement "every commandment" (31:5), that is, every commandment relative to the proper inheritance of a land occupied by pagan nations. In his commentary to Deuteronomy, Bekhor Shor (12th century) listed seven injunctions pertaining to such a situation (in Deuteronomy 7:2-5; 12:3 and 20:16).[37] Quoting him, Hazquni (17th century) limited the reference to the rule of sacred war (the חרם commandment) expressed in 20:16, "but in the cities of these peoples that YHWH your God gives you for an inheritance, you shall not let a soul remain alive," probably out of regard for the military context of Joshua's mission. Lohfink has recently expressed a similar view in contending that 31:2-6 "auf das חרם-Gebot zugespitzt ist."[38]

---

[36] See Ibn Ezra, on Deut 31:2. See especially Num 27:17, 21 (apropos of Joshua); Josh 14:11; 1 Kings 3:7; in Deuteronomy, cf. 28:6.

[37] Bekhor Shor, *ad loc.*, refers to the rules of sacred war (*ḥērem*) in Deut 20:16; to the interdiction of contracting a covenant with the pagan inhabitants of the land (7:2); to the practice of intermarriage (7:3); to the injunction to break down the nations' altars (7:5), to hew down their Asherim (7:5), to dash in pieces their pillars (7:5) and to destroy the gods' names in the place chosen by YHWH (12:3); cf. Driver, *Deuteronomy*, 334; D. E. Skweres, *Die Rückverweise im Buch Deuteronomium* (AnBib 79; Rome: Pontifical Biblical Institute Press, 1979) 73-75.

[38] Lohfink, "Fabel in Dtn 31-32," 262, erroneously attributes a similar comment to Ibn Ezra. Commenting on Deut 31:5, Ibn Ezra discerns in Moses' order a ref-

Is Moses' way of involving God (and Joshua) in Israel's future—
a future without Moses—completely free of resentment? In his
opening speech Moses alluded three times (Deut 1:37-38; 3:26;
4:21-22) to his personal quarrel with God about the issue of his
non-crossing. In 31:2-3 Moses recalls the fateful interdiction,
entrusting the people's fate to YHWH "himself" (הוא) and to
Joshua "himself" (הוא). This may sound like a further echo of
Moses' indignation. The God who intends to do without Moses
will have to care "himself" for the people of Israel. If Joshua, and
not Moses, crosses at the people's head (31:3), it will be because
God has so decided ("as YHWH has spoken"). Is Moses at peace
with God's will? Further hints will point to Moses' protracted inner
conflict.

In Deut 31:7-8 Lohfink has identified (as in 31:23 and in Josh
1:6, 9b) the formula for an appointment to an office, composed
of three elements: a pronouncement of encouragement, a description of the task which the office involves, and a promise of
support.[39] It is my contention, however, that no formal appointment takes place in Deut 31:7-8.[40] The account does not feature
the keyverb of the installation procedure—צוה + a person as direct
object. As Lohfink himself indicates, this verb expresses a "Rechtsakt," i.e., the official installation of someone to a new function.[41]
The phrase "to commission (צוה) someone" occurs in Deut 31:23
(a proper installation); in Josh 1:9 God mentions Joshua's installation as a fact of the past (הלוא צויתיך, "Have I not commissioned you?"). Lohfink's "formula" has thus a larger compass
than the specific installation genre. In Deut 31:7-8, as I shall

---

erence to לשבור מצבותם, i.e., to Deut 7:5, which enjoins the destruction of the religious monuments of the inhabitants of the land.

[39] Lohfink, "Darstellung," 38. In the same article (pp. 36, 42), Lohfink further
maintains that in 31:7-8 Joshua is installed by Moses in the double capacity of
conqueror ("Landeroberer") and allotter of the land ("Landverteiler"); in Deut
31:23 he is appointed by God in the first of the two capacities only; the installation of Joshua by God in his second capacity is deferred until Josh 1:6, 9. In his
essay, "An Installation Genre?," *Institution and Narrative: Collected Essays* (AnBib
108; Rome: Biblical Institute Press, 1985) 182-92, D. McCarthy questions Lohfink's
assumptions as to the *Sitz im Leben* of the so-called "Amtseinsetzung." He suggests
seeing it rather as a hortatory genre originally connected with the cult.

[40] See C. F. Keil and F. Delitzsch, *Biblical Commentary on the Old Testament. Volume III: The Pentateuch* (Grand Rapids: Eerdmans, 1951) 456-57.

[41] Lohfink, "Fabel in Dtn 31-32," 273, apropos of the instances of the verb in
Deut 31:14, 23.

indicate, it takes place within an act of public encouragement.

In Lohfink's view the alleged installation of Joshua by Moses in Deut 31:7-8 is, furthermore, the enactment of God's request formulated in 3:27-28:[42]

> [27]Go up to the top of Pisgah ... [28]and commission Joshua (וצו את יהושע), and encourage and strengthen him; for he shall go over at the head of this people, and he shall put them in possession of the land which you shall see.

YHWH's command, however, appears in Moses' retelling, that is, in Moses' reviewing of events of the past. In telling God's order to appoint Joshua, Moses is indeed retelling the scene previously related in Num 27:12-23, which opens with God's command, "Go up into this mountain of Abarim ..." God next enjoins Moses to "take Joshua" in order to install him as his successor: "and you shall commission him (וצויתה אתו)" (Num 27:19).[43] The narrative in Numbers goes on, and describes the actual installation of Joshua:

> [22]And Moses did as YHWH commanded him; he took Joshua and caused him to stand before Eleazar the priest and the whole congregation, [23]and he laid his hands upon him, and commissioned (ויצוהו) him as YHWH directed through Moses. (Num 27:22-23)

The installation is public, and it involves an *ad hoc* ritual. It is signalled by the verb צוה, with Joshua as direct object (via the pronominal suffix). And the narrator twice reports that Moses acted as requested by YHWH.[44] Moses' quoting of God's demand to *appoint* Joshua in Deut 3:28 is therefore not the announcement, as often thought, of what is carried out in Deut 31:7-8. The formal commissioning has already taken place.[45] What does Moses do on behalf of Joshua in Deut 31:7-8? As stated in the text, he

---

[42] See Lohfink, "Darstellung," 42. The same view is expressed by Buis, *Deutéronome*, 81-82; Skweres, *Rückverweise*, 40 (and the authors listed p. 40 n. 74); and Schäfer-Lichtenberger, *Josua und Salomo*, 185, 370.

[43] In Deut 3:27-28 Moses summarizes and combines in a single quote the two divine speeches in Num 27:12-14 and 27:18-21 (see Dogniez and Harl, *Deutéronome*, 132).

[44] Compare Deut 3:21, where Moses reports an initiative of his own, before God's actual command to install Joshua.

[45] That Deuteronomy's narration knows the account of Numbers 27 will be further evidenced in Deut 34:9, "And Joshua the son of Nun was full of the spirit of wisdom, for Moses had laid his hands upon him," a clear reference to Num 27:23, "And he laid his hands upon him, and commissioned him."

encourages him. Yet in doing so, Moses conforms to God's expressed will. In Deut 3:28 Moses' retelling of God's order to install Joshua includes a double imperative, not documented in Numbers 27: "encourage and strengthen him (וחזקהו ואמצהו)." Beyond the formal installation, God, *in Moses' recollection and retelling*, equally asked him to assure the new leader. This further step occurs in Deut 31:7-8: "Then Moses called Joshua, and said to him in the sight of all Israel, 'Be strong and of good courage' (חזק ואמץ)" (31:7).[46]

In Deuteronomy's narrative the "calling" of Joshua by Moses in Deut 31:7 functions as an official summoning—"Then Moses called Joshua." For the reader of the Pentateuch the summoning in question has, moreover, an echoing quality. The calling of Joshua in Deut 31:7 subtly echoes Moses' renaming of Hoshea in Num 13:16.

Num 13:16

ויקרא משה להושע בן נון יהושע

And Moses called (to) Hoshea son of Nun Joshua

Deut 31:7

ויקרא משה ליהושע

And Moses called (to) Joshua

Between these two scenes, Moses has never "called" (קרא) Joshua. A superimposition of the two scenes in the reader's mind is appropriate at this point. Joshua, formerly Hoshea, from the tribe of Efraim, received his new name when he was dispatched along with eleven other spies to reconnoiter the land: "These were the names of the men whom Moses sent to spy out the land. And Moses called Hoshea the son of Nun Joshua" (Num 13:16). Joshua then—before his first entrance into the land—was called by Moses, and received his "military" name; he now—before his definitive entrance into the same land—is called again by Moses. The first calling apparently took place before few witnesses (the eleven spies sent along with him, all of them now deceased [Deut 2:16] except Caleb [Deut 1:36]).[47] The renaming occurred, more-

---

[46] Regarding the formula חזק ואמץ, "be strong and of good courage" (Deut 31:7) as formula for encouragement (and not for appointment) in Deuteronomy (see 1:29-30; 7:18, 21; 20:1, 3; 31:6) and in the Hebrew Bible, as well as for parallels in ancient Near Eastern literature, see Weinfeld, *School*, 45 n. 5.

[47] Commenting on the reappearance of Joshua's genuine name, הושע, "Hoshea," in Deut 32:44, Ibn Ezra contends that the son of Nun was still known under this

over, without any specified motivation.[48] The calling of Hoshea/
Joshua is still in want of a public enactment, and Joshua's "long"
name is yet to be provided with a rationale. This is, in my view,
what the reader is invited to note in Deut 31:7-8.[49]

The public dimension of the calling is made clear in Deut 31:7:
Joshua is called and addressed "in the sight of all Israel." Yet, how
does Moses' speech endow Joshua's name with a manner of motivation?[50] The point of Moses' encouragement lies in his assertion
of God's assistance to Joshua: "It is YHWH who goes before you;
he will be with you" (31:8). That "YHWH will be with Joshua" is
precisely mirrored in the name יהושע, in its contrast with הושע,
Hoshea. The prefixing of הושע by a single "י" turns "Hoshea" into
a theophoric name, יהו/שע, "Yehoshua."[51] Joshua's "long" name
thus spells out the fact that "YHWH will be with you," not seman-
tically but literally. Joshua's name therefore is the perpetual warrant of God's being with him everywhere he goes (see Josh 1:9;
6:27; cf. Deut 31:6, 23).[52] And this is the token given to the one
who will himself go before the people.[53]

---

name by the people of Israel; only those eleven who were sent along with him
to spy out the land of Canaan witnessed the change to יהושע, "Joshua." Strictly
speaking, this is possible in the book of Numbers since the name "Joshua" is used
either by the narrator or by YHWH and Moses in their mutual conversations; the
addressees of Moses in Deuteronomy, however, are already familiar with the
"long" form יהושע, "Joshua."

[48] Cf. the motivation clause in Gen 15:5, "No longer shall your name be Abram,
but your name shall be Abraham; for I have made you the father of a multitude
of nations."

[49] The subtle link between Deut 31:7 and Num 13:16 will be emphasized, by
way of contrast, by another summoning in Deuteronomy 31, which lacks the echoing quality of Deut 31:7. In 31:14 God's order to Moses to summon Joshua makes
use of another syntactic construction: קרא את יהושע, "Call Joshua."

[50] To be sure, Moses is not said in Deut 31:7 to have articulated Joshua's (new)
name. This has already been done in Num 3:16, and Moses has repeatedly used
Joshua's "long" name in his speeches in Deuteronomy. The narrative accentua-
tion is rather on the recurrence of the calling scene (as קרא ל).

[51] It could even be said that the prefixing of the *yod* brings out the theophoric quality latent in הושע.

[52] As in many cases of biblical puns upon names, there is therefore a tight correspondence between Joshua's name and the function of the character within
Deuteronomy's overall plot. On this issue, see M. Garsiel, *Biblical Names: A Literary Study of Midrashic Derivations and Puns* (Tel Aviv: Bar-Ilan University Press,
1991); see especially Garsiel's sixth chapter, "The Appropriateness of Names to
Literary Units," 212-53; and H. Marks, "Biblical Naming and Poetic Etymology,"
JBL (1995) 29-50.

[53] A further hypothesis is worth considering. The Joshua issue, it could be said,
is an issue of precedence. This is emphasized in Moses' words to "all Israel":

Such a subtle punning in Joshua's commissioning in Deut 31:7-8 may explain the reappearance of Joshua's genuine name in the related passage of Deut 32:44, "Moses came and recited all the words of this song in the hearing of the people, he and Hoshea."[54] The occurrence of הושע would then underscore the new and supererogatory character of Joshua's long name. The fact that the genuine name comes after a narrative reference to the new name is not contradictory. The omniscient narrator is not tied by the change that takes place in the represented world; he always enjoys the latitude of reminding his reader of the past name of his dramatis persona.[55] What the narrator's use of "Hoshea" reminds us is that there has been a change in the character's name. And what the scene of Deut 31:7-8 subtly conveys is that Joshua's theophoric name is linked to his mission as Israel's precursor into the land.

b. *The Written Torah as Torah beyond Moses—Deut 31:9*

The Torah is associated with the movement led by the re-named Joshua in being now entrusted, in its written form, to "moving carriers," the Levites (and to the "elders of Israel"):

Moses had written this Torah;	ויכתב משה את התורה הזאת ויתנה אל
he gave it to the priests the sons of	הכהנים בני לוי הנשאים את ארון ברית

"YHWH said to me, 'You shall not go over this Jordan.' *YHWH your God himself will go over before you* (לפניך); he will destroy these nations before you, so that you shall dispossess them; and *Joshua will go over before you* (לפניך), as YHWH has spoken" (Deut 31:3; see 1:38; cf. 3:28). In Moses' address to Joshua, the double sequence, YHWH < the people, Joshua < the people (the sign < meaning here "precedes") becomes: ויהוה הוא ההלך לפניך ("And YHWH is the one who goes before you" [31:8]). Now, the change from הושע, Hoshea, to יהושע, Yehoshua/Joshua, reflects precisely the same statement, if יהושע is understood as a pun on YHWH's antecedence on הושע: יהו(ה) < הושע = יהושע.

[54] The form הושע, which after all differs from יהושע only by an initial *yod*, is sometimes explained as a textual corruption. On the basis of the LXX, the Vulgate, and the Peshitta, which all read Joshua's full name in 32:44 (the Samaritan Pentateuch can be added to the list), A. Klostermann, *Der Pentateuch: Beiträge zu seinem Verständnis und seiner Entstehungsgeschichte* (Leipzig: Deichert [G. Böhme], 1893) 249, and Driver, *Deuteronomy*, 381, consider it to be a probable scribal error. On this point, however, it is interesting to notice that the Aleppo Codex supports the הושע reading of the Leningrad manuscript. Furthermore, in a narrative rationale such as the one I suggest, the presence or absence of a single *yod* (as in the MT) proves to be a distinctive and meaningful feature.

[55] See the narrator's resumption of Gideon's first name (Jerubbaal) in Judg 7:1; cf. Judg 6:32.

Levi who carried the ark of the covenant of YHWH, and to all the elders of Israel. (Deut 31:9)

יהוה ואל כל זקני ישראל

The phrase ויכתב משה, it can be surmised, plays a key role in the reader's endeavor to make sense of Deuteronomy's theme of communication. For the first time in the book, the root כתב, "to write," is explicitly associated with Moses: Moses did write. For the first time, as a *wayyiqtol* form, it is not associated with YHWH (see Deut 4:13; 5:19; 10:4). In other words, Moses is the first to emulate the God who did write. The curiosity question that arose from the repeated references to a written (כתוב) document (ספר) in Deuteronomy 29-30 finds here a first answer (only as far as writing is concerned; 31:9 does not mention the ספר or written record). Yet the reader must go on in his hermeneutic task, since the temporal value of the ויכתב form in 31:9 calls for interpretation. Moses did write, but when? If the data provided in Deuteronomy 29-30 are to be believed, Moses committed the words of the Torah to writing prior to the ritual recorded in Deuteronomy 29-30. In this ritual Moses referred in several ways to the words of the Torah as "written in this document."[56] In that case the form ויכתב is to be construed as a pluperfect: "Moses had written." Such a reading has been suggested by Lohfink in his essay on the *Fabel* of Deuteronomy 31-32. "Da *wayyiqtol* Zeitabstände zuläßt, [kan] 31,9 ... so verstanden werden, als habe Mose den Leviten (und Ältesten) ein schon zu einem früheren Zeitpunkt angefertigte Niederschrift der Tora übergeben."[57] Lohfink does not use the term "pluperfect," but speaks in terms of temporal intervals ("Zeitabstände"): "Allerdings muß in Kauf genommen werden, daß die Niederschrift der Tora und ihre Übergabe an die Ladeleviten nicht unmittelbar

---

[56] It should be noted here that in the view of some scholars the link between תורה in Deuteronomy 31 and in the previous chapters does not exist. N. Sarna, "Bible," *EJ* 4.821-822, and Fishbane, "Varia Deuteronomica," 350-51, see in the occurrences of תורה in Deuteronomy 31 repeated references to the Song of Deuteronomy 32: "From the context," Fishbane writes, "it seems clear that the *tôrâ* referred to in 31_{9.12} is specifically the 'song' which was to serve as a witness to the Covenant (v. 19)" (p. 350). In my view the communicational context of Deuteronomy 31, following the Mosaic speeches, rather favors an identification of the mentioned Torah with the previously reported covenantal regulations (see 4:44).

[57] Lohfink, "Zur Fabel in Dtn 31-32," 268 (but see already Keil and Delitzsch, *Commentary*, 457). Lohfink also sees in "Deut 31:24s" a reference to an anteriority to the past; see my remark about the improbability of such a reading, p. 123 n. 20 above.

aufeinander folgen."[58] Actually Lohfink does not postulate, in the phrase ויכתב משה, a "simple" antecedence in relation to ויתנה, "and he gave it," but the further recession of the pluperfect:[59] "Moses had [already] written this Torah and [then] gave it to the priests, the sons of Levi …"[60] As is known, the Hebrew verbal system does not have a form that specifically expresses the pluperfect. Anteriority to the past is most often expressed by *qatal* forms[61] or *w-…qatal* forms (so as to break a succession of *wayyiqtols*).[62] In the wake of Qimhi's insights, however, scholars have recognized that in some instances even *wayyiqtol* forms represent pluperfects.[63] "It is clear that in the Massoretic Bible," Randall Buth writes, "the story will often 'repeat' and go back over a temporal segment without using the *waw-X-qatal* structure to signal the temporal break. The standard narrative *wayyiqtol* will be used as though the story is marching forward on its timeline but the story actually does an about-face and picks up the timeline at an earlier point, one already passed."[64] The peculiarity of these instances of pluperfect (as against, for instance, the ones embedded in a *w-…qatal* form interrupting a succession of *wayyiqtols*) is that they lack any formal distinctiveness (they are "unmarked") and result entirely from the reader's assessment in context. Buth in particular has

---

[58] Lohfink, "Fabel in Dtn 31-32," 269.

[59] W. J. Martin appropriately describes the phenomenon of pluperfect: "The pluperfect denotes some event which had already occurred before some specific point in time in the past. It is a sort of doubly expressed relationship of the time-position in the past" ("'Dischronologized' Narrative in the Old Testament," *Congress Volume: Rome 1968* [VTSup 17; Leiden: Brill, 1969] 181).

[60] See Lohfink's reconstruction of the order of events ("Fabel in Dtn 31-32," 270; see pp. 152-53 above).

[61] Joüon—Muraoka, *§ 112 c.*

[62] Joüon—Muraoka, § 118 *d.*

[63] See Martin, "'Dischronologized' Narrative," 179-186; D. W. Baker, *The Consecutive Nonperfective as Pluperfect in the Historical Books of the Hebrew Old Testament* (Regent College Thesis, 1973) (I have not been able to consult this work); Waltke and O'Connor, § 33.2.3; R. Buth, "Methodological Collision Between Source Criticism and Discourse Analysis: The Problem of 'Unmarked Temporal Overlay' and the Pluperfect/Nonsequential *wayyiqtol*," *Biblical Hebrew and Discourse Linguistics* (ed. R. D. Bergen; Dallas: Summer Institute of Linguistics, 1994) 138-54. Num 1:47-49 provides such an instance: "The Levites, however, were not recorded among them by their ancestral tribe. For the Lord *had spoken* [וידבר] to Moses, saying: 'Do not on any account enroll the tribe of Levi or take a census of them with the Israelites'" (NJPSV). In his essay "Jona ging zur Stadt hinaus," *BZ* 5 (1961) 185-203, N. Lohfink had already drawn attention to a like phenomenon in Jon 4:5.

[64] Buth, "Methodological Collision," 139.

tried to make sense of this peculiar syntactic and hermeneutical situation, which he calls "unmarked temporal overlay." "The constraint of adding details to a passage without also demoting them off the mainline," Buth writes, "gives rise to this nonsequential use of the *wayyiqtol*."[65] The unmarked character of the device has accordingly to be made up for by appropriate contextual motivation, especially by lexical reference or repetition signalling a back reference.[66]

How does the form ויכתב make sense in the context of Deut 31:9 and in the context of the Mosaic speeches that preceded? A back reference is signalled by the verbal root כתב, which brings to the reader's mind Moses' previous mentions of a written (כתוב) Torah (see 29:19, 20, 26; 30:10). What induced the narrator to shape the whole sentence of 31:9 as a *wayyiqtol* sequence? The decisive element, in my view, is the paradigm provided by Deuteronomy's foregoing narrative material. The sequence that makes up 31:9 reproduces the sequence in the divine writing of the tables in Deut 5:22 and 10:4:[67]

Deut 5:22

ויכתבם

And he wrote them
עֲל שְׁנֵי לֻחֹת אֲבָנִים
upon two tables of stone,
ויתנם אלי
and gave them to me

10:4

ויכתב עֲל הַלֻּחֹת

And he wrote on the tables
. . .
. . .
ויתנם יהוה אלי
and YHWH gave them to me

---

[65] Buth, "Methodological Collision," 147-48.

[66] See Buth, "Methodological Collision," 147. The nonsequential use of *wayyiqtols* can be encompassed within the general phenomenon of coordination in narrative, which, as Sternberg indicates, can obey various forces and patterns, sometimes jarring against linear temporal sequencing; see M. Sternberg, "Ordering the Unordered: Time, Space, and Descriptive Coherence," *Yale French Studies* 61 (1981) 60-88, with biblical material; see also Sternberg, "Grand Chronology," 141-42 n. 4.

[67] This phenomenon has been noted by C. T. Begg, "The Tables (Deut. X) and the Lawbook (Deut. XXXI)," *VT* 33 (1983) 96-97, but it is assessed exclusively from a genetic perspective. Together with other recurring elements, these parallels between Deuteronomy 10 and 31 (Deuteronomy 5 is not mentioned) lend credence, Begg writes, "to the supposition that xxxi 9-13, 24-29 and ix 7b-10,11 derive from the same author, i.e. the Deuteronomist who would have employed a like verbal schema in his account of the writing and storing up of the two fundamental legal documents, the 'tables of the covenant' and the 'book of the law'" (p. 97).

31:9

Moses had written this Torah;	ויכתב משה את התורה הזאת
he gave it to the priests,	ויתנה אל הכהנים
the sons of Levi	בני לוי

In other words, a sequence thus far associated with God is now transferred to Moses' case.[68] In a certain sense the text of Deut 31:9 is less "fabula"-oriented (it does not trigger or confirm a reconstruction of the order of events) than "sujet"-oriented: it resumes a contextual paradigm, conjugating it now with a new subject.[69] The irony is that Moses himself, in his retelling of the Horeb event, provided the narrator with the pattern of his own course of action.[70] The divine and foundational action is repeated with a shifting forward of the actors: what was written by God and given by him to Moses is in 31:9 written by Moses and given by him to the Levites and the elders. The divine setting apart of the tribe of the Levites in 10:8-9, with the carrying of the ark of the covenant of YHWH as their first mission, launched the people on their journey: "Arise, go on your journey at the head of the people, that they may go in and possess the land, which I swore to their fathers to give them" (10:11). The written Torah is now grafted to this momentum by being entrusted to the Levites, carriers of the ark. The Levites appeared on Deuteronomy's stage as a distinct group when the transfer of written communication—the "ten words" committed to the tables—became an issue. The commissioning of the Levites by Moses, entrusting them with the written Torah, is thus a continuation of the divine commissioning reported in 10:8-9.[71]

After having launched Joshua as Israel's new leader, Moses transmits the written Torah to two groups—the Levitical priests

---

[68] Verbal forms of the root (כתב (על are furthermore associated with God (as subject of the action of writing) in Deut 4:13; 9:10 and 10:2; for (נתן (אל, see also in 9:10, 11.

[69] It is worth noting that in Deut 5:22 the sequence כתב–נתן אל had already embodied a nonsequential use of *wayyiqtols*, due to the proleptic value of ויתנם אלי, "and he gave them to me" = "that he would give me"; see my comments p. 45 above.

[70] For a general theory of the sequencing forces and patterns behind coordination, see Sternberg, "Ordering the Unordered," 60-88.

[71] A further hint of the connection of the Levites with written documents occurred in the so-called "royal law," which stipulates that the *Urtext* for the king's copy will be obtained "from the Levites" (Deut 17:18).

and the elders. Joshua's military leadership is thus concomitant
with the empowerment of other people.[72] This retrospectively
sheds light on the comprehensiveness of Moses' own leadership.
Deut 31:9, it could be said, stages a further projecting and split-
ting of Moses' complex function and identity. The entrusting of
the elders with the written Torah and their commissioning as the
ones responsible for the transmission of this Torah represents
what could be said to be a "looping of the loop." In 5:23, at the
peak of the Horeb event, the elders, together with the heads of
the tribes, intervened on behalf of the people and asked Moses
to mediate between God's voice and themselves. Now that Moses'
mediating mission has come to an end, the elders are reunited
with God's word, receiving it in "proper hands"—"and he gave it
to them." The lethal encounter in face to face, oral communication gives way, thanks to the written medium, to a life-giving transmission and reception (see 31:13).

That the "elders of Israel" are closely associated with Moses,
and with the future of the covenant, was shown in Deut 27:1-8.[73]
The solemn admonition to the people in 27:1 and the injunctions
concerning the erection of the altar and the "large stones" beyond
the Jordan were uttered (the narrator tells us) in two voices: "Now
Moses and the elders of Israel commanded the people saying ..."
Significantly enough, Moses' joint address with the elders is followed in Deut 27:9-10 by another speech in two parts, with the
Levitical priests this time: "And Moses and the Levitical priests
said to all Israel ..." (27:9; see also 27:14 on the leading role of
the Levites in the Ebal ceremony). The two groups who receive
the written Torah from Moses' hands are thus closely associated
with the making of the covenant, in Moab and beyond the Jordan. As Lohfink and Braulik contend, the two groups apparently

---

[72] In Deuteronomy, the issue of the distribution of power is actually mentioned
as early as Deut 1:9-18, where Moses retells the appointment of the ראשים, "heads"
(שרים, "commanders," and שטרים, "officers") and of the שפטים, "judges."

[73] On this issue, see N. Lohfink's subtle analysis of the role of the elders in
Deuteronomy, especially in covenantal contexts, "Ältesten," 26-42. See also idem,
"Bund," 233-37. On a larger scale, and notably on the scale of Moses' cycle in
the Pentateuch, see the survey, "La fonction des anciens dans le récit," in J.-L.
Ska, "Récit et récit métadiégétique en Ex 1-15: remarques critiques et essai d'interprétation en Ex 3,16-22," *Le Pentateuque: recherches et débats* (LD 151; Paris: Cerf,
1992) 165-70. The texts surveyed by Ska "établissent un lien étroit entre les
anciens et la transmission de l'héritage mosaïque. Il n'était donc pas étonnant
de les trouver dès le point de départ aux côtés de Moïse (Ex 3,16.18)" (p. 169).

represent, and are called to continue, two aspects of Moses' mediation. The Levites (Moses' tribal mates) "repräsentieren in der
durch die Geschichte gedeuteten Bundesinstitution den gött-
lichen Partner, die Ältesten den menschlichen."[74]

c. *The Written Torah and the Re-enactment of the Horeb Experience— Deut 31:9-13*

In the so-called "Law of the King," the paradigm "to write—to
read" emerged for the first time in Deuteronomy (17:18-19). In
Deuteronomy 31 the paradigm recurs (31:9, 10), but is broken
down: the writing has already been done by Moses, the reading
will take place in Israel's future in the land. No act of reading
whatsoever, it is important to note, takes place on Deuteronomy's
narrative stage and within Deuteronomy's staged action. The
דברים, "words," that had to be transmitted have been transmitted
by word of mouth. But the mediation of the written Torah enables
Moses to provide for a re-enactment, in the land, and before the
assembled people, of the foundational Horeb event. The *telos* of
Moses' writing is thereby revealed.

A particular aspect of Moses' injunction first needs to be
assessed. Who will read? The traditional Jewish interpretation sees
in Joshua—in Israel's chief leader—the one responsible for the
periodical reading of the Torah[75] (see the singular תקרא, "thou
shalt read" in 31:11).[76] This same interpretation is defended by
Weinfeld:

> The instructions 'assemble the people', 'you shall read this law ...
> in their hearing' pertain to Joshua, who is here deemed to be the
> successor of Moses, and not directed to the priests and elders men-
> tioned in v. 9. The ordinance regarding the reading of the Torah
> in fact follows Moses' address to Joshua (vv. 7-8), but the editor was
> compelled to introduce the detail concerning the writing of the
> Torah before Moses could command Joshua regarding its recitation.
> Verses 11-12 are indeed addressed in the singular: 'to appear before

---

[74] Braulik, *Deuteronomium II*, 223; see Lohfink, "Ältesten," 26-42. A similar observation is already found in Dillmann, *Deuteronomium*, 387, and Driver, *Deuteronomy*,
335.

[75] See *b. Soṭa* 41a; see also Rashi, Bekhor Shor, Sforno, Ḥazquni. Josephus, *Ant*
4 § 209, holds, however, that the reading is incumbent upon the high priest.

[76] The LXX and *Tg. Pseudo-Jonathan* present a reading in the plural, "you shall
read."

the Lord *thy* God (אלהיך)', '*thou* shalt read (תקרא)', 'assemble (הקהל)
the people'. Because of the interpolation of v. 9 original אתו [Moses
commanded *him*] was turned into אותם [Moses commanded *them*] (v.
10).[77]

Lohfink points out that, if the editor really intended to depict the
injunction to Joshua, as contended by Weinfeld, he could turn
the allegedly original אותו, "him," into את יהושע, "Joshua," or omit
the confusing mention of the Levites and elders. Moreover,
Lohfink goes on, Moses, who addressed all the people as (singular) "thou," could have done so for a group of particular Israelites
as well.[78] In Lohfink's view, the periodical reading of the Torah
is thus incumbent upon the elders and the Levites. They are the
(singular) "thou" commanded by Moses—"Thou shalt read". Yet
it is worth noting that elsewhere in Deuteronomy Moses always
addresses particular groups in the plural (the judges in 1:17-18;
the Transjordanian tribes in 3:18-20; the Levites in 31:26, 28).
Therefore, Driver's interpretation of the "thou shalt read" injunction is, in my view, the most plausible: "Israel is addressed (as just
before, in 'thy God'), the command being supposed to be carried
out by the particular members, or representatives of the nation,
whom it may concern (cf. 17[8] [the king])."[79] In other words,
Moses is here less interested in the identity of the official reader
than in the fact that the Torah be read in Israel's future.[80] Moses
entrusts the Levites and the elders with the implementation of
the command as such.[81]

Klaus Baltzer has emphasized the analogy between the provision in Deut 31:9-13 for a periodical reading of the Torah and

[77] Weinfeld, *Deuteronomy*, 65 n. 1.
[78] See Lohfink, "Ältesten," 31.
[79] Driver, *Deuteronomy*, 335; see already Dillmann, *Deuteronomium*, 387.
[80] Ensuing biblical developments bring to the fore various *cas de figure* of
solemn readings of the Torah: Joshua is the reader in Josh 8:34; King Josiah in
2 Kings 23:1-3; Ezra, the scribe and priest (הכהן), in Neh 8:1-6, with the assistance
of the Levites (Neh 8:8; see also 8:9). None of these scenes of public readings
fits the setting projected by Moses in Deut 31:10-13. The closest one is the reading by Ezra, which results in the celebration of the feast of Booths (see Neh
8:13-18).
[81] In that sense the injunction תקרא, "thou shalt read," in Deut 31:10 echoes
the previous injunction וכתבה, "and thou shalt write" in 27:3, 8. Both provisions
are meant for the entire people, whoever the actual agents of the writing and
the reading may be, and are channeled through particular groups (the elders
beside Moses in 27:3, 8; the elders and the Levites in 31:10).

similar stipulations in Hittite treaties.[82] The treaty between Sup-
piluliumas and Kurtiwaza, for instance, says: "At regular *intervals*[83]
shall they read it in the presence of the king of the Mitanni and
in the presence of the sons of the Hurri country."[84] Baltzer notably
dismisses the theory of covenant renewal often attached to the
periodical reading of Deut 31:9-13, in favor of a perspective of
"knowledge of the covenant," as a duty inseparable from the
covenant itself. Lohfink and Braulik have in turn appropriately
emphasized the dimension of "festlichen Lernritual" that underlies the injunction in 31:9-13.[85] In the following paragraphs I will
review this aspect of the gathering projected by Moses, paying special attention to the role of the written medium.

The setting of the solemn reading is the first indication of its
scope. As one of the three pilgrimage festivals to "the place that
YHWH will choose," the feast of Booths brings about a general
gathering of the sons of Israel. The inclusiveness of the assembly
is carefully spelled out in Deut 31:12: "the people, men, women,
and little ones, and the sojourner within your gates."[86] The nature
of the future gathering described in 31:10-13 stems from its taking place "at the end of every seven years, at the set time of the
year of release" (31:10). The release from debts (Deut 15:1-6) and
the manumission of the Hebrew slave (Deut 15:12-18) in the seventh year are meant to restore the people to their original equal-
ity and fraternity before YHWH.[87] Both in its quantity and its quality, this setting is a rehearsal of "the day of the assembly" at Horeb.
The solemn reading of the written Torah brings about a Horeb-
like experience, re-enacting the foundational event.[88] The lexical

---

[82] Baltzer, *Bundesformular*, 91-95 (especially 91-92). See also Weinfeld, *School*,
64-65, and G. E. Mendenhall, "Covenant Forms in Israelite Tradition," *BA* 17
(1954) 66-67.
[83] Uncertain translation.
[84] *ANET*, 205.
[85] The expression stems from Lohfink, "Glaube," 158 (see pp. 144-66, 260-63).
See also Braulik, "Gedächtniskultur," 9-31.
[86] Cf. Moses' enumeration of Israel's constituent participants in the actual law
concerning the observance of Booths (Deut 16:13-15). The making of the
covenant in Moab occasioned an inclusive gathering as well (cf. the listing in
Deut 29:9)—Moses' current audience in Deuteronomy 31.
[87] See Lohfink, "Glaube," 159; Braulik, "Gedächtniskultur," 21.
[88] For a theoretical consideration of such a phenomenon in biblical thinking,
see my *La parole consacrée: théorie des actes de langage, linguistique de l'énonciation et
parole de la foi* (BCILL 25; Louvain: Peeters, 1984) 160-65.

and ideological pattern that lies behind Moses' command is found in his narrative retelling in Deuteronomy 4 and 5.[89] The assembling of the people for the proclamation of the written Torah will echo the "assembling" (see הקהל, 4:10), "your assembly" (קהלכם, 5:22), and "the day of the assembly" (יום הקהל, 9:10; 10:4; 18:16)—in short, the Horeb assembly. A quote of YHWH by Moses in 4:10 (within Moses' first evocation of the Horeb event) is especially pervasive in Moses' convocation in Deut 31:12:

Deut 4:10 (YHWH speaking to Moses)	Deut 31:12 (Moses speaking to the people)
הקהל לי את העם	הקהל את העם
	האנשים והנשים והטף
	וגרך אשר בשעריך
ואשמעם את דברי	למען ישמעו
אשר ילמדון	ולמען ילמדו
ליראה אתי	ויראו את יהוה אלהיכם
	ושמרו לעשות את כל דברי התורה הזאת
כל הימים אשר הם חיים על האדמה	ובניהם אשר לא ידעו ישמעו ולמדו
ואת בניהם ילמדון	ליראה את יהוה אלהיכם
	כל הימים אשר אתם חיים על האדמה

Gather the people to me,	*Gather the people,* men, women, and little ones, and the sojourner within your gates,
that I may let them *hear* my words, so that they may *learn* to *fear* me	that they may *hear* and that they may *learn* and *fear* YHWH your God, and be careful to do all the words of this Torah,
all the days that they *live upon the land,*	and that *their children,* who did not know, may hear and *learn* to fear YHWH your God, *all the days that* you *live on the land*
and that they may *teach their children.*	

Both the gathering at Horeb in Israel's foundational past and the gathering in Israel's recurring future have the people's learning in view. God's purpose at Horeb becomes the purpose of Moses' injunction in 31:10-13: אשר/למען ילמדו, "so that they may learn."[90]

---

[89] Lohfink, "Glaube," 159, refers to an "archetypischer Ort, die Offenbarung am Horeb," as depicted in Deuteronomy 5; see also Braulik, "Gedächtniskultur," 21-22; idem, *Deuteronomium II*, 224; M. A. Zipor, "The Deuteronomic Account of the Golden Calf and its Reverberation in Other Parts of the Book of Deuteronomy," *ZAW* 108 (1996) 31.

[90] In Deut 4:10, the learning (יִלְמְדוּן) of the adults leads to their teaching (יְלַמְּדוּן) of their children; see Rashi, *ad loc.*

In both cases, "hearing" leads to "learning," but the process of learning is in turn oriented toward the instilling of fear: "so that they may learn to fear me" (4:10); "that they may learn and fear YHWH your God" (31:12). The learning perspective also underlay Moses' conveying *in Moab* of the "words" he received *at Horeb* (see 5:1, "Hear, O Israel, the statutes and ordinances which I speak in your hearing this day, and you shall learn them [ולמדתם] and be careful to do them").[91] The connection of "learning" and "fearing" has, however, a special affinity with the extreme stages of God's revelation: the awesome revelation at Horeb (4:10) and the relation to the written "words" (in the king's reading, see 17:19; in the solemn reading to the people, see 31:12, 13).[92] In its setting and staging, the proclamation of the written Torah to the assembled people is thus conceived of as a fear-inspiring experience. However, it would be wrong to associate the fear-inspiring character of the solemn reading with its scenic dimension alone, its ὄψις, "spectacle," in Aristotelian terms.[93] Since Deut 17:19, and the *mise en abyme* of the "royal law," Moses' addressees and Deuteronomy's readers know that the fear of God is also linked, as an intended consequence, with the meditative reading of the Torah:[94] "and [the Torah] shall be with him, and [the king] shall read in [the book] all the days of his life, *that he may learn to fear* (למען ילמד ליראה) YHWH his God, by keeping all the words of this Torah, and doing them" (Deut 17:19). Is a process of understanding and active learning also implied in the "extreme" scenes we are dealing with (the Horeb experience and the solemn reading of the Torah)? An interesting change in Moses' wording is to be observed. A relative ambiguity hangs over God's sentence in 4:10 (thus at Horeb), ואשמעם את דברי אשר ילמדו ליראה אתי. It is not clear whether the connecting word אשר introduces a relative clause ("that I may let them hear my words *which* they will learn [in order] to fear me"), or a consecutive/purpose clause, "that I may let them hear my words *so that/in order that* they may learn to fear me." Is intellectual learning involved in the acquisition of religious fear? Moses' phrasing in 31:12, למען ישמעו ולמען ילמדו ויראו את יהוה אלהיכם, "that they may hear and that they may learn and fear

---

[91] See Braulik, "Gedächtniskultur," 19, 22.
[92] An exception to this setting is found in Deut 14:23.
[93] Aristotle, *Poetics* § 6.
[94] See Fischer and Lohfink, "Diese Worte," 68-69.

YHWH your God," dispels the doubt in question. "Learning" and "fearing" are two juxtaposed purposes, the former coming before the latter. What remained ambiguous in the foundational oral transmission becomes distinct when the written medium is involved: the acquisition of God's fear proceeds from the active understanding and learning of his revealed word.

A hint in favor of the claim just made is provided in Deut 31:13, where the intended effect of the solemn reading on the children is described: "and that their sons, who have not known, may hear and learn to fear (וְלָמְדוּ לְיִרְאָה) YHWH your God." In his commentary on 31:12-13, Nachmanides points out the difference between what is expected from the adults in 31:12, "they will learn and they will fear," and from the children in 31:13, "they will learn to fear." In the latter case, he explains, the acquisition of fear implies an educational process.[95] In my view Craigie and Braulik are more to the point when they contend that what is expected from the children in the solemn proclamation of the Torah is a first acquiring of basic religious fear.[96] While adults are supposed to combine the rational experience of learning with the religious experience of fear, children are expected to be initiated into the Horeb's *tremendus et fascinans*.

In conclusion: what Deut 31:10-13 projects is the successful mediation of the written Torah. The prime quality of the written medium is its ability to be a Torah-beyond-Moses, by overcoming the limitations of space (since the reading shall take place in the land) and especially of time. The oral transmission of the Torah is staged as an ἐφ ἅπαξ ("once and for all"): "And Moses summoned (וַיִּקְרָא) all Israel, and said to them" (5:1). The "singulative" narrative in 5:1 gives way to an "iterative" injunction in 31:10-11, using the same verb: "At the end of every seven years ... you shall read (תִּקְרָא) this Torah before Israel in their hearing."[97] What was conveyed orally once to a particular audience

---

[95] Nachmanides, on Deut 31:13.

[96] Craigie, *Deuteronomy*, 371; Braulik, "Gedächtniskultur," 23. How is the children's "ignorance" to be explained, since Deut 6:7 and 11:19 provide for the daily inculcation of the words of the Torah? As Craigie indicates, what is not yet known or experienced by the children is the Horeb-like, fear-inspiring, communal recitation (in the presence of "all Israel"), as distinct from the daily learning (see p. 371).

[97] For a distinction between "singulative" (a single event is told a single time) and "iterative" (a narrative tells once events that occur many times) narratives,

will be transmitted an indefinite number of times to further generations, thanks to the written medium. "This first passage about
the transfer from oral to written *torah*," Olson writes, "focuses on
the element of time and generations. The periodic reading of the
torah transcends and overcomes the limits of human time and
mortality so that the *torah* may be made new for each generation."[98] Yet the difference in medium does not compromise the
communicational experience. As with the Horeb event it recap-
tures, the Moab Torah was made of "words" to be heard: "Hear
(שמע), Israel, the statutes and the ordinances which I speak in
your hearing (דבר באזניכם) this day" (5:1). The experience *ex audi-
tu* will be repeated in every reading of the same Torah, as 31:11
makes clear: "you shall read this Torah before all Israel in their
hearing (באזניהם)."[99] The written Torah thus diffuses throughout
time the foundational communication of the Torah.

In the first part of Deuteronomy 31 (vv. 1-13) Moses thus makes
arrangements for a successful passage of the people from the
desert to the land, or, one could say, from foundational to modern times. The new regime implies a political leader, Joshua, and
officials in charge of the covenantal "words." The commitment to
writing of the "words" in question emerges as the initiative that
enables the survival of the covenant in its new temporal and spatial frame. Taking this step, Moses contemplates an unquestioned
possession of the land, as his last words imply: "as long as you live
in the land which you are going over the Jordan to possess"

---

see G. Genette, *Narrative Discourse: An Essay in Method* (Ithaca: Cornell University Press, 1980) 113-60.
[98] Olson, *Deuteronomy*, 135. In a comparative essay, "Lessons from the Dying:
The Role of Deuteronomy 32 in its Narrative Setting," *HTR* 87 (1994), 377-93,
S. Weitzman points to interesting analogues to Moses' writing in Deuteronomy
31. In the Syriac version of the *Words of Ahiqar* and in the *Instruction of Ankhsheshonqy* from Egypt, the sage issues his final teaching in two forms: in oral form to a
contemporary audience and in written form to an audience at a spatial or temporal distance. In the case of *Ahiqar*, the closest match in Deuteronomy 31 is
probably found in Moses' writing of the Song (see 31:22), since in both instances
the transcription of the teaching precedes its oral conveying. The main point in
the comparison, however, is that in all three cases a valedictory address is con-
verted into a written record for a future audience. "In all three cases—Deuteronomy 31, Syriac *Ahiqar*, and in the *Instruction of Ankhsheshonqy*," Weitzman writes,
"the sage is said to have composed or commissioned a written edition of his final
teaching rather than relying upon others who were present to transmit the teaching" (387).
[99] See Braulik, "Gedächtniskultur," 22.

(31:13).[100] This is precisely the perspective which will be shattered in the second part of the chapter.

3. *The Turning Point of the Theophany—Deut 31:14-32:47*

a. *The Return of the Repressed—Deut 31:14-15*

In Deut 31:2 Moses carefully avoided the theme of his forthcoming death, putting forward his old age and God's decree, "You shall not go over this Jordan," as reasons for his non-crossing. YHWH's words in 31:14—"And YHWH said to Moses, 'Behold, the days approach when you must die'"—therefore represent the "return of the repressed." When he reported God's fateful decision in his first speech, Moses enjoyed the latitude in rephrasing involved in any retelling. In 4:22, for instance, Moses contented himself with a geographical parameter: "For I must die in this land; I will not go over the Jordan."[101] Narratively speaking, the spatial parameter advanced by Moses brought the narrative to a kind of standstill, since Moses was already standing, while speaking, "in this land." No move was to be expected. Moses' death was (spatially) close, but it had been close from the beginning of Deuteronomy's action. Moses' presentation neutralized, so to speak, the drawing near of death. In 31:14, Moses is no longer the all-reporting speaker, but the addressee of God's first direct (unreported) speech.[102] For the first time in Deuteronomy, the theme of Moses' fate comes up without Moses' verbal mediation. And what YHWH makes clear from the outset is that Moses' death has its temporal parameter: "Behold, the days approach when you must die." By bringing to the fore the temporal dimension, God's words precipitate the perception of a process that Moses kept eluding. Moses' death is close temporally as well, which means that it is *getting* closer.

The conjunction of the temporal and spatial parameters brings

---

[100] A similar promise of blessing in the land concludes the second of the "you shall write" injunctions in Deut 11:18-21, as well as the "royal law" in 17:18-20. On this issue, see Braulik, "Gedächtniskultur," 20.

[101] See my comments, p. 33-34 above.

[102] God's direct speech to Moses, it should be noted, benefits the reader alone, and not Moses' audience.

about a dramatic turn in Moses' mind as well as in the reader's. Still, one could say that God's intervention includes a counter-momentum, since it mentions "days" in the plural, קרבו ימיך למות. The reader has known since Deut 1:3 that Deuteronomy's action—under the guise of Moses' communication act—was completed within a single day, "the first day of the eleventh month." What is the bearing of the plural in God's announcement? I will indicate in the next chapter that a patriarchal paradigm underlies God's statement (cf. Gen 47:29, ויקרבו ימי ישראל למות, "And the days drew near in which Israel had to die"). In Moses' case, further narrative turns possibly still lie ahead and can narrow down the temporal frame to the single day of Deut 1:3.

The divine announcement to Moses brings about the convocation of Joshua in the Tent of Meeting.[103] In Deut 31:7-8 the public encouragement of Joshua by Moses was a presentation of the successor without an avowed *raison d'être*: the death of the leader was the evaded theme. Not so in 31:14-15, where the calling of Joshua proceeds directly from the mention of Moses' forthcoming death. The sudden convocation and the subsequent theophany—"and YHWH appeared in the tent in a pillar of cloud" (31:15)—are wholly unexpected in Deuteronomy's plot; as it will turn out, they are even Deuteronomy's main *peripeteia*.[104] Thus far, whatever point of revelation the people had to learn as new was also ancient: it proceeded from Horeb through Moses. The theophany in Deuteronomy 31 brings Moses back to a point where even the mediator has to learn. Something new was apparently kept in reserve by the God of Horeb.

b. *In the Tent of Meeting—Deut 31:16-22*

God's announcement to Moses in Deut 31:16 includes a temporal element, with a considerable dramatic import:

Behold, you are about to lie with your   הנך שכב עם אבתיך
fathers;

---

[103] In Deuteronomy, the "Tent of Meeting" is mentioned only in 31:14, 15; see, however, the narrative precedents in Exod 33:7-11; 34:34-35; Num 11:24-25, 12:4, 10; 20:6.

[104] As Braulik, *Deuteronomium II*, 221, perspicaciously points out, the theophany is "in gewissen Sinnen der Höhepunkt des Buches—der in 5 nur berichteten Erscheinung am Horeb entsprechend."

then this people will rise
and prostitute themselves after the
strange gods of the land.

וקם העם הזה
וזנה אחרי אלהי נכר הארץ

God's infallible prediction outlines a dire future, made of opposed movements: Moses' lying down with his fathers and the people's rising up (to "lie down" for intercourse with foreign deities!). The theme of Israel's corruption has repeatedly appeared in Moses' speeches (alternating with wishes of faithful occupation of the land). Yet the theme of the people's rebellion, going back to Moses' speech in 4:25, has thus far belonged to either a remote or an indefinite future:

> When you have begotten children and children's children and are long established in the land, should you act wickedly ... (4:25)
> If you forget the Lord your God and follow other gods to serve them or bow to them, I warn you this day that you shall certainly perish. (8:19)
> And later generations will ask [about the future desolation of the land]... Then men would say, "It is because ... they went and served other gods and worshipped them." (29:21)

What YHWH's announcement in 31:16 states is a *post hoc, propter hoc* relationship: Moses' death will not only be followed by, it will even prompt, Israel's uprising.[105] God's revelation thus precipitates (and coordinates with Moses' death) what were so far mere *futurabilia*. The perspective of a happy post-Mosaic age opened in the first part of Deuteronomy 31 is shattered by God's initial statement.

God goes on with his dire prediction. The people's conduct will amount to nothing less than a breaking of the covenant, והפר את בריתי אשר כרתי אתו, "and [they will] break my covenant which I have made with them" (Deut 31:16; see also 31:20).[106] Which covenant? We are still in the part of Deuteronomy that opened in 28:69 with the heading: "These are the words of the covenant which YHWH commanded Moses to make with the people of Israel in the land of Moab, besides the covenant which he made with them at Horeb." The covenant at Horeb has already been transgressed in

---

[105] For the role of הנה in introducing clauses expressing a causal or temporal connection, or the occasion or condition for the ensuing clause, see Waltke and O'Connor § 40.2.1c.d.

[106] The idiom הפר ברית, "to break a covenant," is not found elsewhere in Deuteronomy; previous instances occur in Gen 17:14 and Lev 26:15, 44.

the Golden Calf affair; is the covenant in Moab destined to under-
go the same process? Will (sacred) history repeat itself? The pattern of a dramatic repetition seems to loom in God's words. God's
anger will be expressed in his "hiding his face" (31:17; emphasized in 31:18: ואנכי הסתר אסתיר פני, "And I will surely hide my face").
Yet, the withdrawal of God's face will not leave the people in a
silent void. The injunction in 31:19, "now therefore (ועתה) write
this Song," is in my view logically connected with the prospect of
God's disappearance.[107] The Song in question will do duty for the
hidden God. As YHWH makes clear, it "will be for me (תהיה לי) a
witness (עד) against (ב) the people of Israel" (31:19). Moses is
enjoined to write down the poem,[108] to teach it, and to put it
(שימה) into the mouth of the sons of Israel (31:19). In Deut 6:6
and 11:18 the metaphor of the "heart" (לב) implied that the words
of the Torah were to be committed to memory. The reference to
the "mouth" (פה) in 31:19, 21 has rather in view the actual uttering of the Song. From generation to generation, God announces,
the poem will indeed be uttered: "it will not be forgotten from
the mouth (מפי) of their offspring" (31:21). What the tradition
and the articulation of the Song will prevent is a sense of mute
irrationality when Israel has turned to other gods, broken the
covenant and met an evil fate: "and when many evils and troubles have come upon them, this Song will confront (וענתה) them
as a witness." (31:21). Although YHWH will hide his face (פני,
31:17, 18), the Song will "answer" (וענתה) "in [the people's] face"
(לפניו, 31:21), making it impossible for the people to find the
meaning of their fate elsewhere than in God's omniscient word.
Nothing of the future of the people is irrational, and there is no
rationality beyond or beside God's prophetic word. The "other

---

[107] See Driver, *Deuteronomy*, 341.

[108] Most commentators point out the discrepancy in number between the
injunctions of v. 19: כתבו, "write" (plural) vs. ולמדה, "and teach it," שימה, "put it"
(singular). The disparity is all the odder since one could easily imagine a single
writer of the song and more than one teacher. In the narrated facts, such seems
to be the situation: in v. 22, Moses alone is described as writing down the Song,
whereas in 32:44 he is joined by Hoshea-Joshua in the oral transmission (teaching?) of the same Song. The ancient versions (Peshiṭta, LXX, Vulgate, Vetus Lati-
na) present alternative readings, with all the imperatives either in the plural or
in the singular. The writing down and the teaching of the Song by Moses alone
in 31:22 actually ensures that, although Joshua is now associated with Moses'
prophetic mediation, every bit of revelation within Deuteronomy is written down
by Moses, and therefore transmitted under his sole authority.

gods" Israel will turn to (31:20; see 31:16) are in advance stripped of any pretention whatsoever when the sense of history is at stake: the Song provides its exclusive intelligibility.

Moses' writing down of the Torah, as narrated in Deut 31:9, did not proceed from any recorded divine stipulation. Moses apparently *emulated* God's recourse to writing at Horeb, and he did so for a good reason, i.e., in order to overcome an imminent break in communicational continuity. As for Moses' writing down of the Song, it proceeds directly from God's expressed will.[109] In the Moab covenant, the "words" of the Song (see 31:30; 32:44-45) therefore occupy a situation analogous to the (ten) "words" in the Horeb covenant, whose commitment to writing equally originated at God's initiative. Just as YHWH wanted the people to journey toward the land with the written repository of the Horeb revelation, so he wants them now to be provided with a written record of his dramatic revelation in Moab. Yet, what was possible in foundational times—the writing of the tables with God's finger—is now entrusted to human *savoir faire*. A divine operation, writing, is now divinely enjoined to human agents.

God's revelation to Moses in the theophany opened with the disclosure of the people's infidelity that would follow the leader's death (31:16). What was then still on the horizon of Moses' life draws definitely closer in God's last sentence: "for I know (ידעתי) the purpose which they are forming today (היום), before I have brought them into the land that I swore to give" (31:21). The rebellious future of the people is present *in nuce* on the day God is speaking to Moses—the day that forms the basic frame of Deuteronomy. It is therefore no surprise that, as stated by the narrator in the next verse, "Moses wrote this Song the same day (ביום ההוא), and taught it to the people of Israel" (31:22). The narrator probably summarizes in this sentence a comprehensive process (anticipating, for instance, the conveying of the Song to the people, as represented between 31:30 and 32:44). But the proleptic aspect of the sentence makes one thing clear. As Ibn Ezra on 31:22 points out, in teaching the Song the same day, Moses did not waste time. A literal implementation of God's command, "Now therefore write (plur.) this Song" would have associated Joshua with the act of writing. But Moses wrote alone, "the same day," and taught the

---

[109] See Schäfer-Lichtenberger, *Josua und Salomo*, 50.

Song to the people, as if a personal deadline had to be met.

Hittite, Aramaic and Neo-Assyrian treaties included the invocation of gods and other mighty forces of nature as witnesses, guaranteeing punishment in case of violation of the treaty.[110] In Deuteronomy, heaven and earth are invoked as witnesses by Moses in 4:26; 30:19 and 31:28, in the context of Israel's future fateful choices. Heaven and earth are referred to not as deities—this could hardly fit a speech that extols the one God—but very likely as elements "representing the unchangeable and ever-present fabric of the universe," bearing witness to "the fact that the consequences of Israel's disobedience have thus been foretold to it."[111] If the cosmic elements are no real witnesses in Deuteronomy 31-32, it is also because the Song itself serves as עד, "witness."[112] Since God is a party in the covenant, he cannot be called upon as a witness; yet his Song, objectified in writing, becomes the third party, representing to Israel the truth of its situation in the covenant. The mythic or formulaic convention—the call to natural elements as witnesses—is thus preempted by the illocutionary value of the Song—the established witness. The "textual logic" pervading Deuteronomy finds here a forceful illustration.[113] In other places the Israelites serve as their own witnesses (עדים), i.e., they are to testify against themselves should they violate the covenant (Josh 24:22). A great stone, a pillar or a heap can also be erected and act as a material witness (עד or עדה, see Gen 31:48, 52; Josh 24:27).[114] In Deut 31:19, the written *words* of the Song are elevated to the status of permanent witness. "Persistent repetition," Harold Fisch writes, is the "characteristic of the *'edût* function of the poem": "the text as a nagging presence [will] return upon us in the future like a revenant."[115] The bringing of the linguistic mediation (especially in its written form) to the fore is

---

[110] See Baltzer, *Bundesformular*, 24; Weinfeld, *School*, 62.

[111] Driver, *Deuteronomy*, 72, and M. Delcor, "Les attaches littéraires, l'origine et la signification de l'expression biblique 'prendre à témoin le ciel et la terre,'" *VT* 16 (1966) 8-25.

[112] See Lohfink, "Bundesschluß," 54-55.

[113] See Lohfink, "Bundesschluß," 54 n. 78.

[114] The contrast is particularly interesting in the case of Josh 24:27 since the "great stone," far from being inscribed with the covenantal stipulations, acts as a perpetual representative of their reception, "for it has heard all the words of YHWH which he spoke to us" (Josh 24:27).

[115] H. Fisch, *Poetry with a Purpose: Biblical Poetics and Interpretation* (Bloomington: Indiana University Press, 1990) 58.

Deuteronomy's distinctive trope. Additional provisions by Moses will soon give this phenomenon an even greater import.

The emphasis on the role of the Song as witness coincides with a paradoxical (and temporary) concealment of its content from the reader. Whereas Moses and Joshua are instructed about "this Song" (Deut 31:19), the reader is not made privy to the Song until "all the assembly of Israel" hears it from Moses' mouth (see 31:30—32:44). The withholding of the primary communication of the Song to Moses and Joshua somehow fits the privacy of the theophany in the Tent of Meeting. After all, we also do not know how the regulations of the Torah were entrusted to Moses at Horeb (see 5:31). As it will turn out, the Song already pervades the speeches of God (31:16-21) and of Moses (31:26-29) that preface its rendering.

c. *Leader of a Rebellious People—Deut 31:23*

Deut 31:23 records the installation of Joshua in a speech featuring the verb of the formal appointment (צוה), yet leaving unspecified the identity of the authority who performed the act in question (ויצו, "and he appointed"). The name of Moses occurs as subject in the previous sentence, though both the narrative and the discursive consistency designate God as the agent of Joshua's installation.[116] As commentators point out, YHWH's summoning of Joshua to the Tent of Meeting (in 31:14) in order to install him into office (ואצונו, "and I shall commission him") remains a *totes Motiv* if the announcement is not followed by the enactment in 31:23, "and he commissioned (ויצו) Joshua."[117] The inset quotation, "Be strong and of good courage; for you shall bring the

---

[116] Some witnesses of the Greek version (followed by Rahlfs) mention Moses as subject in Deut 31:23. Yet the oldest LXX witnesses (followed by Wevers)—the Vaticanus, the 963 Papyrus, the manuscripts of the O family—refrain from mentioning any subject. The latter present in my view a reliable *lectio difficilior*, parallel to the MT reading (see Dogniez and Harl, *Deutéronome*, 318).

[117] See already the interpolation of "Dominus" in some witnesses of the Vulgate. That God is the agent of the installation of Joshua in Deut 31:23 has been advocated by most Jewish medieval commentators (Rashi, Bekhor Shor, Nachmanides, Sforno, Ḥazquni; cf. however Ibn Ezra). Among modern exegetes, see for instance Dillman, *Deuteronomy*, 389; Driver, *Deuteronomy*, 338; C. Steuernagel, *Das Deuteronomium* (Göttingen: Vandenhoeck & Ruprecht, 1923) 162; Lohfink, "Fabel Dtn 31-32," 272-73; Schäfer-Lichtenberger, *Josua und Salomon*, 177-80; Nwachukwu, "Textual Differences," 87-88. The opposite view (i.e., Moses is the

sons of Israel into the land I swore to give them" (31:23),[118] further points to a divine locutor.

The installation of Joshua by YHWH[119] in Deut 31:23 is usually seen as a "confirmation of the appointment made previously by
Moses."[120] As I indicated above, the counterpart of Joshua's installation by YHWH is actually found in Joshua's formal appointment
by Moses in Num 27:22-23. What Moses does in Deut 31:7-8 is to
encourage Joshua "in the sight of all Israel." It turns out, however, that Moses' words of encouragement are echoed in God's
installation speech in Deut 31:23. Yet this echoing includes dramatic as well as ironic undertones: Joshua is indeed to be encouraged, for (God now reveals) he is the leader of a rebellious people. The context of Moses' admonitions in 31:1-8 was essentially
military. What threatened the future of the people in the land
was the presence of hostile nations; Moses' encouraging of Joshua
as military leader was the appropriate answer to such a danger.
God's appointment of Joshua in 31:23 comes right after the revelation of a completely different threat to Israel's existence in the
land: Israel's own imminent rebellion against the God of the
covenant. From God's dire announcement in 31:16-21, it can be
gathered that the real danger threatening Joshua's mission will
come from the sons of Israel themselves.

The shift of perspective may explain the slight change in wording between Moses' and God's admonitions to Joshua:

Deut 31:7 (Moses to Joshua)   Deut 31:23 (YHWH to Joshua)

חזק ואמץ כי אתה תבוא את העם הזה אל   חזק ואמץ כי אתה תביא את בני ישראל

---

agent of Joshua's installation in 31:23) is defended by Laberge, "Deutéronome
31," 156-57.

[118] The Greek version reads, "into the land that *the Lord swore* (to give them),
and *he will himself* be with you." See my comment in the introduction about a
possible rationale behind the Greek rendition (p. 39 n. 30).

[119] God's commissioning of Joshua, and promise of assistance to him ("I will
be with you") in Deut 31:23 fits a traditional pattern in the Hebrew Bible. Baltzer,
Bundesformular, 71-90, draws attention to the recurrence of a confirmation of the
covenant when the office of leadership is transferred from one person to another.
Baltzer's survey includes Joshua 23; 1 Samuel 12; Deuteronomy 31-Joshua 1; 1
Chronicles 22-29; 2 Kings 11. See also Lohfink, "Übergang," 42 n. 40. Within the
Mosaic cycle, the promise of assistance to Joshua significantly echoes the initial
promise of God to Moses, "I will be with you" (Exod 3:12) (see Schäfer-Lichten-
berger, *Josua und Salomo*, 180).

[120] Driver, *Deuteronomy*, 339; see also M. Noth, *Überlieferungsgeschichtliche Studien*
(2d ed; Tübingen: Max Niemeyer, 1957) 215; Buis, *Deutéronome*, 403; Mayes, *Deuteronomy*, 378.

הארץ אשר נשבע יהוה לאבותם לתת להם   אל הארץ אשר נשבעתי להם

Be strong and of good courage; for   Be strong and of good courage;
you *shall come* with this people into   for you *shall bring* the sons of
the land which YHWH has sworn to   Israel into the land which I
their fathers to give them.   swore to give them.

The MT reading תבוא, "you shall come" in Deut 31:7 (in the Qal)
is sometimes corrected and brought into alignment with the
Hiphil תביא, "you shall bring" of 31:23.[121] There are, however, good
reasons to keep the MT as it is, understanding the particle את in
31:7 as the preposition "with":[122]

(i) Within Moses' speech in 31:2-8, the root בוא, "to come,"
occurs in the Qal: "I am no longer able to go out and come in
(ולבוא)" (31:2; Moses alludes to what he is no longer able to do,
and to what Joshua will have to do).[123] In the same text the relationship of the divine and of the human leader to the people is
a relationship of precedence (going *before*; see 31:3, 8) or escort-
ing (going *with*; see 31:6, 8). Moses' assertion to Joshua in 31:8,
"for you shall come with this people," accords with this perspective.

(ii) Within God's speech in 31:20-21, which immediately precedes Joshua's appointment, the root בוא is used in the Hiphil,
the people being "brought into the land." See 31:20, "For when
I have brought him (כי אביאנו) into the land"; 31:21, "before I have
brought them (בטרם אביאנו) into the land." The same verbal form
occurs in God's appointment of Joshua: "for you shall bring (תביא)
the sons of Israel into the land." The emphasis אתה תביא, "*you* shall
bring" reinforces the effect: Joshua is to be encouraged because

---

[121] Some ancient versions—the Peshitta, the Vulgate, the Samaritan and one
manuscript of Onqelos—may be referred to as evidencing a Hiphil, תביא in their
Vorlage of Deut 31:7. The rendering of Neofiti 1 cannot be adduced as unequiv-
ocal evidence in this sense. See M. Klein, "Deut 31:7, תבוא or תביא?," *JBL* 92 (1973)
585, answering to B. Grossfeld, "Targum Neofiti 1 to Deut 31:7," *JBL* 91 (1972)
533-34. The form תיעל in *Tg. Neof.* Deut 31:7, Klein writes, "is not the usual haphel
in Neofiti 1." Among modern commentators turning the Qal into a Hiphil in
31:7, see Dillmann, *Deuteronomium*, 386; Driver, *Deuteronomy*, 334-35; Steuernagel,
Deuteronomium, 161; P. Buis—J. Leclercq, *Le Deutéronome* (SB; Paris: Gabalda, 1963)
188; Buis, *Deutéronome*, 31; Craigie, *Deuteronomy*, 370.

[122] The meaning of כי אתה תבוא את העם הזה as "for you will come with this people" is defended by Onqelos and Pseudo-Jonathan, as well as by Rashi, Hazquni
and Ibn Ezra.

[123] Notice the same use in the Qal in the related text of Deut 1:38: "Joshua
the son of Nun, who stands before you, he shall come (יבא) over there."

he is the one who will emulate God and "bring into the land" a people who have already decided to rebel (see 31:21).

Moses' words to Joshua are thus not simply confirmed by God in Deut 31:23. A dramatic turn intervened between the two speeches—the revelation of the people's imminent rebellion.[124] What narratively stands out in God's initiative is therefore his determination to assist Joshua ("I will be with you") and to fulfill his promise ("the land which I swore to give them"), *in spite of* the announced behavior of the beneficiaries of the promise.

d. *A Supplemented Torah—Deut 31:24-26*

As I pointed out in the introduction to the present chapter, both panels of Deuteronomy 31 feature the same sequence: an address to Joshua as "crossing" leader (31:7-8, 23) prefaces injunctions given to the Levites as carriers of the written Torah (31:9, 24-26). In what follows, I will indicate how Moses' instructions to the Levites in regard to the written Torah in 31:24-26 fit the new and dramatic perspective attached to the people's entrance into the land. Supplemented with the Song, the Torah "book" entrusted to the Levites will accompany Joshua as God's device for foiling the people's rebellious purpose.

The narrator's statement about Moses' completion of the writing of the Torah in a "book" (ספר) in Deut 31:24 has proved to be a *crux* for some interpreters. They had trouble with the relevance of a second mention of Moses' writing down of the Torah.

(i) According to Willy Staerk, followed by Carl Steuernagel and Alfred Bertholet, the whole development in Deut 31:24-30 is centered on the Song. "Torah" in v. 24 is therefore to be replaced by "Song."[125] As I indicated above, Sarna and Fishbane have renewed this view, without supposing another reading, but by

<hr />

[124] Baltzer's statement, "In welcher Verhältnis dieser Akt zu dem vorher beschriebenen steht, läßt sich aus dem Text nicht sicher entnehmen" (*Bundesformular*, 77), can thus be overridden on narrative grounds.

[125] See W. Staerk, *Das Deuteronomium, sein Inhalt und sein literarische Form* (Leipzig: Hinrichs, 1894) 75; Steuernagel, *Deuteronomium*, 163; A. Bertholet, *Deuteronomium* (Freiburg: Mohr, 1899) 93. The substitution has been criticized in favor of the actual reading by J. Hempel, *Die Schichten des Deuteronomiums* (Leipzig: Voigtländers, 1914) 96, followed by A. C. Welch, *Deuteronomy: The Framework to the Code* (Oxford: Oxford University Press, 1932) 62-64. von Rad, *Deuteronomy*, 190, puts forward a genetic answer that goes the other way: "It is not the reference

understanding תורה, "teaching," throughout Deuteronomy 31 as implying a reference to the succeeding Song.[126] In my opinion these views miss the communicational dynamic of Deuteronomy, which leads to the writing down of an initially orally transmitted Torah. They equally overlook the communicational dynamic of Deuteronomy 31, which interweaves the function of the written Song with the function of the written Torah. Sarna aptly reminds us that the word תורה "means teaching and is by no means limited to laws."[127] Yet he overlooks the fact that the word תורה has received a determinate meaning in Deuteronomy, especially since 4:44, "This is the Torah." A phrase such as ספר התורה הזה, "this 'book' of the Torah" (31:26), has been used in 29:20 and 30:10 (that is, in the unit of Deuteronomy that includes 31:9-12, 24-26) in a reference to the "words of the Torah" that Moses *previously* delivered. Deut 31:9-32:47 is misunderstood unless Moses' way of combining the Torah and the Song is properly taken into account. The event of the theophany, at the core of Deuteronomy 31, is the event of a textual supplementation: a new piece of revelation, i.e., the Song, is combined with an earlier one, i.e., the Torah.

(ii) Another way of missing the narrative progression that underlies Deuteronomy 31 is to contend, as Lohfink does, that Deut 31:24-26 is a second reporting of Moses' writing of the Torah first recorded in 31:9—one event being twice narrated:

Da 31,24 כ ויהי trotz des zusätzlichen עד תמם einfach an die Niederschrift von 31,9 anknüpft und man kaum auf die Idee kommen wird, die gleiche Tora sei den gleichen Leuten zweimal zur Aufbewahrung

---

to the law in vv. 24-29 which is secondary, but the reference to the song in vv. 16-22. After all, the stereotyped phraseology of the speech in vv. 16ff. 'write', 'teach', 'put in their mouths', 'may be a witness' is not applicable to a song but to a legal document." It can be objected to von Rad's statement that the expression שימה בפיהם, "put it in their mouths," in 31:19 matches the phrase ויתן בפי שיר חדש, "He put a new song in my mouth," in Ps 40:4; songs are likely to be "put in someone's mouth" no less than legal documents. O. Eissfeldt, "Das Lied Moses Dt. 32, 1-43 und das Lehrgedicht Asaphs Ps. 78 samt einer Analyse der Umgebung des Mose-Liedes," *Berichte über die Verhandlungen der Sächsischen Akademie der Wissenschafen zu Leipzig* (Berlin: Akademie Verlag, 1958) 43-54, establishes a kind of identity between the two entities, the Song having been turned into "eine Art Kompendium" of the Torah (p. 54).

[126] See Sarna, "Bible," *EncJud* 4.821-22; Fishbane, "Varia Deuteronomica," 350-51.

[127] Sarna, "Bible," 822.

übergeben worden, muß man bei dem, was folgt, wohl mit dem sel-
ben Geschehen rechnen.[128]

It is out of the question, Lohfink contends, that the same Torah
be twice the object of a transmission. But does 31:26 necessarily
concern the same Torah as in 31:9? What about the traditional
idea that the completion alluded to refers to a supplementation
of the genuine Torah with the Song revealed in the theophany?[129]
In Lohfink's view the situation of the written Song *vis-à-vis* the
written Torah is undecidable, left to the reader's imagination.[130]
Written down, the Song may have supplemented the Torah document; in that case the phrase עד תמם, "to the(ir) end" is a possible hint that the Song has been added to the already written
Torah. Yet the Song may also have eventuated in a parallel document (about which no further notice is given). In that case the
phrase עד תמם, "to the end," in 31:24 concerns the commitment
to writing of the genuine Torah (the Song not included), whereas the same phrase עד תמם, "to the end," in 31:30 signals that, no
less than the Torah, the Song has been conveyed in full to Israel.
Moreover, Lohfink's suggestion accords with the hypothesis of a
distinct tradition for the Song. "Dauer hat die Tora in Schriftlichkeit, das Moselied in Mündlichkeit."[131] Lohfink points to
God's statement in 31:21, that "[the Song] will live unforgotten
in the mouth of their descendants," כי לא תשכח מפי זרעו. In my view,
however, the sentence rather implies a continuity in the recitation ("in the mouth") of the Song; it does not imply an exclusively oral tradition (which would appeal to the heart, as the seat
of the faculty of memory). But if the Song's transmission is to be
ensured by exclusive oral means, what is the sense of Moses' writing it down (see 31:22), as enjoined by YHWH (see 31:19)?[132]

It is true that Deuteronomy 31-32 never particularizes the relation of the Song in its written form to the written Torah. Lohfink's
suggestion of an independent document, however interesting,

---

[128] Lohfink, "Fabel in Dtn 31-32," 264; see also Smith, *Deuteronomy*, 340-41; von
Rad, *Deuteronomy*, 190, who sees in Deut 31:24-26 a doublet rehearsing 31:9.

[129] See Ibn Ezra on Deut 31:23 and Nachmanides on Deut 31:24. In modern
exegesis, see Schäfer-Lichtenberger, *Josua und Salomon*, 182.

[130] See Lohfink, "Fabel in Dtn 31-32," 270-71.

[131] Lohfink, "Fabel in Dtn 31-32," 271.

[132] And what if the plural in Deut 31:19, כתבו לכם, "write for yourself," aims at
a plurality of acts of writing—Moses carrying out his own part "on the same day,"
as reported in 31:22? See Ibn Ezra on Deut 31:19: "Moses is commanded to write
[the Song], as well as anyone who knows how to write."

does not actually fit the communicational dynamic of Deuteronomy 31. It is significant that Moses' writing down of the "words
of this Torah" is presented as completed ("when Moses had finished writing [ככלות]"), and completed "to the end" (עד תמם), only
after the mention in 31:22 of the writing down of the Song.[133]
Ḥaim Gevaryahu and Michael Fishbane have drawn attention to
the scribal value of the phrase עד תמם, "to the end."[134] "This
phrase," Fishbane writes, "is the precise Hebrew correspondence
to the common colophonic notation used in cuneiform literature:
qati,"[135] that is, "the end."[136] As Gevaryahu indicates, the verb כלה,
"to be completed," can also have a colophonic use in biblical
Hebrew.[137] It is, moreover, important to note that the revelation
dispensed by Moses in the plains of Moab has, thus far, not been
provided with a "marker of completion" such as the one specified
by Moses in his report of the revelation of the Decalogue, "and
[YHWH] added no more" (5:22).[138] Only in 31:24—after the Song
is written—does the narrator present Moses' recording of the
Torah as formally carried through. As Schäfer-Lichtenberger indicates, the emphasis in 31:24 on Moses' writing "the words of this
Torah ... *to the very end* (עד תמם)" signals that "das in V.16-22 ange-
kündigte und nach V.22 von Mose aufgeschrieben Lied zur Tora
rechnet."[139] The verb כלה, Piel, "to bring to an end," and the
phrase עד תמם, "to the end," echoing the practice of scribal
colophons, thus portray Moses as a scribe whose communicational
duty has been brought to an end.[140]

What Deuteronomy 31 tells is thus the story of a process of

---

[133] As I indicated, this mention may be seen as a prolepsis, yet with a very short
range.

[134] H. Gevaryahu, "Set of Remarks about Scribes and Books in Biblical Times,"
Beth Miqra 43 (1970) 368-70 (Hebrew); Fishbane, "Varia," 350.

[135] Fishbane, "Varia," 350. See H. Hunger, *Babylonische und assyrische Kolophone*
(AOAT 2; Neukirchen-Vluyn: Neukirchener Verlag, 1968) 2, and the texts listed
p. 172; Leichty, "Colophon," 149.

[136] "Zu Ende," in Hunger's translation (from the verb *qatû*, "Zu Ende sein")
(*Kolophone*, 2).

[137] Gevaryahu, "Remarks," 369-70, cites Ps 72:20, "The prayers of David, the
son of Jesse, are ended (כלו)." Other colophonic expressions are found in Jer
48:48 and 51:64 (עד הנה, "thus far"), and in Job 31:40 (תמו, "are ended").

[138] The formula in Deut 13:1, "Everything that I command you you shall be
careful to do; you shall not add to it or take from it," is meant for Moses'
addressees; it does not qualify Moses' own mediation.

[139] Schäfer-Lichtenberger, *Josua und Salomon*, 182.

[140] For כלה, see also Deut 32:45. In my view this explains why the MT does not

completion—a process turned dramatic by the unexpected theophany and by the ensuing interpolation of the Song in the already
written Torah. The concept of "interpolation" primarily belongs
to the framework of redactional criticism, where it denotes the
insertion of secondary material into a given text. Interestingly
enough, a redactional or editorial interpolation arguably underlies the text of Deuteronomy 31. The genetic approach to Deut
31:14, 15, 23 has long sensed the secondary character of the verses in question[141] and, in the wake of remarks by Martin Noth, the
theophany pericope is increasingly ascribed to a secondary Deuteronomistic redaction.[142] The interpolation hypothesis is strength-
ened by the presence of a repetition framing the theophany peri-

---

have the verbal form ויכל, "and he completed," in 31:1, as in Qumran (1QDeut^b)
or, presumably, in the LXX's *Vorlage* (both of which further add: "to say *all* [כל]
these words" [MT "these words"]). Such a form would have represented an undue
anticipation of the completion of a still ongoing process of communication (the
revelation and the transmission of the Song are yet to come). The MT, as well
as the Samaritan Pentateuch, rather read וילך, "and he went." E. Tov, *The Text-Critical Use of the Septuagint in Biblical Research* (Jerusalem Biblical Studies 3; Jerusalem,:
Simor, 1981), 104, 290, as well as Laberge, "Deutéronome 31," 146, see in the
MT וילך the outcome of a metathesis on a genuine ויכל form. "Je crois," Laberge
writes, "que la tradition massorétique témoigne d'une logique qui trouvait
curieuse [*sic*] l'usage du verbe *compléter* ou *terminer* pour introduire une nouvelle
série de paroles de Moïse" (p. 146). Lohfink, "Fabel in Dtn 31-32," 274, and
"Fabel," 75, tends to prefer, still with hesitation, the ויכל, "and he completed"
reading as genuine. Whatever the genetic development, the MT is narratively consistent in its avoidance of a premature "marker of completion" in 31:1. In regard
to the LXX rendering, however, Harl, *Deutéronome*, 312, points out that συνετέλειν
in 31:1 (cf. 32:25) means "non pas 'achever', 'terminer' (le discours précédent)
mais 'conduire jusqu'à son terme' (continuer à parler)." Accordingly, the LXX
verse is translated: "Et Moïse continua de dire jusqu'au bout toutes ces paroles
à tous les fils d'Israël." On the other hand, the Massoretic וילך does not necessarily require a spatial move, it can mark off the beginning of a process. Lohfink,
"Fabel in Dtn 31-32," 258, similarly wonders whether "וילך vor einem zweiten
finiten Verb nur einfach 'den Vorgang anschaulich' [see *HALAT*, 236b, under 3]
macht, vielleicht als 'mere introductory word' [see BDB, 234a, under I.5] mit der
Nuance des Neuansatzes im Weitergang einer zusammenhängenden Ereignis-
kette." Harl construes it as "'et il alla' (et il dit), au sens inchoatif ('il se mit à
dire')" (p. 312). Therefore, one can say, with Harl, that there is no real contradiction between the Greek rendering and the MT: in both cases, "cette proposition
introduit un nouveau discours" (p. 312).

[141] See already Dillmann, *Deuteronomium*, 388
[142] In his *Überlieferungsgeschichtliche Studien* (Halle: Niemeyer, 1943) 215, M.
Noth first attributed the passage to one of the "ancient sources." In his *Überlieferungsgeschichte des Pentateuchs* (Stuttgart: Kolhammer, 1948) 35 n. 125, he rather
argues in favor of a "sekundär deuteronomistisch" redaction. See M. Rose,
"Empoigner le Pentateuque par sa fin!: L'investiture de Josué et la mort de
Moïse," *Le Pentateuque en question* (ed. A. de Pury; Genève: Labor et Fides, 1989)

cope—the reference to Moses' writing in Deut 31:9, 24:[143]

Torah unit (31:9-13)
"And Moses '*wrote*' (ויכתב) [had written] this Torah"

Theophany unit—revelation of the Song (31:14-23)

Torah unit (31:24-26)
"When Moses had finished *writing* (לכתב) the words of this Torah"

The phenomenon of "resumptive repetition" (*Wiederaufnahme*) has been singled out as an editorial or redactional device both in cuneiform and Israelite literature. Redactors or editors used to bracket the material they interpolated, either in narrative or legal contexts, by framing the secondary text with the (more or less literal) repetition of a sentence.[144] The theophany pericope seems thus to represent a typical interpolation, supplementing a previous account of Moses' last initiatives. The companion text to the theophany pericope, the Song revealed during the theophany, may have had a similar redactional origin (see the second resumptive repetition, framing the Song of Moses, in Deut 31:30; 32:44).

Yet the phenomenon of "interpolation" also applies to the story narrated in Deuteronomy 31. Given its unexpected character, the theophany recorded in Deuteronomy 31 sounds very much like an "interpolated" event in the expected course of things— nothing less than the intervention of a *Deus ex machina*. And what is revealed to Moses and epitomized in the Song looks like a last minute supplementation of an already closed revelation. The two phenomena, actually, are ideologically connected: nothing less

---

139-40; E. Blum, "Israël à la montagne de Dieu: Remarques sur Ex 19-24; 32-34 et sur le contexte littéraire et historique de sa composition," *Pentateuque en question*, 281-82; and idem, *Studien*, 85-88. In his studies on the composition of the Pentateuch, Blum brings out the connection between Deut 31:14-23 and Exodus 33, 34, Numbers 11, 12, and Deut 34:10 [12]. Among the components of this set of related texts, Blum lists the Tent of Meeting outside of the camp, the cloud that goes up and down, Moses' privileged status as an *Überprophet*, and the presence of Joshua, introduced as Moses' assistant. Blum regards the texts in question as part of the so-called *KD* composition (a post-Dtr overall composition of the Pentateuch, still in the Deuteronomistic tradition).

[143] Bernard Levinson has drawn my attention to the redactional aspect of the repetition in Deut 31:9, 24.

[144] See H. M. Wiener, *The Composition of Judges II 11 to 1 Kings II 46* (Leipzig: Hinrichs, 1929) 2; and C. Kuhl, "'Die Wiederaufnahme'—ein literarkritisches Prinzip?," *ZAW* 64 (1952) 1-11. For a full discussion and bibliography of this device, see Levinson's dissertation, *Hermeneutics*, 142-50.

than a divine disclosure was required to authorize a supplementation of the (already) written Torah. In its narrative claim Deuteronomy 31 thus tells of the interpolation of a piece of revelation (the Song) within a previous piece of revelation (the Torah). The repetition of the motif of Moses' writing supports such a narrative claim. In biblical literature the phenomenon of resumptive repetition functions not only as an editorial or redactional "marker" but also as a narrative technique.[145] In the latter capacity, the device is used by the narrator to present motifs in a sequence that departs from the spatiotemporal constraints of the storyworld. Events synchronous to a story's episodes, prospective or retrospective views, and digressions of various kinds are marked off by a repetition that signals the resumption of the main storytelling.[146] For instance, the story of Joseph in Egypt is interrupted in Gen 37:36 by a parallel story that takes place back in the homeland—the story of Judah and Tamar (Genesis 38). The non-sequential relationship of the episodes is indicated, when the narrator reverts to the Joseph saga, by the repetition in Gen 39:1 ("And Joseph was brought down to Egypt and Potiphar bought him") of a motif first stated in 37:36 ("And the Midianites sold him in Egypt to Potiphar"). In some cases resumptive repetitions can presumably do double duty, as a Janus-like device: they can mark an editorial or redactorial interpolation on the one hand, while providing a guideline in a complex narration on the other.[147] This is apparently the case in Deut 31:9, 24. The specific bearing of the narrative technique in this case is not the presentation of non-sequential motifs, but the relationship of an *event* (the theophany) to a *process* (the writing of the Torah). The unexpected revelation brings about the resumption and completion of an action already initiated (see 31:9). The account in 31:22—"So Moses wrote this Song"—signals Moses' second and distinct act of writing. Yet Deut 31:24 describes Moses' further writing as the prolongation of a single process, now brought to completion: "When Moses had finished writing the words of this Torah." Beyond the

---

[145] See S. Talmon's seminal study, "The Presentation of Synchroneity and Simultaneity in Biblical Narratives," *Studies in Hebrew Narrative Art Throughout the Ages* (ed. J. Heinemann and S. Werses; ScrHier 27; Jerusalem: Magnes, 1978) 9-26.
[146] See B. O. Long, "Framing Repetitions in Biblical Historiography," *JBL* 106 (1987) 385-399; and J.-L. Ska, *"Our Fathers,"* 9-12.
[147] See Greenstein, "Formation," 155 n. 16.

temporal interruption (Moses wrote in two sessions), Deuteronomy 31 considers the process: the continued writing of the Mosaic Torah, dramatically relaunched by the extemporaneous theophany.[148]

The reference to a circumscribed *sēper*, and to the deposition of the *sēper* in question by the side of the ark, home of the canonical written tables, rounds off the narrative description of the completion of Moses' integral Torah.[149] A noteworthy difference between Deut 31:9-13 and 31:24-26 is the appearance of the word ‏ספר‎—"inscription, document, book"—in the description of Moses' final writing. Moses' audience and the reader already know that the king has to "write a copy of this Torah on a 'book' (‏על ספר‎)" (17:18) upon his installation, from an original provided by the Levitical priests. This provision now finds its condition of possibility in Moses' writing down of the comprehensive Torah ‏על ספר‎, "on a 'book'" (31:24), entrusted to the keeping of the Levites (31:25). The emphasis on the materiality of the record, and on its preservation, is in sharp contrast to the description of Moses' writing in 31:9-13. In the former scene the Torah is written (v. 9) to be publicly read (v. 11) and to be obeyed (v. 12). The committed reception of the words of the Torah is thus the *raison d'être* of their recording. In 31:24-26 the written Torah is a material document ("Take this 'book' of the Torah"), to be deposited in a specific place ("and put it by the side of the ark of the covenant of YHWH"),[150] where it will be an "objective" witness ("that it may be there for a witness against you"). Supplemented with the Song,

---

[148] In its narrative claim, Deuteronomy 31 thus arguably mirrors its genesis. The text is the outcome of a redactorial interpolation (something "more" was to be said), yet it also tells of a dramatic interpolation in the Horeb-Moab revelation (something more was said by God, and written by Moses). In my final chapter I will return to this and other instances of a phenomenon that pervades the ending of Deuteronomy: the reflection of redactorial practices in the narrative action.

[149] See the discussion in the Talmud, *b. B.Bat.* 14a-b, opposing the view by R. Yehudah that the Torah "book" was kept on a board jutting out of the ark, to the opinion by R. Meir that it was deposited within the ark, "by the side of the tables." The latter interpretation is referred to by Nachmanides (commenting on 31:24-26) in a perspective of canonization: "it was deposited in the ark, on the side, because from now on they would not touch it at all, whether to add to it or to take from it, and this is the point of 'And it came to pass when Moses had finished writing to the end'" (translation mine).

[150] On the custom of depositing official texts in the ancient Near East, see de Vaux, *Institutions*, 132; Baltzer, *Bundesformular*, 28; Weinfeld, *School*, 63.

the written Torah is now a circumscribed and protected "body," ready to accompany the people on their journey.

In his reconstruction of the "fabula" of Deuteronomy 31-32 Lohfink further argues that it would not make sense to hand over the written Torah twice to the same people "zur Aufbewahrung."[151] In my view there is a substantial difference between the two scenes of commissioning, as far as the recipients of Moses' injunctions and their respective missions are concerned. In Deut 31:9 two groups, "the priests, the sons of Levi (כהנים בני לוי), who carried the ark of the covenant of YHWH," and "all the elders of Israel (כל זקני ישראל)," receive the written Torah and are commanded to provide for its periodical reading (31:10-13). The responsibility of the double staff is thus not one of preservation, but of communication of the written Torah.[152] In the scene described in 31:25-26 a single group, the "Levites" (הלוים), is entrusted with what is now the proper keeping of the Torah "book": "Take this 'book' of the Torah, and put it by the side of the ark of the covenant of YHWH, that it may be there for a witness against you" (31:26).[153] This is in agreement with the function of the Levites as it has been outlined in Moses' retelling of

---

[151] Lohfink, "Fabel in Dtn 31-32," 264.

[152] The mission of communication entrusted to the Levitical *priests* (הכהנים) in Deut 31:9-13 echoes their solemn intervention in 27:9 as "Levitical priests" (הכהנים הלוים); and the same is true of the "elders of Israel" (זקני ישראל) in 31:9 and in 27:1 (these cross-references have, paradoxically, been emphasized by Lohfink in his study "Ältesten"; see also idem, "Bund," 233-37).

[153] The difference has been noticed by Dillmann, *Deuteronomium*, 387, by Bertholet, *Deuteronomium*, 93, and by Mayes, *Deuteronomy*, 375. In Lohfink's view ("Ältesten," 29, 39), the difference between Deut 31:9 and 31:24-26 as to the personnel of the written law (the "priests sons of Levi" and the "elders of Israel" vs. the "Levites," who in turn summon the "elders of your tribes" and the "officers" [31:28]) can be explained only "diachronically," not "synchronically" (see p. 29). In 31:24-29 "es handelt sich offenbar um eine Revision der vorgegebenen Konzeption" (p. 39). J. Buchholz, *Die Ältesten Israels im Deuteronomium* (GTA 36; Göttingen: Vandenhoeck & Ruprecht, 1988) 17-21, carries the data of Deuteronomy 31:9, 25 to the point of an opposition between two social groups (the elders of Israel vs. the Levites), which he attempts to explain genetically and historically. A reading more attentive to the stages of Moses' provisions regarding the written Torah brings out, on the contrary, the consistency of Moses' choice of his partners, and the precision of the narrator in his presentation of them. On this issue, see Schäfer-Lichtenberger, *Josua und Salomo*, 51 n. 160; 182 n. 374, who draws attention to the basic identity of the Levitical group—they are twice defined by reference to the carrying of the ark, as well as to their different responsibilities toward the written Torah. In their first task they are primarily "priests" (31:9), called to carry out the public reading of the Torah; in their second office they

the Horeb events (10:8) and in the "royal law" (17:18). In Deuteronomy the Levitical group has a special affinity with the keeping of the written records of the covenant. It can therefore legitimately be said that the written Torah has been entrusted twice, to different staffs (the sons of Levi being involved in both cases), and for different purposes.

It is important to note that only in Deut 31:26 is the written Torah put in relation with the ark: "Take this 'book' of the Torah, and put it by the side of the ark of the covenant of YHWH" (in 31:9, the ark was just mentioned as the responsibility of the Levitical priests). Providing for the deposit of the Torah "book" beside the ark, Moses emulates God's provisions in Horeb for the rewritten tables. Moses' "second" writing of the words of the Torah (by way of supplementation) thus echoes God's second writing of the "ten words." The echoing effects are worth detailing. The occurrence of the verb שׂים, "put," in 31:26—"and you shall put (ושמתם) [the Torah 'book'] by the side of the ark"—echoes God's injunction to put the new set of tables in the ark: "and you shall put them (ושמתם) in the ark" (10:2; cf. 10:5). A further parallelism exists between Deut 10:5 and 31:26; it pertains to the final location of the document, written tables or Torah "book."

Deut 10:5	Deut 31:26
ואשם את הלחת בארון אשר עשיתי <u>ויהיו</u> <u>שם</u> כאשר צוני יהוה	ושמתם אתו מצד ארון ברית יהוה אלהיכם <u>והיה שם</u> בך לעד
And I put the tables in the ark which I had made; *and there they are*, as YHWH commanded me.	Put it by the side of the ark of the covenant of YHWH your God, *that it may be there* as a witness against you.

A special affinity seems therefore to exist in Moses' parlance between the second writing of the tables and the writing of the supplemented Torah.[154] Further hints will enhance the similarity between God's final writing and Moses'.

The most significant sign of the *peripeteia* brought about by the

---

are primarily "Levites" (31:25), entrusted with the preservation of the written document.

[154] Here too a shifting forward of the actors is to be observed. What YHWH did (the writing) is now carried out by Moses; what Moses did (the depositing of the document) is now enjoined upon the Levites. When it comes to the custody of the records of the covenant, the Levites stand out as new Mosaic figures. The two operations enjoined upon the Levites—"to take" (לקח) and "to put" (שׂים)—

theophany is the change in the status of the written Torah. In Deut 31:9-13 the written document received the positive *telos* of catalyzing the people's faithfulness to the covenant in their future in the land. In 31:26 the same document, now supplemented with the Song, is turned into a "witness against" (עד ב) the same people, "for I know," Moses states, "how rebellious and stubborn you are" (31:27).[155] The status of the written record is thus fundamentally transformed by the dramatic revelation—epitomized in the Song—of Israel's imminent breaking of the covenant. Moses transfers the (illocutionary) value attached by God to the Song (31:19, "that this Song may be a witness for me against [לעד ב] the people of Israel") to the now completed "book" (31:26, "that it may be there for a witness against you [בך לעד]"). The contagion is, so to speak, spatial. The embedded Song communicates its value of "witnessing against" to the Torah "book" to which it is attached. The contagion is also mimetic. Moses transposes to his writing of the "book" the finality of writing divinely revealed to him in regard to the Song.[156] As Schäfer-Lichtenberger points out, "Mose erhält keinen Auftrag JHWHs, die Tora aufzuschreiben."[157] Moses therefore finds a point of reference for the recording of the comprehensive Torah "book" in God's purposive injunction about the writing of the Song. As a result, the written

---

correspond to the first and the last actions that Moses performs on the tables (see Deut 9:9 and 10:5).

[155] Although prompted by an unexpected revelation, Moses' writing of the Song and of the Torah as "witnesses against" is somehow prepared by Moses' speeches. The warning illocutionary force (עד ב, "witness against"), conferred upon both the written Song and the Torah "book" (Deut 31:19, 21, 26), has oral precedents. Moses has been "witnessing against" (4:26; 8:19; 30:19) the people in the most insistent parts of his speech, notably while envisaging Israel's (remote) idolatrous future (in 4:15-31 and 8:6-20). What was achieved orally is now an illocutionary force attached by God to a written document, the Song האזינו (31:19), and by Moses to the comprehensive Torah "book" (31:26). The result is an interesting interchange between oral and written communication. The written documents are pervaded with the intensity of oral warnings; the evanescent speech acts receive in their written counterparts an (ever)lasting persistency. The exchange in question is further staged in the oral communication of the written Song. The value attached to the written Song as עד ב, "witness against," is orally performed in Moses' calling of heaven and earth "to witness against" (31:28; see 32:1), as well as in Moses' "warning against" (32:46) in his oral transmission of the Song to the assembly of Israel.

[156] The result of the process is that two witnesses are combined for the same purpose, which is not without recalling Deut 17:6: "On the evidence of two witnesses or of three witnesses ..."

[157] Schäfer-Lichtenberger, *Josua und Salomo*, 50.

Torah, primarily meant to catalyze the people's obedience, now exposes their disobedience. Deuteronomy's "textual thinking" is, once more, unmistakable. Elsewhere, erected stones (that is, fixed landmarks) could be עֵד, "witness" in covenant making.[158] With the Torah "book" attached to the movable ark, the witness will accompany the transgressor wherever he goes. "Putting the *torah* beside the mobile ark of the covenant, which the Levites carried," Olson writes, "underlines the ability of the written *torah* to travel and thus to transcend physical limitations of space as well as time."[159] It will do so as a truthful deponent, evidencing anticipatorily and retrospectively the people's unfaithfulness to God's word.

e. *Moses' Prophetic and Factual Knowledge—Deut 31:27-29*

The Torah "book" will be a "witness against" Israel, Moses warns, "for I know (כִּי אָנֹכִי יָדַעְתִּי) how rebellious and stiff-necked you are" (Deut 31:27). Moses hammers home what sounds like infallible prophetic knowledge: "For I know [כִּי יָדַעְתִּי] that, when I am dead, you will act wickedly and turn away from the path that I enjoined upon you" (31:29). The reader, who watched the encounter in the Tent of Meeting, knows how fresh is Moses' knowledge. He further knows that the prophet's knowledge (כִּי יָדַעְתִּי, "for I know") echoes God's own (כִּי יָדַעְתִּי, "for I know"), just revealed to him (31:21). The unexpected revelation, however, awakens Moses' memory. His denunciation of Israel's imminent behavior is packed with the phrases he coined in his retelling of the Golden Calf affair. In the following paragraphs I will survey the reminiscences of Israel's paradigmatic idolatrous sin in 31:27-29.[160]

---

[158] The "large stones" of Deuteronomy 27 somehow participate in this "geographical thinking." See my remarks p. 92 n. 20 above apropos of Gen 31:46, 51-52. See also Josh 24:27, where a plain stone is erected as "witness" against the people. The contrast between Deuteronomy 31 and Joshua 24 is all the more striking, since Joshua commits the terms of the Shechem covenant to writing, in the "'book' (סֵפֶר) of the Torah of God" (Josh 24:26).

[159] Olson, *Deuteronomy*, 136.

[160] See especially Driver, *Deuteronomy*, 243-44; Fretheim, "Ark in Deuteronomy," 5; and Zipor, "Deuteronomic Account," 31-33.

(a) קשה ערף, "stiff-necked"

Deut 9:6   Deut 31:27

... <u>וידעת</u> כי לא בצדקך
כי עם <u>קשה ערף</u> אתה

כי אנכי <u>ידעתי</u>
את מריך ואת <u>ערפך הקשה</u>

Know that it is not because of your righteousness ...
for you are a *stiff-necked* people

For *I know*
how rebellious and *stiff-necked* you are.

cf. Deut 9:13 (God speaks to Moses)

ראיתי את העם הזה
והנה עם <u>קשה ערף</u> הוא

I have seen this people,
and behold, it is a *stiff-necked* people

(b) המרה, "to be rebellious"[161]

Deut 9:7   Deut 31:27

למן <u>היום</u> אשר יצאת מארץ מצרים
עד באכם עד המקום הזה
<u>ממרים היתם עם יהוה</u>

כי אנכי ידעתי
את <u>מריך</u> ואת ערפך וקשה
הן בעודני חי עמכם <u>היום</u>
<u>ממרים היתם עם יהוה</u>
ואף כי אחרי מותי

From *the day* you came out of the land of Egypt,
until you came to this place, *you have been rebellious against YHWH*

For I know how *rebellious* and stiff-necked you are;
behold, when I am yet alive with you *today*,
you have been rebellious against YHWH;
how much more after my death!

Deut 9:23

<u>ותמרו</u> את פי יהוה אלהיכם

Then you *rebelled* against the command of YHWH your God

Deut 9:24

<u>ממרים היתם עם יהוה</u>
<u>מיום</u> דעתי אתכם

You have been rebellious against YHWH
from *the day* that *I knew* you

---

[161] See also Deut 1:26, 43.

(c) שחת, השחת, "to act corruptly"[162]—סור מן הדרך, "to turn aside from the way"[163]

Deut 9:12 (God speaks to Moses)	Deut 31:29 (Moses speaks)
קום רד מהר מזה	כי ידעתי אחרי מותי
כי שחת עמך אשר הוצאת ממצרים	כי השחת תשחתון
סרו מהר מן הדרך	וסרתם מן הדרך
אשר צויתם	אשר צויתי אתכם
עשו להם מסכה	

Arise, go down quickly from here; for your people whom you have brought from Egypt *have acted corruptly*; they *have turned aside* quickly *from the way which I commanded* them; they have made themselves a molten image	For I know that after my death you will surely *act corruptly*, and *turn aside from the way which I have commanded* you

Deut 9:16 (Moses speaks)

עשיתם לכם עגל מסכה
סרתם מהר מן הדרך
אשר צוה יהוה אתכם

You had made youselves a molten calf;
you *had turned aside* quickly *from the way*
which YHWH *had commanded* you

If the sin of Israel in its "landed" future is patterned after Israel's sin in the desert, what about the Golden Calf itself in Moses' prediction? A cryptic and metaphoric reference to the paradigmatic idol is found in Moses' last phrase, במעשה ידיכם, "through the work of your hands" (Deut 31:30). The reference may be loaded with irony, since the phrase is found in a very positive context in 2:7, "For YHWH your God has blessed you in all the work of your hand (מעשה ידך) [= enterprises]." Contextual hints in 31:29, however, re-orient the reference to idolatrous practices. The expression is preceded by the phrase תעשו את הרע בעיני יהוה, "you will do what is evil in the eyes of YHWH," and by the verbal form להכעיסו, "provoking him to anger," which occur twice in Deuteronomy:

(i) In 9:18b, in a passage where Moses recalls his intercession

---

[162] See also Deut 4:16, 25; see especially the echo in the Song in 32:5, "They have dealt corruptly with him."
[163] See also Deut 11:28.

after the Golden Calf affair: "because of all the sin which you had committed, in doing what is evil in the sight of YHWH (לעשות הרע בעיני יהוה), to provoke him to anger (להכעיסו)."

(ii) In Deut 4:25, in the opening of a passage (4:25-31) that envisions Israel's future idolatry (but postpones it to a remote future):[164]

> [25]When you beget children and children's children, and have grown old in the land, if you act corruptly (והשחתם) by making a graven image in the form of anything, and by doing what is evil in the sight of YHWH your God (ועשיתם הרע בעיני יהוה אלהיך), so as to provoke him to anger (להכעיסו) ... [28]And there [among the peoples] you will serve gods of wood and stone, the work of men's hands (מעשה ידי אדם), that neither see, nor hear, nor eat, nor smell.

No making of a new calf is prophesied in 31:29, but reference is made to "works of (human) hands" of the idolatrous type that provoke God's anger.[165] Israel's degeneracy will happen without delay (see 31:29, "For I know that after my death you will surely act corruptly"), and the imminent character of Israel's corrupt future is not contradicted by the expression באחרית הימים (31:29). Fishbane has made a strong case in favor of the reference of the expression to an impending future—"in the coming days." He draws attention to the fact that cuneiform legal texts frequently conclude "with reference to the possible illegalities and/or binding strictures *ina arkāt ūmē*, 'in the future'," which means, contextually, "after the death (or tenure) of the contracting parties."[166]

Moses' prophetic statement—"For I know"—in Deut 31:27-29 is linked to both the Torah "book" and the Song. In 31:27 Moses

---

[164] Significantly enough, this projection by Moses of Israel's idolatrous future occurs just after Moses' disclosure about his non-crossing of the Jordan River (without any temporal or causal connection being established): "For I must die in this land; I must not go over the Jordan; but you shall go over and take possession of that good land. Take heed to yourselves, lest you forget the covenant of YHWH your God, which he made with you, and make a graven image in the form of anything YHWH your God has forbidden you" (Deut 4:22-23). What Moses dreads in Israel's future is precisely what, according to God's ultimate revelation (in 31:16-21), will happen after his own death.

[165] See Driver, *Deuteronomy*, 344.

[166] Fishbane, "Varia," 351. A precise lexical equivalent is found at the conclusion of Esarhaddon's inscription from Nippur in a phrase—*ina aḫrāt ūmē* (D 18)—"with clear reference to an immediate future following the death of the parties involved" (p. 351).

legitimates the status of the "book" as עד ב, "witness against," in a sentence that subtly superimposes references to Israel's past and future sin: "For I know how rebellious and stiff-necked you are …" Moses' prophetic knowledge is supported by his factual knowledge, gained through the Horeb events. The reference to the Golden Calf affair confirms the hints I pinpointed above: there is an affinity between Moses' conclusive writing of the Torah "book" (the Song now included) and the second writing of the tables.[167] The pattern of a double writing (before and after the Golden Calf sin) at Horeb underlies the telling of a double stage in Moses' writing of the Torah "book" in Moab. Israel's original idolatrous desertion prompted YHWH's second writing of the tables (and their insertion in the ark); the revelation, epitomized in the Song, of Israel's forthcoming desertion brings about Moses' completion of the Torah "book" (and its deposition by the side of the ark).

Initially centered on the Torah "book," Moses' speech in Deut 31:26-29 ends by introducing the rendition of the Song:

> [28]Assemble to me all the elders of your tribes, and your officers, that I may speak these words in their ears and call heaven and earth to witness against them …' [30]Then Moses spoke the words of this Song to the end, in the ears of all the assembly of Israel. (31:28-30)

When it comes to Moses' communication of the Song, Lohfink puts forward the hypothesis of two acts of transmission:[168]

(i) A communication to the assembly of Israel's notables, כל קהל ישראל (31:30). This assembly is formed by "all the elders of your tribes" (כל זקני שבטיכם) and "your officers" (שטריכם), convened by the Levites on Moses' order (31:28), that he "may speak these words in their ears (באזניהם)" (31:28).[169]

---

[167] See Fretheim, "Ark in Deuteronomy," 5, who points out that the necessity for the written Torah "book" "is much the same as that for the second set of tablets, the stubbornness and the rebellion of the people (cf. 31,27-29 with 9,7-8.12-13.16b.23-24, noting the similarity in phraseology)."

[168] See Lohfink, "Fabel in Dtn 31-32," 264-66, 275-78; see also Craigie, *Deuteronomy*, 373.

[169] Instead of the twofold group, the LXX mentions a fourfold group of officials, almost identical to the one listed in LXX Deut 29:10: "the heads of your tribes, your elders (29:9: the elders' council), your judges, and your officers." Laberge, "Deutéronome 31," 158, holds that the listing of the LXX "représente mieux la liste ancienne," whereas the MT "témoigne d'une adaptation ou d'une confusion des quatre termes de la liste." Lohfink, "Fabel in Dtn 31-32," 273, deems it more likely that the enumeration of officials in LXX Deut 32:28 represents a

(ii) A conveying of the Song, by Moses and Joshua (Hoshea), באזני העם, "in the people's ears" (32:44).

The existence of an assembly of Israel's notables as a distinct institution is in itself problematic.[170] The communicational context of Moses' convocation also needs to be properly understood. Does Moses address the Levites throughout his speech in Deut 31:26-29? It is quite possible that, beyond the command explicitly formulated to the Levites in 31:26, Moses is addressing the entire people in 31:27-29 (see the use of "you," "For I know how rebellious and stiffnecked you are," etc.).[171] Moreover, does Moses' injunction that the elders and the officers be assembled (31:28) imply a communication of the Song restricted to the latter, as distinct from the rendition to the "people" attested *post facto* in 32:44? Does Moses' intention, ואדברה באזניהם, "that I may speak in their ears," require that the elders and officers only be addressed? Is an intended communication to the people, the ones who are actually rebuked, necessarily excluded? The Hebrew Bible knows situations where the convocation of representatives catalyzes a communication to the entire people. The paradigm, one could say, of such a communicational situation is found in the Sinai pericope in Exod 19:7-8:

> [7]So Moses came and called the elders of the people and set before them all the these words which YHWH had commanded him. [8]And all the people answered together and said, "All that YHWH has spoken we will do."

In Josh 24:1-2, the formal convocation (ויקרא) by Joshua of the "elders of Israel, the heads, the judges, and the officers," takes place within a general assembling of the tribes of Israel:

> [1]Then Joshua gathered all the tribes of Israel to Shechem, and summoned the elders, the heads, the judges, and the officers of Israel; and they presented themselves before God; [2]and Joshua said to all the people ...

---

secondary harmonization based on LXX Deut 29:9 (Nwachukwu, "Textual Differences," 88, adopts Lohfink's view).

[170] Lohfink's survey in "Fabel in Dtn 31-32," 275-78, does not produce any explicit control for the hypothesis.

[171] See C. J. Labuschagne, "The Song of Moses: Its Framework and Structure," *De Fructu Oris Sui: Essays in Honour of Adrianus van Selms* (Pretoria Oriental Series 11; ed. I. H. Eybers et al.; Leiden: Brill, 1971) 88: "Because of the clear reference to the Song in verses 28 and 29, this section can only be taken as an address directed to the people."

In 2 Kings 23:1-2 the convocation of the elders eventuates in a general assembly of the people:

> ¹Then the king sent, and all the elders of Judah and Jerusalem were gathered to him. ²And the king went up to the house of YHWH, and with him all the men of Judah and all the inhabitants of Jerusalem, and the priests and the prophets, all the people, both small and great; and he read in their hearing all the words of the "book" of the covenant which had been found in the house of YHWH.

I therefore consider it likely that in 31:28 Moses summons the elders and officers as the ones who will facilitate the transmission of the Song "in the ears of all the assembly of Israel" (31:30).

f. The Power of the Song—Deut 31:30-32:44

An element in Deuteronomy's communicational plot is rarely noticed: Moses, who has written down the Song (Deut 31:22), conveys it to Israel without reading it out: "Then Moses spoke (וידבר) the words of this Song to the end in the ears of all the assembly of Israel" (31:30).[172] The pattern of writing ⇒ reading, as it is found in Exod 24:4, 7, "Moses wrote (ויכתב) ... then he took the 'book' of the covenant and he read (ויקרא) [it] in the ears of the people," is foreign to Deuteronomy, as far as Moses is concerned. In Deuteronomy the act of reading is consistently projected into Israel's future in the land (see Deut 17:19; 31:11).[173] No reading whatsoever takes place as long as Moses, the prophetic mediator, is present; the mediation of written records is supererogatory as long as prophetic knowledge and channels of transmission can be relied on. The situation will be completely different in post-Mosaic time, when reference to Moses' Torah will be reference to Moses' "book" (see Josh 1:8). For the time being, however, communication means oral communication, without the support of written records. In the scene of the theophany the reader, eavesdropping on the conversation held in the Tent of Meeting, knows

---

[172] Notice the mimetic overlapping between the narrator's description, "Then Moses *spoke* (וידבר)" (Deut 31:30), and Moses' introductory sentence, "Give hear, O heavens, and I will speak (ואדברה)" (32:1).

[173] As to Lohfink's contention that Deuteronomy 5-26 was read from an already written book to the people gathered in Moab, see my remarks above pp. 114-16.

more than the people.[174] Yet this calculated boost for the reader
does not contradict Deuteronomy's basic rule. When it comes to
the "words" that make up the Torah, the principle of reception
is invariable throughout Deuteronomy: the reader knows what is
known by the people. Only (reported) communication performed
and completed (עד תמם) on the narrative stage, to the benefit of
the (then) parties of the covenant, reaches the reader. The conveying of Deuteronomy's comprehensive Torah (i.e., the Torah
supplemented with the Song) has the general shape of a chias-
mus in which the sequence "oral delivery" ⇒ "commitment to
writing" gets inverted. "Die Tora," Lohfink points out, "wird erst
verkündet, dann aufgeschrieben (und zwar עד תמם). Das Moselied
wird erst aufgeschrieben, dann verkündet (und zwar עד תמם)."[175]
However significant, this pattern does not modify the basic situation: the communication of the Torah on the narrative stage is
performed exclusively orally, without the mediation of written
records.

The Song of Moses is primarily meant for times of God's "withdrawal" in his anger at Israel's unfaithfulness. Yet Moses' immediate communication of the Song to the sons of Israel is an eventful transaction, bearing witness to the Song's power. The
publication of the poem's words first prompts a retrospective
assessment by the reader. Eavesdropping on the Song conveyed
to the assembly of Israel, the reader discovers in retrospect that
a knowledge of the Song showed through the surface of YHWH's
speech that introduced it (Deut 31:16-21), as well as in Moses'
warning (31:26-29) that preluded its rendition. While still concealed from the reader, the Song's content was already present in
God's mind (and for good reason!) and in Moses', as appears in
several allusions.[176]

God's disclosure in Deut 31:16-21 is imbued with definite
themes of the Song. Announcing Israel's idolatrous behavior after
Moses' demise, YHWH refers to a prostitution "after the strange
gods of the land (אלהי נכר הארץ)" (31:16); the unusual expression
(instead of the common "other gods," see 31:18.20) is echoed in

---

[174] For a typology of reading positions, see Sternberg, *Poetics*, 163-72.

[175] Lohfink, "Fabel in Dtn 31-32," 271.

[176] Elements of the survey that follows are found in A. Klostermann, *Der Pentateuch: Beiträge zu seinem Verständnis und seiner Entstehungsgeschichte* (Leipzig,
Deichert, 1907) 227-66, and Driver, *Deuteronomy*, 339-81.

the Song, in a statement that emphasizes the gravity of Israel's offense: "YHWH alone did lead [Jacob], and there was no foreign god (אל נכר) with him" (32:12).[177] The process through which the people, growing fat on the land, turn away from the giver of the land is at the core of God's denunciation in the introduction to the Song, as it is in the Song itself. See, for instance, the echoing effect between 31:20, "they are full and have grown fat," and 32:15, "But Jeshurun waxed fat ... you waxed fat, you grew sleek."[178] God's repeated threat to hide his face from the corrupted people in 31:17, 18 comes also to expression in the Song, אסתירה פני מהם, "I will hide my face from them" (32:20).

The same knowledge shows in Moses' admonition (Deut 31:16-29). Moses' intention to "call heaven and earth to witness against them" (31:28) anticipates the Song's overture, which gives the call in question: "Give ear, O heavens, and I will speak; and let the earth hear the words of my mouth" (32:1). The verbal root שחת, "to act corruptly," that occurs in an emphatic form in Moses' convocation speech, "after my death *you will surely act corruptly* (השחת תשחתון)" not only evokes the Golden Calf affair (see above), but also announces the opening theme of the Song: "*They have dealt corruptly* (שחת) with him, they are no longer his children because of their blemish; they are a perverse and crooked generation" (32:5). Moses' prophecy that the people will provoke God to anger (להכעיסו) through the work of their hands foretells God's judgment in the Song, כעסוני בהבליהם "they have provoked me to anger with their idols" (32:21).[179]

The anticipation of some aspects of the Song in God's speech in Deut 31:16-21, as well as in Moses' address in 31:26-29, is often interpreted as a redactional strategy. So is it in Mayes' commentary:

> The verses [31:16-21] have the purpose of giving an interpretation to the Song making it suitable to its present context in Deuteronomy. The Song is interpreted in the section in wholly negative terms as testifying to Yahweh's destructive anger, an interpretation not adequate to the whole Song (cf. especially 32:36ff.), but deliberately

---

[177] No other occurrence of the expression is found in Deuteronomy.

[178] Recurrences of lexical elements are limited to the word דבש, "honey," and to the verbal root אכל, "to eat," in Deut 31:20 and 32:13.

[179] See also God's retaliation in the same verse, "So I will provoke them to jealousy [אכעיסם] with those who are no people."

intended as a means of adapting the Song to its context.[180]

As some interpreters point out, the anticipatory echoes to the Song all refer to the first part of the poem.[181] Comments of this kind, however, overlook the fact that the Song is transmitted to the people by Moses (and Joshua) as authoritative in all its parts, in God's exposure of the people's perverted ways as well as in God's final revenge on behalf of his people. The emphasis by YHWH on the incriminating value of the Song (as עד ב, "witness against") comes up in Deut 31:19 in a communication to Moses and Joshua alone (in a speech in the Tent of Meeting, eaves-dropped on by the reader, and inaccessible to the people). Moses and Joshua are made privy to the value of the Song in God's view—"this Song will be *for me* (לי תהיה) a witness against the peo-ple" (31:19)—and know that the effectiveness of the Song will pri-marily stem from its incriminating power. Moses consistently intro-duces the Song afterwards, if only to avoid ambiguity, as an accusatory piece of speech, "to witness against them" (31:28).

This basic drive of the Song, however, does not preclude its inner developments. This is all the less so, since the poem unfolds a historical dynamic from past to future, as Fisch points out, rehearsing the biblical foundations of history—"Remember the days of old, consider the years of many generations" (Deut 32:7).[182] The Song first revisits the lexical and metaphoric uni-verse of creation (see the opening mention of the "heavens" and the "earth," the "grass" and the "herb"). Next come the Flood, as the phase of corruption (expressed through the verbal root שחת; compare Deut 32:5 and Gen 6:12, 13, 17), and the immediate aftermath of the Flood story (the separation of nations; compare 32:8 and Gen 10:5, 19). A further great disaster in the Genesis record, namely the overthrow of Sodom and Gomorrah, is then echoed. Besides the image of fire (compare Deut 32:22 and Gen

---

[180] Mayes, *Deuteronomy*, 376.

[181] See, for instance, Lohfink, "Bundesschluß," 53-54, about the "authentisch-er Kommentar" given to the Song in Deut 31:16-22; and Braulik, *Deuteronomium II*, 225. Von Rad, *Deuteronomy*, 191, approaches the issue from the perspective of the integral Song and contends that the interpretation of the Song provided in Deuteronomy 31 "is a very arbitrary one, and it must be said that it diminishes to some extent the purport of the Song. For the comforting statements in the Song (vv. 36; 40ff.), if interpreted in this way, no longer come to fruition."

[182] See Fisch, *Poetry*, 72-79.

19:24), the paradigmatic root linked to the "overthrow," הָפַךְ (see Gen 19:21, 25, 29), appears in 32:20, "for they are a perverse generation (דּוֹר תַּהְפֻּכֹת; cf. Deut 29:23)," before the dreaded names of Sodom and Gomorrah are finally uttered (32:32-33).[183] These reminiscences, Fisch goes on, cast a specific historical logic forward:

> The memory by which the Song of Moses kept its power was one of sudden overthrow, turning gladness into mourning. But sudden overthrow can work both ways. The Song of Moses itself ends with a good miracle—a shout of praise goes up from the nations as God takes vengeance on his enemies, making his arrows drunk with blood and thus the evil done in the Land is made good (Deut 32:41-43). That is the real meaning of *hpk*: not only overthrow but the overthrow of overthrow ... This is not the universe of eternal forms that the Greeks knew, but a created universe, created suddenly by a word of power, and as such it is a place of extraordinary surprises.[184]

One of the surprising aspects of the Song is that the reversal in God's attitude towards his people takes place without any Mosaic intervention. At Horeb, it was Moses' intercession—"And I prayed to YHWH, 'O YHWH God, destroy not your people and your heritage'" (9:26)—which obtained the people's pardon: "And YHWH hearkened to me that time also" (9:19). The motive Moses put forward in his entreaty, that Egypt would misunderstand God's punishment of Israel (see 9:28), is echoed in YHWH's speech in the Song: "I would have said, 'I will scatter them afar, I will make the remembrance of them cease from among men,' had I not feared provocation by the enemy, lest their adversaries should judge amiss, lest they should say, 'Our hand is triumphant, YHWH has not wrought all this'" (32,26-27). God thus seems to have interiorized the Mosaic plea. What Moses obtained at Horeb now belongs to YHWH's attitude towards Israel, and the Song records it for ever.

Since the Song has been explicitly transmitted עַד תֻּמָּם, "to the very end," it must be assumed that the unexpected turn of the Song and its ending, praising God for having vindicated his servants, belongs to its full function as witness. As I shall now indi-

---

[183] On the function of the Sodom-Gomorrah motive in the context of the song as a hint at YHWH's coming judgement and at an imminent catastrophy, see Labuschagne, "Song of Moses," 96-97.

[184] Fisch, *Poetry*, 78-79.

cate, the transmission of the Song *in extenso* leads up to final comments by Moses which have positive accents. In his comments Moses subtly echoes the final developments of the poem. Summing up the importance of the Song and of the Torah for Israel, he concludes: "For it is not a trifling word (דבר) for you, but it is your life (חייכם), and thereby you shall live long in the 'land' (אדמה) which you are going over the Jordan to possess" (Deut 32:47). The theme of "life" belongs to God's final and solemn assertions in the Song; see 32:39, אני אמית ואחיה, "I kill and I make live"; 32:40, ואמרתי חי אנכי לעלם, "and I swear, as I live for ever." In his introduction to the Song Moses saw the people's future from the point of view of death, that is, his own (see 31:27, 29). Moses' final reference to the people's long life in the "land" (אדמה) (32:47) subtly echoes the final words of the Song, inviting the nations to praise God, who "makes expiation for the land [אדמתו] of his people" (32:43). Long life on the land is conceivable, in spite of everything, but only in the wake of God's promise to intervene for that same land. That Moses eventually regains hopeful perspectives on Israel's "long life" in the land may thus be seen as a result of the Song's inner *peripeteia*. The reversal announced in the Song has affected its transmitter.

g. *"All Has Been Heard"—Deut 32:45-47*

Deut 32:45-47 could be paraphrased with Qohelet's sentence: "The end of the matter; all has been heard" (Qoh 12:13). With the rendering of the Song that now supplements the Torah, Moses has brought his mission of transmission to completion. A conclusive exhortation makes this clear, but it also reveals Moses' ultimate change of posture as to the "words" he transmitted. Moses' final words are prefaced with a significant heading by the narrator, a heading which multiplies the "markers of completion": "And when Moses had finished (ויכל) speaking all (כל) these words to all (כל) Israel" (32:45).[185] In the narrator's reporting, the completion of the oral communication of the Horeb-Moab revelation

---

[185] See already the conclusion to the communication of the Song in the previous verse: "Moses came and recited all (כל) the words of this Song in the hearing of the people, he and Hoshea the son of Nun" (Deut 32:44). See also the recurrence of כל in Moses' quoted admonition in 32:46: "all (כל) the words which I attest ... all (כל) the words of this Torah."

parallels the completion of the process through which the same revelation was written down: "And when Moses had finished (ויכל) speaking" (32:45) answers "And when Moses had finished (ככלות) writing" (31:24).[186] Moses' *grand oeuvre* in Deuteronomy—the communication of the Torah (opened in 5:1 [4:44])—has come to an end.

Moses' concluding exhortation in Deut 32:44-47 is a subtle weaving of the theme of the Song with the theme of the Torah,[187] in a way reminiscent of his alternate injunctions in 31:26-29. A reference to the Song paves the way for a reference to "all the words of this Torah."[188] But Moses' final speech is also a surprising combination of the perspective linked to the revelation in the theophany in 31:14-29 with the perspective attached in 31:9-13 to the reading of the written Torah:

From this combined perspective, the illocutionary act of העיד ב, "to witness against," resurfaces in Moses' final exhortation. In Deut 31:28 the verb announced the communication of the Song: "that I may speak these words in their ears and call heaven and earth to witness against them (ואעידה בם)."[189] In 32:46, the appropriate reception of the Song is described by Moses: "Lay heart to all the words that I have attested against you (מעיד בכם) this day" (32:46). The incriminating power of the Song is (still) its *raison d'être*, as God made clear in the revelation in the Tent of Meeting (31:19).

Yet the function of the Song is now subordinated to a further purpose: ""Lay to heart all the words that I have attested against you this day, that you may command them to your children, *that they may be careful to do all the words of this Torah*" (Deut 32:46). Saying so, Moses takes up the perspective that was attached to the written Torah in 31:9-13. A positive link (of implementation) to

---

[186] In both parts, the verb of completion (כלה) is followed by the verb שׂים, "to put, to lay," describing a step toward the reception process. In Deut 31:26, Moses commands the Levites to lay (ושׂמתם) the comprehensive Torah "book" beside the ark (cf. 10:2.5); in 32:46, Moses instructs his addressees to "lay heart (שׂימו לבבכם) to all [his] words" (cf. 11:18).

[187] See von Rad, *Deuteronomy*, 201.

[188] See Lohfink, "Bundesschluß," 51 n. 70: "Während in 31,24-39 zuerst von der Tora, dann vom Lied gehandelt wird, schließt chiastisch hinter dem Moseslied zunächst das Motiv 'Lied' an, dann kommt als äußerer Rahmen das Motiv 'Tora'."

[189] See Lohfink, "Bundesschluß," 51 n. 70.

the Torah "words" is thus restored. Moses' instruction in 32:46 literally echoes his genuine provisions as to the reception of the written Torah (31:12)—הזאת התורה דברי כל את לעשות לשמור / ושמרו, "and that they may be careful to do all the words of this Torah." The "words" of the Torah that in 31:26-27 were reduced to revealing Israel's rebellion are again destined for faithful implementation. As in 31:13, transmission to the next generation constitutes Moses' basic concern.[190] The perspective of "long life in the land," which the revelation of the theophany thoroughly questioned, resurfaces in Moses' final warning. Here too, Moses quotes himself, in a literal echo of 31:13: שמה הירדן את עברים אתם אשר האדמה על לרשתה, "in the land which you are going over the Jordan to possess" (32:47).

Deut 32:45-47 thus appears as the reconciliation of Moses' plain injunctions in 31:9-13, meant for a faithful people prolonging its life in the land, with Moses' agonizing stipulations in 31:24-29, determined by the revelation of the people's imminent unfaithfulness to the covenant. Paradoxically enough, it is apparently the Song which enables such a reconciled perspective. As Casper Labuschagne puts it, Moses' addressees are advised "to take all the words of the *Song* to heart so that they may observe the *law*."[191] In its "cathartic" function, the Song that exposes the people's unfaithfulness is now adjuvant to the people's faithfulness to the Torah.

4. *Conclusion*

Whereas my previous chapters surveyed data distributed over large stretches of Deuteronomy, the present one tackled the whole of Deut 31:1-32:47 as a narrative unit (within the greater unit that opened in 28:69, "These are the words of the covenant ..."). The issue at stake was to verify, precisely, the *narrative* character of the text in question, within the overall context of Deuteronomy. Is Deuteronomy 31 a collection of "débris of tradition" with no "real advance in the narrative," as von Rad contends?[192] Does Deuteron-

---

[190] See Braulik, *Deuteronomium II*, 235-36.
[191] Labuschagne, "Song of Moses," 91. See already Sforno in his comment on Deut 32:45.
[192] Von Rad, *Deuteronomy*, 190.

omy 29-32 really avoid "Erzählung," as Lohfink asserts?[193] Do Deuteronomy 31 and the following chapters constitute a mere "appendix" grafted on to the previous chapters, as Mayes holds?[194] I showed that Deut 31:1-32:47 embodies a proper, albeit subtle, narrative logic, deeply connected with what precedes it in the book. As far as communication is concerned, Deut 31:1-32:47 even features Deuteronomy's most determining *peripeteiae*. They are worth a final summing up.

"Of making many 'books' there is no end," Qohelet warns (Qoh 12:12). In Deuteronomy 31 Moses goes through the agony of bringing a single prophetic "book" to completion. When it comes to the limits of a work, a writing prophet who conveys divine revelation does not enjoy the freedom of other writers. "So I will here end my story," the compiler of the Second Book of Maccabees announces (2 Mac 15:37). Unlike the author who freely puts an end to his account, the prophetic writer is hanging upon God's will to close or supplement what needs to be closed or supplemented. Of prophecy, as of every thing that exists in time, God is the one who knows "the beginning, the end and the middle" (see Wis 7:18); and only the narrator, not the prophet, really knows whether or not "God added no more."

Emulating God's writing of the tables, Moses commits the Torah to the only medium—writing—that guarantees a foolproof transmission of his words beyond himself, that is, beyond the Jordan River. The crossing itself is primarily the work of Joshua, the "one who crosses before [the people]" (Deut 31:3), who himself is preceded by God. In Joshua's wake the Torah will reach the land. It is no wonder that Moses entrusts the precious record to the Levites, the carriers of the ark: the impulse imparted by God to their journey toward the land is thus communicated to the Torah itself. Along with the Levites, the elders are in charge of the periodical and public reading of the Torah, which brings about nothing less than a new Horeb. Such are Moses' provisions, enabling the Torah words to pervade Israel's future time and space.

Convoking Moses and Joshua to the Tent of Meeting, God leaves Israel's leader and his successor with no illusion about the people's future time and space: they are the framework of the peo-

---

[193] Lohfink, "Bundesschluß," 55.
[194] See Mayes, *Deuteronomy*, 371.

ple's unfaithfulness. Moses' departure will prompt the people's infidelity just as his being away on the mountain led to their breach of faith in the Golden Calf affair. Moses, who writes down divine revelation, somehow revisits the story of the written tables and of the Golden Calf. Like Horeb, like Moab: further writing is required. At the close of the people's rebellion at Horeb, God had to write again—he wrote a copy of the first tables; the revelation in Moab of the people's future rebellion eventuates in Moses' further writing—the writing down of the Song. The Song is, so to speak, the reality principle attached to the Torah. Deposited with the Torah on the side of the ark, it will confront the sons of Israel in their unfaithfulness wherever they are. In its incriminating power the Song will turn even the Torah into a witness, attesting against the people who refuse to comply with it. Yet the Song, like the bronze serpent erected in the desert, has also a "cathartic" virtue. It can restore the sons' relationship to the Torah as life-giving commandment.

Announcing the people's rebellion, God presents it as a forthcoming process linked to Moses' imminent death. The revelation to the prophet is therefore also a revelation *ad hominem*, given Moses' reluctance to accept the fate God had imposed on him. What follows in Deuteronomy focuses on the issue of Moses' demise—and so will my next chapter.

CHAPTER FIVE

"BEFORE HIS DEATH" (DEUT 32:48-34:12)

> With peace and consolation hath dismist, and
> calm of mind, all passion spent.
>
> John Milton, *Samson Agonistes*

Moses' concluding exhortation in Deut 32:45-47, setting the Torah
at the center of the people's life, is followed by a blunt speech
by YHWH to his prophet (Deut 32:48-52). In this speech God set-
tles in plain terms the complex issue with which Moses struggled
throughout Deuteronomy: his non-crossing of the Jordan River,
his death at God's command, and the reason for these. Deuteronomy's final chapters then tell how Moses carries out YHWH's
re-expressed will. In other words, the narrative focus has shifted
from the Torah—its communication completed and its transfer to
the land properly assured—to the Torah's prophet. After having
centered on crossing characters and on the Torah "book" as a
crossing device, the narrative now focuses on the one who will
not cross. The difference in narrative relevance is best understood
through a consideration of the status of the words uttered by
Moses. The words of the Torah and the words of the Song were
explicitly meant to be conveyed, copied, read, proclaimed and
memorized in another time and place; the words Moses utters in
Deuteronomy 33—his blessing of the tribes—may have a large
range of futurity, but drive their uniqueness from their being pronounced by Moses in Moab "before his death" (Deut 33:1).
Deuteronomy's central issue—the communication of the Torah—
has been brought to its end. Another issue comes to the fore—
that of Moses' end. As it turns out, Moses' end concurs with the
end of Deuteronomy's narrative. In my last chapter I will bring
out the complex relationship between what is consummated on
the narrative stage—Moses' communication, and Moses' life—and
the ending of the book that reports such conclusive events. In the
present chapter I will draw attention to the narrative dynamics of
Deut 32:48-34:12, that is, the dynamics of what happens after

Moses had finished writing and speaking "all these words" (31:24 and 32:45).

In the general structure of Deuteronomy, marked off by the four headings, Deut 32:48-52 occupies a particular situation. Rather than making sense within the unit opened by the heading in 28:69, "These are the words of the covenant," the passage announces and prepares for what follows the heading of 33:1, "This is the blessing with which Moses the man of God blessed the sons of Israel before his death."[1] Yet this peculiar situation echoes a textual phenomenon already encountered. The heading in 4:44, "This is the Torah," is also preceded by a narratorial intervention that marks a break with the preceding Mosaic speeches. In 4:41-43 the narrator reports the setting apart of the three cities of refuge "in the east beyond the Jordan" (4:41). As I showed above, this setting apart is the first of the Mosaic provisions in Transjordan to be reported in Deuteronomy. In this sense, 4:41-43 provides a stepping-stone to the collection of stipulations that follows. But this first batch of measures concerns the eastern bank of the Jordan River; it is of no relevance, unlike the rest of Moses' decrees, for the "land" west of the Jordan. The specific bearing of Moses' first stipulation is signalled by the fact that Moses' assignment of the cities of refuge in the east is recorded before the heading of 4:44, that is, before the reporting of the Torah "to be carried away" in the west. The function of 4:41-43 is mirrored in the function of 32:48-52, at the close of the communication of the Torah. Starting with 32:48, the Deuteronomic narrative re-focuses on "Moses in Moab," and on the words and deeds that take place there. True, Moses' blessing describes the tribes in their future in the land, but it does so as a prophecy uttered outside the land, and not meant to be "reproduced" in the land. As far as communication is concerned, the general structure of Deuteronomy can therefore be outlined as follows:

1:1-4:43   "Words" not meant to enter the Torah "book"

                        4:41-43
                        Stipulations for Transjordan

4:44-28:68   "Words" destined to make up the Torah "book"

---

[1] See Lohfink, "Bundesschluß," 55: "Wir können 32:48-52 als sachgemäße Überleitung zu dieser Uuberschrift [Deut 33:1] hin betrachten."

28:69-32:47   The covenant "on" the Torah "book," supplemented by
               the Song.

                              32:48-52
                              *God repeats that Moses must die in Trans-
                              jordan*

33:1-34:12   "Words" not meant to enter the Torah "book"[2]

1. *"And Die There on the Mountain"—Deut 32:48-52*

Having completed his prophetic mission, Moses is addressed by
God "that very day" (Deut 32:48). God's speech to Moses in
32:48-52 opens with an order—"Ascend this mountain of Abarim"—which brings Moses and the reader back to well-known
themes. In more than one sense God resumes the story where
Moses ended his retelling of the people's journey after Horeb. In
the final verse of Deuteronomy 3 Moses recalls that the journey
ended at the place of the people's current encampment (and the
place from which Moses is speaking)—"So we remained in the
valley opposite to Beth-peor" (3:29). In the previous verses
(3:26-28), Moses tells how God had asked him, after his abortive
plea to cross over with the people, to "go up to the top of Pisgah" (3:27),[3] to see in all its extent the land into which he will
not enter, to appoint Joshua as a successor, and to encourage him
in his double task as conqueror and allotter of the land. As I indicated in the previous chapter, Moses is thereby retelling a divine
injunction that the narrator first reported in Num 27:12-14—the
order to go up the mountain, see the land, and be reunited with
his people—and the command to appoint Joshua in Num
27:15-51.[4] As far as Joshua's installation is concerned, God's order
has been immediately fulfilled by Moses (see Num 27:22-23). However, God's injunction that Moses ascend "the mountain of

---

[2] Notice the presence of a connective *waw* at the beginning of both Deut 4:44
and 33:1, that is, in both the headings preceded by a brief narratorial account.

[3] About the geographical identity of "Pisgah," "Mount Nebo," and "the mountain of the Abarim," see Weinfeld, *Deuteronomy*, 186 and 191-92: "Pisgah is the top
of Mount Nebo (34:1), which is situated on the heights of the Abarim (cf. 32:49)"
(pp. 191-92).

[4] See Driver, *Deuteronomy*, 61: "Nu. 27[12-14] is parallel to v.[27] here, and Nu. 27[15-21]
to v.[28]." See also Dogniez and Harl, *Deutéronome*, 132.

CHAPTER FIVE

Abarim" (Num 27:12) has not, thus far, been echoed in the narrative. No enactment of such a commandment is recorded in the Book of Numbers.[5] The order, therefore, is still awaiting fulfillment when Moses mentions it in Deut 3:27.

The interesting point in the long sentence of 3:27, whereby Moses communicates to the people what was so far a revelation known to him alone (see Num 27:12, "YHWH said to Moses"), is Moses' way of reproducing God's speech.[6] In rehearsing what he heard from God's mouth, Moses produces a crafty montage summarizing God's double intervention (Num 27:12-14; 18-21), yet omitting the motif of his own death and the rationale for it given by God. These two elements were explicitly stated by God in Num 27:13-14:

> [13]And when you have seen [the land], you also shall be gathered to your people, as your brother Aaron was gathered, [14]because you rebelled against my order (פי) in the wilderness of Zin during the strife of the congregation, to sanctify me at the waters before their eyes.' (These are the waters of Meribat-Qadesh in the wilderness of Zin).

In Deut 32:48-52 God's direct intervention on the narrative stage brings about, once more, a "return of the repressed." Re-expressing his initial command, "Go up into this mountain of Abarim," God fills in the gaps contrived in Moses' quotation. The astute reporter is straightforwardly reminded of the data he has kept back. God is even more direct here than in his original injunction. The periphrasis in Num 27:13, "you also shall be gathered to your people," is now prefaced with a direct "and die on the mountain which you ascend" (Deut 32:50). The rationale for Moses' fate is also adduced, in conformity with what God said in Num 27:13. The reason for Moses' death outside the land has received special attention in source-critical exegesis; it will therefore be discussed at some length in the following paragraphs.

In its formulation in Deut 32:51, the reason for Moses' death in the Transjordan contrasts blatantly with the reason put forward thus far in Deuteronomy (in 1:37; 3:26; 4:21). In the latter passages Moses' non-entering into the land is presented as the price

---

[5] Cf. the immediate enforcement of God's command to go up the mountain when it comes to Aaron's death in Num 20:25-28.

[6] On the highly stategic nature of quotation, that is, of reproduction of speech by speech, see M. Sternberg, "Proteus in Quotation-Land," 107-56.

that he was forced to pay for the people's refusal to go up to the land after the episode of the twelve spies (see 1:20-45). In 32:51, on the contrary, Moses' fate is determined by his (and Aaron's) behavior at Meribat-Qadesh, when God answered the people's contention about the lack of water (see Num 20:1-13; cf. Exod 17:1-7). The difference between the perspective developed in Deuteronomy 1-4 and the view presented in 32:48-52 usually receives an explanation in terms of *Redaktionsgeschichte*: whereas the motif of Moses' non-entering in Deuteronomy 1-4 constitutes a Deuteronomistic elaboration, the notice in 32:48-52 represents a late interpolation by the Priestly redactor.[7] Arguments are produced that establish the motif of Moses' death outside the land undergoing a hermeneutical reinterpretation in order to harmonize it with the "priestly" doctrine of individual responsibility.[8] Yet there is no reason to suppose that the redactors responsible for reinterpretations of this kind were lacking the narrative concern, and genius, of their predecessors. After all, the appropriate way to supplement a narrative is to supplement it narratively. An ideological reinterpretation (such as a new emphasis on individual responsibility) must be artfully woven into the overall narrative[9] in order to be effectively conveyed to the readers.[10] Deuterono-

---

[7] See for instance M. Noth, *Überlieferungsgeschichtliche Studien*, 190-206, and most of the ensuing commentaries. Contrast the divergent opinion expressed by L. Perlitt, "Priesterschrift im Deuteronomium?," ZAW (Supplement) 100 (1988), 65-88. See also P. Stoellger, "Deuteronomium 34 ohne Priesterschrift," *ZAW* 105 (1993) 26-51, who ascribes Deut 32:48-52 to a late Deuteronomistic redaction, presupposing the priestly texts of Numbers 27.

[8] Rose, "Empoigner le Pentateuque," 138, elaborates on the ideological difference between the two traditions: "En comparant [les] textes deutéronomistes avec ceux qui sont empreints du style sacerdotal (Nb 27,12-13 et Dt 32,48-52), il faut constater que selon la pensée sacerdotale Moïse doit porter les conséquences de ses *propres* péchés *individuels* ... . La pensée de P, influencée par l'idée d'une responsabilité *individuelle* qui s'exprime programmatiquement aussi dans le livre du prophète de l'exil, Ezéchiel (ch. 18), ne supporte plus cette réponse à peine suffisante qui recourt aux péchés collectifs. Mourir à l'extérieur du pays promis, c'est (pour la pensée sacerdotale) un malheur éclatant, et ce malheur doit être expliqué de manière individuelle. Un concept théologique précis demande la modification de l'interprétation de l'histoire."

[9] See Alter's considerations on the biblical narrative as "composite artistry," *Biblical Narrative*, 131-54.

[10] This must be especially true if a string of texts, namely Num 20:1-13; 27:12-14 and Deut 32:48-52, derives from the (Priestly) reinterpretation in question. On the relationship of theses texts, see Rose' discussion of Noth's hypotheses ("Empoigner le Pentateuque," 134-37), and Blum, *Studien*, 271-78.

my's implied readers are not supposed to know the other side of
the textual tapestry, i. e., the ideological and hermeneutical history of its making; they are supposed to make sense of the narrative data, however puzzling they may appear. The pinpointing
of redactional or editorial transformations therefore calls for a
greater attention to the thrust, and to the subtleties, of the narrative itself.

The question now is whether the contrasting views of Moses'
non-crossing, coherently explained from a genetic perspective,
also have a narrative rationale. Actually, a major narrative parameter—a difference in level of narration—is here of prime relevance. Deut 1:37; 3:26; 4:21 are voiced by a secondary, and human,
locutor, Moses; in Deut 32:48-52, Deuteronomy's primary locutor,
the omniscient narrator, reproduces God's voice in direct speech.
The difference is, first of all, a difference in reliability.[11] The combination of God's and the narrator's voices in 32:48-52 provides
the reader with an authorized point of reference, to which he
may safely appeal in order to assess and motivate Moses' version
of the facts.[12] Moses' retelling in Deuteronomy 1-3 includes a significant organizational element. The rationale provided by Moses
for God's decision about his fate does not occur within God's
reported speech; it belongs to Moses' appraisal of the matter:
"With me also YHWH was angry because of you (בגללכם)" (1:37);
the same discursive situation is found in 3:26, "but YHWH was
angry with me owing to you (למענכם)," and in 4:21, "YHWH was
angry with me on your account (על דבריכם)." As to YHWH's own
words, "you also shall not go in there" (1:37),they can be read in
two ways. They can first be understood as implying the inclusion
of Moses in the fate of the rebellious generation. This is apparently Moses' interpretation of God's words. By saying "With me
also (גם בי) YHWH was angry" and by putting forward God's state-

---

[11] In his essay, "The Problem of Individual and Community in Deuteronomy
1:6-3:29," *Theology of the Pentateuch: Themes of the Priestly Narrative and Deuteronomy*
(Minneapolis: Fortress, 1994), 227-33, N. Lohfink approaches the issue in a
non-genetic perspective, addressing the texts of Deuteronomy 1-3 *per modum unius*,
yet without taking into account the difference in levels of enunciation I just indicated. Lohfink is accordingly constrained to put forward an unfathomable divine
logic: "Without giving a simple reason, God associates Moses with the sinful generation, but then does not destroy him along with it; instead, God gives him new
tasks in order, finally, to include him once again in the fate of that generation"
(p. 230).
[12] See Sternberg, *Poetics*, 413.

ment, "You also (גַם אַתָּה) shall not go in there," Moses maintains that God has passed to the prophetic leader the judgment that had been laid on the desert generation: "Not one of these men of this evil generation shall see the good land which I swore to give to your fathers" (Deut 1:35; see Num 14:30).[13] This raises, however, the question of God's justice, since, as Lohfink points out, "Moses' innocence [has] been brought out by the earlier text ... It appears that the tradition connected with the narrative of the scouts, as far as we can judge, does not contain a divine punishment pronounced against Moses."[14] But YHWH's words "You also shall not go in there" can equally represent a divine oath that makes clear Moses' final fate and that has no causal relationship with the people's refusal to enter the land in the affair of the spies. What Moses puts forward in his retelling is definitely an explanation of his personal fate by means of Israel's collective fate, that is, by the sin of the desert generation and by the punishment divinely meted out to them.

In his blunt intervention in Deut 32:49-52, God formulates a totally different rationale for Moses' non-entering into the land and for his death in Transjordan. Moses' destiny is now related to another fateful episode of the journey in the wilderness—the affair of the waters of Meribah (see the account of the events in Num 20:1-13, and God's statement in Num 27:12-14).[15] In God's verdict the indictment of Moses has no link at all with the sin of

---

[13] See Driver, *Deuteronomy*, 27-28, who regards the phrase "you also" as a way to include Moses "in the same sentence with the rest." In his third mention of the affair Moses puts forward such a connection without, however, quoting God, but rather by resorting to indirect speech: "Furthermore YHWH was angry with me on your account, and he swore that I should not cross (וַיִּשָּׁבַע לְבִלְתִּי עָבְרִי) the Jordan, and that I should not enter the good land which YHWH your God gives you for an inheritance. For I must die in this land" (Deut 4:21-22).

[14] Lohfink, "Problem," 228; Lohfink goes on: "Here we seem to be facing the author's own contribution. This author's desire to think of history in a thoroughly theological sense, and his ability to consider the most varied elements of the tradition together, in a collection of representative individual narratives, is at work here" (p. 228).

[15] The mention of Meribah in Deut 32:51 is the first occurrence of the toponym in Deuteronomy (a second mention occurs in 33:8, coordinated with Massah, as in Exod 17:7). Two previous references to the incident, with no allusion to Moses' intervention, are found in 6:16 and 9:22, with the simple locative Massah. The spatial determination in 32:51—"the waters of Meribat-Qadesh"—echoes the episode as told in Num 20:1-13: "These are the waters of Meribah, where the people of Israel contended with YHWH, and he showed himself holy among them" (Num 20:13).

the desert generation. On the contrary, it reaches back to an
episode Moses withheld in his retelling.

> Because you broke faith with me in the midst of the people of Israel
> at the waters of Meribath-Qadesh in the desert of Zin; because you
> did not revere me as holy in the midst of the people of Israel. (32:51)

God reminds Moses that it is a personal incident, not the people's sin, that has determined his (and Aaron's) destiny.[16] Was
Moses deliberately misleading his audience when he gave his version of the facts? Did he try to deceive himself as well as the people?[17] The reader has to reassess Moses' claim. This claim is no
forthright lie. Moses' attempt to include himself in the short-
comings of the exodus generation is fairly legitimate, by ideological (if not quite by factual) standards. Prior to the fateful episode
at the waters of Meribah, Moses could believe he was also included in the generation banned from the land (Joshua and Caleb
are the only individuals for whom God explicitly makes an exception [see Num 14:24, 30]). Also, we must not forget it is the people's muttering that led to Moses' eventual striking—hence, again,
a justification of sorts for "on your account." Yet Moses' claim is
also a way of circumventing a most personal and humiliating incident that pertains to his specific call—his vocation of mediating
God's word.

Moses hears God's indictment in Deut 32:51 articulated as a
terse reminder—"for you broke faith with me in the midst of the
people of Israel at the waters of Meribat-Qadesh, in the wilderness of Zin." Moses apparently does not need further elaboration;
the reader's memory may need to be refreshed. Num 20:10-12
refrains from making Moses' offense explicit; yet the narrative is

---

[16] It therefore becomes impossible to construe the three passages of Deut 1:37;
3:26; 4:21 as fostering a theology of vicarious punishment, which presents Moses
as a servant suffering for the sake of the people. On the idea of vicarious punishment, see especially von Rad, *Deuteronomy*, 209-10; Buis, *Deutéronome*, 434; G. W.
Coats, *Rebellion in the Wilderness: The Murmuring Motif in the Wilderness Traditions
of the Old Testament* (Nashville: Abington, 1968) 79-81; Rose, "Empoigner le Pentateuque," 137-38. See especially Olson, *Deuteronomy*, which is entirely built on this
assumption (see pp. 97, 123-124, 150, 158; but cf. 165).

[17] Moses somehow betrays himself when he tells of the fulfillment of God's
judgment on the generation of the desert: "So when all the men of war had per-
ished and were dead from among the people, YHWH said to me ..." (Deut
2:16-17). How come Moses is now dissociated—with no comment about his specific case—from the fate of the punished generation?

fraught with concurrent hints. Discrepancies between God's order
and Moses' execution lead to the identification of Moses' mis-
deed.[18] Moses and Aaron are asked to "speak (ודברתם) to the rock
before the eyes [of the people] to yield its water" (Num 20:8). In
front of the assembled people Moses first utters words that are
best understood as an expression of holy wrath: "Hear now, you
rebels; shall we bring forth water for you out of this rock?" (Num
20:10).[19] Giving way to his anger, Moses next strikes the rock,
rather than faithfully performing God's command; and he does
so repeatedly, "as if to underline the need of a forceful physical
action."[20] "At the waters of Meribat-Qadesh (קדש)," Moses (and,
behind him, Aaron) thus failed to sanctify (קדשתם) YHWH by dis-
trusting the omnipotent power of God's word.[21] "Is this not the
test," Ackerman asks: "Does Moses sufficiently believe in YHWH's
word (see 11:23), and does he believe that his words approximate
the power of that word? Ironically, the sole mediator of YHWH's
words does not fully trust the word he embodies (see 27:14). He
reverts to his wonder-working staff—striking, as he had done
before the divine words were spoken at Sinai."[22]

---

[18] See S. E. Loewenstamm, *From Babylon to Canaan: Studies in the Bible and its Oriental Background* (Jerusalem: Magnes, 1992) 142; Sternberg, *Poetics*, 107.

[19] See Blum, *Studien*, 273-74.

[20] Loewenstamm, *From Babylon*, 142. In Exod 17:6 Moses was explicitly enjoined to hit the rock: "and you shall strike the rock, and water shall come out of it, that the people may drink. And Moses did so, in the sight of the elders of Israel." God's order in Exod 17:6 does not contradict the different request by YHWH in Numbers 20 since the two narratives, in Exodus and in Numbers, claim to record two different events. The "Massah and Meribah" event (Exodus 17) takes place in the wilderness of Sin, that is, in the Sinai Peninsula ("Horeb," see 17:6), at Rephidim, before the giving of the Torah at Sinai; the "Meribah" event (Num 20:1-13; "Meribat Qadesh" in Num 27:14 and Deut 32:51) takes place during the people's journey in the wilderness of Zin, that is, near the southern border of Canaan, after the event at Sinai, and is linked to the people's sojourn in Kadesh. A hypothesis of redactional reinterpretation, referring the two stories to a single "genuine" tradition, cannot obliterate the narrative data. Narratively speaking, the recurrence of an event oddly similar to a previous one is rather the point, and it becomes Moses' test. By hitting the rock in Qadesh (Numbers 20), Moses simply reproduces a successful past performance. He fails to adjust his response to God's new, and different, request.

[21] See God's own interpretation of the facts in Num 27:14, "because you rebelled (מריתם) against my voice (פי) in the wilderness of Zin during the strife of the congregation, to sanctify me at the waters before their eyes."

[22] J. S. Ackerman, "Numbers," *The Literary Guide to the Bible* (ed. R. Alter and F. Kermode; Cambridge: Harvard University Press, 1987) 84. See also Loewenstamm, *From Babylon*, 142.

When it comes to Moses, the divine justice thus hinges entirely on the faithfulness of the mediator to God's expressed word
(and not, for instance, on the achievements of the leader). Is it
partiality (after all, the affair of the spies in Numbers 13-14 is of
greater national import)? Or is it, on the contrary, paradoxical
divine "fair play"—God's resolution to incriminate Moses only on
that which really counts in his personal mission, his faithfulness
to the divine word?[23] God's reminder in Deut 32:51, coming just
after the transmission of the Song, and after Moses' final remarks
about the lifegiving power of the word—"for it is no trifling word
(דבר רק) for you, but it is your life" (32:47)—is all the more acute.
It is God now who strikes the blow, and, once more, gets things
straight in Moses' conscience and memory. Yet Moses, now that
he has brought his mission as mediator of the Torah to completion and has transmitted the awesome Song,[24] is also a man ready
to hear blunt truths on his life and on his death. He is, as he will
be called in Deut 33:1, "the man of God."

2. "So Moses, the Servant of YHWH, Died There"—Deut 33:1-34:7

The very fact that Moses blesses the "sons of Israel" (Deut 33:1,
בני ישראל), that is, the Israelite tribes, testifies to his readiness to
comply with God's fateful order. In the biblical world the blessing of "sons"[25] is a valedictory speech act through which someone prepares for his own death.[26] In auguring to each tribe its
respective destiny in the land, and in entrusting it to YHWH's
care,[27] Moses expresses his acceptance of the parting of the ways.
Whereas the Song delivered in Deuteronomy 32 somehow accord-
ed with the agony of its transmitter, the blessing breathes the

---

[23] This, in my view, would represent the narrative embodiment of the redactional hypothesis concerning individual responsibility discussed above.

[24] Is it a mere coincidence if God is repeatedly called "the rock" (צור) in the
Song (see 32:4, 15, 18, 30, 31)? Num 20:1-13, indeed, uses the synonym סלע; yet
the latter also occurs in the Song in Deut 32:13, "and [YHWH] made him suck
honey out of the rock (סלע), and oil out of the flinty rock (צור חלמיש)."

[25] Although Moses does not stand in the position of the tribes' "father," he
somehow complies with the patriarchal genre. On this issue, see my next chapter.

[26] See Gen 27:4, 7, 10 (Isaac); 49:28-30 (Jacob), and my next chapter.

[27] The dimension of prayer, whereby Moses associates most of the tribes with
YHWH's benediction or protection (as against the more "secular" blessing of
Jacob in Genesis 49) has been emphasized by von Rad, *Deuteronomy*, 208.

serenity of the one who is giving the blessing.[28] "Happy are you, O Israel! Who is like you, a people saved by YHWH, the shield of your help, and the sword of your triumph!" (33:29).

Moses' acceptance of God's will is especially salient in the narrative of his death in Deuteronomy 34. The narrator presents Moses' last deeds as a literal fulfillment of God's orders.[29] No longer stalling or rephrasing, Moses straightforwardly complies with God's word:

Deut 32:48-52 (God to Moses)			Deut 34:1-6 (the narrator)		
v.49a	עלה	"Go up"	v.1a	ויעל	"And [Moses] went up"
v.49b	וראה	"and see"	v.1b	ויראהו	"And [YHWH] made him see"
v.50a	ומת	"and die"	v.5	וימת	"and [Moses] died"

Moses' literal complying is further emphasized by the narrator's comment: "Moses died there ... *at the 'command' of YHWH* (עַל פִּי יהוה)" (34:5). Moses is thereby "inverting" the point of God's accusation in Num 27:14, "because you rebelled against my 'word' (מרמתם פִּי) in the wilderness of Zin." Moses indeed breathes his last, in total obedience to God's word—to the divine imperative ומת, "and die" (32:50). This in itself represents a climax in biblical and human experience.[30] Aaron was given notice of his imminent death (Num 20:24); the order to die falls to Moses' lot. God's immediacy to his prophet and the prophet's adherence to God's word could hardly go further.[31] The narrator dispels any misunderstanding as to the quality of Moses' determination to obey. Moses' readiness is in no way mixed with the pragmatic motives of someone whose natural death draws near: "Moses was a hundred and twenty years old when he died; his eye was not dim, nor his natural force abated" (34:7).[32] In so saying, the narrator also

---

[28] See Driver, *Deuteronomy*, 385-89.

[29] See R. Lux, "Der Tod des Moses als 'besprochene und erzählte Welt': Überlegungen zu einer literaturwissenschaftlichen und theologischen Interpretation von Deuteronomium 32:48-52 und 34," *ZTK* 84 (1987) 401.

[30] In the Hebrew Bible, a second occurrence of the imperative is found in Job 2:9, on the lips of a human character, Job's wife, and in a rather different "language game": "Do you still hold fast your integrity?," she says, needling her husband, "Bless [curse] God, and die (וָמֻת)" (Job 2:9).

[31] Moses' undivided obedience is answered by God's burying of his prophet; on this issue, see the considerations in my next chapter, pp. 224.

[32] See my comments on this verse in the next chapter, p. 208, n. 23.

corrects what Moses gave in 31:2 as a motive for his being suc-
ceeded by Joshua, "I am a hundred and twenty years old this day;
I am no longer able to go out and come in" (31:2). Moses was
then trying to impress his audience, evading the real issue that
his forthcoming death is at God's order. We see him now in his
true light. Far from being an ailing veteran, he is still *dans la force
de l'âge*. It is thus in his full vigor that Moses goes up the mountain to deliberately meet his fate, that is, God's order: "and die
on the mountain!" (32:50). Prophetic faithfulness is brought to
perfection in silent and wholehearted obedience.

A geographic element further enhances Moses' allegiance to
YHWH. Moses is buried "in the valley ... opposite Beth-Peor"
(Deut 34:6). Within Deuteronomy's narrative this note brings out
the spatial unity of Deuteronomy's action, since Moses is buried
exactly where he started speaking in Deut 1:5.[33] Within the greater
Pentateuchal narrative Moses' burial place "in the valley ... opposite Beth Peor" drops a broad hint. "Beth-Peor is Beth Baal-Peor
(the house of Baal Peor)," Weinfeld stresses, "the site of the
Israelites' first encounter with cultic prostitution, part of the Baal
worship (cf. Num 25:1-9; Hos 9:10)."[34] Opposite the place of
Israel's transgression, the obedient prophet is buried. Sacred, or
rather desecrated, history is not doomed to repeat itself.

3. *"So the People of Israel Listened to Joshua"—Deut 34:8-12*

Moses' faithfulness gives a specific tone to the end of Deuteronomy. Is it therefore surprising if the narrative closes with the
progressive disclosure of a happy *peripeteia*? God's announcement
in the Tent of Meeting apparently implied that the people would
rebel immediately after Moses' death: "Behold, you are about to
sleep with your fathers; then this people will rise and play the har-
lot after the strange gods of the land" (Deut 31:16). God's statement has been dramatically echoed by Moses in his admonition
to the people in 31:26-29: "For I know that after my death you

---

[33] See Deut 3:29, "So we remained in the valley opposite Beth-Peor"), which
refers back to 1:5, "Beyond the Jordan in the land of Moab, Moses undertook to
expose this Torah."
[34] Weinfeld, *Deuteronomy*, 192.

will surely act corruptly, and turn aside from the way which I have commanded you" (Deut 31:29). A first surprise comes with the people's behavior at Moses' death. "And the people of Israel wept for Moses in the plains of Moab thirty days" (34:8). Instead of denying the memory of the deceased leader and lawgiver, the people honor Moses' memory with a month-long period of mourning.[35] Is it conventional behavior—Aaron too was mourned for thirty days (Num 20:29)? Is it a tactical interim prior to the outburst of idolatrous prostitution? Or is it a sincere move, and a striking inversion of the people's apostasy with the Golden Calf during Moses' previous absence "on the mountain"? The last hypothesis is confirmed by the next narratorial statement. In Deut 34:9, in a preview of ensuing history, the narrator discloses that the generation led by Joshua "listened to him (וישמעו אליו), and did as YHWH had commanded Moses." In other words, throughout Joshua's lifetime Moses's persistent call that Israel "obey" (in listening—שמע) God's revelation was answered. What the narrator announces is not *per se* the invalidation of God's dire prediction in 31:16; it is rather a delay in the fulfillment of the prophecy.[36] Is it irony? Moses died without knowing the happy turn that the immediate future would take. Yet he is directly implied in the course of things, because the authority of Joshua, which proves so successful, derives from Moses' own. In Num 27:18, 20, God ordered Moses to lay his hands upon Joshua and to invest him with some of his authority "that all the congregation of Israel *may*

---

[35] In Deuteronomy's represented history the mention of Joshua's (exercised) leadership follows the reference to the mourning for Moses. Such a notice rules out any form of co-regency in Moses' lifetime, as Deut 31:14-15, 23 might have implied. See Schäfer-Lichtenberger, *Josua und Salomo*, 188; *contra* Baltzer, *Bundesformular*, 89.

[36] The one generation delay announced at the end of Deuteronomy is borne out throughout the book of Joshua and is retrospectively confirmed in Josh 24:31, and especially in Judg 2:7-10: "And the people served YHWH all the days of Joshua, and all the days of the elders who outlived Joshua, who had seen all the great work which YHWH had done for Israel. And Joshua the son of Nun, the servant of YHWH, died at the age of one hundred and ten years ... And all that generation also were gathered to their fathers; and there arose another generation after them; who did not know YHWH or the work which he had done for Israel." What immediately follows (without the mention of mourning; see Judg 1:1 and 2:10-11) is, indeed, another chapter in Israel's history: "And the people of Israel did what was evil in the sight of YHWH and served the Baals" (Judg 2:11).

listen/obey (יִשְׁמְעוּ)" (Num 27:20). God's purpose is realized in the people's allegiance to Joshua: "Joshua the son of Nun was full of the spirit of wisdom, for Moses had laid his hands upon him; so the people of Israel *listened* to him (וַיִּשְׁמְעוּ אֵלָיו), and did as YHWH had commanded Moses" (34:9). The effect of Moses' authoritative commissioning of Joshua (in Num 27:22-23) comes to the fore only after Moses' demise, and thus after the prophet's struggle as to the future of the covenant. Moses' "blind obedience" in death is hence all the more impressive.

But it would be hasty to conclude that the impact of Joshua's authority proved greater than the impact of Moses'. On the one hand Joshua fully qualifies as the prophet "like Moses" announced by God in Deut 18:15-22.[37] Israel's future military leader, Joshua has also been progressively initiated into the prophetic function. Summoned with Moses to the Tent of Meeting,[38] he joins Moses in the communication of the Song (32:44). In a proleptic summary, the narrator adds that the sons of Israel "listened to Joshua (וַיִּשְׁמְעוּ אֵלָיו)", and "did as YHWH had commanded Moses" (34:9). God's portrait of the announced prophet—Deut 18:15, "to him you shall listen (אֵלָיו תִּשְׁמָעוּן)"[39]—is thereby verified in Joshua. On the other hand, Joshua is *at best* a "prophet like Moses," that is, second to him. Joshua's spiritual authority derives from Moses'— "for Moses had laid his hands upon him" (34:9).[40] And if the peo-

---

[37] See the opening of Ben Sira's praise: "Joshua the son of Nun was mighty in war, and was the successor of Moses in prophesying" (Sir 46:1). See also Bekhor Shor and Ḥazquni on Deut 31:3. As it will arise from further developments (beyond Deuteronomy), Joshua is, more precisely, "the first 'prophet like Moses'," so Blenkinsopp, *Prophecy and Canon*, 48. See Blenkinsopp's overall treatment of the issue of "Mosaic" prophecy in Deuteronomy and in the Deuteronomistic History [pp. 39-53]). Joshua is the first of a line of figures whose function is "to mediate the covenant between the LORD and his people and 'speak' the laws which guarantee its survival" (p. 45). Upon his death Moses receives the title of "servant of YHWH" (Deut 34:5), which is also granted to Joshua on the same occasion (Josh 24:29). This title, Blenkinsopp, p. 166 n. 96, indicates, is "a standard synonym for prophet in Deuteronomic writings" (p. 48), where the phrase "my servants the prophets" stands for the prophetic succession as a whole (see 1 Kings 14:18; 15:29; 18:36; 2 Kings 9:7, 36; 10:10; 14:25; 17:13, 23; 21:10; 24:2; Jer 7:25; 25:4; 26:5; 29:19; 35:15; 44:4).

[38] In a kind of fulfillment of young Joshua's attendance in the same Tent; see Exod 33:11.

[39] See also Deut 18:18: "I will put my words in his mouth, and he shall speak to them all that I commanded him."

[40] See G. W. Coats, "Legendary Motifs in the Moses Death Reports," *CBQ* 39 (1977) 34-44; and Schäfer-Lichtenberger, *Josua und Salomo*, 188.

ple obeyed, it was not him they obeyed (they just "listened to him," as the preposition אֶל, "towards," suggests),[41] but the orders that were given to Moses.[42] The introduction of Joshua as "prophet like Moses" prompts a dialectical reassertion of Moses' incomparability:[43] "But there has not arisen a prophet since in Israel like Moses, whom YHWH knew face to face" (34:10).[44] As Schäfer-Lichtenberger indicates, there is no contradiction whatsoever between the promise in 18:15,18 and the narrator's statement in 34:10.[45] The promise of a "prophet like Moses" means that the objective criteria of "Mosaic prophecy" will be met again. What 34:10 emphasizes is the uniqueness of Moses as a subject known by God. Coming from a narrator who almost systematically resorted to the "showing" mode of narration, the intrusive comment of 34:10 is remarkable. After a narration that focused on Moses' last day, the narrator now formulates a statement that comprehends the whole of Israel's post-Mosaic history.[46] The narrator lends all the weight of his authority to Moses' own, sanctioning his uniqueness in Israel's existence. What God achieved through Moses, from beginning to end,[47] remained and will remain unmatched in Israel's existence—as long as Deuteronomy is read.

4. *Conclusion*

The section of Deuteronomy surveyed in this chapter brings the reader beyond Deuteronomy's main concern—the communica-

---

[41] For a narrative staging of the difference between שׁמע + direct object, and שׁמע אֶל (in Gen 23:2-20), see Sternberg, "Double Cave, Double Talk: The Indirections of Biblical Dialogue," *"Not in Heaven": Coherence and Complexity in Biblical Narrative* (ed. J. P. Rosenblatt and J. C. Sitterson, Jr.; Bloomington: Indiana University Press, 1991) 49.

[42] See Schäfer-Lichtenberger, *Josua und Salomo*, 187-89, 370.

[43] See J. Blenkinsopp, *The Pentateuch: An Introduction to the First Five Books of the Bible* (New York: Doubleday, 1992) 232.

[44] The intransitive verb קם, "has arisen," in Deut 34:10 echoes the causative forms יקים, "he will raise," and אקים, "I will raise," in the promise of a prophet in 18:15, 18.

[45] Schäfer-Lichtenberger, *Josua und Salomo*, 188 n. 399.

[46] Long-range statements are the hallmark of Deuteronomy's ending. See the comment in Deut 34:6 about the (unknown) location of Moses' burial place (see my next chapter) and the announcement of the obedience of Joshua's generation in 34:9.

[47] In Deut 1:5 Moses started his retelling at Horeb; the narrator ends up with a summary that goes further back in time, covering Moses' *début* in Egypt.

tion of the Torah. The narrative relevance of Deut 32:48-34:10
emphasizes, by way of contrast, the status of the previous parts of
the book. A communicational difference comes out: the distinction between the "words" meant for transfer to the land (by being
recorded in the Torah "book") and duplication in the land, and
the "words" (in this case, Moses' blessing) that occur as singular
speech acts in the action's *hic et nunc*.[48] Deuteronomy's implied
readers are supposed to be acquainted with the Torah (supplemented by the Song) because they enjoy, as sons of Israel, the
channels of transmission established by Moses in Deuteronomy
31, and because specific acts of reception have been enjoined on
them (6:4-9; 11:18-21; 17:18-20). The same readers know of Moses'
blessing exclusively because they are readers, eavesdropping on
what Moses once said to their forefathers in the plains of Moab.

There is a clear duality throughout Moses' speeches in Deuteronomy. These speeches, on the one hand, testify to Moses' faithfulness in his transmission of that which he is to transmit—"Moses
spoke to the people of Israel according to all that YHWH had giv-
en him in commandment for them" (Deut 1:3). This he does "to
completion," in both oral communication (32:45) and actual writing (31:24) of Israel's essential "words." On the other hand, the
Mosaic speeches also illustrate Moses' use of the teller's or
reteller's latitude—to reshape what is told or retold. In the speeches of Deuteronomy 1-4 and in Deuteronomy 31, Moses at times
phrases or designs the (re)telling in a way that betrays his human,
all too human, point of view. The narrator's final account reports
how God eventually educates his prophet, so that he may come
to terms with those issues which had proved painful. The narration, thus, does not close without a full correction of the data that
Moses has somehow distorted. Moses' silent obedience is his
way—a most telling way—of correcting in his death what went
awry in his speech.

---

[48] An intermediate category is constituted by the speeches uttered in reference
to the Torah "book" (in Deuteronomy 29-30) or with a view to its transmission
and conservation (in Deuteronomy 31).

CHAPTER SIX

MOSES AND MOSES' "BOOK"
IN BIBLICAL TIME AND SPACE

> I will not lodge thee by
> Chaucer or Spenser, or bid Beaumont lie
> A little further to make thee a room:
> Thou art a monument without a tomb,
> And art alive still while thy book doth live,
> And we have wits to read and praise to give.
>
> Ben Jonson, "To the Memory of
> My Beloved, the Author
> Mr. William Shakespeare"

"The end of the matter; all has been heard" (Qoh 12:13). How, among many other ways, can the words of the end prompt the reader that "all has been heard"? By being themselves already heard. Endings can make the most of the phenomenon of *déjà lu*. In this chapter I intend to show that the ending of Deuteronomy echoes Pentateuchal and especially patriarchal motifs. The previous chapter had centered on plot developments. This one will give heed to what could be called in Saussurian fashion, "the characters under the characters."[1] Determining figures of the Pentateuch underlie the characterization of Moses in his last words and deeds, enhancing the singularity of Israel's founding prophet by way of contrast.

The more history and narrative paradigms precede a biblical *dramatis persona*, the more this figure is likely to have to answer for, knowingly or unknowingly. Josiah, for instance, is a new Joshua who, in turn, is a new Moses. Whatever Josiah does or says can be measured in relation to his illustrious predecessors.[2] The stake that

---

[1] See J. Starobinski, *Les mots sous les mots: Les anagrammes de Ferdinand de Saussure* (Paris: Gallimard, 1971).

[2] To mention just a few analogies: Josiah reads the Torah "book" (2 Kgs 22-23) that Joshua was commanded to read (Josh 1:8). Joshua writes down the covenant words (Josh 24:26) just as Moses did before (Deut 31:9, 24). Josiah's praise by the narrator echoes Moses'; compare 2 Kgs 23:25, "Before him there was no king like him ... and there has not arisen any like him after him," and Deut 34:10, "There has not arisen a prophet since in Israel like Moses."

the Bible's poetics has in iterative phenomena (parallelism, repetition, inclusion, and the like) is not to be explained on formal grounds alone, especially when the technique bears on plot development or characterization.[3] Literary iteration goes along with a historiographical claim. In the Bible, history progresses by revisiting itself. A late-coming figure may very likely be haunted by a previous one. At the end of the book of Samuel, David utters his "last words" (2 Sam 23:1), opening his speech as a new Balaam:

Num 24:15   2 Sam 23:1

נְאֻם בִּלְעָם בְּנוֹ בְעֹר   נְאֻם דָּוִד בֶּן יִשַׁי
וּנְאֻם הַגֶּבֶר   וּנְאֻם הַגֶּבֶר

The oracle of Balaam *the son of* Beor,   *The oracle of* David, *the son of* Jesse,
the oracle of the man   *the oracle of the man*

Is David playing the prophet, the one who utters oracles? A new Balaam, he seems, however, to have forgotten his classics. More likely, David unknowingly leads the reader to recall that tradition. When YHWH says to David "Go, number (מנה) Israel and Judah" (2 Sam 24:1), the king hurries to do so and falls straight into the trap. The oracle seems ironically unaware of Balaam's rhetorical question: "Who can count (מנה) the dust of Jacob, or number the dust cloud of Israel?" (Num 23:10). At times, the characters may be the conscious agents of such resumptions. Blessing Joseph's sons in the wrong order, Jacob apparently remembers his own blessing scene. "I know, my son," Jacob replies to Joseph who whispers, "Not so, father, for the other is the first-born" (Gen 48:18-19). The reader, in any case, is the one who records the winding of history within the individual and successive stories. He is the one who hopes and fears: is what will be what has been?

In the previous examples, and throughout this chapter, the highlighting of similarities and contrasts between (distant) nar-

---

[3] For the use of parallelism and opposition in the shaping of biblical characters, see Y. Zakovitch, "Mirror-Image Story—An Additional Criterion for the Evaluation of Characters in Biblical Narrative," *Tarbiz* 54 (1985) 165-76 (Hebrew); idem, "Through the Looking Glass: Reflections/Inversions of Genesis in the Bible," *BibInt* 1 (1993) 139-152; F. Polak, *Biblical Narrative: Aspects of Art and Design* (The Biblical Encyclopaedia Library 11; Jerusalem: Mossad Bialik, 1994) 277 (Hebrew).

rative characters pertains primarily to the hermeneutics of reading, and not to the reconstruction of textual geneses.[4] The iterative patterns that mark out the Pentateuch undoubtedly stem from
complex redactional and editorial phenomena (literary dependency, organization of texts in macro-sequences, alterations and
interpolations, etc.). The elucidation of the composite nature of
the Pentateuch, however determinant in the exegetical project,
has a critical counterpart—a "helpful mate" (Gen 2:18)—in the
description of the Pentateuch as a (well) composed work. What
is gathered from the whole in the reading process is perforce distinct from what genetic hypotheses put forward about the parts.
Yet both approaches eventually shed light on each other. The ideological configuration of echoes and recurrences throughout the
Pentateuch, for instance, may reveal something of the strategies
that underlie the redactional history of the text. In the following
pages the identification of iterative patterns will be viewed "as a
general approach to *reading*: making meaning through the inter-
nal comparison of relations among characters, motifs, and narrative sequences."[5] From its opening to its concluding verses, the
Pentateuch offers a rich collection of narrative characters. These
characters are inevitably understood according to their order of
appearance, that is, serially and cumulatively. In that sense this
collection of characters has in itself a narrative dimension.

As he departs, Moses is depicted as Moses in the extreme, and
eventually alone, on "the top of Pisgah" (Deut 34:1) with the One
God. Still he is "narratively" revisiting a long history of depart-
ings. Determinate figures are haunting each of Moses' final words

---

[4] See above pp. 6-9, and A. Berlin's judicious remarks in "Literary Exegesis of
Biblical Narrative: Between Poetics and Hermeneutics," *"Not in Heaven": Coherence
and Complexity in Biblical Narrative* (ed. J. P. Rosenblatt and J. C. Sitterson; Bloomington: Indiana University Press, 1991) 120-28.

[5] E. L. Greenstein, "On the Genesis of Biblical Prose Narrative," review of *The
Narrative Covenant: Transformations of Genre in the Growth of Biblical Literature*, by D.
Damrosch, *Prooftexts* 8 (1988) 351. Because of its narrative parameters, the hermeneutics of reading illustrated in these pages departs from other interpretive ven-
tures, and notably from the Midrash. "Although the Midrashists did assume the
unity of the text," Alter writes, "they had little sense of it as a real narrative continuum, as a coherent unfolding story in which the meaning of earlier data is
progressively, even systematically, revealed or enriched by the addition of subsequent data" (*Biblical Narrative*, 11). The non-narrative stance of the Midrash is
somehow epitomized in the Rabbinic interpretative guideline, "There is no earlier and later in the Torah" (see Sternberg, "Grand Chronology," 83). See also
Berlin, *Poetics and Interpretation*, 17-19.

and deeds. None of the narrative parameters of Deuteronomy
31-34 can be said to be unprecedented. The place Moses is standing on, the moment of life he is coming to grips with, the speeches he utters—all of these narrative "slots," I shall show, belong to
previous stories. Either on the omniscient narrator's part or on
Moses' own, the Moses of Deuteronomy 31-34, however, has it out
with his national, and especially patriarchal, past history. The chal-
lenge, in the end, is communicational. Facing a people, and not
a family clan, and facing it as a prophet, and not as a father, Moses
creates a new type of social communication that eventuates in the
production of the Torah "book."

1. Patriarchal Death Scenes

In the Pentateuchal narrative Moses is not the first leading figure
to die. When YHWH tells him "the days approach for you to die"
(Deut 31:14), the reader is reminded of the opening of the story of Jacob's last moments: "When the days approached for Israel
to die" (Gen 47:29). Taking the hint contained in God's words to
Moses—the subtle reference to Jacob's story , I will examine the
patriarchal background to the narrative of Moses' death. Properly speaking, no type-scene of "patriarchal death" is found in Genesis.[6] The reader, rather, records the progressive unfolding of what
is at first a short obituary.

> [7]These are the days of the years of Abraham's life, a hundred and
> seventy-five years. [8]Abraham breathed his last and died in a good
> old age, an old man full of years, and was gathered to his people.
> [9]Isaac and Ishamel, his sons, buried him in the cave of Machpelah,
> in the field of Ephron the son of Zohar the Hittite, east of Mamre,
> [10]the field which Abraham purchased from the Hittites. There Abra-
> ham was buried, with Sarah his wife. [11]After the death of Abraham
> God blessed Isaac his son. (Gen 25:7-11)

The account of Isaac's death echoes two elements of Abraham's
end: the demise in old age, "full of days," and the burying by the
sons:

> [28]Now the days of Isaac were a hundred and eighty years. [29]And Isaac
> breathed his last; and he died and was gathered to his people, old

---

[6] See Alter's review of biblical type-scenes in *Biblical Narrative*, 47-62.

and full of days; and his sons Esau and Jacob buried him. (Gen 35:28-29)

The obituary note is shorter than the one in Genesis 25; it is pre-fixed, however, with another scene, substantially expanding the benediction motif. What belonged to God in Gen 25:11 ("After the death of Abraham, God blessed Isaac his son") now becomes a paternal prerogative. "When Isaac was old and his eyes were dim so that he could not see, he called Esau his older son ... 'Behold, I am old; I do not know the day of my death'" (Gen 27:1-2). Esau the hunter is asked to provide his father with game, "that I may bless you before I die" (Gen 27:4). Retelling the scene to Jacob, and preparing the tricky inversion, Rebekah redirects the bless-ing: "so that he may bless you before he dies" (Gen 27:10).

What was separated by eight chapters in the case of Isaac (the ultimate blessing in Genesis 27; the actual death in Genesis 35) is reunited in four chapters in the case of Jacob (Genesis 47-50). The patriarchal benediction is now fully integrated within the nar-rative of the forefather's demise. It is also considerably expand-ed, not only because of the spelling out of the individual bless-ings, but also because of the doubling of the scene: Jacob blesses Joseph and Joseph's sons just before he blesses his own twelve sons, Joseph included. The genealogical and patriarchal logic implies that Jacob's blessing of the twelve sons is final. An epony-mous father is perforce a historical hapax. After Jacob's death, the reader would not expect any reenactment of the confronta-tion of the one and the twelve.

The closing of the patriarchal age with Jacob's death is spatially figured by the burying of all three patriarchs in the same bur-ial-place, the cave of Machpelah.[7] In his valedictory speech Jacob makes it clear: "There they buried Abraham and Sarah his wife; there they buried Isaac and Rebekah his wife; and there I buried Leah" (Gen 49:31; see also 47:29-30). And so it happened to Jacob: "His sons ... buried him in the cave of the field at Machpelah" (50:13). The phrase בניו .... אתו ויקברו, "his sons ... buried him," occurs in each of the patriarchal stories (25:9; 35:29; 50:13). The burying of the father by the reunited sons (Isaac and Ishamel;

---

[7] By being the first to refer to the patriarchal triad (in his mention of God's promise "to Abraham, to Isaac, and to Jacob" [Gen 50:24]), Joseph adds to the closure. The opening of Exodus confirms that the Pentateuch's story is the saga of Jacob's sons—and not of Joseph's own lineage.

Esau and Jacob; the twelve brothers) is therefore to be counted among the parameters of a patriarchal death.

In Isaac's and Jacob's case the death of a patriarch is also the death of a patriarch's son. The growing old and the passing away of Isaac and Jacob illustrate the general "like father, like son" principle. Like Abraham, Isaac dies at a good, ripe age—see the motif of "satiety (of days)" ([ימים] שבע) in Gen 25:8; 35:29. Jacob's story drops the motif in question,[8] but picks up the feature relating to Isaac of poor sight due to old age: "When Isaac was old and his eyes grew heavy so that he could not see" (Gen 27:1). So also: "Now the eyes of Israel were dim with age, so that he could not see" (48:10). The overall patriarchal pattern goes along with individual father-son similarities. The peculiar way biblical history revisits itself from father to son[9] could not fail to underlie the national and theological "fatherhood" called "Abraham, Isaac, and Jacob."

2. Reading Deuteronomy 31-34 in a Patriarchal Key

The figures of Abraham, Isaac, and Jacob belong to Moses' speech since its opening (Deut 1:8),[10] and the reference to the promise to the "fathers" is a recurrent theme in Moses' rhetoric.[11] Yet, the patriarchs also cryptically pervade the narration of Moses' depart-

---

[8] When introduced to the Pharaoh, seventeen years before his death, Jacob declares: "Few and evil have been the days of the years of my life, and they have not attained to the days of the years of the life of my fathers in the days of their sojourning" (Gen 47:9).

[9] Biblical history does so in either moral way, as is shown again and again in the royal successions recorded in 2 Kings: "PN did what was right/evil in the sight of YHWH, as his father had done."

[10] On the narrative import of this initial reference, tying the ensuing mentions of the "fathers" to the three patriarchs, see N. Lohfink, *Die Väter Israels im Deuteronomium—Mit einer Stellungnahme von Thomas Römer* (OBO 111; Freiburg Schweiz: Universitätsverlag; Göttingen: Vandenhoeck & Ruprecht, 1991) 1-6, 27-30. Lohfink's essay primarily addresses a genetic issue, disputing Römer's claim that the names "Abraham, Isaac, and Jacob" have been interpolated in Deuteronomy by the final redactors of the Pentateuch, and that "the fathers" in Deuteronomy first referred to the Exodus generation. See Th. Römer, *Israels Väter: Untersuchungen zur Väterthematik im Deuteronomium und in der deuteronomistischen Tradition* (OBO 99; Freiburg Schweiz: Universitätsverlag; Göttingen: Vandenhoeck & Ruprecht, 1990).

[11] See Deut 1:8, 35; 4:31; 6:10, 18, 23; 7:8, 12, 13; 8:1, 18; 9:5; 10:11; 11:9, 21; 13:18; 19:8; 26:3, 15; 28:11; 29:12; 30:20; 31:7, 20 (21); 34:4.

ing in Deuteronomy 31-34. Literal allusions and narrative situations reminiscent of the patriarchal regime provide the narration
with a specific background. A narrative and historical contrast
between Moses and the "fathers" is thus created, enhancing the
originality of Moses' accomplishment.

The first divine speech in Deuteronomy that is non reported
by Moses, that is, the first speech by YHWH directly recorded by
the narrator (Deut 31:14), awakens in the reader's mind specific
memories related to Jacob.

Gen 47:29	Deut 31:14
ויקרבו ימי ישראל <u>למות</u>	<u>קרבו ימיך למות</u>
And when *the days approached* for Israel *to die*	*The days approach* for you *to die*
<u>ויקרא</u> לבנו ליוסף	<u>קרא</u> את יהושע
he *called* his son Joseph	*call* Joshua

In the Pentateuch, the phrase "the days approached for X to die"
occurs only in the two verses just quoted.[12] A subtle analogy is
thus created between Moses and the last of the Patriarchs in the
ultimate turn of their lives. In a second, and now properly theophanic, intervention (Deut 31:14 was mere summoning), YHWH
appropriates Jacob's own words (neither used elsewhere in the
Pentateuch):[13]

Gen 47:30	Deut 31:16
<u>ושכבתי עם אבתי</u>	הנך <u>שכב עם אבותיך</u>
When *I lie down with my fathers*	Behold, you are soon *to lie with your fathers*

In Genesis 47 Jacob means "lying with his fathers" literally, that
is, spatially: "to be buried in their burying place." "Do not bury
me in Egypt," he enjoins his son Joseph, "but when I lie down
with my fathers, carry me out of Egypt and bury me in their burying place (וקברתני בקברתם)" (Gen 47:29-30). Using the same word-

---

[12] See Dillmann, *Deuteronomium*, 388; Driver, *Deuteronomy*, 338; Steuernagel,
Deuteronomium, 162. A third occurrence is found in 1 Kgs 2:1 (about David's
impending death). Most of the parallels between Deuteronomy and Genesis
reviewed in the following pages have been pinpointed (but not interpreted) by
either Dillmann or Driver.

[13] Elsewhere, see 2 Sam 7:12, and frequently in 1-2 Kings.

ing in his statement to Moses, YHWH seems to promise him a
"patriarchal" death (the lying with the fathers).[14] However, the
phrase will know another fulfillment: Moses will lie only metaphorically "with his fathers," in a place known by God alone:
ולא ידע איש את קברתו, "But no one knows the place of his burial"
(Deut 34:6).[15]

Another "patriarchal" hapax recurs in Deuteronomy 31. Moses
introduces the song YHWH has just revealed to him with a phrase
that echoes the introduction to Jacob's blessing:

Gen 49:1   Deut 31:29

ואגידה לכם את אשר יקרא אתכם   וקראת אתכם הרעה באחרית הימים
באחרית הימים

That I may tell you what is *to befall*   And evil *will befall you in the days to*
you in the days to come   *come*

As Driver points out, the same dire announcement—"many evils
and troubles shall befall you"—occurs twice in previous verses
(Deut 31:17,21; YHWH speaks to Moses); in those instances, however, the verb מצא, here "to come upon," is used, and not קרא, "to
befall," as in Gen 49:1 and Deut 31:29.[16] When addressed to the
"you" of the people (in Deut 31:29), Moses' speech closely matches Jacob's words, addressed to the "you" of the gathered sons (Gen
49:1). The introduction to a patriarchal blessing now prefaces a
prophetic exposure of the people's wickedness (this is, at least,
the way the Song is presented by YHWH to Moses in 31:21). In
Deuteronomy 31-34 Moses' audience is twice the addressee of
"lyrical" developments: the Song of Moses (Deuteronomy 32) and
the blessing (Deuteronomy 33). Rhetorically speaking, this duplication makes sense within a distribution of tasks. Jacob's words
about Israel's future ("in the days to come") include, beside the
appropriate blessings, the expression of blame (Gen 49:4), rebuke
(49:5-7), irony (49:15), and even a curse (49:7). Jacob's hetero-

---

[14] Compare God's statement in Num 27:13, "you also shall be gathered to your
people (אל עמיך), as your brother Aaron was gathered" (see also Num 20:24; 31:8).
[15] Compared with קבר, "grave, sepulchre," קבורה is a rare word in the Hebrew
Bible. In the Pentateuch it is only used for the burial places of Jacob (Gen 47:30),
Rachel (Gen 35:20, twice), and Moses (Deut 34:6).
[16] *See* Driver, *Deuteronomy*, 344; the parallelism between Gen 49:1 and Deut
31:29 is all the more remarkable since the verb קרא, and not the more common
קרה, is used on both sides.

geneous style gets broken down in Moses' double intervention. The blessings in Deuteronomy 33 are "wholly eulogistic,"[17] whereas the exposure of Israel's infamy and punishment is anticipated in the Song (Deuteronomy 32): "evil will befall you in the days to come" (31:29).

3. Whose Fatherhood?

The cryptic presence of a patriarchal valedictory scene in Deuteronomy 31 sheds indirect light on a feature of the Song recorded in Deuteronomy 32: the pervasiveness of the father-son category (and of other metaphors related to generation) throughout the poem.[18] Patriarchal valedictory sayings are perforce paternal speech acts. They may, as in Jacob's blessing, glorify the speaker's fatherhood (see Gen 49:3, 26), associating his paternity with God's might (see Gen 49:24-26). When Moses, facing the imminence of his death (31:27, 29), addresses the "assembly of Israel" in Deuteronomy 32, he speaks like Jacob (31:29), yet without being Israel's father. The patriarchal genre somehow needs to be redirected. This is significantly ensured by the Song, where the father's position is occupied by the divine figure, and not by the human speaker.

The Song of Moses apprehends the whole of history within a theological framework, from creation through YHWH's final victory on behalf of his servants. What feeds the drama of history is Israel/Yeshurun's lack of wisdom in response to God's creative and providential love for him (see the wisdom overtones in vv. 2, 6, 21, 28-29). The drama of lack of intelligence towards the "Rock, [whose] work is perfect" (32:4) is cast in the father-mother/son-daughter relationship.[19] In Deut 32:6, exploiting the word

---

[17] Driver, *Deuteronomy*, 385.

[18] The genealogical aspect of the Song of Moses has been rightly emphasized in recent scholarship, yet without paying sufficient attention to its relationship to the narrative context of Deuteronomy 31-32. See for instance J. Luyten, "Primeval and Eschatological Overtones in the Song of Moses (Dt 32,1-43)," *Das Deuteronomium: Entstehung, Gestalt und Botschaft* (BETL 68; ed. N. Lohfink; Louvain: University Press, 1985) 341-43.

[19] God's motherhood is implied by Deut 32:18a, "You were unmindful of the Rock that bore you (ילדך), and you forgot the God who gave you birth (מחללך)." The verbal form ילדך, however, can equally mean "begot." In that case, "the verse

pair אב, "father" / קנה, "to acquire,"[20] the poem superimposes creation and fatherhood into the figure of YHWH:[21]

Is not he your father who created you,   הלוא הוא אביך קנך
who made you and established you?   הוא עשך ויכננך

Facing such a genitor, Moses' addressees are the "sons" (vv. 5,
20[22]), the "sons and the daughters" (v. 19), the "generation" (דור,
cf. v. 5, 20), whose lack of intelligence receives manifold expression. The generational relationship between YHWH and Israel is
the core of the people's existence. Conversely, human generation,
as it appears in 32:7, is primarily a channel for tradition: "Remember the days of old, consider the years of many generations; ask
your father, and he will show you; your elders, and they will tell
you."

In his addressing the people, Moses is no longer in a position
to appeal to paternal authority. Life is transmitted through him,
yet not through generation (compare Jacob praising Reuben as
"the first fruits of my strength" [Gen 49:3]).[23] A further paral-

---

may be understood to combine images of both fatherhood and motherhood in
order to express how Israel owes its origin completely to Yahweh" (Mayes,
Deuteronomy, 388). The "son-daughter" pair is explicitly mentioned in 32:19.

[20] As in Gen 14:19, 22 the verb קנה here designates God as the originator of
creation. Interestingly enough, the same verb is used by Eve in Gen 4:1 to express
her motherhood: "I have gotten (קניתי) a man with YHWH."

[21] The representation of the God-creator as a parental figure is as old as religion; it has its specific history in the ancient Near Eastern religious complex. See
Th. Jacobsen, "Second Millennium Metaphors. The Gods as Parents: Rise of Personal Religion," *The Treasures of Darkness: A History of Mesopotamian Religion* (New
Haven: Yale University Press, 1976) 145-64; Cross, *Canaanite Myth*, 1-75. In Moses'
Song, as often in ancient Near Eastern and biblical sources, wisdom overtones
add to the motivation of the metaphor (see 32:5-6, 19-21, 28-29).

[22] And possibly v. 43, see 4QDeut[q] and LXX.

[23] Yet Moses is in no way a shadowy figure. Deut 34:7 will specify not only that
Moses'"eye was not dim" (contrary to Isaac's and Jacob's), but also that
ולא נס לחה, a statement which is rendered in modern translations by "his natural
force" (RSV) or "his vigor" (NJPSV) "was unabated," and that may conceal a sexual hint. There is no other occurrence of the word in the Hebrew Bible, though
the related adjective לַח does occur with the meaning "moist, fresh," of fruit (Num
6:3), of growing or freshly-cut wood (Gen 30:37; Ezek 21:3; 17:24), of ropes (Judg
16:7, 8). All this suggests for the noun לֵחַ the fresh, moist character of vital trees
and fruit. G. W. Coats sums up: "At one hundred and twenty years Moses would
have been as supple as a youth" ("Legendary Motifs in the Moses Death Reports,"
CBQ 39 [1977] 35). On the use of the root in two passages in the Ugaritic Legend of Aqht (2 Aqht 1:29 and 6:28), W. F. Albright deems its precise connota-
tion, both in Aqht and in Deuteronomy, to be "sexual power" ("The 'Natural
Force' of Moses in the Light of Ugaritic," *BASOR* 94 [1944] 32-33, n. 7). Albright's

lelism enhances the asymmetry between the two founding figures. Jacob's ultimate injunctions (49:29, 33) pertain to his being buried with his fathers "in the cave that is in the field at Machpelah to the east of Mamre" (49:30). No ultimate words could be more down-to-earth.[24] In a wording that echoes Genesis, Deuteronomy also features the completion of its character's speech:

Gen 49:33	Deut 32:45-46
<div dir="rtl">ויכל יעקב לצות את בניו</div>	<div dir="rtl">ויכל משה לדבר את כל הדברים האלה אל כל ישראל</div>
When Jacob *finished commanding his sons*	When Moses *finished* reciting all these words to all Israel
	<div dir="rtl">ויאמר אלהם ... תצום את בניכם</div>
	He said to them: "... *command them to your sons*"

Moses and Jacob are brought once more into alignment. Yet the prophet's final trope differs from the patriarch's. In his ultimate words to "all Israel," Moses recalls his previous communication: "Lay to heart all the words which I enjoin upon you this day, that you may command them to your children, that they may be careful to do all the words of this law" (Deut 32:46). The self-reflexive logic of a speech alluding to itself is characteristic of Moses' discourse in Deuteronomy and of prophetic discourse in general.[25] Jacob's speech-acts do without any similar logic: patriarchal authority is straight, needing no discursive credentials. Prophetic authority, in contrast, proves itself in the saying of prophetic words. It is therefore no surprise that Moses' prophetic speech refers back to itself in its final development. The life-giving power Moses transmits lies in the words he is prophetically conveying: "For it [= "all the words of this Torah"] is no trifle for you, but is your life, and thereby you shall live long in the land which you are going over the Jordan to possess" (Deut 32:47).

---

rendering of the Ugaritic has been disputed by H. L. Ginsberg ("The North-Canaanite Myth of Anath and Aqhat," *BASOR* 98 [1945] 19).

[24] Jacob's speech similarly gives way to a matter-of-fact notice: "When Jacob finished enjoining upon his sons, he drew up his feet into the bed, and breathed his last, and was gathered to his people" (49:33).

[25] On this phenomenon, see my next chapter, pp. 254-59.

4. *Blessing: Patriarchal vs. Prophetic*

The life-giving Torah has been duly transmitted; Moses, directed by YHWH, now faces his death. And, once more, he is revisiting patriarchal (hi)story. "This is the blessing with which Moses the man of God blessed the sons of Israel before his death" (Deut 33:1). Such a heading echoes two patriarchal scenes, both related to Jacob. The former is Isaac's blessing of Esau/Jacob in Genesis 27:

Gen 27:7	Deut 33:1
<div dir="rtl">ואברככה לפני יהוה <u>לפני מותי</u></div>	<div dir="rtl">וזאת <u>הברכה</u> אשר <u>ברך</u> משה ... לפני מותו</div>
That I may *bless* you before YHWH *before I die*	This is the *blessing* with which Moses blessed ... *before his death*

Gen 27:10

<u>יברכך לפני מותו</u>

So that he [Isaac] may *bless* you *before his death*

The latter scene is Jacob's blessing of his twelve sons:[26]

Gen 49:28	Deut 33:1
<div dir="rtl"><u>ויברך</u> אותם איש אשר <u>כברכתו ברך</u> אתם</div>	<div dir="rtl">וזאת <u>הברכה</u> אשר <u>ברך</u> משה איש האלהים את בני ישראל לפני מותו ...</div>
As he *blessed* them, *blessing* each with *the blessing* suitable to him	This is *the blessing* with which Moses the man of God *blessed* the sons of Israel before his death[27]

More than any other text, Genesis 49—Jacob/Israel's blessing of his twelve sons—provides the reader with a precedent to Deuteronomy 33.[28] A subtle reminder of the *Ur*-scene is found in

---

[26] With the blessing of Ephraim and Manasseh (Genesis 48) as a prologue; see Gen 48:9 (Jacob to Joseph:) "Bring them to me, I pray you, that I may bless them (ואברכם)"; see also Gen 48:15, 20.

[27] The phrase "before his death" occurs as well in Jacob's cycle in Gen 50:16, (the brothers to Joseph:) "Your father gave this command before his death." No further occurrence of the phrase is found in the Pentateuch.

[28] The repetition of the benediction scene is here considered as a fact within the represented world, and as a signal for the reader of the Pentateuch. A very

the designation of Moses' audience: "This is the blessing with which Moses the man of God blessed *the sons of Israel* (בני ישראל)" (Deut 33:1). Although not uncommon in Deuteronomy, the idiom "sons of Israel" has a pertinence of its own in the context of Moses' valedictory blessing. Since 29:20 the reader is acquainted with the distributive appellation (כל) שבטי ישראל, "(all) the tribes of Israel," which would have best described the recipients of the benediction. Moses' use of the phrase שבטי ישראל, "the tribes of Israel" in the opening lines of his utterance (33:5, "when the heads of the people were gathered, *the tribes of Israel* together") retrospectively enhances the narrator's use of the alternative phrase "sons of Israel" in Deut 33:1. Facing the tribes as "sons of Israel," and cast as the one vis-à-vis the twelve, Moses in Deuteronomy 33 revisits a previous fateful moment of the people's history. Standing in Jacob/Israel's place, Moses is yet far from impersonating Israel's forefather.[29] Within the background of the archaic setting, Moses stands out as a new social persona.

The appellation "sons of Israel" gains special relevance from its conjunction with Moses' designation in the same verse. Deut 33:1 presents him as איש האלהים, "the man of God," an unprecedented expression in the Pentateuch.[30] The combination איש + אלהים situates Moses in a sphere of divine immediacy, not directly akin to the generational and familial sphere of the "patriarchal blessing." In Genesis 49 a father blesses his sons ("Get together and hear, O sons of Jacob, and hearken to Israel your father" 49:2)—

---

different set of assumptions is implied in C. M. Carmichael's claim that Deuteronomy 33 and the whole of Deuteronomy are a composition patterned after Genesis 49 (*The Laws of Deuteronomy* [Ithaca and London: Cornell University Press, 1974] 17, 23-25, 171-173, 257). In my opinion, the complex growth of both Genesis and Deuteronomy calls for more analytical assessment. As far as Genesis 49 and Deuteronomy 33 are concerned, Carmichael's thesis, though plausible, still calls for appropriate controls. Further factors can be brought into the picture. As Carmichael acknowledges, the parallel setting of the two chapters may originate in a common cultural background [see p. 23]). Moreover, the (relatively few) literary points of contact between Genesis 49 and Deuteronomy 33 may stem, all or in part, from editorial harmonizations. For an overall assessment of Carmichael's project, see B. M. Levinson, "Calum M. Carmichael's Approach to the Laws of Deuteronomy," *HTR* 83 (1990) 227-57.

[29] The name of Jacob appears in Deut 33:4, "the assembly of Jacob."

[30] Moses is designated as "the man of God" in Josh 14:6, in the title of Ps 90, in Ezra 3:2; 1 Chr 23:14 and 2 Chr 30:16. This designation is used for messengers of God (Judg 13:6,8), and frequently for prophets (1 Sam 2:27; 9:6; 1 Kgs 12:22; 13:1; 2 Kings 4-8 passim; etc.).

indulging himself in some rebukes *ad hominem*. In Deuteronomy
33 a "man of God" awakens in a twelvefold nation the happiness
of her being YHWH's people: "Happy are you, O Israel! Who is
like you, a people saved by YHWH!" (Deut 33:29). Genesis 49
opens with a celebration of blood relationship and virile fecun-
dity, "Reuben, you are my first-born, my might, and the first fruits
of my strength, pre-eminent in pride and pre-eminent in power"
(Gen 49:3), whereas Deuteronomy 33, uttered by the "man of
God," has an unmistakable theological opening: "YHWH came
from Sinai, and dawned from Seir upon us" (33:2). The constitution of Israel, as Moses views it, is far from genealogical. A theocratic confederation, the Israel of Deuteronomy 33 proceeds from
the Mosaic giving of the Torah: "When Moses commanded us a
Torah, as a possession for the assembly of Jacob. Then [YHWH]
became king in Yeshurun, when the heads of the people gathered, the tribes of Israel together" (33:5).

That Moses' so-called blessing of "the sons of Israel" recasts a
previous model can be read in the generic tensions that underlie Deuteronomy 33.[31] On the one hand, a benediction such as
Asher's is in full agreement with the genealogical substratum of
the "patriarchal blessing" genre: "Blessed above sons be Asher; let
him be the favorite of his brothers" (33:24). The brotherhood pattern is similarly used in the case of Joseph: "Let these [gifts] come
upon the head of Joseph ... who was separate from his brothers"

---

[31] The relationship of the two blessings (in Genesis 49 and Deuteronomy 33)
is here considered as a fact within the represented world. As the outcome of a
literary production, Deuteronomy 33 is also possibly the result of a generic recasting, though of another type: the integration of individual sayings on the tribes
into a "valedictory blessing." The recasting may be entirely editorial, stemming
from the re-contextualization of independent sayings within Moses' blessing. It
may well be authorial as well, if the blessings, far from being a collection of archaic pieces, are a literary creation. A. Caquot has called into question the traditional ascription of Deuteronomy 33 to an early stage of biblical poetry (see, for
instance, F. M. Cross and D. N. Freedman, "The Blessing of Moses," *JBL* 67 [1948]
191-210; I. L. Seeligmann, "A Psalm from Pre-Regal Times," *VT* 14 [1964] 75-92;
H. J. Zobel, *Stammesspruch und Geschichte* [BZAW 95; Berlin: de Gruyter, 1965]; D.
N. Freedman, *Pottery, Poetry and Prophecy: Studies in Early Hebrew Poetry* [Winona
Lake; Eisenbrauns, 1980] 90-92, 167-78). Caquot strongly criticizes the "romantic
assumption," given respectability by comparative linguistics (via Ugarit), that a
piece such as Deut 33:6-25 can help us reconstruct the earliest Israelite history
and origins. He concludes that Deut 33:6-25 is not a collection of ancient scraps
of folklore but rather a composition of the Deuteronomic school, of no greater
antiquity than the end of the sixth century ("Les bénédictions de Moïse
[Deutéronome 33,6-25]," *Sem* 32 [1982] 67-81; *Sem* 33 [1983] 59-76).

(33:16). In these instances the "patriarchal" genre still lends its logic and metaphors. On the other hand, the blessing of Levi explicitly goes against the genealogical stream when it extols, "Your faithful one, whom you tested at Massah, challenged at the waters of Meribah; who said of his father and mother, 'I consider them not.' His brothers he disregarded, ignored his own children" (33:8-9). The sentence significantly goes on (shifting to plural): "For they observed your precepts, and kept your covenant" (33:9). Whatever the identity of the "faithful one,"[32] the very praise of an "a-genealogical" figure betrays the fact that the "patriarchal blessing" genre has been overridden—and even, in this case, undermined.[33]

The literal echoes between Jacob's and Moses' sayings are found in the respective blessings of Joseph (Gen 49:22-26; Deut 33:13-17).[34]

Gen 49:25

ברכת שמים מעל
ברכת תהום רבצת תחת

Blessings of *heaven* above,
blessings of *the deep that crouches beneath*

Gen 49:26

על ברכת הורי עד
תאות גבעת עולם

Deut 33:13

ממגד שמים מטל
ומתהום רבצת תחת

With the choicest gifts of *heaven* with the dew,[35]
and of *the deep that crouches beneath*

Deut 33:15

ומראש הררי קדם
וממגד גבעות עולם

---

[32] Is the איש חסידך the high priest, the one who wields the Urim-Tummim (see 33:8)? Rabbinic interpretation refers to Aaron (*Exod. Rab.* 5:10; 15:4; 35:1; *Num. Rab.* 19:9; *Tanhuma Exod.* 8b). Following the MT (to be literally translated "the man of your faithful"), Caquot prefers to distinguish between two individuals: "Il est préférable de suivre les rares exégètes qui ont fait de *hasîd* un déterminant de *'îš* et pensent que, si 'l'homme' est le grand prêtre, 'le fidèle' n'est autre que Moïse" ("Bénédictions," [1983] 74-75).

[33] See J. Wellhausen, *Prolegomena zur Geschichte Israels* (6th ed.; Berlin: de Gruyter, 1927) 129 (about Deut 33:8-11): "Die Priester erscheinen hier als ein fest geschlossener Stand... . Jedoch beruht diese so sehr hervortretende Solidarität des Standes keineswegs auf der natürlichen Grundlage der Geschlechts- oder Familieneinheit, den Priester macht nicht das Blut, sondern im Gegenteil die Verleugnung des Blutes, wie mit großem Nachdruck betont wird."

[34] See also the recurrence of גור אריה, "lion's whelp" in Gen 49:9 (on Judah) and Deut 33:22 (on Dan).

[35] The alternative reading שמים מעל, "heaven above," documented in the Peshitta is often suggested, because of the parallelism with תחת, "beneath," in the same

Beyond the blessings of the eternal *mountains* and the lust of the everlasting hills	From the top of the ancient *mountains* and the abundance of *the everlasting hills*
Gen 49:26	Deut 33:16
תהיין לראש יוסף ולקדקד נזיר אחיו	תבואתה לראש יוסף ולקדקד נזיר אחיו
May they be *on the head of Joseph, and on the brow of him who was separate from his brothers*	May they come *on the head of Joseph, and on the brow of him who was separate from his brothers*

The recurrences I have just reviewed may be ascribed, as Mayes avers, to "a common background in traditional formulaic blessings on the tribe"[36] (a background which, strangely enough, does not surface in the sayings on the other tribes). Yet how can these echoing effects be understood in their narrative relevance? It can be observed that the blessing of Joseph in Genesis is the saying that extols God's power as well as the power of Jacob's own fatherly blessing (see Gen 49:24, "the Mighty One of Jacob"; 49:25, "El Shaddai who will bless you"; 49:26, "the blessings of your father are mighty beyond the blessings of the eternal mountains and the lust of the eternal hills"[37]). This is the only blessing that Moses echoes, yet with a significant change. Divine munificence, invoked upon Joseph, is no longer combined with divine power and with the paternal power of the blesser; it is now associated with "the favor of him that dwelt in the bush" (Deut 33:16)—in other words, with the favor of the God of the Mosaic covenant. Moses seems thus to intentionally echo the most patriarchal of Jacob's utterances, only to endow it with the new paradigm of God's relationship to Israel.

The point therefore is the subversion of a patriarchal piece by another voice, that of "the man of God" (Deut 33:1) (whom the

---

verse, and because of the similar formulation in both Gen 49:26 and Gen 27:39 (another patriarchal saying on a son, namely of Isaac on Esau). Interestingly enough, the Massoretic reading in Deut 33:13, "of heaven with the dew (מטל)," equally echoes Gen 27:39, "from the dew (ומטל) of heaven above." The MT has been respected for this reason.

[36] Mayes, *Deuteronomy*, 405.

[37] The sexual hints encroach on the female side: "By El Shaddai (שדי) who will bless you ... with blessings of the breasts (שדים) and of the womb" (Gen 49:25).

narrator eventually designates as "prophet" in 34:10).[38] Moses
somehow fits into the paradigm progressively built up in the patriarchal narratives—blessing the "twelve," he is a new Jacob. Acting
in Jacob's *persona*, Moses gains something of the stature of a genitor. Coming to his end, Moses, the leader and the prophet, dons
the mantle of the father. What YHWH brought about through
him—the birth of a nation—borders on fathering. Still, no doubt
is possible: when it comes to Moses, fatherhood is nothing more
than a forceful metaphor. Insofar as he is post-patriarchal, Moses
radically recasts the patriarchal paradigm. A blood-related gesture,
the blessing is turned into the oracle of the "man of God," the
prophet Moses. Jacob has twice been the trickster in blessing ven-
tures (in Genesis 27 and 48); this time, with the help of the narrator, it is Moses who makes the most of an existing institution,
the valedictory patriarchal blessing.

5. *Balaam vs. Moses: What prophecy?*

Is the patriarchal setting the exclusive background of Deuteronomy 31-34 (and especially of Moses' blessing in Deuteronomy 33)?
A prophetic, rather para-prophetic, figure also appears behind the
scene, next to the patriarchal figure of Jacob. This time the invo-
catory device is no longer temporal but spatial. Moses blesses the
"sons of Israel" at a certain point of time: לפני מותו, "before his
death" (33:1). So did Jacob and Isaac.[39] Moses' blessing and death,
however, take place at a point in space that calls to the reader's
mind another figure related to blessing. Balaam faced the people
of Israel encamped in the plains of Moab (Num 22:1), where
Moses now faces them. From the top of the hills Balaam saw "a
people *dwelling alone* (עם לבדד ישכן)" (Num 23:9), just as Moses
eulogizes Israel's dwelling alone (Deut 33:28, וישכן ישראל בטח בדד

---

[38] Moses designated himself, yet indirectly, as a prophet in Deut 18:15, "YHWH
your God will raise up for you a prophet like me."

[39] In the case of Isaac, the overlapping with Deut 33:1 is literal: "so that [Isaac]
may bless you before his death (לפני מותו)" (Gen 27:10); see also Gen 27:7,
לפני מותי, "before my death." The phrase "before his death" appears in relation to
Jacob in the brothers' plea to Joseph: "Your father gave this command before his
death, 'Say to Joseph, Forgive, I pray you, the transgression of your brothers and
their sin'" (Gen 50:16).

עֵין יַעֲקֹב, "So Israel *dwelt* in safety, the fountain of Jacob *alone*").[40] This is the singular nation Balaam is thrice compelled to bless. "How can I curse whom God has not cursed? How can I denounce whom YHWH has not denounced?" (Num 23:8).

The spatial and textual parameters deserve closer reading. YHWH's command to Moses in Deut 32:49 to go up (עֲלֵה) "the mountain of the Abarim, Mount Nebo" echoes Deut 3:27, that is, Moses' retelling of God's request in Num 27:12. In Moses' words, God's order is rendered into עֲלֵה רֹאשׁ הַפִּסְגָּה, "Go up to the top of Pisgah." This is the very place where Balak brought Balaam, in his second attempt to get him to curse the people of Israel: "'Come with me to another place from which you can see them—you saw only a part of them, you did not see them all—then curse them for me from there.' And he took him to the field of Zophim [watchers' point], to the top of Pisgah (אֶל רֹאשׁ הַפִּסְגָּה)" (Num 23:13-14).[41] Contemplating the people of Israel from this vantage point, Balaam cannot but bless them: "My message was to bless: when [YHWH] blesses, I cannot reverse it" (Num 23:20). In Deuteronomy Moses does not have to overlook the people from afar to bless it; he faces the "sons of Israel" in the plains of Moab. His blessing, however, takes place between YHWH's command to go up the mountain (Deut 32:49) and his actual ascent to "the top of Pisgah" (34:1), that is, to the mountain linked to Balaam's irresistible blessing.[42]

---

[40] See the comparative analysis in H. Rouillard, *La péricope de Balaam (Nombres 22-24): la prose et les "oracles"* (Ebib 4; Paris: Gabalda, 1985) 224-28.

[41] In his third attempt, Balak takes Balaam "to the top of Peor" (Num 23:28), a place that serves as a landmark in the account of Moses' burial, "opposite Beth-Peor" (Deut 34:6).

[42] That Moses and Balaam were held close together in the narrative memory and imagination of biblical authors and readers is shown by Mic 6:4-5, which associates Moses and Balaam on the same Exodus-Conquest axis: "For I brought you up out of the land of Egypt, and redeemed you from the slave-house. I sent before you Moses, Aaron and Miriam with him. Remember the scheme of Balak, king of Moab, and the answer he got from Balaam, son of Beor ... from Shittim to Gilgal. That you may know the saving acts of Yahweh" (translation by D. R. Hillers, *Micah* [Hermeneia; Philadelphia: Fortress, 1984] 75). The discovery of the Balaam text of Deir 'Allā from about 700 BCE and the evidence of Num 25:1-3 and 31:16 (Balaam's role in the "matter of Peor") make it plain, Hillers adds, "that the figure of Balaam loomed even larger in legend of Micah's time than the Numbers story suggests" (*Micah*, 78). Hillers refers to "Micah's time" (late 8th century); scholars who rely more than Hillers on redaction-criticism vary greatly in their assessment of the dating of Mic 6:1-8, from pre-exilic to post-exilic times (see the discussion in H. W. Wolff, *Dodekapropheton 4: Micha* [BKAT 14/4; Neukirchen-Vluyn: Neukirchener Verlag, 1982] 144-45).

The figure of Balaam, "the man whose eye is opened, ... who hears the words of God" (Num 24:3.15-16) appears therefore behind Moses', "the man of God" (Deut 33:1).[43] The blessing of the sons of Israel by Balaam, the non-Israelite prophet, is at any rate a-patriarchal and a-genealogical.[44] By this measure, Balaam shares Moses' non-genealogical but prophetic relationship to the "sons of Israel" who benefit from his blessing. In other respects, the same Balaam is, as Margaliot puts it, an "anti-Moses."[45] The hired prophet who, upon completion of his paradoxical mission, rises and goes back "to his place" (Num 24:25), is hardly the type of the prophetic "servant of YHWH" (Deut 34:5). Balaam is the mere receptacle of a divine switching of curse into blessing; Moses, although occasionally recalcitrant, hangs upon YHWH's word from birth to death, and from Egypt to the promised land. Both Balaam and Moses meet their fate at God's command, and as a divine sanction. Yet the slaying of Balaam and the Midianites by the men of Israel, executing God's vengeance on Midian (Num 31:1-8), is quite different from Moses' death in exile, in God's hands (see Deut 34:6).

Balaam, the foreign prophet, haunts Moses' benediction, as does Jacob, the patriarch. The benediction of the sons of Israel is a speech act already "invested." To bless the sons of Israel "before one's death," and to bless them in the plains of Moab, is to stand in someone else's shoes.[46] The blessing of Jacob the patriarch leads up to his ultimate entry into the land, as a mummy embalmed by Egyptian physicians (Gen 50:2). The blessing of Balaam the prophet is followed by his return to "his place" (Num 24:25). Is Moses condemned to conform to the fate of any of his

---

[43] The Balaam figure not only belongs to the Pentateuchal macro-(hi)story, it is also a figure mentioned in Deuteronomy—as the one whose curse was turned into blessing (23:5-6), in relation to the exclusion of the Ammonite and Moabite from "the assembly of YHWH"; cf. Neh 13:1-2. For a presentation of Balaam as an "anti-Moses" figure, see M. Margaliot, "The Connection of the Balaam Narrative with the Pentateuch," *Proceedings of the Sixth World Congress of Jewish Studies (13-19 August 1973)*, (vol. 1; Jerusalem: World Union of Jewish Studies, 1977) 279-90.

[44] Balaam comes significantly from ארץ בני עמו, the "land of the sons of his people" (Num 22:5; MT): he bears no relation to the sons of Israel and to their land.

[45] Margaliot, "Balaam," 285.

[46] Blessing the people of Israel, Moses falls within Balaam's own blessing: "Blessed be every one who blesses you, and cursed be every one who curses you" (Num 24:9).

predecessors? In the Pentateuchal narrative, blessings are a highly strategic locus, e.g. the dramatic reversals in Balaam's story or
Jacob's ploys as the blessed one (Genesis 27) or as the blessing
one (Gen 48:13-20). Moses' revisiting of the blessing genre creates a third, properly Mosaic, way that cunningly combines the
Jacob-patriarchal and Balaam-prophetic features. The combination, on the one hand, has a formal aspect. In the frame of his
poem (Deut 33:2-5; 26-29) Moses faces the whole of Israel ("Happy are you, O Israel!" 33:29), just as Balaam does in his triple oracle. In the core of his utterance Moses dispenses a distributive
benediction in the style of Jacob: "And this he said of Judah ...
And of Levi he said ..." The combination, on the other hand,
pertains to Moses' very fate. Moses' end combines the final journey of the two blessing figures, that is, Balaam's non-entry into
Canaan, and Jacob's ultimate entry into the same land, beyond
his death, as an embalmed mummy. Moses dies out of Canaan,
yet, as I shall soon indicate, he dispatches in the land the memorial of his, and YHWH's, words.

6. *Visionary Prophets: Abraham and Moses*

YHWH's command to Moses to ascend the mountain and to see
the promised land (Deut 32:49) evokes a further figure of the
patriarchal cycle. Moses is enjoined to see "the land of Canaan."
This is the first and only time in Deuteronomy that the promised
land is presented as "land of Canaan." In the Pentateuch the
expression occurs mainly in Genesis 12-50 and has therefore a
patriarchal flavor.[47] Moses is commanded to "see" (ראה) such a
land. Among the patriarchs Abraham is the one whose relationship to the land is markedly "sight related."[48] The most conspicuous text is Gen 13:14-15: "Lift up your eyes, and look (ראה) from

---

[47] The first occurrence of "Canaan" (as a reference to the land) in Genesis
slightly precedes Genesis 12-50, but is already related to the patriarchal history:
"Terah took Abram his son and Lot the son of Haran, his grandson, and Sarai,
his daughter-in-law, his son Abraham's wife, and they went forth together from
Ur of the Chaldeans to go into the land of Canaan" (Gen 11:31). The expression ארץ כנען, "land of Canaan" occurs 35 times in Genesis, 2 times in Exodus, 3
times in Leviticus and 12 times in Numbers.

[48] The verb ראה, "to see," as M. Buber has pointed out, constitutes a *Leitwort*
in Abraham's cycle ("Abraham, the Seer," *Judaism* 5 [1956] 291-305).

the place where you are, northward and southward and eastward
and westward; for all the land which you see (הָאָר) I will give to
you and to your descendants forever."[49] The hints of an Abra-
hamic background in Deut 32:49 receive confirmation in Moses'
actual seeing of the land in Deuteronomy 34.[50] Deut 34:1 echoes
Gen 13:15:

Gen 13:15	Deut 34:1
כי את כל הארץ אשר אתה ראה לך אתננה ולזרעך עד עולם	ויראהו יהוה את כל הארץ
For *all the land* which you *see* I will give to you and to your descendants for ever	And YHWH *made* him *see all the land*

The echoing goes further in Deut 34:4, which includes a partial
quote as well. The authoritative utterance behind the quote is
found in YHWH's solemn declaration to Abra(ha)m when the
patriarch first entered the "land of Canaan":[51]

Gen 12:7	Deut 34:4
וירא יהוה אל אברם ויאמר לזרעך אתן את הארץ הזאת	ויאמר יהוה אליו זאת הארץ אשר נשבעתי לאברהם ליצחק וליעקב לאמר לזרעך אתננה והראיתיך בעיניך

---

[49] In Deuteronomy the order given to Moses to ascend the mountain and see
the land first appears in 3:27, in Moses' retelling of God's command formulated
in Num 27:12-14. In Deut 3:27, just as in the case of Abraham in Gen 13:14,
Moses is enjoined by YHWH to look in the four cardinal points (note, however,
the lexical variations as to the appellation of the "south" and the "east," and the
difference in the order of the cardinal points).

[50] For an analysis of the data according to genetic parameters, see F. García
López, "Deut 34, DTR History and the Pentateuch," *Studies in Deuteronomy* (F.S.
C. J. Labuschagne; ed. F. García Martínez et al.; VTSup 53; Leiden: Brill, 1994)
54-56.

[51] God's promise to Abraham is repeated in Gen 15:18 and 17:8. In N.
Lohfink's view, it is to the description of the land in Gen 15:18 that Deut 12:1
refers ("Dtn 12,1 und Gen 15,18: Das dem Samen Abrahams geschenkte Land
als der Geltungsbereich der deuteronomischen Gesetze," *Die Väter Israels: Beiträge
zur Theologie der Patriarchenüberlieferungen im Alten Testament. Festschrift für Josef Scharbert zum 70. Geburtstag* [ed. M. Gourg; Stuttgart: Katholisches Bibelwerk, 1989]
183-210). A further link between the promise to Abraham and Moses' mission is
therefore discernible.

Then YHWH appeared [*was seen*] to *Abram* and *said, "To your descendants I will give this land"*

And YHWH *said* to him, *"This* is the *land* of which I swore to *Abraham*, to Isaac, and to Jacob, '*I will give* it *to your descendants.*' I *have let* you *see* it with your eyes"

The echoing between Genesis and Deuteronomy includes a play on the root ראה ("to see"). Whereas the root is used in the Niphal in Gen 12:7 (YHWH being the object of Abraham's vision) and in the Qal in Gen 13:14 (the land being now the object of the vision), it occurs in the Hiphil in Deut 34:1, 4—YHWH making Moses see the land.

The theme of seeing is emphasized again in the final note about Moses: "Moses was a hundred and twenty years old when he died; his eye grew not dim, nor his natural force abated" (Deut 34:7). Is Balaam, "the man whose eye is opened [?]" (Num 24:3, 15), once more the *persona* behind the *persona*?[52] The negative formulation of "his eye did not grow dim" seems rather to hint at characters whose eyes, at least in their old age, did grow dim. This was the case of both Isaac and Jacob. In the case of the former, a lexical parallelism is to be noted:[53]

Gen 27:1	Deut 34:7
ויהי כי זקן יצחק <u>ותכהין עיניו מראת</u>	<u>לא כהתה עינו</u>
When Isaac grew old and *his eyes were dim* so that he could not see	*His eye* did not *grow dim*

In the case of Jacob it is specified that "Israel's eyes grew heavy with age, so that he could not see (ועיני ישראל כבדו מזקן לא יוכל לראות)" (Gen 48:10). Of Abraham, nothing similar is ever said. That Moses is clear-sighted providentially fits YHWH's order enjoining him to see the land as far as Dan and the "hinder" Sea (הים האחרון), that is, the Western or Mediterranean Sea. Moses dies on the top of the mountain, his eyes open on the land, revisiting Abraham's eye contact with the land (Gen 13:14). In other words,

---

[52] The meaning of MT שְׁתֻם הָעָיִן in Num 24:3, 5 is uncertain; שתם has been rendered as "open," "closed," and "malevolent;" see the discussion in Rouillard, *Péricope*, 347-51.

[53] The root כהה, "to be or grow dim, faint," it is worth noting, does not occur elsewhere in the Pentateuch narrative. A subtle signal is thus provided to the reader.

an (almost) overall thematic structure of the Pentateuch becomes apparent here: "In Gen 12:1-3 an arch is opened which closes— but only partially—in Deut 34."[54] Is Moses taking up again something of Abraham's function and *persona*, while somehow dissociating himself from Jacob's and Isaac's? Abraham, it is worth remembering, is a patriarch without being the son of a patriarch; in other words, he is a patriarch "by vocation." Being installed by God's word in his mission, Abraham is not far from Moses the prophet.[55] The parallels between Moses and Abraham that I am referring to significantly concern the opening of the Abraham cycle, that is, the non-genealogical face of Abraham's story.

Despite his being a type of the visionary Moses, Abraham is in other respects, and along with the other patriarchs, an antitype of the one who died outside of the land. Abraham, Isaac and Jacob all entered the land, the access to which is denied to Moses. Their entry (or re-entry)—whether as migrant, returnee, or corpse—makes the difference between the patriarchs and the prophet. In that sense, the ban שמה תעבור לא, "you shall not cross over there," לא תבוא, "you shall not enter," put on Moses inverts what the narrator tells of Abraham:[56]

Gen 12:5-6	Deut 34:4
ויבאו ארצה כנען <u>ויעבר</u> אברם בארץ	ויאמר יהוה אליו זאת הארץ ... ושמה לא <u>תעבר</u>
When they had come to the land of Canaan, Abram *passed* through the land	And YHWH said to him, "This is the land ... but you shall not *pass* over there"

Retrospectively, a difference emerges within the "visionary paradigm" shared by Abraham and Moses. Abraham sees the land from

---

[54] García López, "Deut 34," 50; García López sums up D. J. A. Clines, *The Theme of the Pentateuch* (JSOTSup 10; Sheffield: Sheffield University Press, 1978) 25-29.

[55] Abraham himself has been called a "prophet," capable of efficient intercession (Gen 20:7). YHWH's "knowing" of Abraham and Moses represents a further contact between the two figures; compare Gen 18:19, "I have known him (ידעתיו)," and Deut 34:10, "Moses whom YHWH knew (ידע)."

[56] See the coordinated use of בוא and עבר in Deut 4:21-22: "Furthermore, YHWH was angry with me on your account, and he swore that I should not cross (לבלתי עברי) the Jordan, and that I should not enter (ולבלתי בוא) the good land which YHWH your God gives you for an inheritance. For I must die in this land, I must not cross (עבר) the Jordan; but you shall cross (עברים) and take possession of that good land."

within, after having entered it (12:5-6). Looking toward the four cardinal points of the land Abraham is looking around: "Lift up your eyes, and look *from the place where you are* (וראה מן המקום אשר אתה שם), northward and southward and eastward and westward" (13:14). Significantly, Moses intends first to match Abraham's way, that is, to see the land from within: אעברה נה ואראה את הארץ הטובה אשר בעבר הירדן, "Let me go over, I pray, and see the good land beyond the Jordan" (Deut 3:25). In his angry answer God inverts the order of actions, "seeing" occurring now before (the hence-forth forbidden) "crossing": "Go up to the top of Pisgah, and lift your eyes westward and northward and southward and eastward, *see it with your eyes, for you shall not go over this Jordan* (וראה בעיניך כי לא תעבר)" (Deut 3:27). The phrase לא תעבר, "You won't go over," quoted by Moses in 31:2, will become YHWH's last words to his prophet in 34:4. In this final statement Moses' fate is significant-ly thrown against the dynamic of the promise to the patriarchs: "This is the land of which I swore to Abraham, to Isaac, and to Jacob, 'I will give it to your descendants.' I will make you see it with your eyes, but you shall not go over there."

The verb עבר can be termed one of Deuteronomy's *Leitwörter*.[57] In his retelling of Israel's past and in his telling of its imminent future, Moses repeatedly describes the people's history as a "cross-ing" journey. From Deut 2:29 on, the root עבר tends to specialize in a double expression: עבר את הירדן, "to cross the Jordan";[58] עבר שמה, "to go over there" (into the land).[59] A "crossing" momentum toward the land seems therefore to carry Deuteronomy's charac-ters forward. The theme of passage is emphasized, however, while both speaker and addressees are at a standstill. And it is brought forward by the one who, he knows already, and we have known since 3:27, will not cross over. Moses is enjoined by God to see the land he will not enter from הר העברים, "the mountain 'of the parts beyond'" (32:49), as Driver translates.[60] A subtle irony is thus

---

[57] See Alter, *Biblical Narrative*, 95: "Through abundant repetition, the seman-tic range of the word-root is explored, different forms of the root are deployed, branching off at times into phonetic relatives (that is, word-play), synonymity, and antonymity; by virtue of its verbal status, the *Leitwort* refers immediately to meaning and thus to theme as well."

[58] Deut 2:29; 3:27; 4:21, 22, 26; 9:1; 11:31; 12:10; 27:2, 4, 12; 30:18; 31:2; 31:13; 32:47.

[59] Deut 3:21; 4:14; 6:1; 11:8, 11; 34:4.

[60] Driver, *Deuteronomy*, 383; see Num 27:12; 33:47, 48.

discernible in this unique occurrence of the toponym in Deuteronomy. In Deut 29:11 the verb עבר picks up a further meaning: "You stand this day all of you ... that you may *pass over into the sworn covenant of YHWH your God* (לעברך בברית יהוה ובאלתו) , which YHWH your God makes with you this day." As I have indicated in Chapter Three, the phrase "to pass over (עבר) into the sworn covenant" in 29:11 probably implies an actual crossing within in a prescribed ritual.[61] The overall perspective of the people's crossing in Moses' speeches, linked to the verbal root עבר, strengthens the hypothesis. To be sure, no equivalence is made by the text between "crossing into the covenant" and "crossing the Jordan." Yet the unity of time that, in Moses' view, holds together both operations (see 9:1, "You are to pass over the Jordan this day") brings about a symbolic overlapping of the two steps. At any rate, the people who will write down "all the words of this Torah" on the very day of the crossing, according to Moses' command in Deut 27:2-3, are the people who, by that time, will have "crossed into" the covenant as well. This assumption by Moses, however, supposes the actual transmission, from one bank of the Jordan to the other, of "all the words of this Torah" (28:58) and of the "sanctions of the covenant (אלות הברית)" (29:20). This brings us back to the issue of the ספר-record that ensures such a transmission.

7. *From Burial Place to Crossing Book*

A further parallelism between the ending of Genesis and the final chapter of Deuteronomy calls for examination. The issue of burying place that comes to the fore in the ending of Genesis also surfaces in Deuteronomy 34. Jacob's double request to be buried "with his fathers" (Gen 47:29-30; 49:29-32) is repeated by Joseph after his father's death (50:5); the translation of Jacob's embalmed corpse and its burying "in the cave of the field at Machpelah" are next told at length (50:6-14). In his valedictory speech (49:29-32) Jacob endows a common expression—נאסף אל עמיו, "to be gathered to his people"—with a definite spatial bearing. The idiom נאסף אל עמיו originally derives from the practice of collecting the bones of

---

[61] See p. 115 above.

the deceased, and of burying them anew, gathered to the family ossuary.[62] In Biblical Hebrew, however, the expression seems to have lost its spatial implication, and to be used metaphorically to express the death of family figures.[63] Yet Jacob seems to restore the set phrase to its genuine meaning when he says: "I am to be gathered with (אל = "to, unto") my people; bury me with (אל) my fathers in (אל) the cave that is in the field of Ephron the Hittite" (49:29). The repeated use of אל makes clear that in Jacob's view, "to be gathered to his people" is literally to be *spatially* gathered to his fathers' burying place. Moses, by contrast, does not make any arrangement concerning his grave place; in his last moments, far from being surrounded by sons anxious to comply with a father's last will, Moses faces God, who directs his servant's death even to the point of taking care of his burying: "And he buried him in the valley in the land of Moab opposite to Beth-Peor; and no one knows his burial place to this day" (Deut 34:6).[64]

The plain sense of Deut 34:6 implies in the first place what the post-biblical tradition repeatedly failed to record: Moses did die and was actually buried.[65] As to the mode of departure, Moses is in no way a precursor of Elijah. Elijah's ascension into heaven from the place where Moses died—the far side of the Jordan,

---

[62] See E. M. Meyers, "Secondary Burials in Palestine," *BA* 33 (1970) 15. Cf. the parallel expression נאסף אל קברתיו "to be gathered to his tombs" (2 Kgs 22:20; 2 Chr 34:28).

[63] The idiom נאסף אל עמיו "to be gathered to his people" occurs in the Pentateuch in connection with Abraham (Gen 25:8), Ishmael (Gen 25:17); Isaac (Gen 35:29); Jacob (Gen 49:29, 33); Aaron (Num 20:24; see 27:13 and Deut 32:50); Moses (Num 27:13; 31:2; Deut 32:50).

[64] The second part of the verse sheds light on the first as to the identity of the subject of ויקבר, "he buried," showing that it was YHWH who buried Moses: Moses' gravesite has remained forever a secret to men *because* God—and he alone—attended to Moses' burial (YHWH, to be sure, is not the subject of the previous sentence; God's name, however, occurs as the verse's last word). See in this sense Driver, *Deuteronomy*, 423; Lux, "Tod des Mose," 421; Loewenstamm, *From Babylon*, 146-147; Mayes, *Deuteronomy*, 413. Others replace the MT with a plural ("they buried") or a Nifal ("he was buried"). See Steuernagel, *Deuteronomium*, 130; M. Noth, *Überlieferungsgeschichte des Pentateuchs*, 188-89 n. 482; von Rad, *Deuteronomy*, 210. The incongruity proposed by these scholars in order to discredit the MT is overridden, in my view, by the specific narrative context of Deut 34:5-6.

[65] See the survey of the Jewish post-biblical developments on the issue of Moses' death in Loewenstamm, *From Babylon*, 136-66 and 167-73; see also (concerning Christian typology) R. M. Schwartz, "Joseph's Bones and the Resurrection of the Text: Remembering in the Bible," *The Book and the Text: The Bible and Literary Theory* (ed. R. Schwartz; Oxford: Blackwell, 1990) 40-59, esp. 55.

opposite Jericho (see 2 Kgs 2:1-12)— can be seen as a mythological variation on the theme of "the prophet's death," not as a
further rendering of the story of Deuteronomy 34. Moses' recorded death (34:5, וימת שם משה, "so Moses died there") echoes God's
unmistakable command, ומת בהר אשר אתה עלה שמה, "and die on the
mountain which you ascend" (32:50). Moses did die, witness the
fact that his burying place (קברה) exists somewhere, within an area
that can be spelled out: "in the valley in the land of Moab opposite to Beth-Peor" (34:6). These parameters are sufficient to rule
out the construing of Moses' disappearance as an ascension; yet
they are not sufficient to found a grave-site cult. Such a cult cannot be content with an area ("in the valley ... opposite to ..."); it
must, by definition, be founded on the *ipsissimus* grave site. Its
location, the narrator states, is not known and will never be
known. In Deut 34:6 the omniscient narrator conveys proper
nescience to the reader: "no one knows [ידע] the place of his burial to this day."[66] This nescience is imparted as perpetual: עד היום
הזה, "up to this day," that is, up to the day of Deuteronomy's reception. What is recorded as a fact (the burying place has not been
located) is turned, by the addition of "up to this day," into a "perpetual fact": the site will never be located. In other words, it is
not to be looked for.[67] Whereas the book of Genesis ended by
focusing on the patriarchal grave-site at Machpelah,[68] Deuteronomy takes pains to defuse any similar expectation. The ending of
the Jacob cycle in Genesis obeys a patriarchal logic: the burying
of the fathers in a "possession" (אחזת קבר, "burial holding," in Gen
23:4, 9, 20; 49:30; 50:13) within the promised land is the pledge
of the promise of the whole land to the sons.[69] In being freed

---

[66] Note the contrast with 34:10, "Moses, who YHWH knew (ידעו) face to face";
see Craigie, *Deuteronomy*, 406.

[67] See M. Greenberg, "Moses," *EncJud* 12.387.

[68] Yet, as Sternberg points out, the biblical narrative is far from promoting any
form of cult of the dead patriarchs, in line with its war against idolatry (no mention of Machpelah occurs beyond Genesis) ("Double Cave," 53).

[69] A "burial holding" in a cave at the edge of a field, begged from "the people of the land" (Genesis 23), represents a paradoxical pledge, to be sure, when
brought into alignment with God's promise to give "all the land ... to *you* [Abra-
ham] and to your descendants for ever" (Gen 13:14; cf. 15:7; 17:8). See Sternberg's presentation of Genesis 23 as the last of Abraham's trials ("Double Cave,"
55-57).

from any grave-site connection, Moses' death and burying can be said to be anti-patriarchal.[70]

The theme of burying—in the characters' last wills or in the narrator's own account—endows the final chapters of Genesis with a determined dynamism. The translation of the embalmed Jacob "out of Egypt" (Gen 47:30), "beyond the Jordan" (50:10, 11), and to the "land of Canaan" (49:30; 50:5, 13) functions as a proto-exodus within Genesis: a rehearsal by the "sons of Jacob" (50:12) of the future migration of the "sons of Israel" (Exod 1:1-7). Joseph's injunction to the sons of Israel, "You shall carry up my bones from here" (50:25) launches another movement along the same axis. The book of Genesis closes with the placing of Joseph in his coffin (50:26). The theme resurfaces in Exod 13:19, when the sons of Israel depart from Egypt: "And Moses took the bones of Joseph with him; for Joseph had solemnly sworn the people of Israel, saying, 'God will visit you; then you must carry my bones with you from here.'" The translation of Joseph's bones is "silently" carried on throughout the four ensuing books and comes to an end with the end of the book of Joshua: "The bones of Joseph which the people of Israel brought up from Egypt were buried at Shechem, in the portion of ground which Jacob bought from the sons of Hamor the father of Shechem for a hundred pieces of money; it became an inheritance of the descendants of Joseph" (Josh 24:32). At the other end of his journey Joseph is, once again, reunited with Jacob. By true patriarchal logic, the reunion of both "patriarchal" father and son is mediated by a "portion of ground" purchased from the Canaanites.

Joseph's coffin—אָרוֹן (Gen 50:26)—did not travel alone. From the book of Exodus on (Exod 25:10), another אָרוֹן, the ark, begins a parallel journey. Both containers will eventually cross the Jordan river and reach the land, having analogically journeyed from book to book, across the book limits. Much has been said about

---

[70] Actually, Deuteronomy smuggles its own logic into the patriarchal ways of speaking. The (rare) word used for Moses' grave echoes the Jacob cycle. Outside Deut 34:5, the word קְבֻרָה, "burial place," occurs three times in the Pentateuchal narrative. It refers twice to Rachel's tomb (Gen 35:20) and is used once by Jacob in reference to the patriarchal tomb in Hebron (47:30). In Jacob's valedictory speech (Gen 47:30), קְבֻרָה is preceded by the finite verb קבר (קְבַרְתַּם) וּקְבַרְתַּנִי בִּקְבֻרָתָם, "and bury me in their burial place"). The same sequence is found in Deut 34:6, וַיִּקְבֹּר ... קְבֻרָתוֹ, "and he buried... . his burial place." Deuteronomy's narrator redirects the patriarchal discourse to achieve his own narrative purpose.

the themes which make up the overall unity of the Pentateuch (or of the Hexateuch). Not much attention has been paid to the fact that on the narrative stage this unity is intermittently signalled by two objects "on the move," Joseph's coffin and the ark of the covenant. Both items fit the crossing of borders and call for appropriate "crossing characters" (Moses and the Exodus generation for the way from Egypt, Joshua and the Levites for the crossing of the Jordan). However, the two "vehicles" also embody very different conceptions of the inheritance of the land.

The ark and the Torah "book" come to be associated with each other before Moses' death, and before the impending crossing of the Jordan river.[71] "By the side" of the ark (see Deut 31:26), Moses' Torah "book" is therefore meant to enter the land where Moses was denied entry. A look at the book of Joshua reveals that, along with the ark, "Moses" did enter the land, yet as the name attached to the Torah "book" he wrote down: "Then Joshua built an altar on Mount Ebal to YHWH, the God of Israel, as Moses, the servant of YHWH had commanded the people of Israel, as it is written in *the Torah 'book' of Moses* (בספר תורת משה)" (Josh 8:31; see also Josh 8:32 and 23:6). The story of Deuteronomy can therefore be read as the genesis of a "crossing book." The two initiatives told in Deuteronomy 31—the public designation of Joshua as the "crossing" leader and the writing down of the Torah "book"—are teleogically related insofar as they make possible the passage of both the people and the "words of the Torah" into the land, and their reunion in the land. The wooden ark is therefore a kind of Israelite Trojan Horse. No decoy, but a *machina* to be translated *intra muros*, to echo Virgil,[72] it ensures the driving into the land of Israel's vital "words." Moses' Torah "book" transcends its spatial and temporal birthplace—the plains of Moab and the long day of its genesis—as much as it survives its "author's" death.

In its close reading and in its attention to long-range motifs, early Jewish interpretation could not fail to pick up the analogy of the two journeying ארונות ("coffin-" and "ark- chests"):

> *And Moses Took the Bones of Joseph with Him...* . Furthermore, the coffin of Joseph (ארונו של יוסף) went alongside of the ark (ארון) of the

---

[71] See my remarks pp. 64-67 above about the ark in Deuteronomy as "container," and about its affinity with the kinematics of the "book."

[72] Virgil, *Aeneid*, 2:33, 46.

Eternal. And the nations would say to the Israelites: What are these
two chests (ארונות)? And the Israelites would say to them: The one
is the ark of the Eternal, and the other is a coffin with a body in it.
The nations then would say: What is the importance of this coffin
that it should go alongside of the ark of the Eternal? And the
Israelites would say to them: The one lying in the coffin has fulfilled
that which is written on what lies in that ark. On the tablets lying
in this ark is written: "I am the Lord thy God" (Ex. 20.2), and of
Joseph it is written: "For, am I in the place of God?" (Gen. 50.19)
[etc.].[73]

The Midrash rightly emphasizes the concurrence, within an overall economy, of the two "bodies" that journeyed with the sons of
Israel toward the promised land. Yet the bias of the Tannaitic sages
in favor of biblical consonance prevents them from lending an
ear to the "counterpoint" that underlies such a symphony. The
common journeying of the two ארונות is also the signal that *two* different, yet convergent, economies actually run across the Pentateuchal narrative. Joseph's coffin can be said to be the last token
of the patriarchal economy; the ark that conveys both the Tables
and the Torah "book" is the lasting token of Moses' prophetic
economy. The former economy requires the ultimate entering of
the patriarchs, and of the "patriarchal son," into the land and
their burying in a portion of the land they unquestionably own.
Expansion throughout time (the genealogical continuity) and
space (the inhabiting of the land) has its warrant in the patriarchal holding.[74] The latter economy, superimposed on the former,
has no similar "physics." Moses' burial may remain out of the picture, and even out of the land. The principle of life, superimposed on generational continuity, is now located in the Torah
(Deut 32:47, "for it is your life"). The enjoying of the land, still
the object of the promise to the patriarchs, is mediated by obedience (שמע) to the Torah injunctions.[75] It is Moses' Torah "book"
that enables and ensures the enforcement of the covenantal economy throughout time and space, i.e., among the generations in

---

[73] *Mek. Beshallaḥ* 1:122-30 (transl. by J. Z. Lauterbach, *Mekilta de-Rabbi Ishmael*
[vol. 1; Philadelphia: Jewish Publication Society of America, 1976] 178-79).
[74] See Cooper and Goldstein, "Cult of the Dead," 296-97.
[75] Genesis closes with the oath taken by Joseph's brothers to carry his bones
to their proper place (50:25); the last verses of Deuteronomy announce the obedience of the people: "So the people of Israel listened (וישמעו) to [Joshua], and
did as YHWH had commanded Moses" (34:9).

the land. In other words, a Mosaic, that is, legal and prophetic, logic is grafted onto the patriarchal one.

The affinity between Moses and writing, as against the background of the patriarchal "pre-scriptural" economy, comes under new light in the ending of Deuteronomy. Albeit living in relatively sophisticated societies, the patriarchs are never depicted as writing characters. The patriarchal covenant knows a bodily inscription— the circumcision, and mute stelae.[76] Its lasting documents are the buried bodies of the fathers. The patriarchal grave at Hebron may be a "grave-register," as Nohrnberg writes,[77] both a land-register, and a genealogical register, yet it is a register that goes without writing, none of Israel's forefathers partaking in Moses' status as a scribe. Moses, on the contrary, to quote Nohrnberg again, is "in charge of Israel's papers, which are like a certificate of adoption,"[78] the opposite of the Mosaic "bill of divorcement" (Deut. 24:1, 3). The written Torah is far from sharing the fate of those ancient documents deposited as archives in temples and royal libraries.[79] Deuteronomy ultimately emphasizes in the ספר-record phenomenon what I would call its ark-aspect: its movability.[80] The book is to be "taken-away" (see 31:26: "Take this book of the Torah, and put it by the side of the ark"); it is what, with the ark, goes over. Spatial transcendence is a sign of temporal pervasiveness.[81] The book can be read over and over again; day after

---

[76] See the survey by Cooper and Goldstein, "Cult of the Dead," 285-303.

[77] J. Nohrnberg, *Like Unto Moses: The Constituting of an Interruption* (Bloomington: Indiana University Press, 1995) 60.

[78] Nohrnberg, *Like Unto Moses*, 3.

[79] See Oppenheim, *Ancient Mesopotamia*, 243-44, 286-87; W. G. Lambert, "A Catalogue of Texts and Authors," *JCS* 16 (1962) 59-81, who reconstructs and discusses the Ashurbanipal catalogue.

[80] The opposite aspect—immovability—is illustrated in the inscription on the "large stones" prescribed in Deuteronomy 27.

[81] The phenomenon of mutual conversion of time and space in the ending of Deuteronomy is finely broached by J. Gold, who missed however the role of the Torah book in such a process: "The future which Moses surveys is magnificently captured [...] as a spatial metaphor, an image startlingly appropriate to Israel's history. Time is seen as apprehensible only by events played out in a spatial dimension. Events are metaphors of time, and language is the synthesis. There is little to say about the marvels of a metaphor in which the leader of people, the servant of God, looks and points to a future which he has helped make possible but which he cannot live himself because of the very humanity that marks him at every point" ("Deuteronomy and the Word: The Beginning and the End," *The Biblical Mosaic: Changing Perspectives* [ed. R. M. Polzin and E. Rothman; Philadelphia: Fortress, 1982] 56-57).

day in the case of the king (Deut 17:19), every seven years in the
case of all the congregation (Deut 31:10-13). The ספר medium
gives Moses' Torah entry to the land that the fathers entered and
re-entered, up to their respective burying. The same medium,
through the act of reading, enters the time of the "sons," i.e. the
time of the generations in the land. Banning Moses from the land,
YHWH metes divine justice; yet God's refusal is the reverse side
of a divine *laissez-passer*: written by Moses in the "book," the words
of the Torah will reach the land. The actual removal of Moses'
burial place from public knowledge (34:6, "and no one knows")
is, analogically, the reverse of the actual publication of his Torah
"book" throughout time and space (31:8, "and their sons who have
not known will hear").[82]

8. *The Mosaic Communication*

The patriarchal-Mosaic complex has been recently singled out by
de Pury as a key to the understanding of the growth of the Pentateuch.[83] The point of departure and the initial control of de
Pury's hypothesis is provided by Hos 12:3-15. In his poem Hosea

---

[82] Not surprisingly, the scribal culture of the ancient Near East developed the
theme of the scribe's surviving in his written work. The following lines (probably from Thebes, about 1300 BCE) are particularly telling. "They [the scribes]
made themselves no pyramids of metal, with their tombstones of iron. Though
they could not leave heirs in children, ... pronouncing their names, they did
make heirs for themselves in the writings and in the (books of) wisdom which
they composed. They gave themselves [*the papyrus-roll* as a lector] priest, the writ-
ing-board as a son-he-loves, (books of) wisdom (as) their pyramids, the reed-pen
(as) their child, and the back of a stone for a wife. From great to small were
made into his children. (As) for the scribe, he is the foremost of them. If there
were made for (them) doors and buildings, they are crumbled; their mortuary
service is [*gone*]; their tombstones are covered with dirt; and their graves are forgotten. (But) their names are (still) pronounced because of their books which
they made, since they were good and the memory of them (lasts) to the limits
of eternity" (Papyrus Chester Beatty IV, verso ii 5- iii 11; *ANET* 431-32).

[83] See A. de Pury, "La tradition patriarcale en Genèse 12-35," *Le Pentateuque en
question* (ed. A. de Pury; Genève: Labor et Fides, 1989) 259-70; idem, "Le cycle
de Jacob comme légende autonome des origines d'Israël," *Congress Volume Leuven 1989* (VTSup 43; ed. J.A. Emerton; Leiden: Brill, 1991) 78-96; idem, "Osée
12 et ses implications pour le débat actuel sur le Pentateuque," *Le Pentateuque:
recherches et débats* (LD 151; ed. P. Haudebert; Paris: Cerf, 1992) 175-207; idem,
"Las dos leyendas sobre el origen de Israel (Jacob y Moisés) y la elaboración del
Pentateuco," *EstBib* 52 (1994) 95-131.

exposes Israel's present misbehavior by resorting to the opposition between the fraudulent or cowardly eponymous ancestor Jacob/Israel, and God's kindness to the patriarch or the people of Israel. In the last section (12:12-15) Jacob's story is opposed to another story, which is seen in a positive light: the exodus from Egypt under the leadership of a prophet, that is, the Mosaic story:[84] "Jacob fled to the land of Aram; there Israel did service for a wife, and for a wife he herded sheep. By a prophet YHWH brought Israel up from Egypt, and by a prophet it was preserved" (Hos 12:12-13). Hosea's audience, de Pury sums up, is placed before two foundational stories. Each one claims to account for the presence of Israel in Canaan, yet they compete with each other. The first legend of origins features an ancestor as mediate link, and the second a prophet. The former brings lineage and inheritance into play, whereas the latter, basically antitribal and anti-genealogical, implies prophetic vocation and speech (see Hos 12:11, "I spoke to the prophets; it was I who multiplied visions, and through the prophets gave parables"). Hosea the prophet invites his audience to make a choice between the two, and in favor of the Exodus history rather than Jacob's. In de Pury's view, the Pentateuch is the outcome of an exilic combination of Israel's two foundational legends, at a time when the normativity of the Mosaic tradition no longer had to fear the appending of a patriarchal "prologue"—the Joseph story providing the link between the two units. The patriarchal covenant was thus combined with the Mosaic one, the former providing the prologue and the infrastructure for the latter.[85] However, a subtle antagonism centered on the figure of Jacob still underlies the texts we now read. It is notably de Pury's contention that strict Deuteronomistic theology was hostile to the tradition of Jacob, the unnamed "wandering Aramaean" of Deut 26:5.[86]

---

[84] See E. Jacob, "Der Prophet Hosea und die Geschichte," *EvT* 24 (1964) 281-90.

[85] In the patriarchal camp, Abraham may have been enhanced as the beneficiary of an almost prophetic vocation, and of a promise particularly meaningful for exilic or even post-exilic readers.

[86] See de Pury, "Cycle de Jacob," 82-83; idem, "La dos leyendas," 128: "La historiografía deuteronomistica rezuma todavía una hostilidad radical hacia la tradición jacobiana, tradición que procura ocultar por todos los medios." If this is the case, later redactors and editors must have turned the figure of Jacob into a kind of *felix* necessity.

De Pury's hypothesis is appealing, and, interestingly enough, it ties up many of the themes *narratively* spun against the patriarchal background in Deuteronomy 31-34. The whole issue could represent an instance of mutual confirming between a poetic and a genetic approach. The redactional and editorial process, however, may have been more complex than in de Pury's reconstruction.[87] In my view, moreover, the represented story is less dramatic than the genetic process proposed by de Pury. Deuteronomy 31-34 does not stage a hostility or the overcoming of a hostility. In particular, these chapters do not imply that Moses relates traumatically to the figure of his patriarchal ancestor(s). The echoes of Jacob's words in Moses' own (see Deut 31:29 and Gen 49:1; Deut 33:13-16 and Gen 49:25-26), or Moses' reference to Israel as "Jacob" (32:9; 33:4, 10, 28), are no proof of Moses' psychological entanglement with his forefather. The narrator and God are responsible for many of the echoing effects between Deuteronomy 31-34 and Genesis, thus exonerating Moses from being *the* voice or character struck with a "patriarchal complex."[88] Moses seems well aware of his revisiting of previous scenes and speeches of the national history. Yet no psychologically (let alone pathologically) marked turn can be discerned in his final words and deeds, as far as the patriarchs or Balaam are concerned. It is rather the reader who records, thanks to concurrent hints in the text, the metamorphosis of a familiar "genre"—the departing of patriarchal figures—into an unprecedented one—the departing of a national prophet and Torah-giver.

The Mosaic valedictory communication differs from Jacob's in that it implies a different authority. Fatherhood gives way to prophetic mandate; life-giving might (see Gen 49:2) is replaced by life-giving words (see 32:47; 30:19-20). The difference in communication is also shaped by the difference of the audience, in quantity as in quality. In his last words, Jacob is surrounded by a

---

[87] L. M. Eslinger, for instance, points to an ideological contrast between the "canonical" figure of Jacob in Genesis 32 and Hosea's representation of it ("Hosea 12:5a and Genesis 32:29: A Study in Inner Biblical Exegesis," *JSOT* 18 [1980] 91-99).

[88] The narrator echoes Genesis in Deut 31:1 (Gen 27:7, Isaac's words, and Gen 49:28, the narrator's), in Deut 32:45-46 (Gen 49:33, a narratorial statement), in Deut 34:7 (Gen 27:1, idem). God echoes the narrator in Deut 31:14 (Gen 47:29) and in Deut 34:4 (Gen 12:5-6), Jacob in Deut 31:16 (Gen 47:30), and himself in Deut 34:4 (Gen 12:7; 15:18; 17:8).

restricted clan—his twelve sons. Moses faces an organized nation (see Deut 29:9-10), defined in Deuteronomy 31-34 as "all Israel" (31:1; 32:45), "the people" (32:44), "the sons of Israel" (33:1), "all the assembly of Israel" (31:30).[89] Moses' Song projects the history of an elected, rebuked, and vindicated people (see the use of עַם, "people," and גּוֹי, "nation," in 32:6, 8-9, 28, 36, 43). The distributive blessing of the tribes in Deuteronomy 33 is prefaced with a reminder of Israel's birth as a theocratic nation (33:5); the individual sayings are followed by Moses' final salute to Israel as a distinct people: "Happy are you, O Israel! Who is like you, a people (עַם) saved by YHWH!" (33:29).[90] Addressing the "sons of Israel" as a people, Moses brings specific communicational ways and means into play. He alternates second-person singular and second-person plural references to Israel;[91] he speaks "in two voices," with the elders or the Levitical priests as co-speakers (27:1, 9); he appeals to communication "mediators" (the "elders of your tribes" and the "officers" in 31:28).

A distinctive element of the new, properly Mosaic, communication is his recourse to writing. Emulating God's initiative at Horeb, Moses provides the people with a written record of the covenantal "words." This initiative represents a definite leap forward, when compared with the "sayings" of the fathers. So does Moses at Sinai, as reported in Exodus 24. Yet the "'book' of the Covenant" has no other use than its reading in the covenantal ritual at Sinai (Exod 24:3-8). In his retelling of Sinai/Horeb in Deuteronomy, Moses significantly passes over this record in silence, thus preparing the entrance of another document, endowed with a different import. The Deuteronomic Torah "book" is meant to perpetually accompany the people. It will do so in its quality of Israel's *politeia* ("national constitution")—as

---

[89] See Moses' command in 31:28, הַקְהִילוּ, "assemble," and compare the "gathering" in Genesis 49 (49:1, הֵאָסְפוּ, "gather yourselves together"; 49:2, הִקָּבְצוּ, "group together").

[90] In his blessing, Balaam too addresses Israel as a nation. Yet he merely speaks "on" the people, hailing it from afar, whereas Moses confronts the "you" of his addressees.

[91] Moses thus relates to Israel as "both a corporate entity and a collectivity of the individual selves who comprise its membership" (S. Dean McBride, Jr., "Polity of the Covenant People: The Book of Deuteronomy," *Interpretation* 41 [1987] 237). On the rhetorical (rather than exclusively redactional) significance of this alternation, see Lohfink, *Hauptgebot*, 244-51.

Josephus puts it,[92] spelling out Israel's "divinely authorized social order."[93] In the ancient Near East law-books are state documents, and so is Moses' Torah "book." The written record matches the scope of Moses' address: it is meant to be solemnly read to "all Israel" assembled (31:9-13). The "book" has its arch-reader in Israel's future king (17:18-20), thus revealing its inclusive compass in Israel's new society. When it attains its written form, the Mosaic communication, it can be said, appears in its full social import.

The Pentateuch can be broached as a history of communication, of which Deuteronomy represents the final stage. A major change intervenes in the transition between the patriarchal age and the Mosaic one. Since his calling in Exodus 3, Moses has to speak to the ones who are no longer the "sons of Israel" (Exod 1:1) but "the people of the sons of Israel" (Exod 1:9). Moses' communicational venture gets a further, idiosyncratic turn in Deuteronomy, the book made of his "words" in the land of Moab. As the present chapter endeavored to show, the originality of Moses' communication is best understood in the contrast of the departing scenes of two foundational figures, the eponymous patriarch and the founder of the nation. Moses does not cross over to the land, yet he does not die without bringing a new kind of communication to completion: "when Moses had finished writing the words of this Torah in a 'book'" (Deut 31:24); "when Moses had finished speaking all these words to all Israel" (32:45).

---

[92] *J. Ant.* 4 § 184, 193, 198, 302, 310, 312. Josephus' view is the starting point of S. Dean McBride, Jr.'s penetrating study, "Polity of the Covenant People: The Book of Deuteronomy," *Int* 41 (1987) 229-44.

[93] McBride, "Polity," 233.

CHAPTER SEVEN

"TAKE THIS 'BOOK'"
THE TORAH "BOOK" AND THE BOOK OF DEUTERONOMY

> The words were spoken
> as if there was no book,
> Except that the reader
> leaned above the page.
>
> Wallace Stevens, "The House Was Quiet
> and the World Was Calm"

The previous chapters centered on Deuteronomy's communication process as it unrolls "on stage," that is, in the represented history. Yet from the outset Moses' voice and the representation of Moses' scribal activity are the inner side of another communication endeavor: the conducting of the tale by the book's narrator. The present chapter will bring this further dimension—the framing narration—into the picture and will examine the relationship between Deuteronomy's "inner" and "outer" voices, Moses' and the narrator's. As before, the investigation will follow Deuteronomy's thread from beginning to end, as much as possible. In so doing I will review the modulations of the narrative voice in Deuteronomy, from self-effacement, through specific intrusions, to intrusive commentary. A remarkable analogy exists between Moses' voice and the narrator's. Yet, as made clear at the end of Deuteronomy, the analogy is just an analogy. The difference between Israel's arch-prophet and Deuteronomy's narrator is not one of degree only; it is essential. The narrator is not the "prophet like Moses," and Moses, though a gifted (hi)storyteller, is not the narrator's peer. The difference is essential, and, as such, it makes Deuteronomy's narrative possible.

Behind the narrator, Deuteronomy's final chapters may evoke further figures. The silhouette of the scribes responsible for the making of Deuteronomy can arguably be discerned in Moses-the-scribe, who commits the "book" of the Torah to writing. What could be the purport of an analogy of this kind? Does it threaten Deuteronomy's narrative model, or does it support it? The

assessment of Moses' analogical stance vis-à-vis Deuteronomy's
makers is the object of an excursus appended to the present chapter.

Deuteronomy's opening verse—אלה הדברים אשר דבר משה, "These
are the words that Moses spoke"—makes it clear: Deuteronomy
bears upon a world of words. "This is a book about words and
the covenant form is a form of words."[1] The phrases that preface
Deuteronomy's three ensuing sections bear out the initial indication. "And this is the Torah that Moses set before the sons of
Israel" (Deut 4:44); "These are the words of the covenant which
YHWH commanded to make with the sons of Israel" (28:69); "And
this is the blessing with which Moses the man of God blessed the
sons of Israel" (33:1). Verbal communication ("words," "Torah,"
"words of the covenant," "blessing") is the represented action on
which Deuteronomy focuses. Yet Deuteronomy itself, as a book, a
piece of linguistic communication, is also made of "words." The
book traditionally called in Hebrew דברים, "Words," is therefore
characterized by an overall homogeneity between the represented action (Moses' linguistic communication) and the representing medium (the book as linguistic communication). Is this
homogeneity a mere coincidence, without special relevance, or
does it make sense within a purposeful literary design? Were
Deuteronomy's represented action "X begot Y" or "X waged war
against Y," the question would not arise. Yet in Deuteronomy language represents language. In the following sections I will review
the aspects of Deuteronomy's analogy between represented and
"representing" communication. In my introduction, drawing on
Ezekiel's vision of the divine "chariot" (merkābâ), I described
Deuteronomy's communicational "mechanics" as based on the
"wheel within the wheel" effect. Deuteronomy, I will now show, is
indeed a singular literary "chariot" or "machine."

---

[1] Gold, "Deuteronomy and the Word," 52.

1. *So Spoke Moses*

How to *prendre la parole* by handing it over: this seems to be the issue at stake in Deuteronomy's opening. What the narrator places in the foreground is Moses' voice, not his. Most of the interventions of Deuteronomy's narrative voice either launch or re-launch Moses' represented speech acts. This is the function of the four major headings (Deut 1:1-5; 4:44-5:1; 28:69-29:1a; 33:1). Within these units speech is at times re-launched by narratorial intervention (27:1, 9, 11). This is especially the case in Deuteronomy 31-33 (see 31:1(2), 7, 10, 14, 16, 23, 25, 30; 32:44-45(46), 48; 33:1). In these chapters the only mentions (by the narrator) of non-vocal actions are found in 31:9, 24 and 31:14-15—the double reference to the writing of the Torah "book" and the telling of YHWH's theophany. Both events, however, are related to communication. The major exception to this communicational pattern is found in Deuteronomy 34, where a silent Moses is the subject and the object of non-verbal, ultimate actions ("Moses went up ... . YHWH made him see ... . Moses died ... . He buried him ... . The sons of Israel wept for Moses").[2] Most of the narratorial phrases thus have a relaying function, introducing the reader to the real action—Moses' speech act—on the scene. This represents a peculiar form of narratorial self-effacement to the benefit of the speaking *dramatis persona*.[3] Yet the narrator's reticence is apparently not equally distributed over the Mosaic speeches. Narratorial comments of a further kind occur within Deuteronomy 1-11 (that is, before Moses' transmission of legal stipulations). These comments call for a specific assessment.

---

[2] The minor exception is constituted by Deut 4:41-43, narrating the establishment by Moses of cities of refuge in Transjordan; on this section, see above p. 37 and pp. 184-85.

[3] Self-effacement of the narrative voice does not mean disappearance. Deuteronomy does not open immediately with Moses' voice. A narratorial *ouverture* precedes it, which immediately gives precedence to the prophet's דברים, "words".

2. *Frame-Breaks*

A second set of narratorial interventions is found in the so-called "frame-breaks" in the first and second Mosaic speeches.[4] They have the form of explanatory notes interpolated within Moses' reported speech or even within God's words quoted by Moses. In Moses' first speech five texts, often described as "antiquarian notices"[5] or "ethnographic sections,"[6] belong to this category: Deut 2:10-12, 20-23; 3:9, 11, 13b-14; in Moses' second discourse, one text pertains to the same group of inserted notices: 10:6-9. A clear instance of "frame-break" is found in Deut 3:8-12:

> [8]So we took the land at that time out of the hands of the two kings of the Amorites who were beyond the Jordan, from the valley of the Arnon to Mount Hermon
>> —[9]*The Sidonians call Hermon Sirion, while the Amorites call it Senir—*
> [10]all the cities of the tableland and all Gilead and all Bashan, as far as Salecah and Edrei, cities of the kingdom of Og in Bashan
>> —[11]*For only Og the king of Bashan was left of the remnant of the Rephaim; behold his bedstead was a bedstead of iron; is it not in Rabbah of the Ammonites? Nine cubits was its length, and four cubits its breadth, according to the common cubit*[7]
> [12]When we took possession of this land at that time ...

The interpolations in question are commonly regarded as secondary explanatory notes, that is, as redactional interpolations.[8] Yet these notices also and primarily represent discursive interpolations—interruptions in the flow of discourse—and they need to be assessed as such.[9] In his *Moses and the Deuteronomist* Polzin

---

[4] The category of "frame-break" goes back to E. Goffman, *Frame Analysis: An Essay on the Organization of Experience* (Cambridge: Harvard University Press, 1974). The category has been used by Polzin to describe the narratorial interventions in Deuteronomy 1-11 (see *Moses*, 30-36, 38-39).

[5] Driver, *Deuteronomy*, 36.

[6] C. J. Labuschagne, "Divine Speech in Deuteronomy," *Das Deuteronomium: Entstehung, Gestalt und Botschaft* (BETL 68; ed. N. Lohfink; Louvain: University Press, 1985) 113.

[7] In Weinfeld's view (*Deuteronomy*, 184), "This clause seems to refer to [Og's] sarcophagus, where he was buried." An interesting contrast would then be created between Og's burial place, the location of which belongs to public knowledge, and Moses' tomb, the place of which is removed from knowledge "up to this day" (Deut 34:6).

[8] See for instance (regarding the notices in Deut 2:10-12, 20-23) von Rad, *Deuteronomy*, 42; Mayes, *Deuteronomy*, 137, 139; Perlitt, *Deuteronomium*, 178.

[9] See the remarks by Labuschagne, "Divine Speech," 112-114. In Labuschagne's view the "ethnographic notices" in Deut 2:10-12, 20-23 serve "to bridge the gap

describes them as intrusions by Deuteronomy's narrator, and he endows them with a subtle communicational function.[10] The so-called "frame-breaks," Polzin argues, represent self-assertions by the Deuteronomistic narrator in his dialectical stance vis-à-vis Moses. By supplementing Israel's greatest prophet (see Deut 34:10), the narrator reveals the limits of Moses' prophetic authority. Through the narrator's frame-breaks,

> the unique status of Moses, emphasized in the other parts of the reporting narrative, is undermined. The narrator's utterances are spoken in two ideological voices which interfere with one another: an overt, obvious voice that exalts Moses and plays down its own role, and a hidden voice that will soon exalt itself at the expense of Moses' uniqueness.[11]

Polzin's contention that the narratorial interpolations bespeak a dialectical, dissonant relationship between the narrator and Moses is, in my view, farfetched, lacking adequate controls. In the following paragraphs I will answer Polzin's claim by enhancing what is, in my view, the point in the narrator's interpolated notices.

What the interpolated comments make clear is that Deuteronomy unfolds a double act of communication: (1) from Moses to his addressees in the plains of Moab; (2) from the narrator to the readers.[12] The starting point is that each group remains in its own sphere of communication (Moses never addresses the readers as such). The latter-day readers are in the position to receive information that is denied to Moses' "historical" addressees. In the so-called frame-breaks the readers, indeed, are provided with practical updatings (see the use of the phrase "[even] to this day" in Deut 2:22; 3:14 and 10:8). The quality of the speaker also makes the difference. In the interpolations pieces of encyclopedic knowledge are communicated, as befits an omniscient narrator; the communication of the same data would sound inappropriate in the mouth of a limited (albeit prophetic) character. For instance, the mention of the Sidonian name for Mount Hermon or the Ammonite name for the Rephaim does not obviously suit Moses'

---

created by the contrast between the command to Moses [before the notices] and that to the people [after the notices]" (p. 113). Labuschagne does not, however, address the question of a change of "voice" in these notices.

[10] See Polzin, *Moses*, 30-36, 38-39.

[11] Polzin, *Moses*, 34.

[12] This is stressed by Polzin, *Moses*, 31-32.

speech—Moses tells the story in a national perspective. Yet the same mention is appropriate to the narrator's parlance, since the latter sets Israel's story against its international background. Thus, while reproducing Moses' address to the sons of Israel in the plains of Moab, the narrator at times produces his own (offstage) voice in a direct disclosure to the reader.

The phenomenon of "frame breaks" highlights Deuteronomy's preference for dramatic presentation. Reported speech is the norm. In what goes before Deuteronomy 31, introductory statements excepted, the narrator's voice is only heard against the background of the character's speech. The primacy of reported speech stands out in that the point commented upon in the interpolation is always provided by the character's speech. Moses' mention of Og triggers the narratorial comment on "king Og" (Deut 5:11); Moses' account of the making of the ark prompts the narrator's notice on the setting apart of the tribe of Levi "to carry the ark of the covenant of YHWH" (10:8-9); etc. The same primacy of reported speech shows in the narrative representation of time. In a study on "Die Stimmen in Deuteronomium 2," Lohfink addresses an intriguing point in Moses' retelling of the people's movement toward the promised land.[13] How is Israel's "leap" over Moab to be explained? In Deut 2:14 the people cross the Wadi Zered, i.e., Moab's southern border. In 2:24 the people is enjoined by God to cross the Wadi Arnon, that is, Moab's northern border. Between these two verses, Moses has nowhere directly reported the people's journey through Moab:

> [13]So we crossed the Wadi Zered ... . [16]So when all the men of war had perished and were dead from among the people, [17]YHWH said to me, [18]"This day you are to pass over the boundary of Moab at Ar; [19]and when you approach the frontier of the sons of Ammon, do not harass them or contend with them, for I will not give you any of the land of the sons of Ammon as a possession, because I have given it to the sons of Lot for a possession.
>
> —[20]*That also is known as a land of Rephaim; Rephaim formerly lived there, but the Ammonites called them Zamzummim,* [21]*a people great and many, and tall as the Anakim; but YHWH destroyed them before them; and they dispossessed them, and settled in their stead;* [22]*as he did for the sons of Esau, who live in Seir, when he destroyed the Horites before them, and they dispossessed them, and settled in their stead even to this deay.* [23]*As for the Avvim, who lived in villages as far as Gaza,*

---

[13] N. Lohfink, "Die Stimmen in Deuteronomium 2," *BZ* 37 (1993) 227-31.

the Caphtorim, who came from Caphtor, destroyed them, and settled in their stead—
[24]Rise up, take your journey, and cross the Wadi Arnon; behold, I have given into your hand Sihon the Amorite, king of Heshbon, and his land; begin to take possession and contend with him in battle." (Deut 2:14-24)

Lohfink perspicaciously solves the conundrum by pointing to the temporal relevance of the interpolation in Deut 2:20-23. The representational time (*Erzählzeit,* or "narrating time") required by the narrator's comment enables the sons of Israel, in the represented time (*erzählte Zeit,* or "narrated time"), to go from the southern border of Moab to its northern border.[14] Lohfink, however, underrates one fact: the represented time he relies upon is actually Moses' representational time, in his own rendering of the story (by quoting God). What the interpolation covers is the time of the people's journey *in Moses' retelling.* An interesting dimension of these interpolations is therefore their reversal of the "wheel within the wheel" effect: the narrator's act of communication now revolves within the character's. The themes and the tempo of the narrative are set up by the secondary speaker (Moses), while the primary speaker (the narrator) models his interventions on the dramatis persona's art of telling.

The narratorial comments, however, have a narrative function of their own. They cast their proper authority on specific points of Moses' retelling. This is especially perceptible in the international aspect of Israel's settlement history. Leaving the wilderness, Israel enters inhabited areas, the *concert des nations,* stepping into a "mapped" district where landmarks receive different names. As the narrator points out, "The Sidonians call Hermon Sirion, while the Amorites call it Senir" (Deut 3:9). The map is far from reading *No Man's Land,* let alone *Terra Incognita.* In the area in question, lands and peoples, at least some of them, have been matched by YHWH himself, the God of Israel. God commands Israel to refrain from contention with the people of Edom, Moab, and Ammon, because he is the one who gave them these lands as a possession (see 2:5, 9, 19). In his interpolations the narrator provides historical notes for each of the cases (Edom: 2:12, 22; Moab:

---

[14] For the distinction between *Erzählzeit* and *erzählte Zeit,* see G. Müller, *Morphologische Poetik: Gesammelte Aufsätze* (ed. E. Müller; Darmstadt: Wissenschaftliche Buchgesellschaft, 1968) 269-86. See also Genette, *Narrative Discourse,* 33-35; and Ska, *"Our Fathers,"* 7-8.

2:10-11; Ammon: 2:20-21). He further echoes YHWH's intervention in the national history of Edom (2:22; compare 2:12) and
Ammon (2:21). What the narrator adds to Moses' account is the
point of view of the peoples in question in their national history.
We hear that the Moabites used to call the former inhabitants of
their land "Emim" (2:11), and that the Ammonites called their
giant predecessors in Ammon "Zamzummim" (2:20). Alternative
names and foreign languages remind the reader of Israel's movement into a regional history lived by other peoples. In addition,
the narrator specifies which of these other national histories took
place with or without YHWH's blessing. The latter case is illustrated in the notice on the Caphtorites (Philistines) (2:23), with
no mention whatsoever of YHWH's intervention in their own
"exodus" and "settlement" history.[15] As for Og, king of Bashan,
he is presented by the narrator as the last remnant of the Rephaim
(3:11), a people evicted by YHWH (see 2:21-22). What is thus
revealed is a map with divinely protected areas (Edom, Moab,
Ammon), and others, like Bashan or the land settled by the
Philistines, liable to dispossession.

The narrator thus puts his own authority behind Moses' account
in the "frame-breaks" in Deuteronomy 2, completing the picture
with those elements Moses could not provide. The situation therefore is not as described by Polzin: "The [narrator's] voice that
tends to diminish Moses' status tends to diminish Israel's uniqueness also."[16] We rather hear the narrator confirming with his own
authority and knowledge that which Moses reports. Moses tells of
God's involvement in Israel's settling process; that this involvement is objectively reflected in the (then) "state of the world,"
and even in current landmarks,[17] is clarified by the narrator. In
his interpolations the narrator corroborates Moses' account by
affixing to it pre-Mosaic data (Deut 2:10-12, 20-23) as well as
post-Mosaic (3:11, 14; 10:8-9), and national facts (the alternative
names for Mount Hermon, 3:9). The narrator, in *these* instances,

---

[15] See Buis, *Deutéronome*, 67-68; Mayes, *Deuteronomy*, 139-40. Interestingly
enough, the opposite view is presented in Amos 9:7, "Did I not bring up Israel
from the land of Egypt, and the Philistines from Caphtor and the Syrians from
Kir?"

[16] Polzin, *Moses*, 38.

[17] See Og's iron bed (Deut 3:11), and the name of "Havvoth-jair" (3:14), which
bespeaks "to this day" Jair's conquest of what was once "the land of Rephaim,"
that is, a land liable to dispossession.

finds it important to support Moses' knowledge with his own
omniscience. A section of Moses' speech interpolated with a narratorial comment is thus a section enhanced in its reliability. No
doubt whatsoever can remain in the reader's mind on these
points.

If these points in Moses' retelling are narratorially affirmed,
what about other points? Does the narrator's voiceless stance in
certain cases provide the reader with an evaluative clue? Does it
indicate matters of secondary importance? Possible tamperings
with the truth by Moses? Moses' retelling—concerning the issue
of and the reason for the prophet's ultimate fate—showed,
indeed, a certain amount of tampering. In those passages the narrator refrained from intruding (in order to avoid any ironic distance vis-à-vis his *dramatis persona*?), leaving the reader the sole
judge of the matter. Interestingly enough, the contrast between
statements with and without narratorial interpolation is limited to
the non-legal section of Moses' speech (that is, within Deuteronomy 1-11). The narrator falls silent during Moses' transmission of
the Torah's legal stipulations (starting with Deut 12:1).[18] Is it surprising? The narrator has already declared himself in the matter.
As made clear in 1:3, "Moses spoke to the people of Israel according to all that YHWH had commanded him to them (ככל אשר צוה
יהוה אתו אלהם)." Everything received by Moses as "commandment
to the people" has been unerringly conveyed to them. There is
no place here for contrasts in matter of truth: reliability is *de
rigueur*.

3. *"The Torah I Am Setting before You"*

The absolute reliability that prevails in the transmission of
YHWH's commandments is echoed in the narrator's and Moses'
respective parlances: "This is the Torah ... . These are the oaths,
the statutes and the ordinances" (4:44-45) announces the narrator; "This is the commandment, the statutes and the ordinances"
(6:1), "These are the statutes and ordinances" (12:1), says Moses.
Is it Moses who speaks "like" Deuteronomy's narrator, or is it the

---

[18] The narrator was equally silent during Moses' re-uttering of the "ten words"
in Deuteronomy 5.

latter who anticipates stylistically Moses' opening statements?[19] For anyone who goes by the book's claim to represent history, the latter alternative is the right one. By resorting to "This/these (אלה/ זאת)" + *verba dicendi* opening syntagms, the book echoes Moses' presentation of Israel's essential words. In so doing, the book makes perennial ("This is the Torah ...") that which Moses uttered once, in a specific time and place: "This is the commandment ..." The concord between primary and secondary locutors reaches its climax here. The two of them concur in "setting before" their respective audiences words of vital importance (see 32:47).

Like YHWH's words at Horeb—"YHWH spoke with you face to face (פנים בפנים)" (Deut 5:4)—Moses' words face their historical addressees, the sons of Israel, in the plains of Moab. The frontal character of the address is lexically echoed in the preposition לפני, "at the face of, in front of," which is associated with Moses' communication: "The Torah I am setting *before you* (לפניכם) this day" (4:8; see also 4:44; 11:26, 32; 30:1, 15, 19). The extensive use of verbal adjectives further contributes to this mode of presentation ("The Torah I *am setting* (נֹתֵן) before you this day" [4:8, and *passim*]).[20] This stylistic element endows Moses' speech with a dramatic quality: in their contextual use, the verbal adjectives echo Moses' "present" facing of the people. Concurrently, Moses multiplies rhetorical calls for a committed reception of his, and YHWH's, words—the verb שמע, "to listen—to obey," being the hall-

---

[19] A redactional phenomenon possibly explains, at least in part, these lexical and syntactic echoes. Lohfink sees in Deut 4:45, "These are the 'testimonies' (עדת) ... which Moses spoke to the sons of Israel when they came out of Egypt," "vermutlich die älteste uns erhaltene Überschrift zum dt Gesetz" (Lohfink, "'ed(w)t im Deuteronomium," 89). See also N. Lohfink, "Deutéronome et Pentateuque: état de la recherche," in *Le Pentateuque: débats et recherches* (Lectio Divina 151; Paris: Cerf, 1992) 56-57. The progressive diversification of the superscripts is the object of another study by Lohfink: "Die *huqqîm ûmišpāṭîm* im Buch Deuteronomium und ihre Neubegrenzung durch Dtn 12,1," *Bib* 70 (1989) 1-30. The "These (אלה) are ..." pattern could therefore have provided the *matrix* for ensuing developments, and notably for the prefacing of the book. Yet redactional phenomena also serve poetic purposes; the (partial) homology between frame and inset, between the narrator's way of speaking and Moses', is, in my view, primarily an element of Deuteronomy's overall poetics.

[20] See Lohfink, "Fabel," 74 n. 24. Moses' speeches also feature several performatives in perfect form (see for instance Deut 30:15, 18, 19). These verbal forms have their way of stressing the actuality of discourse. See Lohfink, "Bund," 221-228; see also my review of Lenchak, *"Choose Life!"*, *Bib* 76 (1995) 96-97.

mark of such a reception. The poetic means matches the ideological content: Moses' "present" speech hanging upon the audience's reception reflects the very essence of the conditional
covenant offered to the people in Moab.[21] A covenant of this kind
is never to be taken for granted and depends upon the recipient's continued faithfulness. This effect is reinforced by a remarkable narratorial strategy in Deuteronomy. No reception of Moses'
words is ever *told* in the embedding narrative. Whereas Moses multiplies the call to listen-and-obey (שמע), it is never reported in the
framing narrative that Moses' addressees *did* listen (to God's word
and to him). This is all the more remarkable, since the representation of a discourse's reception (its being "heard") is a typical feature of biblical narrative.[22] In Deuteronomy, the addressees'
reception is represented in Moses' speeches and point of view,
either in his retelling of the Horeb events (4:12, 33, 36; 5:23; 24,
26), or in warnings (see 29:18) and prophecies (4:30; 7:12; 30:2,
8, 10) about the future of the covenant: "you *did* listen," "you *will*
listen." Yet nowhere is it told: "And the people of Israel listened"
(to Moses' voice). Interestingly enough, the reception left untold
in the case of Moses' conveying is explicitly reported when it
comes to Joshua's mediation: "So the sons of Israel listened to
[Joshua] (וישמעו אליו), and did as YHWH had commanded Moses"
(Deut 34:9). The gap in the narration of the Mosaic covenant in
Moab is thus, retrospectively, all the more conspicuous. The
engagement of the people in the Moab covenant is the object of
a similar gap. This engagement is *implied* by the statements reported in 26:17-18;[23] it is *reflected* (as imminent) in Moses' admonition
in 29:11, 13. Yet it is never told by the narrator, as in Josh 24:25
or in 2 Kings 23:3,[24] that the people, or their leader in their name,

---

[21] Moses' proposition to the people is recapitulated in his "setting before"
the people the blessing and the curse; see Deut 11:26, "Behold, I set before you
(אנכי נתן לפיכם) this day a blessing and a curse," and 30:15, "I (have) set before
you (נתתי לפניך) life and death, blessing and curse" (see also 30:15).

[22] See M. Sternberg, "The World From the Addressee's Point of View: Reception as Representation, Dialogue As Monologue," *Style* 1986 (20) 295-317.

[23] In Lohfink's view the engagement of the people is equally implied by the
declaration by Moses and the elders in Deut 27:1. See Lohfink, "Ältesten," 31-32,
35-36; "Bund," 233-37.

[24] See Josh 24:25, "On that day at Shechem, Joshua made (ויכרת) a covenant
for the people"; 2 Kings 23:3, "And [the king] made the covenant (ויכרת את הברית)
before YHWH ... and all the people joined (ויעמד) in the covenant" (compare 2
Chr 34:31-32; see also Exod 24:7-8).

made a covenant with YHWH.[25] Deuteronomy's recourse to the "showing" mode of narration reaches its climax here.

The point now is that Moses' presentation of the covenantal words is duplicated by the book of Deuteronomy. The book sets before its readers—"This is the Torah" (Deut 4:44)—the legal teaching that Moses set before his addressees in the plain of Moab. Thanks to Deuteronomy's recourse to the "showing" mode of narration, Moses' *hapax legomenon* gains eternity in a way that preserves the "suspended" character of the mediator's covenantal proposal. Deuteronomy's implied reader, living on the land in post-Mosaic times, quite obviously stands *after* the undeniable, yet never told, Moab covenant. This covenant, however, is fully conditional; and, though sealed in the past, it is, and always will be, in need of continued endorsement. Deuteronomy achieves the *tour de force* of recording a covenant that took place once and for all while presenting it as still dependent on the reader's reception.

4. *The Book within the Book*

Moses' and the narrator's respective "voices" concur in the presentation of Israel's vital "words." Starting with Deuteronomy 28:58, and, even more clearly, Deuteronomy 29:19, this concurrence becomes yet more explicit due to the mention of the ספר, or "written record." The analogy in medium between Deuteronomy and that communication represented in Deuteronomy is thereby further determined. Deuteronomy is not only a book about "words," it is also a book that tells of another "book." Moses's reference to הספר הזה, "this 'book'," and the telling about Moses' making of the Torah "book" are not meant to confuse the reader. The "book" in question, being an element of Deuteronomy's represented world, is distinct from Deuteronomy's framing book. Never is it stated, or even suggested, that Moses' Torah "book" is one and the same with the Book of Deuteronomy. Still, the parallelism in medium is striking and precipitates the awareness of a meaningful analogy.

The motif of "the book within the book" is not uncommon in

---

[25] See Lenchak, *"Choose Life!,"* 203, apropos of the people's "choice."

the Hebrew Bible. In the Pentateuch, before Deuteronomy, the motif appears in both its possible forms: as an element of the framing narrative and as an element of the represented world.

(a) The "book" can be a part of the frame, as a segment ("book-let") within the greater unit, or as a source of information quoted, or mentioned, by the narrator. The former case is illustrated in Gen 5:1-32, where the listing of genealogies from Adam to Noah is headed with the phrase זֶה סֵפֶר תּוֹלְדֹת אָדָם, "This is the 'book' of the generations of Adam" (Gen 5:1).[26] The "book" may also be a source quoted by the narrator,[27] as in Num 21:14, where a few lines from the "Book of the Wars of YHWH" are cited.

(b) The "book within the book" can be a written record coex-isting with the protagonists of the story, as an element of the rep-resented world. This is the case in Exod 17:14; 24:7; 32:32, 33 and Num 5:23, where YHWH, the narrator, or Moses, refer to a *sēper*, present or future, in the characters' world.

The סֵפֶר mentioned in Deuteronomy 28-31 as an "inscription on stone" or as a "record" belongs to the latter type: it is within the reach of the protagonists. Yet Deuteronomy's "book within the book" is paradoxically accessible to the reader. It is a "book" made accessible by the narrative stratagem of letting the reader hear its content before it is committed to writing.[28] In that sense the clos-est equivalent to Deuteronomy's "'book' of the Torah" is the "'book' of the covenant" (Exod 24:7), which similarly records a body of covenantal legal stipulations communicated to the audi-ence, and through them to the reader, beforehand.[29] In both cases the same policy of openness is carried out.

---

[26] See S. Tengström, *Die Toledotsformel und die literarische Struktur der priesterlichen Erweiterungsschicht im Pentateuch* (ConBib 17; Lund: Gleerup, 1981) 71. See also G. M. Tucker, "Prophetic Superscriptions and the Growth of a Canon," *Canon and Authority: Essays in Old Testament Religion and Theology* (ed. G. W. Coats and B. O. Long; Philadelphia: Fortress, 1977) 58. Compare the re-use of the phrase in Mat 1:1, "The book of the genealogy (Βίβλος γενέσεως)."

[27] The narrator's reference to a record, as well as to its content, is an issue entirely distinct from the genetic question of the interpolation of a "document" into a given text. That the redactor of Genesis 5 made use of an older document, "the book of the generations of Adam," is commonly held. See, for instance, Cross' study on the Priestly Work (*Canaanite Myth*, 301-302).

[28] Deuteronomy's Torah "book" is thus not a record removed from the read-er's access, as is God's heavenly "book" mentioned in Exod 32:32-33. In 2 Kings 22, the "book" found in the Temple is read by and to the *dramatis personae* with-out being read by the reader; see, however, the importance of the narratorial comment in 2 Kings 23:25. On this issue, see my study, "Livre trouvé," 857.

[29] See my study "Le Sinaï dans l'événement de sa lecture," 338-43.

Deuteronomy, however, goes a step further than Exodus in this
policy of openness by explicitly linking the "book" and what the
"book" transmits. An interesting phenomenon underlies the use
of demonstratives in Deuteronomy 31. When Moses entrusts the
Levites with the Torah book, he says: "Take *this* Torah book
[ספר התורה הזה]" (31:26). The demonstrative "this" functions (as a
deictic) within the represented world; its reference is determined
by Moses' speech act then and there. Deuteronomy's readers are
not able to see, let alone to peruse, the "book" in question. Yet
the same "this" is endowed with another function when used by
the narrator: "And Moses wrote *this* Torah [התורה הזאת]" (31:9).
The demonstrative "this" is then used as an anaphoric, referring
to a previous mention of "Torah" in the text, or to a previous
stretch of discourse representing "this Torah."[30] Back-reference
suggests that "this Torah (התורה הזאת)" is that which the reader
perused within a definite part of the book of Deuteronomy, starting with 4:44, וזאת התורה, "This is the Torah." The anaphoric phrase
התורה הזאת, "this Torah," in 31:9 is thus presumably the counterpart of the cataphoric (i.e., forward-looking) one התורה וזאת, "This
is the Torah" in 4:44 (the occurrence of "this Torah" in 31:9 is
the first use of the phrase *by the narrator* since 4:44). Whatever its
exact extent, the Torah, now transcribed by Moses, is thus found
between the two markers. By combining the deictic use of "this"
("this Torah book") by Moses and its anaphoric use by the narrator ("this Torah"), Deuteronomy 31 points to the overlapping
between the record on the narrative stage and a foregoing portion of the Book of Deuteronomy. No similar recourse to demonstratives by the narrator is found in Exod 24:3-8 in regard to the
"'book' of the covenant."[31] What is designated by Moses on stage

---

[30] On the anaphoric use of זה - זאת, "this," see Waltke - O'Connor, § 17.4.2e.
The anaphora in Deut 31:24—"When Moses had finished writing the words of
this Torah on a 'book' [התורה הזאת]"—has a slightly different contextual determination since it presupposes the written "Torah" of 31:9 and the supplementation
that has occurred in the meantime.

[31] Deuteronomy 31 presents a further case of such coordination. In 31:19 God
enjoins Moses and Joshua to write down "this Song," which thus exists between
them as a piece of revelation. In 31:22, 30 and 32:44, it is now the narrator who
makes use of the phrase "this Song." The last two occurrences of the expression
frame the rendering of the Song in Deut 32:1-43. God's reference to the poem
by the phrase "this Song" addressed to Moses and Joshua in the Tent of Meeting is echoed in the narrator's parlance: no doubt is left as to the overlapping
between the song now spelled out and the "Song" referred to by God.

is also designated by the narrator for the reader's attention. The demonstratives that resonate in the represented world (Moses: "Take this 'book' of the Torah") are echoed by other demonstratives resonating in the reader's world (the narrator: "This is the Torah," "this Torah"). Deuteronomy thus enhances at the level of the frame an element of the represented world. Definitely a book in the characters' world, the Torah 'book' is not far from being also a book in the frame.

Deuteronomy's focus on the "book" represents a remarkable step in the Pentateuchal narrative. The Pentateuch does not open like the *Gilgamesh Epic* (in its standard version), which presupposes writing from the start: "All his toil he [engra]ved on a (stone) stela."[32] The protagonists of Genesis, God and the patriarchs, are never presented as writers, and the story of the "fathers" is marked off by unwritten signs (the bow in the clouds, circumcision) and plain steles. Moses is the first protagonist enjoined by YHWH to write (Exod 17:14), and the first who is reported to have done so (Exod 24:4). The writing prophet turns out to be the counterpart of a writing God (Exod 24:12; 31:18; 32:16, 32-33; 34:1). The issue of written communication further develops in Deuteronomy. Moses' "words" of the Torah are imbued with the logic of writing. The Torah "book" is almost a partner in the making of the covenant in Moab. Deuteronomy 31 stages the *archē* as well as the *telos* of the written record in question. Deuteronomy thus represents a definite step in what Ska terms "le passage d'une narration simple à une narration réflexive, avec l'apparition de l'écrit dans la narration elle-même."[33] The Pentateuchal narration

---

[32] L. i:8; translation in J. H. Tigay, *The Evolution of the Gilgamesh Epic* (Philadelphia: University of Philadelphia Press, 1982) 141.

[33] J.-L. Ska, "Un nouveau Wellhausen?," *Bib* 72 (1991) 259. Ska pertinently points to a difference in poetics between Genesis and in that which starts with the Sinai event: "Les traditions patriarcales sont très proches des récits populaires. Il n'est pas étonnant que la plupart des exégètes sensibles à l'art narratif de la Bible aient davantage étudié la Genèse que l'Exode (cf. déjà Gunkel lui-même). Narrateur, narrataire, événements et personnages appartiennent au même univers. Avec l'exode s'instaure une distance esthétique et critique. Le récit devient un écrit qui apparaît dans le récit lui-même (Ex 24,3-8; Dt 17,18; 31,9-14.24-29; cf. Jos 8,30-35; 24,26-27). La réponse du peuple est spécifiée. Le livre met devant un choix existentiel (cf. les bénédictions et les malédictions). N'y aurait-il pas là comme une référence implicite à deux identités d'Israël, deux façons d'établir la solidarité d'un peuple? D'une part, l'histoire patriarcale insiste sur les liens du sang avec tout ce que cela signifie pour une société antique. D'autre part, la tradition de l'exode met l'accent sur la liberté et le choix (devant

that first dealt with its "other"—everything that can be made without writing, from creation to procreation—comes to grips through Moses (especially in Deuteronomy) with that which is made exclusively through writing. In so doing, the narrative comes to reflect its own condition of possibility as written communication. Yet, as I shall indicate in the next section, the reflection is not total—Moses is not represented as writing Deuteronomy—and it cannot be so, given the narrative model which governs the Pentateuchal narrative, Deuteronomy included.

5. *Moses vs. the Narrator: The Limits of the Analogy*

Deuteronomy 34 represents a turning point in Deuteronomy's mode of narration: Moses' voice is no longer heard. The prophetic spokesman is now exclusively the object of *telling*. As the Talmud already points out, a basic historiographic requirement—no one *tells* his or her own death—underlies the switch to narratorial telling: "Now, is it possible that Moses, being dead, could have written the words, 'Moses died there'?"[34] Much more, however, than compliance with historiographic verisimilitude is at stake in Deuteronomy's ending. The relationship between Moses and the narrator, in particular, comes out in its true and final light.

If Deuteronomy's final chapter represents the supplanting of Moses' voice by the narrator's, it is certainly not at the former's expense. The narrator is not playing off, in a kind of authorial irony, his omniscience against Moses' prophetic knowledge.[35]

---

la "Tora"). La structure narrative différente et le passage d'une narration simple à une narration réflexive, avec l'apparition de l'écrit dans la narration elle-même, va plutôt dans ce sens" (p. 259).

[34] *b. B. Bat.*, 15a. The opinion is attributed either to R. Judah or to R. Nehemiah. Compare R. Simeon's alternative view that Moses took down "with tears" God's dictation of the final verses of Deuteronomy. If it allegedly provides an answer to a given question ("Who wrote the last verses of Deuteronomy?"), the appeal to divine inspiration, as Sternberg points out, opens holes everywhere else by invalidating human canons of probability: at this rate, "Moses could compose the rest of the Bible as well as the Pentateuch to the last letter" (*Poetics*, 61).

[35] The limits of prophetic knowledge can be illustrated by the data of Deuteronomy 31-34. Prophetic knowledge is anything but innate. It wholly depends on God. The theophany in Deuteronomy 31 stages this process of revelation: Moses' knowledge (ידעתי, "I know," 31:27, 29) of Israel's future rebellion derives from God's previous disclosure (ידעתי, "I know," 31:21). Furthermore, being a prophet does not preclude the prophet's own rebellion, as YHWH's indictment of Moses recalls (32:51).

A unique narratorial statement enhances the uniqueness of Moses' prophetic stance: "And there has not arisen a prophet since in Israel like Moses, whom YHWH knew face to face" (Deut 34:10). The comment of 34:10 represents a forceful intrusion of the otherwise reserved narrating voice. For the most part, this voice hides itself behind the voice of its main and only speaking human character, Moses. In keeping with his policy of self-effacement, the narrator has refrained from passing judgment by way of commentary. Now that Moses' death is told, the narrating voice is heard *en force*, in a unique self-assertion, and in what is perhaps the most forceful narratorial statement in the Hebrew Bible. In his omniscience the narrator bows to Moses' prophetic status, and for good reason: Moses is prophet (נביא) *par excellence* in the way God knows him—face to face.[36]

The statement in Deut 34:10 implies an analogy between the narrating voice and Moses-the-prophet. The voice declaring Moses the greatest of the prophets cannot operate at a lesser level of knowledge than the prophets themselves.[37] Yet the commentary of Deut 34:10 also represents the parting point between Moses and the narrating voice. The narrator is not a character "on stage," endowed with an above-average clear-sightedness; he is an offstage historian, and as such, remains omniscient. His statement, ולא קם נביא עוד בישראל כמשה, "And there has not arisen a prophet since in Israel like Moses" (34:10), is a panoramic historical statement. The narrator does not prophesy, "No prophet will rise (יקום)"; he retrospectively assesses the whole of Israel's history: "There has not arisen a prophet since (ולא קם ... עוד)." The narrator's statement belongs to the (divine) framing of the world and records a constant in all post-Mosaic history.

Moses is thus, without any doubt, the arch-prophet of Israel's history. Yet he is a prophet *in* history, and so who will be the "prophet like Moses" promised by God in Deut 18:17. This point is missed by Polzin in his *Moses and the Deuteronomist*, when he

---

[36] On the issue of Moses' excellence, see Numbers 12. Concerning the possibility of genetic links between Deuteronomy 34 and Numbers 11, see Blum, "Israël à la montagne de Dieu," 281-83; *Studien*, 76-88.

[37] "It is inconceivable," Sternberg writes, "that a storyteller who keeps in closer touch with God's doings and sentiments than the very prophets who figure among his dramatis personae would operate as their inferior in divine sanction" (Sternberg, *Poetics*, 79).

identifies the "prophet like Moses" promised by YHWH with the
Deuteronomist, i.e., the narrator of Deuteronomy and the ensuing books in the so-called Deuteronomistic History.[38] Such an
equation represents an infringement of the rule separating the
two spheres of communication: the sphere where limited, albeit
in some cases prophetic, protagonists convey true or false information, and the sphere of omniscience that belongs to the master of the tale. No more and no less than Moses-the-prophet can
the "prophet like Moses" be equated with the narrating voice,
whose transcendence in regard to history is irreducible. The relationship between the prophetic *dramatis persona* and the narrator
of the drama is at its most analogical, as I have just indicated in
the case of Moses. In other words, the prophetic figure foretold
in Deuteronomy 18 requires a figurative fulfillment in history.
Deuteronomy is in keeping with this principle, when it recounts
a first realization of God's promise in the person of Moses' first
successor, Joshua.[39]

6. *Explicit Liber Helleaddabarim Id Est Deuteronomium*[40]

The limits of the analogy between Moses and the narrator have
their counterpart in that which brings together the Torah "book"
and the Book of Deuteronomy. Both documents strive to publicize the same "words of the Torah" (in future readings, in the
case of the Torah "book"). Deuteronomy presents to the reader
what Moses presents to the people. Sharing the same finality, the
two records develop a kind of asymptotic proximity. Yet Deuteronomy's ending foregrounds the irreducible difference of the two
records. What is true about "voices" is borne out when it comes
to written communication.

In Deuteronomy 31-32 the narrator takes pains to let the reader know that Moses is bringing his oral and written communication to an end (see the use of כלה in 31:24; 32:45). The coming
to an end of the narrator's act of communication in Deuteronomy 34 occurs without any similar signal. The narrator rather takes

---

[38] Polzin, *Moses*, 61.
[39] See Deut 34:9 and my comments pp. 196-97 above.
[40] "*The Book Helleaddabarim*, that is, Deuteronomy, has come to an end" (colophon to Deuteronomy in Jerome's Vulgate).

pains not to flaunt himself as a book-maker.[41] He notably refrains from presenting himself as the writer who is putting an end to his work. Whatever points to the particularity of storytelling or book-making—and would jar with the omniscient and disembodied character of the narrative voice—is carefully avoided. This is not, for instance, the concern of the narrator-compiler of the Second Book of Maccabees, who declares in the last verses of the work:

> [37]This, then, is how matters turned out with Nicanor. And from that time the city had been in the possession of the Hebrews. So I too will here end my story. [38]If this is well told and to the point, that is what I myself desired; if it is poorly done and mediocre, that was the best I could do. [39]For just as it is harmful to drink wine alone, or, again, to drink water alone, while wine mixed with water is sweet and delicious and enhances one's enjoyment, so also the style of the story delights the ears of those who read the work. And here will be the end. (2 Macc 15:37-39; RSV)

Before his final prayer, Ben Sirach writes similarly: "Instruction in understanding and knowledge I have written in this book, Jesus the son of Sirach" (Sir 50:27; RSV). Closer to Deuteronomy, within the Hebrew Canon, the book of Qohelet conforms to a poetics of its own by including in its ending: "Of making many books there is no end, and much study is weariness of the flesh. The end of the matter; all has been heard" (Qoh 12:12b-13). Deuteronomy comes to its end without such statements. The book ends with Moses' end, and Moses ends on God's order. After an outstanding exercise of omniscience ("There has not arisen a prophet since in Israel like Moses ..."), the narrator refers to what is totally out of his range of performance, that is, God's omnipotence in history through his prophet: "... for all the signs and the wonders which YHWH sent him to do in the land of Egypt, to Pharaoh and to all his servants and to all his land, and for all the mighty power and all the great and terrible deeds which Moses wrought in the sight of all Israel" (Deut 34:11-12). The double sequence האתות והמופתים, "the signs and the wonders,"—המורא ... היד החזקה

---

[41] Such a reticence conforms to the narrator's mode of presence elsewhere in the biblical narrative. See Sternberg's remark: "the storyteller appears only as a disembodied voice, nameless and faceless... . He avoids all reference to the act of storytelling—to himself as maker, recorder, editor, or even narrator—nor does he betray the least consciousness of facing an audience by way of direct address and the like" (*Poetics*, 71).

הגדול, "the mighty hand ... the (great) awesome deed," echoes Moses' description of God's action at the exodus (see Deut 4:34; 6:22; 7:19; 11:2-3; 26:8 and 29:2). In Moses' retelling, the *mirabilia* in question are directly attributed to God's agency. In Deut 34:11-12 the narrator does not hesitate to restore that which Moses passed over in silence—here probably out of humility: Moses' own puissance at God's order. So is it in Exodus, where God's agency does not exclude Moses': "And you shall take in your hands this rod, with which you shall do (תעשה) the signs (האתת)" (Exod 4:17). By enhancing Moses' deeds, the master of the tale links the prophet to God's omnipotence in history, in which he himself, as narrator, has no part. The *poiesis*,[42] so to speak, on which Deuteronomy closes, is not the making of the literary artifact, but the making of "signs and wonders" by Moses at God's initiative. Deuteronomy is thus a *poema* foregrounding another *poeisis* than its own.[43]

The opposite situation is found in many literary creations of the ancient Near East, which include, especially in their endings, a trope of self-presentation (via the narrator or one of the protagonists). Resorting to deictics ("*this*"), to descriptives ("*a song*"), or to a combination of both ("*this song*"), the text refers to itself and exhibits its own identity, genesis, or virtues. So is it at the end of the Instruction of Amen-em-Opet:

---

[42] Using the Greek term *poiesis*, I echo the Septuagint which uses twice the verb ποεῖν, "to make," in Deut 34:11-12 to describe Moses' memorable activity.

[43] Although Deuteronomy takes pains not to call attention to itself as a book coming to completion, the end of a book cannot conceal that the book is ending. L. Wittgenstein's category of *zeigen* ("to show") adequately applies to the phenomenon. "What signs fail to express," he writes, "their application shows (das *zeigt* ihre Anwendung)" (*Tractatus Logico-Philosophicus* [with English translation by D. F. Pears and B. F. McGuinness; 2nd ed.; London: Routledge, 1971] 24-25). What Deuteronomy refrains from making explicit is "shown" anyway in the drawing to an end of the representational medium—witness the colophons found in Aramaic, Greek, and Latin manuscripts of Deuteronomy: חזק הכותב ואמיץ הקורא ("Strong is the writer and valiant the reader"), τελος του δευτερονομιου ("The end of Deuteronomy"), *Explicit Liber Helleaddabarim Id Est Deuteronomium,* ("The Book *Helleaddabarim*, that is, Deuteronomy, has come to an end"), etc. The book of Deuteronomy is a discrete linguistic unit, endowed with formal integrity. The *clausula*-like statement that starts with Deut 34:10 ("There has not arisen in Israel ...") contributes to the rounding off of Deuteronomy's long narrative period. Thus, far from being a section within a narrative continuum, and without being a totally independent unit, Deuteronomy is within the Pentateuch's macro-narrative a narrative of its own. Yet it is a narrative work that foregrounds another *poiesis* than its own.

See you *these* thirty *chapters*: they entertain; they instruct; they are the foremost of all books; they make the ignorant to know. (27:10)[44]

In its final verses the Akkadian epic of creation, *Enûma eliš*, mentions its own writing, synthesizes itself as "the song of Marduk" (8:161), and refers to future (ritual) readings:

> The *revelation* (*taklimtu*) which the "first one"
>   discoursed before him (Marduk),
> *He wrote down* and preserved for the future to hear,
> The [wo]rd of Marduk who created the Igigi-gods,
> [His/Its] let them [ ], his Name let them invoke.
> Let them sound abroad the *song* of Marduk,
> How he defeated Tiamat and took kingship. (8:157-162)[45]

The climax of self-referential logic is probably found in the *Erra Epic* (*Erra and Ishum*). In the epilogue the composer introduces himself by name and tells about the inspiration of the poem, while Erra-the-warrior, the main character and speaker in the story (like Moses in Deuteronomy), extols the apotropaic virtue of the reading of the same poem:

> The composer of *its tablet* (of the poem)[46] was Kabti-ilani-Marduk,
>   of the family Dabibi.
> He revealed it at night, and, just as he (the god?)
>   had discoursed it while he (K.) was coming awake,
>   he (K.) omitted nothing at all,
> Nor one line did he add.
> When Erra heard it he approved ...:
> "In the sanctuary of the god who honors *this poem*,
>   may abundance accumulate, ...
> Let the singer who chants (it) not die from pestilence,
> But his performance be pleasing to king and prince.
> The scribe who masters it shall be spared in the enemy country
>   and honored in his own land, ...
> The house in which *this tablet* is placed,
>   though Erra be angry and the Seven be murderous,
> The sword of pestilence shall not approach it,
>   safety abides upon it.
> Let *this poem* stand forever, let it endure till eternity. (5:42-59)[47]

---

[44] *ANET*, 424 (my emphasis); compare Prov 22:20.

[45] Translation in Foster, *Muses*, 1.401 (my emphasis).

[46] For the interpretation of *kam-mì-šú*, "its tablet," as the tablet of the poem, see L. Cagni, *L'Epopea di Erra* (Rome: Istituto di Studi del Vicino Oriente, 1969) 126-127, 280.

[47] Translation in Foster, *Muses*, 2.804 (my emphasis).

Through the narrator's voice, as through Erra's, the text presents itself in its material identity ("this tablet") as in its formal one (*zamâru*, "this song"). Self-reference goes with the flaunting of the work as literary artifact, either in its origins (inspiration, attribution, composition, canonization) or in its *telos* (future reception).[48] Not so in Deuteronomy, the conclusion of which is everything but self-referential. In its ending the narrative avoids any allusion to itself as literary artefact; instead, it centers on the accomplishments of God and Moses in represented history. The sole completion of a work mentioned in Deuteronomy is thus that of the Torah "book": "When Moses finished writing the words of this Torah in a 'book'" (31:24). Moses is the one represented as a book-maker, stealing the show from the (consenting) book narrator.

Another literary corpus in the ancient Near East is particularly fond of self-reference: the corpus of oath and treaty literature. The oath or treaty text usually presents itself as a constitutive token, in present and in future, of the social reality it helps to bring into being. For instance, the ending of the treaty between Muršiliš II and Duppi-Tešup (ca. 1350 BCE) reads :

> These are the words of the covenant and imprecation *written in this tablet*. If Duppi-Tešup will not observe the words of the covenant and oath-imprecation, (then) these curses will destroy Duppi-Tešup, his wife, his son, his son's son, his house, his city, his land, and all his possessions. (§ 20)[49]

---

[48] The opening of the *Gilgamesh Epic* represents a borderline case. The anonymous narrator refers to Gilgamesh's writing down of his adventures—"All his toil he [engra]ved on a (stone) stela / an inscription [*narû*]" (i.8)—and calls upon the reader to search for Gilgamesh's inscription in the walls of Uruk, and to read from it: "[Take out] and read aloud from the lapis-lazuli tablet" (i.25; translation in Tigay, *Evolution*, 141). Does Gilgamesh's inscription coincide with the narrative body of the *Gilgamesh Epic*? Given the lack of explicit coordination between frame and inset "inscriptions," the question must remain open. Once the epic is launched, Gilgamesh's inscription no longer surfaces, and turns into an archaeological token. In Tigay's view, it "is presumably meant to be understood as the source of the epic's information" (*Evolution*, 142 n. 3).

[49] Translation in Weinfeld, *Deuteronomy*, 107 (my emphasis); text and German translation in J. Friedrich, "Staatsverträge des Hatti Reiches", *MVAG* 31/1 (1926) 25. Paradoxically enough, S. Amsler, "Loi orale et loi écrite," 51, refers to the same text to emphasize, by way of contrast, that written communication is foreign to Deuteronomy: "A la différence des contrats de vassalité qui se présentent eux-mêmes, tôt ou tard, comme des 'paroles et serment inscrits sur cette tablette', le testament de Moïse dans le Deutéronome est une collection d'enseignements oraux."

Closer in time to Deuteronomy, the vassal treaty of Esarhaddon (672 BCE) displays the same logic (the treaty is very likely the *matrix* of some parts of Deuteronomy 28). After the formulation of the stipulations, Esarhaddon enjoins his addressees: "*This treaty* ... you shall speak to your sons and grandsons ... : 'Guard *this treaty*'" (l. 283-292).[50] Slightly older, but linguistically very close to Deuteronomy, the Aramaic treaties of Sefire (ca. 754 BCE) multiply self-referential expressions that include the term ספר, "inscription, record": "Let not one of the words of *thi[s] inscription* (מלי ספרא זנ[ה]) be silent" (IB, l. 8);[51] "The gods of the treaty which is in *this inscription* (אלהי עדיא זי בספרא זנה)" (IB, l. 33).[52] And in all of these examples the trope of self-reference ("this tablet," "this inscription," "this treaty") implies a reference to the literary record as a whole. In Deuteronomy, self-designation is systematically avoided at the level of the framing narrative, that is, at the level of Deuteronomy's Book. What is common in oath and treaties—the focus on the centrality of the written record—is out of place in biblical omniscient narration (at the level of the representational medium). Yet, throughout his speeches in Deuteronomy, Moses multiplies that which the narrator does not allow himself: references to his own act of communication. Moses' way of speaking often evokes the style of the oath and treaty just quoted, when he refers to "these words of mine," or to "the words of this Torah written in this 'record' (ספר)." In these instances, however, reference is systematically made to the represented act of communication, and not to the representational medium.

This basic constituent of Deuteronomy's poetics is not always perceived. In his *Deuteronomy and the Death of Moses*, Olson erroneously points to a logic of self-designation at the level of the Book of Deuteronomy. Olson repeatedly calls attention to "Deuteronomy's self-designation of the form of the whole work as *torah*."[53] "Deuteronomy," he writes, "is in fact the only book of the Pentateuch that refers to itself as *torah*."[54] In this Olson confuses

---

[50] Text and translation in S. Parpola and K. Watanabe, eds., *Neo-Assyrian Treaties and Loyalty Oaths* (State Archives of Assyria 2; Helsinki: Helsinki University Press, 1988) 40 (my emphasis).

[51] Text and translation in Fitzmyer, *Aramaic Inscriptions*, 17 (my emphasis).

[52] Text and translation in Fitzmeyer, *Aramaic Inscriptions*, 19 (my emphasis). See also IA l. 6; IB l. 23; IC l. 17; IIC l. 2, 4, 6, 9, 13; III l. 4, 14, 17, 23.

[53] Olson, *Deuteronomy*, 139.

[54] Olson, *Deuteronomy*, 8; see also pp. 2, 6, 11, 15, 40, 135, 157.

what Deuteronomy carefully distinguishes: the narrator's way of speaking, and Moses'. Never calling attention to himself, the narrator always directs the reader's attention to the *mirabilia* that take place on the narrative stage, the foremost of these being Moses' conveying of the Torah. Deuteronomy does not therefore refer to itself as Torah; it rather refers to the Torah delivered "there and then" (see Deut 1:5; 4:44; 31:9, 24). Moses, on the book's stage, is properly the one who qualifies his own speech, or rather a part of it, as "Torah."[55]

In Deuteronomy, furthermore, Moses not only speaks but constantly says that he speaks, calling his audience's attention to the content and the formality of his own speech. As Beauchamp points out, Moses reports in Deuteronomy his own sayings of the past (besides God's and the people's): "Le Moïse du Deutéronome, rapporteur des paroles de Dieu, est aussi rapporteur de ses propres discours: '*Je vous ai dit* en ce temps-là: Je ne peux pas porter seul la charge de vous tous' (Dt 1,9-18; à comparer avec la forme objective de Ex 18,13-26). Le discours se prend lui-même comme thème!"[56] The latter phenomenon—discourse becoming its own theme—actually pervades the whole of Moses' speech. In an almost obsessive fashion, Moses reminds his audience of his speaking to them, beseeching his addressees to heed, and eventually observe, the "words" or "commandments" he is uttering and enjoining upon them.[57] Starting with Deuteronomy 28, reference to communication includes reference to written communication, that is, to the various embodiments of the ספר, as (fixed) "inscription" (Deut 28:58, 61) or (movable) "record" (Deut 29:20, 21, 26; 30:10; 31:24). In other words, the designation of communicational *realia* does pervade Deuteronomy, but only at the level of the represented speech and of the represented covenantal document.

---

[55] See Deut 4:8; 17:18, 19; 27:3, 8, 26; 28:58, 61; 29:20, 28; 30:10; 31:11, 12, 26; 32:46; about the occurrence of "torah" in 17:11, and its reference to Levitical legal instruction, see G. Braulik, "Ausdrücke," 36 n. 115.

[56] Beauchamp, *Testament (2)*, 315. Backward reference in Deuteronomy is the subject of D. E. Skweres' study, *Die Rückverweise im Buch Deuteronomium* (AnBib 79; Rome: Biblical Institute Press, 1979). On Moses' mentions of his own previous statements, see pp. 69-75 and 192-95. On the specific issue of Moses' quotes of his own words, see G. Savran, *Telling and Retelling: Quotation in Biblical Narrative* (Bloomington: Indiana University Press, 1988) 113-16.

[57] See Deut 4:2, 40; 6:2, 6; 7:11; 8:1, 11; 10:13; 11:8, 13, 22, 27, 28; 12:11, 14, 28; 13:1, 19; 15:5, 11, 15; 19:7, 9; 24:18, 22; 27:1, 4, 10; 28:1, 14; 30:2, 8, 11, 16; 32:46-47.

Deuteronomy thus has its own way of coordinating frame and inset communication, carrying to an extreme the biblical narrative's policy in the matter. The "representing" medium denies itself the explicitness it grants to the represented medium. Moses says "Take *this* 'book' of the Torah" (31:26) in a book that avoids any similar self-foregrounding.

7. Conclusion

Deuteronomy's narrative and communicational efficiency results from the skillful balance between various literary elements: the respective roles of Deuteronomy's primary and secondary voices, the successive representation of oral and written communication by Moses, the recourse first to the showing mode and then to the telling mode of narration, the staging of "the book within the book." All these components make sense within a single paradox. The essence of this study lies in the formulation of that paradox.

In a book like Deuteronomy, prophetic communication on the narrative stage is, and must be, the driving force (in the "wheel within the wheel" analogy, the inner wheel is thus the one that drives). Deuteronomy claims to represent not only history but foundational history—deeds and words which underlie Israel's existence for all the generations to come. Moses' address to the people "on the first day of the eleventh month" (Deut 1:3) is thus (foundational) history in the making, outweighing any concomitant communicational venture, most particularly that of the narrator.[58] This absolute primacy of represented history in Deuteronomy combines with the rules of biblical omniscient narration. Although an omniscient history teller, the narrator is nevertheless incapable of "making" history through words or deeds. Moses did so, for it was through him that YHWH wrought great and terrible deeds in Egypt in the sight of all Israel (34:11-12). Although the master of the tale, the narrator is unable to intervene directly to exhort the characters on stage. Moses does so, as when he

---

[58] The centrality of represented history in biblical narrative stands out when compared with other genres where the interpretation of history (by the "reporter") measures history itself. In ancient Jewish literature the latter stance is found, for instance, in the *Pesher* literature at Qumran or in Josephus' historical and apologetic writings.

confronts his addressees with ultimate choices: "Choose life!"
(30:19). Moses' act of communication on Deuteronomy's historical stage is the one that matters—and this explains the narrator's
policy of self-effacement. The Torah "book" records the normative and essential part of Moses' teaching in Moab, so as to dif-
fuse it in post-Mosaic Israel (see 31:9-13). By being bound to the
ark, the Torah "book" is launched as the communicational device
meant to pervade and shape Israel's existence in the land. The
(framing) book of Deuteronomy must therefore, and inevitably,
focus on the represented "book," enhancing it as the effective
medium of the Torah. The narrator tells of its making by Moses
(31:9, 24), as a particular document (31:24, על ספר, "on a book").
Moses repeatedly points to it (29:19, 20; 30:10; 31:26), designat-
ing it as the repository of the words of the covenant (in Deuteronomy 29-30), as the vehicle of the Torah words in Israel's future
(31:9-13), and as the witness for the prosecution in Israel's forthcoming rebellion (31:26). While Moses foregrounds the Torah
"book," Deuteronomy recedes into the background, refraining
from calling attention to itself. By flaunting itself as a particular
artifact, Deuteronomy would compromise the omniscient status of
its disembodied narrative voice (books are particulars, and made
by particulars). By referring to itself as a book, Deuteronomy
would compete with, and in the end endanger, the uniqueness of
Moses' Torah "book."

On the other hand, the content of Moses' Torah "book" is not
accessible elsewhere than within Deuteronomy. One could argue
that the people (Moses' addressees, once arrived in the land, and
their descendants) would know the Deuteronomy's Torah, thanks
to its periodical reading and its daily learning—in other words,
thanks to channels independent of Deuteronomy. For whomever
exists in history, however, as against represented history, the Book
of Deuteronomy is the unique channel through which the Torah
"book" may be apprehended.[59] In the readers' world, Moses'

---

[59] To tell the truth, Moses' addressees, once settled in the land (as well as their
descendants), and Deuteronomy's implied readers look very much alike. Both are
sons of Israel, required to implement the Torah in the land promised to the forefathers. They are the addressees of (almost) the same address. No ironic distance
separates Deuteronomy and the Torah "book," in their parallel thrust to convey
the "words" of the Torah to the concerned audiences. The "sons" who will enjoy
the proclamation of the Torah "book" thus somehow parallel Deuteronomy's
readers, and the readers of Deuteronomy can align themselves with the "sons" in

Torah "book" is never "read" outside of the Book of Deuteronomy. The aim of the inset "book"—to be read to the sons—is thus
fulfilled by the reading of the framing book.[60] Deuteronomy
therefore achieves the *tour de force* of enabling its reader to peruse
the content of a book which one would assume to be out of the
reader's range. The Torah "book" to which Moses points within
Deuteronomy's represented world—"If you obey the voice of
YHWH your God, to keep his commandments and his statutes
which are written in this 'book' of the Torah" (30:10); "Take this
'book' of the Torah" (31:26)—is a record on the narrative scene,
and, as such, it is not "open" (or, rather, "unrolled") to the eyes
of the reader. Elsewhere, such a designation on stage in the character's domain would be the reader's despair—the book becoming inaccessible, as far as its content is concerned, precisely when
exhibited. Yet in Deuteronomy the aporia is overcome by the narrative's architectonics. The reader makes his acquaintance with
the Torah *as spoken* by Moses, before it is committed to writing.
As much as Moses' addressees on stage, the reader finds himself
in the know. Far from being an opaque record, "this 'book'" is
fully revealed to all. Deuteronomy's paradox goes even further.
Deuteronomy is the *surrogate* of another "book," disclosing the
content of the latter while not assuming its formal identity. But
Deuteronomy does so in being a surrogate *book*. The reader comes
to know the Torah as spoken by Moses, but Moses's spoken word
is, from the outset, a written word within the book of Deuteronomy. If irony is to be found in Deuteronomy, it is that irony of
the unavoidable character of the written form. Deuteronomy
makes a powerful virtue of such an ironical necessity.

As in a *Gestalt* riddle, Deuteronomy thus oscillates between two
designs. On the one hand, it has to establish the centrality of
Moses' Torah "book," and it cannot do so except by representing

---

question. Yet this does not imply, in Deuteronomy's claim, a coexistence of the
two systems of transmission. The reading to the "sons" is not described in
Deuteronomy as carried out "up to this day"; it may have been jeopardized by
historical tribulations. In its canonical status, moreover, Deuteronomy figures as
the exclusive representative of the Torah "book," and thus as its surrogate. The
reading of an independent Torah "book" to the "sons" does not belong to the
context of Deuteronomy's readers; it belongs to Deuteronomy's represented history.

[60] See on this point E. W. Conrad's (general) considerations in "Heard but
not Seen: The Representation of 'Books' in the Old Testament," *JSOT* 54 (1992)
53-59.

it (hence the crucial character of Deuteronomy 31). On the other hand, it has to foreground the very דברים, "words," of which the Torah "book" is made (hence the crucial character of the chapters prior to Deuteronomy 31). This second goal is achieved by a series of literary devices—the "showing" mode, the narrator's self-effacement, the echoing effects between frame and inset communication, etc. A rare balance is thus created, from which the reader cannot but profit.

Both traditional and critical interpreters felt the need to account for Deuteronomy's peculiar architectonics and to address the issue of Moses' authorship. Despite some dissenting voices, the traditional stance generally extends Moses' authorship to the surrogate book of Deuteronomy. The critical approach neutralizes the book's claim and poetics in favor of cogent or less cogent genetic hypotheses. While each of these is an internally consistent and thus legitimate approach, neither deals with Deuteronomy's poetics as such, least of all with the communicational pattern it implies. While exploring Deuteronomy's poetics, this study encountered a meaningful paradox. By displaying the דברים, "words," (Torah, oaths, statutes, ordinances) of Moses' Torah "book," Deuteronomy aims at a total openness (offering itself by the same token to any exegetical skill, whether traditional or critical). Yet Deuteronomy equally protects Moses' rights for ever by framing his Torah "book" within an ark-like shrine: another book.

Excursus: The Shadow of the Scribes

Like none of the preceding books in the Pentateuch, Deuteronomy is imbued with "scribal thinking." The protagonists in the story (God, the people, Joshua and Moses) all appear at some point, either in Moses' retelling or in the narrator's telling, in the role of scribes. They all come to be associated with the act of writing, and, at times, with more specific scribal procedures or techniques. God, the heavenly scribe, writes down the "ten words" on stone "tables" (לחות) which definitely resemble the scribes' tablets (see the use of לחות / לוח in Hab 2:2 and Isa 30:8).[61] A distinctly

---

[61] See also the well-documented use of lēʾu as "writing board, document," in Akkadian (CAD 9.157-159).

scribal formula, the canon formula, is attached by Moses to God's
foundational writing: "and he added no more" (Deut 5:22). After
Moses' shattering of the tables, God reproduces their content on
new ones, in a way that is reminiscent of the scribal making of
duplicates: "and he wrote on the tables as in the first inscription
(כמכתב הראשון)" (10:4). The deposit of the new tables in the ark,
finally, echoes the scribal practice of storing tablets or documents
in archive cases (see Baruch's deposit of the deed of purchase in
an earthenware vessel in Jer 32:14).[62] The people's passage into
the land is to be marked off by their inscribing "all the words of
this Torah" on large stones coated with plaster (27:3-8). The liminality of the inscription is echoed in the people's future copying
of the same words "on the doorposts of your house and on your
gates" (6:9; 11:20). No more than God on the mountain, the people will not avail themselves of the services of professional scribes.
To go by Moses' injunctions, they are the scribes *de service*, in
charge of the public display of the Torah. Israel's future king, too,
is described in his making of a duplicate (משנה) "on a 'book'"
(17:18). The king is to peruse a Torah "book" that he has written. Joshua equally falls under the injunction to write when he is
divinely ordered with Moses to write "this Song" (31:19). And no
less than all of these is Moses portrayed as a scribe, responsible
for the Torah's *editio princeps*.

Throughout Deuteronomy 31 the reader follows step by step
the process through which the Torah became the written document that is to be normative for Israel's future. Deut 31:9 makes
explicit what the reader has already gathered: the Torah has been
turned into a written document, the one that served as the basis
of covenant-making in Deuteronomy 29-30. What the account in
31:9 adds to the reader's inference is that Moses himself wrote
down that Torah, and that he engages the document in a communicational dynamic mediated by the Levites and the elders.
The background in the Deuteronomy 31 narrative is thus the existence of an already written authoritative work. What comes next
is the story of the sudden revelation by God of Israel's future,
epitomized in the revelation of the Song of Moses (31:14-22). The
process follows a prophetic logic. God summons his prophet to

---

[62] See also the ancient Near Eastern analogues I surveyed in Chapter Two, pp.
79-82.

the Tent of Meeting, shares with him data that have not been communicated so far, and reveals to him "this Song," which the prophet is to commit to writing and to convey to the people. In Deut 31:24-26, the focus shifts back from the Song to the Torah which, the reader understands, is now supplemented by the Song. The formula עַד תֻּמָּם, "to the end," and the verb כלה, (Piel), "to bring to an end," echo scribal formulae through which the completion of writing is signalled. The deposit of the comprehensive Torah next to the ark, house of the canonical tables, further marks the canonical closure of the new, and final, Torah.[63] The Torah that will make its way to the land is thus no longer the document mentioned in 31:9 *sans plus*; it is the same document *plus* the Song. In other words, it is a supplemented Torah. Deut 31:14-32:47 is the story of a last-minute addition.

In this, Deuteronomy 31-32 arguably mirrors something of the genesis of Deuteronomy as a canonical book. As I indicated in Chapter Four, Deut 31:1-32:47 is truly narrative, playing a crucial role in Deuteronomy's overall narrative. What is narrated is the dramatic revelation, epitomized in the Song, of the people's future rebellion against the covenant just sealed. This unexpected turn engages the prophet in a complex turmoil that eventuates in his final exhortation in 32:47-51, "[this word] is your life" (32:47). Deut 31:1-32:47, however, possibly releases a further, indirect message. It may hint at the Book of Deuteronomy as the product of scribal activity, especially of scribal continuous writing and rewriting of that book. The analogical counterpart of Moses "the scribe" is then no longer the narrator—a disembodied voice, which never presents himself as a writer or as a "maker of books." Moses' counterpart is now rather formed by the historical writers of Deuteronomy, that is, the scribes who were responsible for its making. The Book of Deuteronomy bears the strong imprint of scribal traditions, as Weinfeld has cogently argued.[64] The specific phenomenon of scribal interventions in the redactional growth of Deuteronomy has been recently reassessed, characterized as an

---

[63] Dohmen and Oeming, *Biblisher Kanon*, 67, see in Moses' death a further marker of canonization, the passage from "die *Geburt der Kanonidee* im engeren Sinne, das heisst, an dieser Stelle ist der Übergang vom *kanonischen Prozess* zur *Kanonisierung* greifbar."

[64] See Weinfeld, *Deuteronomy*, 158-71, esp. p. 64.

expression of "inner-biblical exegesis."[65] The expression "inner-biblical exegesis" designates the phenomenon of textual innovation and supplementation within a received, already authoritative, textual tradition: "The problematic of justifying innovation over against authoritative texts, the use of pseudepigraphy to camouflage innovation, the attribution of the innovation to the 'canonical' text which is in fact being substantially transformed: these are fully developed hermeneutical issues prior to the closure of the canon."[66] Particularly salient in Deuteronomy is the use of Moses' valedictory speech to "voice" the revising and the updating of a previous legal tradition. "In fact," Fishbane writes, "[the Mosaic voice]—pseudepigraphic in the Book of Deuteronomy—is a composite of many teaching voices, deriving from the many teachers of the Deuteronomic tradition."[67] Throughout the Deuteronomic speeches, "Moses' traditional authority as guardian and teacher of the traditions is thus capitalized upon."[68]

By a remarkable move the scribes responsible for the making of Deuteronomy projected their working silhouette in the book. The scribal acts of writing down and copying haunt Deuteronomy's world. These acts are granted divine precedents; they are royally exemplified; they are linked to the proper inhabitancy of the land; they receive a powerful paradigm in Moses' writing activity. Is all this an inadvertent reflection of the authors in their work? Or is it, to the contrary, a purposeful measure taken by the scribes? And to what purpose? The questions intensify when they turn on the *mise en scène* of Moses' scribal activity. Moses is the one who produces the Torah "book" and thus parallels the scribes in their making of the framing Book of Deuteronomy. Did Deuteronomy's scribes have a hidden agenda when they staged Moses as a scribe?

Redactional criticism has detected signs of interpolation in the text of Deuteronomy 31-32. As I indicated in Chapter Four, the resumptive repetitions in Deut 31:9, 24 and 31:30; 32:44 appar-

---

[65] See the literature p. 48 n. 15 above.

[66] B. M. Levinson, "The Human Voice in Divine Revelation: The Problem of Authority in Biblical Law," *Innovation in Religious Traditions: Essays in the Interpretation of Religious Change* (Religion and Society, 31; ed. M. A. Williams *et alii*; Berlin and New York: Mouton de Gruyter, 1992) 38.

[67] Fishbane, *Interpretation*, 436.

[68] Fishbane, *Interpretation*, 436.

ently point to the insertion of material related to the Song. What
has not been sufficiently noticed, however, is the fact that
Deuteronomy 31-32 equally *tells* about an interpolation process.
An interesting parallelism can therefore be discerned between
Moses' "further writing" and the scribal redactors' emblematic
operation— interpolation. By staging the supplementation and
the canonization of the Torah, did the scribes foreground a kind
of etiological account, setting their own activity under Moses'
patronage? Has Deuteronomy been built so as to include a para-
bolic *discours de la méthode* toward its end, emphasizing the
prophetic character of scribal supplementation? If Moses supplements the Torah, it is indeed only as a consequence of God's initiative in communicating a further piece of revelation. Does it
mean that the revision and the supplementation of God's Torah
are not left to human initiative (in later theological parlance: that
it presupposes God's inspiration)? And do we have to infer that
the scribes, in their being Moses-like, lay claim to a similar "inspiration"?

The staging of Moses' scribal activity may also play within another, subtler literary strategy. It may function as a kind of apotropaic device, dispelling any impertinent inquisitiveness on the reader's part. The bringing into the limelight of that which took place
behind the scene—the making of a "book"—can be a way to direct
or redirect the reader's curiosity. Deuteronomy is in no way parallel to Gide's novel *Les Faux-Monnayeurs* (and even less to the subsequent *Journal des Faux-Monnayeurs*). Because of the overall poetics they adopted, the scribes had nothing to gain in calling
attention to their intrusive *poeisis*. Rather, the focus on Moses'
authority and authorship was intended. Instead of inquiring about
the genesis of Deuteronomy,[69] Deuteronomy's implied readers are

---

[69] The role of the scribes in the making (redacting? copying?) of Deuteronomy apparently surfaces in Jeremiah's interpellation, "How can you say: 'We are
wise,' and 'The Torah of YHWH is with us'? Truly, the pen (of the scribes) has
worked for naught; in vain (have) the scribes (laboured)" (Jer 8:8; I follow the
translation by Fishbane, *Interpretation*, 34). In Weinfeld's interpretation, the
prophet is not denouncing the Deuteronomic Torah as such, that is, as being
the product of scribal forgery; he is rather condemning the "sages" for not observ-
ing the teaching that they themselves had committed to writing (Weinfeld, *School*,
160; see the similar comments in Fishbane, *Interpretation*, 33-36). Even in this case
the participation of the scribes in the making of Deuteronomy is acknowledged
(see also R. N. Whybray, *The Intellectual Tradition in the Old Testament* [BZAW 135;
Berlin: de Gruyter, 1974] 22-24).

invited to follow the genesis authoritatively represented on the narrative stage:[70] the Mosaic making of the Torah "book" is the genetic process that matters.

---

[70] This, of course, may be interpreted the other way around, and it can be contended that the *mise en scène* in Deut 31 reveals what it is intended to conceal: that a process of *Fortschreibung* indeed underlies the making of Deuteronomy. Did the scribes write to give the game away to future scribes (i.e., today's critical scholars)? This is rather unlikely in an enterprise of pseudepigraphy, and in the context of "sacred scripture."

BIBLIOGRAPHY

Ackerman, James. "Numbers." In *The Literary Guide to the Bible*, edited by R. Alter and F. Kermode, 78-91. Cambridge: Harvard University Press, 1987.

Albright, William Foxwell. "The 'Natural Force' of Moses in the Light of Ugaritic." *BASOR* 94 (1944) 32-35.

Alter, Robert. *Partial Magic: The Novel as a Self-Conscious Genre.* Berkeley: University of California Press, 1975.

_____. *The Art of Biblical Narrative.* New York: Basic Books, 1981.

Amsler, Samuel. "Loi orale et loi écrite dans le Deutéronome." In *Das Deuteronomium: Entstehung, Gestalt und Botschaft*, edited by N. Lohfink, 51-54. BETL 68. Louvain: University Press, 1985.

Anbar, Moshe. "The Story About the Building of the Altar on Mount Ebal: The History of Its Composition and the Question of the Centralization of the Cult." In *Das Deuteronomium: Entstehung, Gestalt und Botschaft*, edited by N. Lohfink, 304-309. BETL 68. Louvain: University Press, 1985.

Aristotle. *The Poetics.* With an English Translation by W. Hamilton Fyfe. Loeb Classical Library 199. Cambridge: Harvard University Press, 1932.

Auerbach, Eric. *Mimesis: The Representation of Reality in Western Literature.* Princeton: Princeton University Press, 1953.

Baker, D. W. "The Consecutive Nonperfective as Pluperfect in the Historical Books of the Hebrew Old Testament." Regent College Thesis, 1973.

Bakhtin, Mikhail [Voloshinov, V. N.: published pseudonym]. *Marxism and the Philosophy of Language.* New York: Seminar Press, 1973.

_____. *Problems of Dovstoevsky's Poetics.* Ann Arbor: Ardis Pubs, 1973.

Bal, Mieke. *Femmes imaginaires: L'Ancien Testament au risque d'une narratologie critique.* Utrecht and Paris: Hes; Nizet, 1986.

_____. *On Story-Telling: Essays in Narratology.* Sonoma, CA: Polebridge Press, 1991.

Balogh, Josef. "'Voces paginarum': Beiträge zur Geschichte des lauten Lesens und Schreibens." *Philologus* 82 (1926) 83-109; 83 (1927) 202-40.

Baltzer, Klaus. *Das Bundesformular.* WMANT 4. Neukirchen-Vluyn: Neukirchener Verlag, 1960.

Beauchamp, Paul. *L'un et l'autre Testament.* Paris: Seuil, 1976.

_____. *L'un et l'autre Testament: 2. Accomplir les Ecritures.* Paris: Seuil, 1990.

Beer, Georg. *Exodus—mit einem Beitrag von Kurt Galling.* HAT 1.3. Tübingen: J. C. B. Mohr, 1939.

Begg, Christopher T. "The Tables (Deut. x) and the Lawbook (Deut. xxxi)." *VT* 33 (1983) 96-97.

Bekhor Shor. *Commentary of Rabbi Bekhor Shor on the Torah*, edited by Y. Nebo. Jerusalem: Mossad Harav Kook, 1994.

Berlin, Adele. "Literary Exegesis of Biblical Narrative: Between Poetics and Hermeneutics." In *"Not in Heaven": Coherence and Complexity in Biblical Narrative*, edited by J. P. Rosenblatt and J. C. Sitterson, Jr., 120-28. Bloomington: Indiana University Press, 1991.

Bertholet, Alfred. *Deuteronomium.* KHC 5. Freiburg: J. C. B. Mohr, 1899.

Beyerlin, Walter. *Origins and History of the Oldest Sinaitic Traditions.* Oxford: Basil Blackwell, 1965.

Blenkinsopp, Joseph. *Prophecy and Canon: A Contribution to the Study of Jewish Origins.* Notre Dame: University of Notre Dame Press, 1977.

_____. *The Pentateuch: An Introduction to the First Five Books of the Bible.* New York: Doubleday, 1992.

Blum, Erhard. "Israël à la montagne de Dieu: remarques sur Ex 19-24; 32-34 et sur le contexte littéraire et historique de sa composition." In *Le Pentateuque en question: les origines et la composition des cinq premiers livres de la Bible à la lumière des recherches récentes,* edited by A. de Pury, 271-95. Le Monde de la Bible 19. Geneva: Labor et Fides, 1989.

_____. *Studien zur Komposition des Pentateuchs.* BZAW 189. Berlin and New York: de Gruyter, 1990.

Booth, Wayne C. *The Rhetoric of Fiction.* 2d ed. Chicago: The University of Chicago Press, 1983.

Boyarin, Daniel. "Placing Reading: Ancient Israel and Medieval Europe." In *The Ethnography of Reading,* edited by J. Boyarin, 10-37. Berkeley: University of California Press, 1993.

Braulik, Georg. "Die Ausdrücke für 'Gesetz' im Buch Deuteronomium." *Bib* 51 (1970): 39-66. Reprinted in idem, *Studien Zur Theologie Des Deuteronomium,* 11-38. Stuttgarter Biblische Aufsatzbande 2. Stuttgart: Verlag Katholisches Bibelwerk, 1988.

_____. *Die mittel deuteronomischer Rhetorik, erhoben aus Deuteronomium 4,1-40.* AnBib 68. Rome: Biblical Institute Press, 1978.

_____. *Deuteronomium I: 1-16,17.* Die Neue Echter Bibel. Würzburg: Echter Verlag, 1986.

_____. *Deuteronomium II: 16,18-34,12.* Die Neue Echter Bibel. Würzburg: Echter Verlag, 1992.

_____. "Das Deuteronomium und die Gedächtniskultur Israels: Redaktionsgeschichtliche Beobachtungen zur Verwendung von למד." In *Biblische Theologie und gesellschaftlicher Wander: Für Norbert Lohfink SJ,* edited by G. Braulik, W. Gross, and S. E. McEvenue, 9-31. Freiburg: Herder, 1993.

Brinkman, John Anthony. "Kudurru." *Reallexikon der Assyriologie und vorderasiatischen Archäologie 6* (1983) 267-74.

Buber, Martin. "Abraham, the Seer." *Judaism* 5 (1956) 291-305.

Buchholz, Joachim. *Die Ältesten Israels im Deuteronomium.* GTA 36. Göttingen: Vandenhoeck & Ruprecht, 1988.

Buis, Pierre. *Le Deutéronome.* Verbum Salutis; Ancien Testament 4. Paris: Beauchesne, 1969.

Buis, Pierre, and Jean Leclercq. *Le Deutéronome.* SB. Paris: Gabalda, 1963.

Buth, Randall. "Methodological Collision Between Souce Criticism and Discourse Analysis: The Problem of 'Unmarked Temporal Overlay' and the Pluperfect/nonsequential *wayyiqtol.*" In *Biblical Hebrew and Discourse Linguistics,* edited by R. Bergen, 138-54. Dallas: Summer Institute of Linguistics, 1994.

Cagni, Luigi. *L'Epopea di Erra.* Rome: Istituto del Vicino Oriente, 1969.

Cairns, Ian. *Word and Presence: A Commentary on the Book of Deuteronomy.* International Theological Commentary. Grand Rapids: Eerdmans, 1992.

Caquot, André. "Remarques sur la 'loi royale' du *Deutéronome* (17/14-20)." *Sem* 9 (1959) 21-33.

_____. "Les bénédictions de Moïse (Deutéronome 33, 6-25). I—Ruben, Juda, Lévi, Benjamin." *Sem* 32 (1982) 67-81.

_____. "Les bénédictions de Moïse (Deutéronome 33, 6-25). II—De Joseph à Asher." *Sem* 33 (1983) 59-76.

Caquot, André, and André Lemaire. "Les textes araméens de Deir 'Alla." *Syria* 54 (1977) 189-208.

Carmichael, Calum M. *The Laws of Deuteronomy.* Ithaca: Cornell University Press, 1974.

Childs, Brevard S. *Exodus: A Commentary.* OTL. London: Westminster Press, 1974.

Clarke, E. G., ed. *Targum Pseudo-Jonathan of the Pentateuch: Text and Concordance.* Ktav. Hoboken, NJ, 1984.

Clines, David J. A. *The Theme of the Pentateuch.* JSOTSup 10. Sheffield: Sheffield University Press, 1978.

Coats, George W. *Rebellion in the Wilderness: The Murmuring Motif in the Wilderness Traditions of the Old Testament.* Nashville: Abington, 1968.

————."Legendary Motifs in the Moses Death Report." *CBQ* 39 (1977) 34-44. Reprinted in *A Song of Power and the Power of Song: Essays on the Book of Deuteronomy,* edited by D. L. Christensen, 181-91. Winona Lake: Eisenbrauns, 1993.

Cohen, David. *Dictionnaire des racines sémitiques.* Paris: Mouton, 1976.

Conrad, Edgar W. "Heard but not Seen: The Representation of 'books' in the Old Testament." *JSOT* 54 (1992) 45-59.

Cooper, Alan, and Bernard R. Goldstein. "The Cult of the Dead and the Theme of Entry Into the Land." *BibInt* 1 (1993) 285-303.

Couroyer, Bernard. "La tablette du cœur." *RB* 90 (1983) 416-34.

————. "*'édût:* stipulation de traité ou enseignement?" *RB* 95 (1988) 321-31.

Craigie, Peter C. *The Book of Deuteronomy.* NICOT. Grand Rapids: Eerdmans, 1976.

Cross, Frank Moore. *Canaanite Myth and Hebrew Epic: Essays in the History of the Religion of Israel.* Cambridge: Harvard University Press, 1973.

Cross, Frank Moore, and David Noel Freedman. "The Blessing of Moses." *JBL* 67 (1948) 191-210.

Crüsemann, Frank. *Die Tora: Theologie und Sozialgeschichte des alttestamentlichen Gesetzes.* Munich: Chr. Kaiser, 1992.

Dällenbach, Lucien. *Le récit spéculaire: essai sur la mise en abyme.* Paris: Seuil, 1977.

Damrosch, David. *The Narrative Covenant: Transformations of Genre in the Growth of Biblical Literature.* Ithaca, NY: Cornell University Press, 1987.

Delcor, Mathias. "Les attaches littéraires, l'origine et la signification de l'expression biblique 'Prendre à témoin le ciel et la terre'." *VT* 16 (1966) 8-25.

Dhorme, Edouard, trans. *La Bible: L'Ancien Testament I.* Collaborators F. Michaéli and A. Guillaumont. Paris: Gallimard, 1956.

————, trans. *La Bible: L'Ancien Testament II.* Collaborators J. Koenig, F. Michaéli, J. Hadot, and A. Guillaumont. Paris: Gallimard, 1959.

Díez Macho, Alejandro, ed. and trans. *Neophyti 1: Targum Palestinense Ms de la Biblioteca Vaticana 5. Deuteronomio. Edición príncipe, introdución y versión castellana.* Textos y Estudois 11. Madrid: Consejo Superior de Investigaciones Cientificas, 1978.

Dietrich, Manfried, and Oswald Loretz. "Akkadische *siparru* 'Bronze', ugaritisch *spr, ǵprt* und hebräisch *spr, ʿprt.*" *UF* 17 (1986) 401.

Dillmann, August. *Numeri, Deuteronomium, und Josua.* 2d ed. Leipzig: S. Hirzel, 1886.

Dogniez, Cécile, and Marguerite Harl. *La Bible d'Alexandrie: 5. Le Deutéronome.* Paris: Cerf, 1992.

Dohmen, Christoph. "Der Tod des Moses als Geburt des Pentateuch." In *Biblischer Kanon: warum und wozu? Eine Kanontheologie,* edited by C. Dohmen and M. Oeming, 54-68. QD 137. Freiburg: Herder, 1992.

Donner, Herbert, and W. Röllig. *Kanaanäische und aramäische Inschriften.* 3 vols. Wiesbaden: O. Harrassowitz, 1962-4.

Driver, Samuel Rolles. *A Critical and Exegetical Commentary on Deuteronomy.* 3d ed. ICC. Edinburgh: T. & T. Clark, 1902.

Durham, John I. *Exodus.* WBC 3. Waco: Word Books, 1987.

Eissfeldt, Otto. *Das Lied Moses Deuteronomium 321-43 und das Lehrgedicht Asaphs*

Psalm 78 samt einer Analyse der Umgebung des Mose-Lied. Berichte über die Ver-
    handlungen der Sächsischen Akademie der Wissenchaften zu Leipzig 104/5.
    Berlin: Akademie-Verlag, 1958.
————. *The Old Testament: An Introduction.* New York: Harper & Row, 1965.
Eslinger, Lyle M. "Hosea 12:5a and Genesis 32:29: A Study in Inner Biblical Exe-
    gesis." *JSOT* 18 (1980) 91-99.
Fisch, Harold. *Poetry with Purpose: Biblical Poetics and Interpretation.* Bloomington:
    Indiana University Press, 1988.
Fischer, Bonifatio, et al., ed. *Biblia Sacra Iuxta Vulgatam Versionem.* Stuttgart: Würt-
    tembergische Bibelanstalt, 1969.
Fischer, Georg, and Norbert Lohfink. "'Diese Worte sollst du summen': Dtn 6,7
    wedibbartā bām—ein verlorener Schlüssel zur meditativen Kultur in Israel."
    Theologie und Philosophie 62 (1987) 59-72. Reprinted in N. Lohfink. *Studien
    zum Deuteronomium und zur deuteronomistischen Literatur III,* 181-203. Stutt-
    garter Biblische Aufsatzbände 20. Stuttgart: Verlag Katholisches Bibelwerk,
    1995.
Fishbane, Michael. "Varia Deuteronomica." *ZAW* 84 (1972) 349-50.
————. *Biblical Interpretation in Ancient Israel.* Oxford: Clarendon Press, 1985.
Fitzmyer, Joseph A. *The Aramaic Inscriptions of Sefire.* BibOr 19. Rome: Pontifical
    Biblical Institute, 1967.
Foster, Benjamin R. *Before the Muses: An Anthology of Akkadian Literature. Volume I:
    Archaic, Classical, Mature.* Bethesda, MD: CDL Press, 1993.
————. *Before the Muses: An Anthology of Akkadian Literature. Volume II: Mature,
    Late.* Bethesda, MD: CDL Press, 1993.
Freedman, David Noel. *Pottery, Poetry and Prophecy: Studies in Early Hebrew Poetry.*
    Winona Lake: Eisenbrauns, 1980.
Fretheim, Terence A. "The Ark in Deuteronomy." *CBQ* 30 (1968) 1-14.
Gadd, Cyril John. "Tablets from Kirkuk." *RA* 23 (1926) 49-161.
García López, Felix. "Analyse littéraire de Deutéronome V-VI." *RB* 84 (1977)
    481-522; 85 (1978) 5-49.
————. "Deut. VI et la tradition-rédaction du Deutéronome." *RB* 85 (1978)
    161-200; 86 (1979) 59-91.
————. "Le roi d'Israël: Dt 17:14-20." In *Das Deuteronomium: Entstehung, Gestalt
    und Botschaft,* edited by N. Lohfink, 277-97. BETL 68. Louvain: University
    Press, 1985.
————. "Deut 34, Dtr History and the Pentateuch." In *Studies in Deuteronomy in
    Honour of C. J. Labuschagne on the Occasion of His 65th Birthday,* edited by F.
    García Martínez, A. Hilhorst, J. T. A. G. M. van Ruiten, and van der Woude
    A. S, 47-61. VTSup 53. Leiden: E. J. Brill, 1994.
Garsiel, Moshe. *Biblical Names: A Literary Study of Midrashic Derivations and Puns.*
    Ramat-Gan: Bar-Ilan University Press, 1991.
Genette, Gérard. *Narrative Discourse: An Essay in Method.* Ithaca: Cornell Univer-
    sity Press, 1980.
Gennep, Arnold van. *The Rites of Passage.* Chicago: University of Chicago Press,
    1960.
Gevaryahu, Ḥaim. "A Set of Remarks about Scribes and Books in Biblical Times."
    Bet Miqra 43 (1970) 368-74 (Hebrew).
Gide, André. *Journal 1889-1939.* Paris: Gallimard, 1948.
Ginsberg, Harold Louis. "The North-Canaanite Myth of Anath and Aqhat." *BASOR*
    98 (1945) 15-23.
Goffman, Ervin. *Frame Analysis: An Essay on the Organization of Experience.* Cam-
    bridge: Harvard University Press, 1974.
Gold, Joseph. "Deuteronomy and the Word: The Beginning and the End." In *The*

Biblical Mosaic: Changing Perspectives, edited by R. M. Polzin and E. Rothman, 49-59. Semeia Studies 10. Philadelphia: Fortress, 1982.

Goody, Jack R. *The Logic of Writing and the Organization of Society.* Cambridge: Cambridge University Press, 1986.

Graesser, Carl F. "Standing Stones in Ancient Palestine." *BA* 35 (1972) 34-63.

Graham, William A. *Beyond the Written Word: Oral Aspects of Scripture in the History of Religion.* Cambridge: Cambridge University Press, 1987.

Greenberg, Moshe. "Some Postulates of Biblical Criminal Law." In *Studies in Bible and Jewish Religion: Yehezkel Kaufmann Jubilee Volume,* edited by Menahem Haran, 5-28. Jerusalem: The Magnes Press, 1960. Reprinted in *A Song of Power and the Power of Song: Essays on the Book of Deuteronomy,* edited by D. L. Christensen, 283-300. Winona Lake: Eisenbrauns, 1993.

_____. "Moses." *EncJud* 12 (1971) 372-87.

Greenstein, Edward L. "On the Genesis of Biblical Narrative Prose." Review of *The Narrative Covenant: Transformations of Genre in the Growth of Biblical Literature,* by D. Damrosch. *Prooftexts* 8 (1988) 347-54.

_____. "The Formation of the Biblical Narrative Corpus." *Association for Jewish Studies Review* 15 (1990) 151-78.

Grelot, Pierre. "La légende d'Hénoch dans les Apocryphes et dans la Bible: origine et signification." *RSR* 46 (1958) 5-26, 181-210.

Grossfeld, Bernard. "Targum Neofiti 1 to Deut 31:7." *JBL* 91 (1972) 533-34.

_____, ed. and trans. *The Targum Onqelos to Deuteronomy.* The Aramaic Bible 9. Wilmington, Del: Glazier, 1988.

Gurney, Oliver Robert. *The Hittites.* London: Penguin, 1952.

Haran, Menahem. *Temples and Temple-service in Ancient Israel: An Inquiry Into the Character of Cult-phenomena and the Historical Setting of the Priestly School.* Oxford: Clarendon Press, 1978.

_____. "Book-scrolls in Israel in Pre-exilic Times." *JJS* 33 (1982) 161-73.

_____. "On the Diffusion of Literacy and Schools in Ancient Israel." In *Congress Volume: Jerusalem 1986,* edited by J. A. Emerton, 81-95. VTSup 40. Leiden: E. J. Brill, 1988.

Hendrickson, George Lincoln. "Ancient Reading." *The Classic Journal* 25 (1929) 182-96.

Hillers, Delbert R. *Micah.* Hermeneia. Philadelphia: Fortress Press, 1984.

_____. *Treaty-Curses and the Old Testament Prophets.* BibOr 16. Rome: Pontifical Biblical Institute, 1964.

Hossfeld, Frank-Lothar, and Eleonore Reuter. "סֵפֶר *sepær.*" TWAT 5 (1986) 929-44.

Hossfeld, Frank-Lothar, and H. Lamberty-Zielinski. "קָרָא, *qārā' VI.*" TWAT 7 (1993) 133-36.

Hunger, Herbert. *Babylonische und assyrische Kolophone.* AOAT 2. Kevelaer: Butzon & Bercker; Neukirchen-Vluyn: Neukirchener Verlag, 1968.

Iser, Wolfgang. *The Act of Reading: A Theory of Aesthetic Response.* Baltimore: Johns Hopkins University Press, 1974.

Jacob, Ernest. "Der Prophet Hosea und die Geschichte." *EvT* 24 (1964) 281-90.

Jacobsen, Thorkild. *The Treasures of Darkness: A History of Mesopotamian Religion.* New Haven: Yale University Press, 1976.

Jean, Charles-François, and Jacob Hoftijzer. *Dictionnaire des inscriptions sémitiques de l'ouest.* Leiden: E. J. Brill, 1965.

Jefferson, Ann. "*Mise en abyme* and the Prophetic in Narrative." *Style* 17 (1983) 196-208.

Joüon, Paul, and T. Muraoka. *A Grammar of Biblical Hebrew. Part One: Orthography and Phonetics; Part Two: Morphology.* Subsidia Biblica 14.1. Rome: Editrice Pontificio Istituto Biblico, 1991.

————. *A Grammar of Biblical Hebrew. Part Three: Syntax.* Subsidia Biblica 14.2. Rome: Editrice Pontificio Istituto Biblico, 1991.

Keel, Othmar. "Zeichen der Verbundenheit: zur Vorgeschichte und Bedeutung der Forderungen von Deuteronomium 6,8f. und Par." In *Mélanges Dominique Barthélémy: études bibliques offertes à l'occasion de son 60ᵉ anniversaire,* edited by P. Casetti, O. Keel, and A. Schenker, 159-240. OBO 38. Freiburg: Universitätsverlag/Göttingen: Vandenhoeck & Ruprecht, 1981.

Keil, Karl Friedrich, and Franz Delitzsch. *Biblical Commentary on the Old Testament: Volume III The Pentateuch.* Grand Rapids: Eerdmans, 1951.

Kermode, Frank. *The Sense of an Ending: Studies in the Theory of Fiction.* Oxford: Oxford University Press, 1966.

Klein, Michael. "Deut 31:7, תבוא or תביא?" *JBL* 92 (1973) 584-85.

Kleinert, Paul. *Das Deuteronomium und der Deuteronomiker: Untersuchungen zur alttestamentlichen Rechts- und Literaturgeschichte.* Bielefeld and Leipzig: Velhagen & Klasing, 1872.

Klostermann, August. *Der Pentateuch: Beiträge zu seinem Verständnis und seiner Entstehungsgeschichte.* Leipzig: Deichert (G. Böhme), 1893.

Knapp, Dietrich. *Deuteronomium 4: literarische Analyse und theologische Interpretation.* GTA 35. Göttingen: Vandenhoeck & Ruprecht, 1987.

Knoppers, Gary N. *Two Nations Under God: The Deuteronomistic History of Solomon and the Dual Monarchies. Volume 1: The Reign of Solomon and the Rise of Jeroboam.* HSM 53. Atlanta: Scholars Press, 1994.

Korošec, V. *Hethitische Staatsverträge: ein Betrag zu ihrer juristischen Wertung.* Leipzig: Weicher, 1931.

König, Eduard. *Das Deuteronomium eingeleitet, übersetzt und erklärt.* KAT. Leipzig: A. Deichertsche, 1917.

Kuhl, Curt. "'Die Wiederaufnahme'—ein literarkritisches Prinzip?" *ZAW* 64 (1952) 1-11.

L'Hour, Jean. "L'alliance de Sichem." *RB* 69 (1962) 5-36, 161-84.

Laberge, Léo. "Le texte de Deutéronome 31 (Dt 31,1-29; 32,44-47)." In *Pentateuchal and Deuteronomistic Studies: Papers Read at the XIIIth IOSOT Congress Leuven 1989,* edited by C. Brekelmans and J. Lust, 143-60. BETL 94. Louvain: Peeters Press/University Press, 1990.

Labuschagne, Casper Jeremiah. "The Song of Moses: Its Framework and Structure." In *De Fructu Oris Sui: Essays in Honor of Adrianus van Selms,* edited by I. H. Eybers, C. J. Fensham, C. J. Labuschagne, W. C. van Wyk, and A. H. van Zyl, 85-98. Leiden: E. J. Brill, 1971.

————. "קרא, qrʾ, Rufen." *THAT* 2 (1976) 666-74.

————. "Divine Speech in Deuteronomy." In *Das Deuteronomium: Entstehung, Gestalt und Botschaft,* edited by N. Lohfink, 111-26. BETL 68. Louvain: University Press, 1985. Reprinted in *A Song of Power and the Power of Song: Essays on the Book of Deuteronomy,* edited by D. L. Christensen, 375-93. Winona Lake: Eisenbrauns, 1993.

Lambert, Wilfred G. *Babylonian Wisdom Literature.* Oxford: Clarendon Press, 1960.

————. "A Catalogue of Texts and Authors." *Journal of Cuneiform Studies* 16 (1962) 59-81.

————. "The Fifth Tablet of the Erra Epic." *Iraq* 24 (1962) 119-26.

Lauterbach, Jacob Z., ed. and trans. *Mekilta De-Rabbi Ishmael.* Philadelphia: The Jewish Publication Society of America, 1933.

Leichty, Erle. "The Colophon." In *Studies Presented to A. Leo Oppenheim,* edited by

R. D. Biggs and J. A. Brinkman, 147-54. Chicago: University of Chicago Press, 1964.

Lemaire, André. *Les écoles et la formation de la Bible dans l'ancien Israël.* OBO 39. Fribourg: Editions Universitaires/Göttingen: Vandenhoeck & Ruprecht, 1981.

_____. "Vom Ostrakon zur Schriftrolle: Überlegungen zur Entstehung der Bibel." In *XXII. Deutscher Orientalistentag Tübingen 21-25 März 1983,* 110-23. ZDMGSup 6. Stuttgart: F. Steiner Verlag, 1985.

_____. "Les inscriptions sur plâtre de Deir ʿAlla et leur signification historique et culturelle." In *The Balaam Text from Deir ʿAlla Re-Evaluated: Proceedings of the International Symposium Held at Leiden 21-24 August 1989,* edited by J. Hoftijzer and A. van der Kooij, 33-57. Leiden: E. J. Brill, 1991.

_____. "Writing and Writing Materials." *ABD 6* (1992) 999-1008.

Lemaire, André, and Jean-Marie Durand. *Les inscriptions araméennes de Sfiré et l'Assyrie de Shamshi-Ilu.* Hautes Etudes Orientales 20. Genève and Paris: Librairie Droz, 1984.

Lenchak, Timothy A. *"Choose Life!": A Rhetorical-Critical Investigation of Deuteronomy 28,69-30,20.* AnBib 129. Rome: Editrice Pontificio Istituto Biblico, 1993.

Levine, Baruch A. *Numbers 1-20.* AB 4a. New York: Doubleday, 1993.

Levinson, Bernard M. "Calum M. Carmichael's Approach to the Laws of Deuteronomy." *HTR* 83 (1990) 227-57.

_____. *The Hermeneutics of Innovation: The Impact of Centralization upon the Structure, Sequence, and Reformulation of Legal Material in Deuteronomy.* Ann Arbor, Mi: University Microfilms, 1991.

_____. "The Human Voice in Divine Revelation: The Problem of Authority in Biblical Law." In *Innovation in Religious Traditions: Essays in the Interpretation of Religious Change,* edited by M. A. Wiliams, M. S. Jaffee, and C. Cox, 35-71. Studies in Religion and Society. Berlin: Mouton de Gruyter, 1992.

_____. *Deuteronomy and the Hermeneutics of Legal Innovation.* Oxford: Oxford University Press. Forthcoming.

Loewenstamm, Samuel E. "The Formula *baʿet hahiʾ* in the Introductory Speeches in Deuteronomy." *Tarbiz* 38 (1968) 99-104 (Hebrew). Translated in and cited according to idem, *From Babylon to Canaan: Studies in the Bible and Its Oriental Background,* 42-50. Jerusalem: The Magnes Press, 1992.

_____. "The Death of Moses." In *Studies on the Testament of Abraham,* edited by G. W. E. Nickelsburg, 185-217. Missoula: Scholars Press: 1976. Reprinted in and cited according to idem, *From Babylon to Canaan: Studies in the Bible and Its Oriental Background,* 136-66. Publication of the Perry Foundation for Biblical Research in the Hebrew University of Jerusalem. Jerusalem: The Magnes Press, 1992.

_____. "The Testament of Abraham and the Texts Concerning Moses' Death." In *Studies on the Testament of Abraham,* edited by G. W. E. Nickelsburg, 219-225. Missoula: Scholars Press: 1976. Reprinted in and cited according to idem, *From Babylon to Canaan: Studies in the Bible and Its Oriental Background,* 167-73. Jerusalem: The Magnes Press, 1992.

Lohfink, Norbert. "Wie stellt sich das Problem Individuum—Gemeinschaft in Deuteronomium 1,6-3,29?" *Scholastik* 35 (1960) 403-407. Reprinted in idem, *Studien zum Deuteronomium und zur deuteronomistischen Literatur I,* 45-51. Stuttgarter Biblische Aufsatzbände 8. Stuttgart: Verlag Katholisches Bibelwerk, 1990. Translated as and cited according to "The Problem of Individual and Community in Deuteronomy 1,6-3,29." In idem, *Theology of the Pentateuch: Themes of the Priestly Narrative and Deuteronomy,* 227-33. Minneapolis: Fortress Press, 1994.

_____. "Jona ging zur Stadt hinaus (Jon 4,5)." *BZ* 5 (1961) 185-203.

_____. "Der Bundesschluß im Land Moab: Redaktionsgeschichtliches zu Dt 28,69-32,47." *BZ* 6 (1962) 32-56. Reprinted in idem, *Studien zum Deuteronomium und zur deuteronomistischen Literatur I*, 53-82. Stuttgarter biblische Aufsatzbände 8. Stuttgart: Verlag Katholisches Bibelwerk, 1990.

_____. "Die deuteronomistiche Darstellung des Übergang der Führung Israels von Moses auf Josue: Ein Beitrag zur alttestamentlischen Theologie des Amtes." *Scholastik* 37 (1962): 32-44. Reprinted in idem, *Studien zum Deuteronomium und zur deuteronomistischen Literatur I*, 83-97. Stuttgarter Biblische Aufsatzbände 8. Stuttgart: Verlag Katholisches Bibelwerk, 1990. Translated as "The Deuteronomistic Picture of the Transfer of Authority from Moses to Joshua: A Contribution to an Old Testament Theology of Office." In idem, *Theology of the Pentateuch: Themes of the Priestly Narrative and Deuteronomy*, 234-47. Minneapolis: Fortress Press, 1994.

_____. *Des Hauptgebot: Eine Untersuchung literarischer Einleitungsfragen zu Dtn. 5-11*. AnBib 20. Rome: Pontifical Biblical Institute Press, 1963.

_____. "Die Sicherung der Wirksamkeit des Gotteswortes durch das Prinzip der Schriftlichkeit der Tora und durch das Prinzip der Gewaltenteilung nach den Ämtergesetzen des Buches Deuteronomium (Dt 16,18-18,22)." In *Testimonium Veritati: Festschrift Wilhelm Kempf*, edited by H. Wolter, 143-55. Frankfurt: Knecht, 1971. Reprinted in idem, *Studien zum Deuteronomium und zur deuteronomistischen Literatur I*, 305-23. Stuttgarter Biblische Aufsatzbände 8. Stuttgart: Verlag Katholisches Bibelwerk, 1990. Translated as "Distribution of the Functions of Power: The Laws Concerning Public Offices in Deuteronomy 16:18-18:22." In *A Song of Power and the Power of Song: Essays on the Book of Deuteronomy*, edited by D. L. Christensen, 336-52. Winona Lake: Eisenbrauns, 1993.

_____. "Zur deuteronomischen Zentralisationsformel." *Bib* 65 (1984) 297-328. Reprinted in idem, *Studien zum Deuteronomium und zur deuteronomistischen Literatur II*, 147-77. Stuttgarter Biblische Aufsatzbaunde 12. Stuttgart: Verlag Katholisches Bibelwerk, 1991.

_____. "Der Glaube und die nächste Generation: Das Gottesvolk der Bibel als Lerngemeinschaft." In *Das Jüdische am Christentum: Die Verlorene Dimension*, 144-66, 260-63. Freiburg: Herder, 1987.

_____. "Dtn 12,1 und Gen 15,18: Das dem Samen Abrahams geschenkte Land als der Geltungsbereich der deuteronomischen Gesetze." In *Die Väter Israels: Beiträge zur Theologie der Patriarchenüberlieferungen im Alten Testament. Festschrift für Joseph Scharbert zum 70. Geburtstag*, edited by M. Görg, 183-210. Stuttgart: Katholisches Bibelwerk, 1989. Reprinted in idem, *Studien zum Deuteronomium und zur deuteronomistischen Literatur II*, 257-85. Stuttgarter Biblische Aufsatzbände 12. Stuttgart: Verlag Katholisches Bibelwerk, 1991.

_____. "Die *huqqîm ûmišpāṭîm* und ihre Neubegrenzung durch Dtn 12,1." *Bib* 70 (1989) 1-30. Reprinted as "Die *huqqîm ûmišpāṭîm* im Buch Deuteronomium und ihre Neubegrenzung durch Dtn 12,1" in idem, *Studien zum Deuteronomium und zur deuteronomistischen Literatur II*, 229-56. Stuttgarter Biblische Aufsatzbände 12. Stuttgart: Verlag Katholisches Bibelwerk, 1991.

_____. "Das Deuteronomium: Jahwehgesetz oder Mosegesetz? Die Subjektzuordnung bei Wörtern für 'Gesetz' im Dtn und in der dtr Literatur" *TP* 65 (1990) 387-91. Reprinted in idem, *Studien zum Deuteronomium und zur deuteronomistischen Literatur III*, 157-65. Stuttgarter Biblische Aufsatzbände 20. Stuttgart: Verlag Katholisches Bibelwerk, 1995.

_____. *Die Väter Israels im Deuteronomium—Mit einer Stellungnahme von Thomas*

Römer. OBO 111. Freiburg: Universitätsverlag/Göttingen: Vandenhoeck & Ruprecht, 1991.

_____. "*"ed(w)t* im Deuteronomium und in den Königsbüche." 35 (1991) 86-93. Reprinted in idem, *Studien zum Deuteronomium und zur deuteronomistischen Literatur III,* 167-77. Stuttgarter Biblische Aufsatzbaunde 20. Stuttgart: Verlag Katholisches Bibelwerk, 1995.

_____. "Dtn 28,69—Überschrift oder Kolophon?" 64 (1992) 40- 52. Reprinted in idem, *Studien zum Deuteronomium und zur deuteronomistischen Literatur III,* 279-91. Stuttgarter Biblische Aufsatzbände 20. Stuttgart: Verlag Katholisches Bibelwerk, 1995.

_____. "Deutéronome et Pentateuque: état de la recherche." In *Le Pentateuque: débats et recherches,* edited by P. Haudebert, 35-64. LD 151. Paris: Cerf, 1992.

_____. "Opfer und Säkularisierung im Deuteronomium." In *Studien zu Opfer und Kult im Alten Testament,* edited by Adrian Schenker, 15-43. Forschungen zum Alten Testament 3. Tuubingen: J. C. B. Mohr (Paul Siebeck), 1992.

_____. "Zur Fabel in Dtn 31-32." In *Konsequente Traditionsgeschichte: Festschrift für Klaus Baltzer zum 65. Geburtstag,* edited by R. Bartelmus, T. Krüger, and H. Utzschneider, 255-79. OBO 126. Freiburg: Universitätsverlag/Göttingen: Vandenhoeck & Ruprecht, 1993.

_____. "Die Ältesten Israels und der Bund zum Zusammenhang von Dtn 5,23; 26,17-19; 27,1.9f und 31,9." BN (1993) 26-42.

_____. "Die Stimmen in Deuteronomium 2." BZ 37 (1993) 209-35.

_____. "Moab oder Sichem—wo wurde Dtn 28 nach der Fabel des Deuteronomiums proklamiert?" In *Studies in Deuteronomy in Honour of C. J. Labuschagne on the Occasion of His 65th Birthday,* edited by F. García Martínez, A. Hilhorst, J. T. A. G. M. van Ruiten, and A. S. van der Woude, 139-53. Leiden: E. J. Brill, 1994.

_____. "Zur Fabel des Deuteronomiums." In *Bundesdokument und Gesetz: Studien zum Deuteronomium,* edited by G. Braulik, 65-78. Herders Biblische Studien 4. Freiburg: Herder, 1995.

_____. "Bund als Vertrag im Deuteronomium." ZAW 107 (1995) 215-39.

Long, Burke O. "Framing Repetitions in Biblical Historiography." *JBL* 106 (1987) 385-99.

_____. "Two Question and Answer Schemata in the Prophets." *JBL* 90 (1971) 129-39.

Luckenbill, Daniel David. *Ancient Records of Assyria and Babylonia. Volume I: Historical Records of Assyria from the Earliest Times to Sargon.* Chicago: The University of Chicago Press, 1926.

_____. *Ancient Records of Assyria and Babylonia. Volume II: From Sargon to the End.* Chicago: The University of Chicago Press, 1927.

Lux, Rüdiger. "Der Tod des Moses, als 'besprochene und erzählte Welt'." ZTK 84 (1987) 395-425.

Luyten, Jos. "Primeval and Eschatological Overtones in the Song of Moses (Dt 32,1-43)." In *Das Deuteronomium: Entstehung, Gestalt und Botschaft,* edited by N. Lohfink, 341-47. BETL 68. Louvain: University Press, 1985.

McBride, S. Dean, Jr. "Polity of the Covenant People: The Book of Deuteronomy." Int 41 (1987) 229-44. Reprinted in *A Song of Power and the Power of Song: Essays on the Book of Deuteronomy,* edited by D. L. Christensen, 62-77. Winona Lake: Eisenbrauns, 1993.

McCarthy, Dennis J. *Treaty and Covenant: A Study in Form in the Ancient Oriental Documents and in the Old Testament.* New Edition Completely Rewritten. AnBib 21a. Rome: Biblical Institute Press, 1981.

_____. *Institution and Narrative: Collected Essays.* AnBib 108. Rome: Biblical Institute Press, 1985.

Margaliot, Mordechai. "The Connection of Balaam Narrative with the Pentateuch." In *Proceedings of the Sixth World Congress of Jewish Studies Held at the Hebrew University of Jerusalem 13-19 August 1973 under the Auspices of the Israel Academy of Sciences and Humanities. Volume I,* 279-90. Jerusalem: Jerusalem Academic Press, 1977.

Marks, Herbert. "Biblical Naming and Poetic Etymology." *JBL* 114 (1995) 29-50.

Martin, W. J. "'Dischronologized' Narrative in the Old Testament." In *Congress Volume: Rome 1968,* 179-86. VTSup 17. Leiden: E. J. Brill, 1969.

Mayes, Andrew D. H. *Deuteronomy.* NCBC. London: Marschall, Morgan & Scott, 1979.

_____. "Deuteronomy 4 and the Literary Criticism of Deuteronomy." *JBL* 100 (1981) 23-51.

Mechonnic, Henri. *Le signe et le poème.* Paris: Gallimard, 1975.

Meier, Samuel A. *Speaking of Speaking: Marking Direct Discourse in the Hebrew Bible.* VTSup 46. Leiden: E. J. Brill, 1992.

Mendenhall, George E. "Covenant Forms in Israelite Tradition." *BA* 17 (1954) 49-76.

Merril, Eugene H. *Deuteronomy.* The New American Commentary 24. Nashville: Broadman & Holman, 1994.

Meyers, Eric M. "Secondary Burials in Palestine." *BA* 33 (1970) 2-29.

Milgrom, Jacob. "The Alleged Demythologization and Secularization in Deuteronomy." *IEJ* 23 (1973) 156-61.

Millard, Alan Ralph. "An Assessment of the Evidence of Writing in Ancient Israel." In *Biblical Archaeology Today: Proceedings of the International Congress of Archaeology, Jerusalem, April 1984,* 301-12. Jerusalem: Israel Exploration Society, 1985.

Mittmann, Siegfried. *Deuteronomium 1.1-6.3: Literarkritisch und traditionsgeschichtlich Untersucht.* BZAW 139. Berlin and New York: de Gruyter, 1975.

Moberly, R. W. L. *At the Mountain of God: Story and Theology in Exodus 32-34.* JSOTSup 22. Sheffield: JSOT Press, 1983.

Moran, William L. "The Ancient Near Eastern Background of the Love of God in Deuteronomy." *CBQ* 25 (1963) 77-87.

_____. "The Epic of Gilgamesh: A Document of Ancient Humanism." Unpublished Paper. Oriental Institute, University of Chicago, 1980.

Morrisette, Bruce. "Un héritage d'André Gide: la duplication intérieure." *Comparative Literature Studies* 8 (1971) 125-42.

Müller, Günther. *Morphologische Poetik: Gesammelte Aufsätze,* edited by E. Müller. Darmstadt: Wissenschaftliche Buchgesellschaft, 1968.

Nohrnberg, James. *Like Unto Moses: The Constitution of an Interruption.* Bloomington: Indiana University Press, 1995.

Noth, Martin. *Überlieferungsgeschichtliche Studien.* 2d ed. Tübingen: Max Niemeyer Verlag, 1943.

_____. *Überlieferungsgeschichte des Pentateuchs.* Stuttgart: Kohlhammer, 1948.

Nwachukwu, Fortunatus. "The Textual Differences Between the MT and the LXX of Deuteronomy 31: A Response to Leo Laberge." In *Bundesdokument und Gesetz: Studien zum Deuteronomium,* edited by G. Braulik, 79-92. Herders Biblische Studien 4. Freiburg: Herder, 1995.

Olson, Dennis T. *Deuteronomy and the Death of Moses: A Theological Reading.* OBT. Minneapolis: Fortress, 1994.

Ong, Walter J. *Orality and Literacy.* London: Routledge, 1982.

Oppenheim, A. Leo. *Ancient Mesopotamia: Portrait of a Dead Civilization.* Rev. ed. Chicago: University of Chicago Press, 1977.

Otto, Eckart. "Aspects of Legal Reform and Reformulation in Ancient Cuneiform and Israelite Law." In *Theory and Method in Biblical and Cuneiform Law: Revision, Interpolation and Development,* edited by B. M. Levinson, 160-96. JSOT-Sup 181. Sheffield: Sheffield Academic Press, 1994.

Palache, J. L. *Semantic Notes on the Hebrew Lexicon.* Leiden: E. J. Brill, 1959.

Parpola, Simo, and Kazuko Watanabe. *Neo-Assyrian Treaties and Loyalty Oaths.* State Archives of Assyria 2. Helsinki: Helsinki University Press, 1988.

Perlitt, Lothar. *Bundestheologie im Alten Testament.* WMANT 36. Neukirchen-Vluyn: Neukirchener Verlag, 1969.

————. "Ein einzig Volk von Brüdern: zur deuteronomischen Herkunft der biblischen Bezeichnung 'Bruder'" In *Kirche. Festschrift für Gunther Bornkamm zum 75. Geburtstag,* edited by D. Lührmann and G. Strecker, 27-52. Tübingen: J. C. B. Mohr (Paul Siebeck), 1980.

————. "Deuteronomium 1-3 im Streit der exegetischen Methoden." In *Das Deuteronomium: Entstehung, Gestalt und Botschaft,* edited by N. Lohfink, 149-63. BETL 68. Louvain: University Press, 1985.

————. "Priesterschrift im Deuteronomium?" *ZAW (Supplement) 100* (1988) 65-88.

————. *Deuteronomium.* V1. Biblischer Kommentar AT. Neukirchen: Neukirchener Verlag, 1990.

————. *Deuteronomium.* V2. Biblischer Kommentar AT. Neukirchen: Neukirchener Verlag, 1991.

Perry, Menakhem. "Literary Dynamics: How the Order of a Text Creates Its Meanings." *Poetics Today* 1 (1979) 35-64.

Polak, Frank. *Biblical Narrative: Aspects of Art and Design.* The Biblical Encyclopaedia Library 11. Jerusalem: Mossad Bialik, 1994 (Hebrew).

Polzin, Robert. *Moses and the Deuteronomist: A Literary Study of the Deuteronomistic History. Part One: Deuteronomy, Joshua, Judges.* New York: The Seabury Press, 1980.

————. "Reporting Speech in the Book of Deuteronomy: Toward a Compositional Analysis of the Deuteronomic History." In *Traditions in Transformation: Turning Points in Biblical Faith,* Festschrift honoring Frank Moore Cross, edited by B. Halpern and J. D. Levenson, 192-211. Winona Lake: Eisenbrauns, 1981. Reprinted in *A Song of Power and the Power of Song: Essays on the Book of Deuteronomy,* edited by D. L. Christensen, 355-74. Winona Lake: Eisenbrauns, 1993.

————. "Deuteronomy." In *The Literary Guide to the Bible,* edited by R. Alter and F. Kermode, 92-101. Cambridge, Harvard University Press, 1987.

Posner, Ernst. *Archives in the Ancient World.* Cambridge: Harvard University Press, 1972.

The Postmodern Bible: The Bible and Culture Collective, edited by E. A. Castelli, S. D. Moore, and R. M. Schwartz. New Haven: Yale University Press, 1995.

Preuß, Horst Dietrich. *Deuteronomium.* ErFor 164. Darmstadt: Wissenschaftliche Buchgesellschaft, 1982.

————. "Zum deuteronomischen Geschichtswerk." *TRu* 58 (1993) 229-64, 341-95.

Pritchard, James B., ed. *Ancient Near Eastern Texts Relating to the Old Testament.* 3d ed. with supplement. Princeton: Princeton University Press, 1969.

Pury, Albert de. "La tradition patriarcale en Genèse 12-35." In *Le Pentateuque en question: les origines et la composition des cinq premiers livres de la Bible à la lumière des recherches récentes*, edited by A. de Pury, 259-70. Le Monde de la Bible 19. Geneva: Labor et Fides, 1989.

_____. "Le cycle de Jacob comme légende autonome des origines d'Israël." In *Congress Volume: Leuven 1989*, 78-96. VTSup 43. Leiden: E. J. Brill, 1991.

_____. "Osée 12 et ses implications pour le débat actuel sur le Pentateuque." In *Le Pentateuque: débats et recherches*, edited by P. Haudebert, 175-207. LD 151. Paris: Cerf, 1992.

_____. "Las dos leyendas sobre el origen de Israel (Jacob y Moisés) y la elaboración del Pentateuco." *EstBib* (1994) 95-131.

Rad, Gerhard von. *Studies in Deuteronomy*. SBT 9. London: SCM Press, 1953.

_____. *Deuteronomy*. OTL. Philadelphia: The Westminster Press, 1966.

Rahlfs, Alfred. *Septuaginta I: Leges et Historiae*. Stuttgart: Württembergische Bibelanstalt, 1979.

Reuter, Eleonore. "'Nimm nichts davon weg und füge nichts hinzu!': Dtn 13,1, seine alttestamentlichen Parallelen und seine altorientalischen Vorbilder." *BibNot* 47 (1990) 107-14.

Richter, David H. *Fable's End: Completeness and Closure in Rhetorical Fiction*. Chicago: The University of Chicago Press, 1974.

Rofé, Alexander. *Introduction to Deuteronomy: Part I and Further Chapters*. Jerusalem: Akademon, 1988 (Hebrew).

Römer, Thomas. *Israels Väter: Untersuchungen zur Väterthematik im Deuteronomium und in der deuteronomistichen Tradition*. OBO 99. Freiburg: Universitätsverlag/Göttingen: Vandenhoeck & Ruprecht, 1990.

_____. "Le Deutéronome et la quête des origines." In *Le Pentateuque: débats et recherches*, edited by P. Haudebert, 65-98. LD 151. Paris: Cerf, 1992.

Rooy, Herculaas F. van. "Deuteronomy 28,69: Superscript or Subscript?" *JNSL* 14 (1988) 215-22.

Rose, Martin. *Deuteronomist und Jahwist: Untersuchungen zu den Berührungspunkten beider Literaturwerke*. ATANT 67. Zürich: Theologische Verlag, 1981.

_____. "La croissance du corpus historique de la Bible: une proposition." *Journal de Théologie et de Philosophie* 118 (1986) 217-326.

_____. "Empoigner le Pentateuque par sa fin! L'investiture de Josué et la mort de Moïse." In *Le Pentateuque en question: les origines et la composition des cinq premiers livres de la Bible à la lumière des recherches récentes*, edited by A. de Pury, 129-47. Le Monde de la Bible 19. Geneva: Labor et Fides, 1989.

Rouillard, Henri. *La péricope de Balaam (Nombres 22-24): la prose et les "oracles"*. EB 4. Paris: Gabalda, 1985.

Rudolph, Wilhelm. *Micha—Nahum—Habakuk—Zephanja*. KAT. Gütersloh: Gerd Mohn, 1975.

Rüterswörden, Udo. *Von der politischen Gemeinschaft zur Gemeinde: Studien zu Dt 16,18-18,22*. BBB 55. Frankfurt: Athenäum, 1987.

Sarna, Nahum. "Bible." *EncJud* 4 (1971) 816-36.

Savran, George W. *Telling and Retelling: Quotation in Biblical Narrative*. Bloomington: Indiana University Press, 1988.

Schäfer-Lichtenberger, Christa. *Josua und Salomo: eine Studie zu Autorität und Legitimät des Nachfolgers im alten Testament*. VTSup 58. Leiden: E. J. Brill, 1995.

Schwartz, Regina M. "Joseph's Bones and the Resurrection of the Text: Remembering in the Bible." In *The Book and the Text: The Bible and Literary Theory*, edited by R. M. Schwartz, 40-59. Oxford: Blackwell, 1990.

Seeligmann, Isaac Leo. "A Psalm from Pre-Regal Times." *VT* 14 (1964) 75-92.

Seow, Choon L. "Ark of the Covenant." *ABD 1* (1992) 386-93.

Ska, Jean-Louis. *Our Fathers Have Told Us: Introduction to the Analysis of Hebrew Narratives*. Subsidia Biblica 13. Rome: Pontifical Biblical Institute Press, 1990.

_____. "Un nouveau Wellhausen?" *Bib* 72 (1991) 253-63.

_____. "Récit et récit métadiégétique en Ex 1-15; remarques critiques et essai d'interprétation." In *Le Pentateuque: débats et recherches*, edited by P. Haudebert, 135-71. LD 151. Paris: Cerf, 1992.

Skweres, Dieter Eduard. "Das Motiv der Strafgrunderfragung in biblischen und neuassyrischen Texten." *BZ* 14 (1970) 181-97.

_____. *Die Rückverweise im Buch Deuteronomium.* AnBib 79. Rome: Biblical Institute Press, 1979.

Smith, George Adam. *The Book of Deuteronomy.* CBC. Cambridge, 1918.

Smith, Wilfred Cantwell. "Scripture as Form and Concept: Their Emergence for the Western World." In *Rethinking Scripture: Essays from a Comparative Perspective*, edited by M. Levering, 29-57. Albany: State University of New York Press, 1989.

Soden, W. von. "Zu einigen akkadischen Wörtern." *ZA* 67 (1977) 237-39.

Soggin, Alberto J. *Old Testament and Oriental Studies.* BibOr 29. Rome: Biblical Institute Press, 1975.

Sonnet, Jean-Pierre. *La parole consacrée: théorie des actes de langage, linguistique de l'énonciation et parole de la foi.* Bibliothèque des Cahiers de l'Institut de Linguistique de Louvain 25. Louvain: Peeters, 1984.

_____. "Le Sinaï dans l'événement de sa lecture: la dimension pragmatique de Exode 19-24." *NRT* 111 (1989) 322-44.

_____. "'Le livre trouvé': 2 Rois 22 dans sa finalité narrative." *NRT* 116 (1994) 836-61.

_____. "Le Deutéronome et la modernité du livre." *NRT* 118 (1996) 481-96.

Sperber, Alexander. *The Bible in Aramaic.* Leiden: E. J. Brill, 1959.

Spinoza, Benedictus de. *Tractatus Theologico-politicus.* Gebhardt Edition 1925. Translated by Samuel Shirley. Leiden: E. J. Brill, 1989.

Staerk, Willy. *Das Deuteronomium: sein Inhalt und sein literarische Form.* Leipzig: Hinrichs, 1894.

Starobinski, Jean. *Les mots sous les mots: les anagrammes de Ferdinand de Saussure.* Paris: Gallimard, 1971.

Steinkeller, Piotr. "Studies in Third Millenium Paleography, 2. Signs ŠEN and ALAL." *OrAnt* 20 (1981) 243-49.

Sternberg, Meir. *Expositional Modes and Temporal Ordering in Fiction.* Baltimore: Johns Hopkins University Press, 1978.

_____. "Ordering the Unordered: Time, Space, and Descriptive Coherence." *Yale French Studies* 61 (1981) 60-88.

_____. "Point of View and the Indirections of Direct Speech." *Language and Style* 15 (1982) 67-117.

_____. "Proteus in Quotation-land: Mimesis and the Forms of Reported Discourse." *Poetics Today* 3 (1982) 107-56.

_____. *The Poetics of Biblical Narrative.* Bloomington: Indiana University Press, 1985.

_____. "The World from the Addressee's Viewpoint: Reception as Representation, Dialogue as Monologue." *Style* 20 (1986) 295-317.

_____. "Time and Space in Biblical (Hi)story Telling: The Grand Chronology." In *The Book and the Text: The Bible and Literary Theory*, edited by R. Schwartz, 81-145. Oxford: Blackwell, 1990.

_____. "Double Cave, Double Talk: The Indirections of Biblical Dialogue." In *"Not in Heaven": Coherence and Complexity in Biblical Narrative*, edited by J. P. Rosenblatt and J. C. Sitterson, Jr., 28-57. Bloomington: Indiana University Press, 1991.

_____. "How Indirect Discourse Means: Syntax, Semantics, Poetics." In *Liter-*

ary Pragmatics, edited by R. D. Sell, 62-93. London: Routledge, 1991.

Steuernagel, Carl. *Das Deuteronomium*. 2d ed. HKAT 1.3.1. Göttingen: Vandenhoeck & Ruprecht, 1923.

Steymans, Hans Ulrich. "Eine assyrische Vorlage für Deuteronomium 28,20-44." In *Bundesdokument und Gesetz: Studien zum Deuteronomium*, edited by G. Braulik, 119-41. Herders Biblische Studien 4. Freiburg: Herder, 1995.

Stoellger, Philipp. "Deuteronomium 34 ohne Priesterschrift." *ZAW* 105 (1993) 26-51.

Talmon, Shemaryahu. "The Presentation of Synchroneity and Simultaneity in Biblical Narratives." In *Studies in Hebrew Narrative Art Throughout the Ages*, edited by J. Heinemann and S. Werses, 9-26. ScrHier 27. Jerusalem: The Magnes Press, 1978. Reprinted in idem, *Literary Studies in the Hebrew Bible: Form and Content. Collected Studies*. Jerusalem: The Magnes Press; Leiden: E. J. Brill, 1993.

Tengström, Sven. *Die Toledotsformel und die literarische Struktur priesterlichen Erweiterungsschicht im Pentateuch*. ConBib 17. Lund: Gleerup, 1981.

Tigay, Jeffrey H. *The Evolution of the Gilgamesh Epic*. Philadelphia: University of Philadelphia Press, 1982.

Todorov, Tzvetan, and Oswald Ducrot. *Encyclopedic Dictionary of the Sciences of Language*. Baltimore: Johns Hopkins University Press, 1979.

Toeg, Arie. *Lawgiving at Sinai: The Course of Development of the Traditions Bearing on the Lawgiving at Sinai within the Pentateuch, with a Special Emphasis on the Emergence of the Literary Complex in Exodus xix-xxiv*. Jerusalem: The Magnes Press, 1977 (Hebrew).

Tomashevsky, Boris. "Thematics." In *Russian Formalist Criticism: Four Essays*, Edited by L. T. Lemon and M. J. Reis, 61-95. Lincoln: University of Nebraska, 1965.

_____. "Thématique." In *Théorie de la littérature*, edited by T. Todorov, 263-307. Paris: Seuil, 1965.

Torat Ḥaim Ḥumash. Jerusalem: Mossad Harav Kook, 1993 (Hebrew).

Tov, Emanuel. *The Text-critical Use of the Septuagint in Biblical Research*. Jerusalem Biblical Studies 3. Jerusalem: Simor, 1981.

Tucker, Gene M. "Prophetic Superscriptions and the Growth of a Canon." In *Canon and Authority: Essays in Old Testament Religion and Theology*, edited by G. W. Coats and B. O. Long, 56-70. Philadelphia: Fortress Press, 1977.

Vaux, Roland de. *Les institutions de l'Ancien Testament*. Paris: Cerf, 1958.

_____. *Bible et Orient*. Cogitatio Fidei 24. Paris: Cerf, 1967.

Veijola, Timo. "Principal Observations on the Basic Story in Deuteronomy 1-3." In *"Wünschet Jerusalem Frieden": IOSOT Congress, Jerusalem 1986*, edited by M. Augustin and K.-D. Schunck, 249-59. Beiträge zur Erforschung des Alten Testaments und des Antiken Judentums 13. Frankfurt: Peter Lang, 1988. Reprinted in *A Song of Power and the Power of Song: Essays on the Book of Deuteronomy*, edited by D. L. Christensen, 137-46. Winona Lake: Eisenbrauns, 1993.

Viberg, Åke. *Symbols of Law: A Contextual Analysis of Legal Symbolic Acts in the Old Testament*. CB 34. Stockholm: Almqvist & Wiksell International, 1992.

Vogels, Walter. "The Literary Form of 'the Question of the Nations'" *EgT* 11 (1980) 159-76.

Walker, C. B. F. "The Second Tablet of *ṭupšenna pitema*: An Old Babylonian Naram-Sin Legend?" *JCS* 33 (1981) 191-95.

Waltke, Bruce K., and M. O'Connor. *An Introduction to Biblical Hebrew Syntax*. Winona Lake: Eisenbrauns, 1990.

Weber, R., ed. B. Fischer, I. Gribomont, H. F. D. Sparks, and W. Thiele, collab-

BIBLIOGRAPHY   283

orators. *Biblia Sacra Iuxta Vulgatam Versionem. Tomus I: Genesis-Psalmi.* Stuttgart: Württembergische Bibelanstalt, 1969.
Weinfeld, Moshe. *Deuteronomy and the Deuteronomic School.* Oxford: Clarendon Press, 1972."
————. On 'Demythologization and Secularization' in Deuteronomy." *IEJ* 23 (1973) 230-33.
————. "The Pattern of the Israelite Settlement in Canaan." In *Congress Volume: Jerusalem 1986,* edited by J. A. Emerton, 270-84. VTSup 40. Leiden: E. J. Brill, 1988.
————. *Deuteronomy 1-11.* AB 5. New York: Doubleday, 1991.
————. "Deuteronomy, Book of." *ABD* 2 (1992) 168-83.
Weitzman, Steven. "Lessons from the Dying: The Role of Deuteronomy 32 in Its Narrative Setting." *HTR* 87 (1994) 377-93.
Welch, Adam C. *Deuteronomy: The Framework to the Code.* Oxford: Oxford University Press, 1932.
Wellhausen, Julius. *Prolegomena zur Geschichte Israels.* 6th ed. Berlin: de Gruyter, 1927.
————. *Die Composition des Hexateuchs und der historischen Bücher des Alten Testaments.* 4th ed. Berlin: Reimer, 1963.
Westenholz, J. Goodnick. "Writing for Posterity: Naram-Sin and Enmerkar." In *kinattūtu ša dārâti: Raphael Kutscher Memorial Volume,* edited by A. F. Rainey, 205-18. Tel Aviv; occasional publications 1. Tel Aviv: Tel Aviv University, 1993.
Wevers, John William, ed. *Deuteronomium.* Septuaginta—Vetus Testamentum Graece 3.2. Göttingen: Vandenhoeck & Ruprecht, 1977.
Whybray, Roger Norman. *The Intellectual Tradition in the Old Testament.* BZAW 135. Berlin: de Gruyter, 1974.
Widengren, Geo. *The Ascension of the Apostle and the Heavenly Book.* UUÅ 7. Uppsala: Lundequistska, 1950.
Wiener, Harold Marcus. *The Composition of Judges II 11 to 1 Kings II 46.* Leipzig: Hinrichs, 1929.
Wiseman, Donald J. "A Gilgamesh Epic Fragment from Nimrud." *Iraq* 37 (1975) 157-63.
Wittgenstein, Ludwig. *Tractatus Logico-Philosophicus.* 2d ed. London: Routledge, 1971.
Wolff, Hans Walter. *Dodekapropheton 4: Micha.* BKAT 14.4. Neukirchen-Vluyn: Neukirchener Verlag, 1982.
Zakovitch, Yair. "Mirror-image Story—an Additional Criterion for the Evaluation of Characters in Biblical Narrative." *Tarbiz* 54 (1985) 165-76 (Hebrew).
————. "Through the Looking Glass: Reflections/Inversions of Genesis Stories in the Bible." *BibInt* 2 (1993) 139-52.
Zimmern, Heinrich. *Akkadische Fremdwörter als Beweis für babylonischen Kultureinfluß.* 2d ed. Leipzig: Hinrichs, 1917.
Zipor, Moshe A. "The Deuteronomic Account of the Golden Calf and its Reverberation in Other Parts of the Book of Deuteronomy." *ZAW* 108 (1996) 20-33.
Zobel, Hans-Jürgen. *Stammesspruch und Geschichte.* BZAW 95. Berlin: de Gruyter, 1965.

INDEX OF AUTHORS

Ackerman, J. S. 191
Albright, W. F. 208
Alter, R. 14, 121, 187, 201, 202, 222
Amsler, S. 5-6, 31, 40, 256
Anbar, M. 87, 91
Aristotle 144
Auerbach, E. 11

Baker, D. W. 136
Bakhtin, M. 16
Bal, M. 11, 79
Balogh, J. 77
Baltzer, K. 125, 141-142, 152, 154, 156, 163
Beach, J. W. 13
Beauchamp, P. 4, 14, 22, 58, 76, 258
Beer, G. 44
Begg, C. T. 137
Bekhor Shor 129, 140, 153, 196
Berlin, A. 201
Bertholet, A. 156, 164
Beyerlin, W. 63
Blenkinsopp, J. 46, 118, 196, 197
Blum, E. 23, 161, 187, 191, 251
Booth, W. C. 13
Boyarin, D. 77
Braulik, G. 15, 37, 52, 69, 74, 75, 78, 90, 91, 122, 139, 140, 142-147, 148, 180, 258
Brinkman, J. A. 94
Buber, M. 218
Buchholz, J. 164
Buis, P. 74, 131, 154, 155, 190, 242
Buth, R. 136-137

Cagni, L. 255
Cairns, I. 5
Caquot, A. 74, 75, 82, 101, 212, 213
Carmichael, C. M. 211
Cazelles, H. 29
Childs, B. S. 44
Clines, D. J. A. 221
Clements, R. E. 61, 63
Coats, G. W. 190, 196, 208
Cohen, D. 29
Coleridge, S. T. 21
Conrad, E. W. 261

Cooper, A. 92, 228, 229
Couroyer, B. 55, 115
Craig, J. C. 50
Craigie, P. C. 91, 96, 145, 155, 171, 225
Cross, F. M. 64, 208, 212, 247
Crüsemann, F. 31, 72, 74

Dällenbach, L. 79, 80
Damrosch, D. 201
Delcor, M. 152
Delitzsch, F. 130, 135
Dhorme, E. 31, 60, 90
Dietrich, M. 101
Dillmann, A. 87, 125, 140, 153, 155, 160, 164, 205
Dogniez, C. 22, 131, 153, 185
Dohmen, C. 29, 46, 264
Driver, S. R. 8, 35, 45, 62, 74, 83, 87, 88, 91, 102, 129, 134, 140, 141, 150, 152, 153, 154, 167, 170, 174, 185, 189, 193, 205-207, 222, 224, 238
Ducrot, O. 15
Durand, J.-M. 114
Durham, J. I. 44

Eissfeldt, O. 48, 118, 157
Ellis, R. S. 64
Eslinger, L. M. 232

Fisch, H. 152, 176-177
Fischer, G. 52, 57, 58, 69, 74, 77, 81, 144
Fishbane, M. 46, 48, 135, 156, 157, 170, 265, 266
Fitzmyer, J. A. 28, 51, 73, 100, 257
Fohrer, G. 118
Foster, B. R. 50, 255
Freedman, D. N. 212
Fretheim, T. A. 61, 63, 167, 171
Friedrich, J. 256

Gadamer, H. G. 4
Gadd, C. J. 84
Garciá López, F. 23, 52, 72, 219, 221
Garsiel, M. 133
Genette, G. 146, 241
Gennep, A. van 88-89

Gevaryahu, H. 159
Gide, A. 79
Ginsberg h. L. 209
Goethe, J. W. 19
Goffman, E. 238
Gold, J. 229, 236
Goldstein, B. R. 92, 228, 229
Goody, J. R. 40, 76, 84
Graesser, C. F. 93
Graham, W. A. 57, 77
Greenberg, M. 50, 73, 225
Greenstein, E. L. 9, 162, 201
Grelot, P. 73
Grossfeld, B. 155
Gurney, O. R. 78

Haran, M. 56, 63, 75
Harl, M. 22, 131, 153, 160, 185
Hazkuni 44, 140, 153, 155, 196
Hendrickson, G. L. 77
Hempel, J. 156
Hillers, D. R. 108, 216
Hossfeld, F.-L. 8, 77, 84, 116
Hunger, H. 159

Ibn Ezra 2, 10, 44, 52-53, 90, 122, 129-130, 132, 153, 155, 158
Iser, W. 6

Jacob, E. 231
Jacobsen, T. 208
Jakobson, R. 15
Jefferson, A. 25, 80
Joüon, P. 31, 136
Josephus 140, 259

Keel, O. 52, 53, 57
Keil, K. F. 130, 135
Kermode, F. 25
Klein, M. 155
Kleinert, P. 17
Klostermann, A. 118, 134, 174
Knapp, D. 109
Knoppers, G. N. 24
Korošec, V. 106
Kuhl, C. 161

L'Hour, J. 88
Laberge, L. 39, 154, 160, 171-172
Labuschagne, C. J. 77, 172, 177, 180, 238-239
Lambert, W. G. 46
Lamberty-Zielinski, H. 77, 116

Leclercq, J. 155
Leichty, E. 75, 159
Lemaire, A. 30, 56, 101, 114
Lenchak, T. A. 4, 6, 14, 15, 102, 104, 244, 245
Levinson, B. M. 43, 46, 48, 161, 211, 265
Loewenstamm, S. E. 66, 191, 224
Lohfink, N. 7, 11, 14, 15, 17, 19-20, 33, 39, 48, 49, 52, 53, 55, 57, 58, 69, 71, 74, 75, 77, 78, 81, 85, 96, 97-98, 101, 102, 106, 108, 112-116, 118, 119-125, 126, 129, 130, 131, 135, 136, 139, 140-141, 142-144, 152, 153, 154, 157-158, 160, 164, 171-172, 173-174, 176, 179, 181, 184, 188, 189, 204, 219, 233, 240-241, 244, 245
Long, B. O. 108, 162
Loretz, O. 101
Lux, R. 193, 224
Luyten, J. 207

McBride, S. D., Jr. 233, 234
McCarthy, D. J. 93, 96, 99, 102, 130
Margaliot, M. 217
Marks, H. 133
Martin, W. J. 136
Mayes, A. D. H. 5, 29, 33, 59, 60, 61, 67, 90, 108, 154, 154, 176, 181, 208, 214, 224, 238, 242
Mechonnic, H. 77
Meier, S. A. 12
Mendenhall, G. E. 142
Merril, E. H. 2
Meyers, E. M. 224
Milgrom, J. 49
Millard, A. R. 56
Mittmann, S. 29-31
Moberly, R. W. L. 44
Moran, W. L. 66, 108
Morrisette, B. 79
Müller, G. 241
Muraoka, T. 31, 136

Nachmanides 44, 128, 145, 153, 158
Nohrnberg, J. 229
Noth, M. 118, 154, 160, 187, 224
Nwachukwu, F. 39, 153, 172

O'Connor, M. 136, 149, 248
Oeming, M. 29, 46, 264
Olson, D. T. 3, 17, 117, 167, 190, 257
Ong, W. J. 57

Oppenheim, A. L. 75, 229
Otto, E. 48

Palache, J. L. 29
Parpola, S. 28, 257
Perlitt, L. 4, 7-8, 11, 22, 30, 31, 78, 187, 238
Perry, M. 6, 15, 62
Polak, F. 200
Polzin, R. 2-3, 13, 16, 23, 24, 125, 238-239, 242, 252
Posner, E. 94
Preuss d. 8
Puech, E. 91
Pury, A. De 230-232

Rad, G. Von 4, 59, 61, 63, 118, 124, 156-157, 158, 176, 179, 180, 190, 192, 224, 238
Rahlfs, A. 153
Rashi 39, 140, 143, 153, 155
Reuter, E. 8, 46, 84,
Richter, D. H. 22
Rofé, A. 118
Römer, T. 5-6, 11, 22, 204
Rooy, H. F. Van 17, 102
Rose, M. 21-22, 118, 160, 187, 190
Rouillard, H. 216, 220
Rudolph, W. 31
Rüterswörden, U. 72

Saadia 44
Sarna, N. 135, 156, 157
Savran, G. W. 258
Schäfer-Lichtenberger, C. 72, 73, 131, 151, 153, 154, 158, 159, 164, 166, 195, 196, 197
Schiller, F. 19
Schwartz, R. M. 224
Seeligmann, I. L. 212
Seow, C. L. 63
Sforno 140, 153, 180
Shmuel Ben Meir 44
Ska, J.-L. 79, 139, 162, 241, 249-250
Skweres, D. E. 108, 129, 131, 258
Smend, R. 118
Smith, G. A. 8, 158
Smith, W. C. 46
Soden, W. VON 65
Soggin, A. 100-101
Sonnet, J.-P. 13, 79, 142, 247

Spinoza, B. De 10
Staerk, W. 156
Starobinski, J. 199
Steinkeller, P. 65
Sternberg, M. 10, 11, 12, 13, 22, 32, 62, 68, 111, 121, 124, 137, 138, 174, 186, 188, 197, 201, 245, 250, 251, 253
Steuernagel, C. 153, 155, 156, 205, 224
Steymans, H. U. 99
Stoellger, P. 187

Talmon, S. 162
Tengström, S. 247
Tigay, J. H. 249, 256
Todorov, T. 15
Toeg, A. 47
Tomashevsky, B. 18
Tov, E. 160
Tucker, G. M. 247

Vaux, R. DE 56, 64, 163
Veijola, T. 3
Viberg, Å. 115-116
Virgil 227
Vogels, W. 108

Walker, C. B. F. 65
Waltke, B. K. 136, 149, 248
Watanabe, K. 28, 257
Weinfeld, M. 3, 20, 31, 35, 36, 43, 45, 46, 49, 57-58, 59, 60, 61, 62, 63, 64, 68, 69, 75, 76, 77, 83, 93, 99, 108, 109, 132, 141, 142, 163, 185, 194, 238, 256, 264
Weitzman, S. 146
Welch, A. C. 156
Wellhausen, J. 62, 213
Westenholz, J. G. 65, 66, 72, 73
Wevers, J. W. 153
Whybray, R. N. 266
Widengren, G. 50
Wiener, H. M. 161
Wiseman, D. J. 65
Wittgenstein, L. 254
Wolff, H. W. 216

Zakovitch, Y. 200
Zimmern, H. 101
Zipor, M. A. 143, 167
Zobel, H.-J. 212

INDEX OF SCRIPTURAL REFERENCES

GENESIS

1:1   10
2:4   87
2:18   201
4:1   208
4:7   107
5:1-32   247
5:1   247
6:12   176
6:13   176
6:17   176
10:5   176
10:19   176
11:31   218
12-50   218
12:1-3   221
12:5-6   221-222, 232
12:7   219-220, 232
13:14-15   218
13:14   219-220, 222, 225
13:15   219
14:19   208
14:22   208
15   115-116
15:5   133
15:7   225
15:13   115
15:17   115-116
15:18   219, 232
17:8   219, 225, 232
17:14   149
18:19   221
19:21   177
19:24   177
19:25   177
19:29   177
20:7   221
23   225
23:2-20   197
23:4   225
23:9   225
23:20   225
24:4   192
24:7   192
24:10   192
25   203

25:8   204, 224
25:9   203
25:11   203
25:7-11   202
25:17   224
27   34, 203, 210, 215, 218
27:1-2   203
27:1   204, 220, 232
27:4   203
27:7   23, 210, 215, 232
27:10   23, 203, 210, 215
27:13   206
27:39   214
28:18   92
28:22   92
30:37   208
31:45-52   92
31:46   167
31:48   93, 152
31:51-52   167
31:52   93, 152
32   232
33:20   92
35   203
35:7   92
35:14   92
35:20   92, 206, 226
35:28-29   203
35:29   203-204, 224
37:36   162
37-47   23
38   162
39:1   162
47-50   203
47   205
47:9   204
47:29-30   203, 205, 223
47:29   202, 205, 232
47:30   205-206, 226, 232
48   210, 215
48:9   210
48:10   204, 220
48:13-20   218
48:15   210
48:18-19   200
48:20   210
49   23, 192, 210-212, 233

49:1 206, 232-233
49:2 211, 232-233
49:3 207-208, 212
49:4 206
49:5-7 206
49:7 206
49:9 107, 213
49:14 107
49:15 206
49:22-26 213
49:23 209
49:24-26 207
49:24 214
49:25-26 232
49:25 213, 214
49:26 207, 213-214
49:28-30 192
49:28 210, 232
49:29-32 223
49:29 209, 224
49:30 209, 225
49:31 203
49:33 209, 224, 232
50 23
50:5 223, 226
50:6-14 223
50:10 226
50:11 226
50:12 226
50:13 203, 225-226
50:16 210, 215
50:19 228
50:24 203
50:25 226, 228
50:26 226

EXODUS

1:1-7 226
1:1-2 12
1:1 234
1:2 12
1:9 234
3 234
3:12 154
3:16 139
3:18 139
4-11 38
4:10 38
4:17 254
13 43
13:19 226
16 43

17 191
17:1-7 187
17:6 191
17:7 189
17:14 42, 247, 249
18:13-26 258
19-24 79
19-20 36
19:7-8 172
19:16 36
19:19 36
19:25 47
20:1 47
20:2-17 43, 47
20:2 228
20:18 36
20:22-23:33 46
20:22-23:19 42
20:22 47
20:25 90
21:1 47
23:5 107
23:24 92
24 92, 95, 106, 114, 116, 233
24:3-8 114, 116, 233, 248, 249
24:3 116
24:4-8 114, 116
24:4-7 173
24:4 42, 48, 92-93, 95, 106, 249
24:7-8 245
24:7 42, 48, 76, 106, 247
24:12 43, 249
25-31 43
25 64
25:1-9 194
25:10 63, 226
25:16 61
28:29 55
28:30 55
31:18 43, 249
32:16 249
32:19 59
32:25-29 67
32:32-33 247, 249
32:32 247
32:33 247
33 161
33:7-11 148
33:7 63
33:11 196
34 43, 161
34:1 43-44, 60, 249
34:14-26 43

34:27-28 43
34:27 43
34:28 43-44, 61
34:34-35 148
35:30 62
36:2 62
37 64
37:1-16 63
37:1-9 62
37:1 62-63
39:35 61
40 64
40:20 61

LEVITICUS

26:15 149
26:44 149

NUMBERS

1:47-49 136
1:50 67
3:1 87
3:6-8 67
3:16 133
5:23 84, 247
6:3 208
10:33-36 61
11-12 23
11 161, 251
11:23 191
11:24-25 148
12 161, 251
12:4 148
12:10 148
13-14 192
13:16 132-133
14:24 190
14:30 189-190
14:42-44 61
20 191
20:1-13 187, 189, 191-192
20:6 148
20:8 191
20:10-12 190
20:10 191
20:13 189
20:24 193, 206, 224
20:25-28 186
20:29 195
21:21-35 21, 23

21:14 247
22:1 215
22:5 217
22:27 107
23:8 216
23:10 200
23:13-14 216
23:20 216
23:28 216
24:3 217, 220
24:5 **220**
24:9 217
24:15-16 217
24:15 200, 220
24:25 217
25:1-3 216
27 131-132, 187
27:12-14 131, 185-187, 189, 219
27:12-13 34, 128, 131, 187
27:12 186, 216, 222
27:13-14 186
27:13 186, 224
27:14 191, 193
27:15-51 185
27:17 129
27:18-21 131, 186
27:18 23, 195
27:19 131
27:20 195-196
27:21 129
27:22-23 131, 154, 185, 196
27:23 23, 131
31:1-8 217
31:2 224
31:8 206
33:47 222
33:48 222

DEUTERONOMY

1-11 237, 243
1-4 18, 20, 22, 187, 198
1:1-4:43 184
1-3 124, 188
1 17
1:1-5 9, 237
1:1-2 5
1:1 2, 10, 12, 17-18, 24, 27, 40
1:2 88
1:3 10, 12, 16, 25, 32, 34, 148, 198, 243, 259
1:4-5 21
1:4 23

1:5 7, 12, 20, 24, 29-32, 37, 194, 197, 258
1:6-3:29 18
1:6-7 35
1:6-8 32
1:6 35
1:8 204
1:9-18 139, 258
1:9 66
1:17-18 141
1:16 66, 126
1:18 66
1:20-45 187
1:26 168
1:29-31 35
1:29-30 132
1:34-36 11
1:35 189, 204
1:37-38 33, 130
1:37 186, 188, 190
1:38 33, 134, 155
1:42-43 61
1:43 168
2 242
2:24-3:22 23
2:5 241
2:7 169
2:8 31
2:9 241
2:10-12 238, 242
2:10-11 242
2:11 242
2:12 241-242
2:14-24 241
2:14 240
2:16-17 190
2:16 132
2:19 241
2:20-23 238, 241-242
2:20-21 242
2:20 242
2:21-22 242
2:21 242
2:22 239, 241-242
2:23 242
2:24 240
2:29 222
2:34 66
3 185
3:4 66
3:8-12 238
3:8 66
3:9 238, 241-242

3:11 2, 238, 242
3:12 66
3:13-14 238
3:14 239, 242
3:18-20 141
3:18 66
3:21-22 35
3:21 66, 126, 131, 222
3:23-26 33
3:23 66
3:25 222
3:26-28 185
3:26 33, 130, 186, 188, 190
3:27-28 33, 131
3:27 34-35, 95, 185-186, 219, 222
3:28 33, 131-132, 134
3:29 35, 185, 194
4-5 6
4 18, 36, 143
4:1 36-37, 47
4:2 35, 45-46, 81, 258
4:5 37, 47
4:6 53, 81
4:8 14, 244, 258
4:10-14 42
4:10 35, 69, 81, 143-144
4:12 35-36, 59, 245
4:13 35, 42, 44-45, 51, 59, 135, 138
4:14 4, 36-37, 47, 66-67, 222
4:15-31 166
4:15 36
4:16 169
4:21-22 130, 189, 221
4:21 186, 188, 190, 222
4:22-23 170
4:22 34, 128, 147, 222
4:23 83
4:25-31 170
4:25 149, 169-170
4:26 152, 166, 222
4:29-31 109
4:30 109, 245
4:31 204
4:33 36, 245
4:34 254
4:36 35-36, 245
4:40 81-82, 258
4:41-44 116
4:41-43 18, 21, 37, 116, 184, 237
4:41 37, 184
4:44-28:68 184
4:44-5:1 237
4:44-49 17

4:44-45   17-18, 36
4:44   14, 86, 109, 157, 179, 184-185, 236, 244, 246, 248, 258
4:45   114-115, 244
4:46   35, 37
5-28   18-20, 41, 82, 85, 107, 112-114, 116
5-26   41, 53, 173
5-11   22, 70
5-6   69
5   42, 69, 95, 124, 143, 148, 243
5:1   36, 81, 113, 116, 126, 145-146, 179
5:2   51, 83
5:3   55, 83
5:4   47, 244
5:5   47, 66-67
5:6-21   42, 68
5:11   240
5:12   49
5:13   49
5:16   82
5:19   84, 135
5:22   36, 42, 45-46, 48, 58-59, 69, 137-138, 143, 263
5:23-33   126
5:23-31   38
5:23   54, 139, 246
5:25-27   37
5:27   47
5:29   81-82
5:31   37-38, 47, 54, 153
5:32   81-82
5:33   82
6   69, 81, 87
6:1-2   54
6:1   17, 37, 47, 54, 222, 243
6:2   54, 81-82, 258
6:3   81
6:4-9   75, 78, 80, 87, 198
6:4-5   52-53
6:4   54
6:5-6   53
6:6-9   51-52, 54-57, 68
6:6-8   56
6:6-7   96
6:6   52-56, 58, 150, 258
6:7   77, 145
6:8-9   57
6:8   52, 55-57
6:9   52-53, 56, 69-70, 75, 89, 111, 263
6:10   204
6:16   189
6:17   81

6:18-19   91
6:18   204
6:22   254
6:23   204
6:25   81
7:2-5   129
7:2   83, 129
7:3   129
7:5   59, 89, 129-130
7:8   204
7:11   81, 258
7:12   81, 204, 245
7:13   204
7:18   132
7:19   254
7:21   132
8:1   81, 91, 204, 258
8:6-20   166
8:6   81
8:11   81, 258
8:13   82
8:14   81
8:18   204
8:19   149, 166
8:20   39
9-10   124
9:1-10:11   64
9:1   222-223
9:5   204
9:6   168
9:7-10   137
9:7-8   171
9:7   168
9:9-11   45
9:9   59, 83, 166
9:10   42, 49, 59, 84, 138, 143
9:11   59, 137-138
9:12-13   171
9:12   82, 169
9:13   168
9:15   59-60
9:16   82, 169, 171
9:17   59
9:18-29   64
9:18   169
9:19   177
9:20   66
9:21   31
9:22   189
9:23-24   171
9:23   168
9:24   168
9:26   177

9:28 177
10-11 69
10 63, 69, 137
10:1-5 60-61, 66
10:1-2 61
10:1-3 62
10:1 59, 60, 66-67
10:2 59, 60, 63, 70, 138, 165, 179
10:3 59, 61
10:4 42, 59-61, 69, 84, 135, 137, 143, 263
10:5 59, 67, 70, 165-166, 179
10:6-9 66, 238
10:6-7 66
10:8-9 66-67, 138, 240, 242
10:8 66-67, 75, 165, 239
10:10 64
10:11 67, 138, 204
10:12-13 53
10:13 81, 258
11 69, 81, 87
11:1 81
11:2-3 254
11:8 55, 81, 91, 222, 258
11:9 82, 204
11:11 222
11:13-15 39
11:13 53-54, 258
11:16 82
11:18-20 53
11:18-21 53, 69, 75, 78, 80, 87, 147, 198
11:18-19 96
11:18 53, 54, 69-70, 150
11:19 77, 145
11:20 53, 56, 69-70, 75, 89, 111, 263
11:21 82, 204
11:22-25 91
11:22 53, 81, 258
11:26 14, 244-245
11:27 258
11:28 169, 258
11:29-30 88
11:30 88
11:31 222
11:32 14, 81, 244
12 54, 89
12:1 17, 54, 74, 81, 243
12:3 59, 89, 129
12:10-11 89
12:10 222
12:11 258
12:14 258

12:28 81-82, 258
13:1 46, 81, 159, 258
13:4-5 53
13:5 39, 81
13:15 31
13:18 204
13:19 39, 81, 110, 258
14:23 144
15:1-18 78
15:1-6 142
15:5 39, 81, 110, 258
15:11 258
15:12-18 142
15:15 258
16:12 81
16:13-15 142
16:18-18:22 71
16:18-19 91
16:21-22 89
16:22 91
17:4 31
17:6 166
17:8 141, 165
17:10 81
17:11 74
17:14-20 71, 77
17:14 71, 73, 78
17:15 71, 78
17:16-17 71, 82
17:17 82
17:18-20 63, 71-72, 80, 87, 147, 198, 234
17:18-19 140
17:18 73-75, 79, 80, 84, 91, 96, 105, 111-112, 138, 163, 249, 258, 263
17:19-20 80
17:19 75-81, 144, 173, 230, 258
17:20 78, 81-82
18 252
18:15-22 196
18:15 196-197
18:16 143
18:17 251
18:18 196-197
19:7 258
19:8 204
19:9 53, 258
19:14 94
19:18 31
20 61
20:1 132
20:3 132
20:16 129

23:5-6 217
24 83-84
24:1-4 83
24:1 56, 83-84, 229
24:2 84
24:3 56, 83-84, 229
24:18 258
24:22 258
24:26 245
26-27 113
26:1-19 96
26:3 204
26:5 231
26:8 254
26:13-15 98
26:14 39
26:15 204
26:16-19 86, 113-114
26:16 114
26:17-19 28
26:17-18 245
26:17 39
27-30 41
27-28 19, 26, 82-83, 101-102, 104, 110
27 85-87, 90, 92-95, 97, 99, 101-111, 167, 229
27:1-8 2, 86, 95, 139
27:1 86, 96, 98, 113-114, 126, 139, 164, 233, 237, 245, 258
27:2-8 86-91, 94-96, 100, 104, 110
27:2-3 87, 90, 223
27:2 86-89, 91, 94, 101, 222
27:3-8 88, 263
27:3 58, 85, 90, 99-100, 102, 104, 111, 141, 258
27:4 87, 88-89, 91, 94, 101, 222, 258
27:5-7 89
27:8 30-31, 58, 85, 87, 91, 94, 99-100, 102, 104, 111, 141, 258
27:9-10 139
27:9 96, 113-114, 126, 139, 164, 233, 237
27:10 39, 98, 110, 114, 258
27:11-14 97
27:11 97, 102, 237
27:12-26 97-98
27:12 98, 222
27:13 104
27:14 98, 102, 139
27:15-26 104
27:17 94
27:26 258
28-31 247

28 97, 98-99, 101-102, 104, 257-258
28:1-68 97
28:1 39, 98, 110, 258
28:2 39, 110
28:3-14 98
28:6 129
28:11 204
28:14 258
28:15-68 104
28:15-17 99
28:15 39, 99, 104, 110
28:45 39, 104
28:58-61 97, 99, 110
28:58 8, 85, 97, 99-104, 109, 223, 258
28:61 85, 97, 99-100, 102, 104, 258
28:62 39
28:69-32:47 185
28:69-29:1 237
28:69 17, 18, 102, 103, 105-106, 117, 119, 149, 180, 184, 236
29-32 181
29-30 14, 19-20, 25, 85, 103-107, 110-116, 119, 122, 135, 198, 260, 263
29:1-31:8 123
29:1-14 113
29:1 113, 126
29:2 254
29:4-5 39
29:4 39
29:5 39
29:8 115
29:9-11 113
29:9-10 233
29:9 14, 121, 142
29:10 171
29:11 115, 223, 245
29:12 204
29:13 115, 245
29:14-15 116
29:14 11
29:15-27 8
29:15 114
29:16-21 110
29:16-19 115
29:17-20 107
29:17 109
29:18 115, 245
29:19-20 107-108
29:19 85, 103-104, 109-110, 114, 116, 123, 137, 246, 260
29:20 8, 85, 103-104, 110-111, 114, 116, 123, 137, 157, 210, 223, 258, 260

29:21-24 108
29:22-28 108
29:22-27 108
29:21 108-109, 149, 258
29:22 109, 177
29:23 108
29:24 108
29:26 8, 85, 103-104, 108, 110, 123, 137, 258
29:27 109, 116
29:28 106, 258
29:69 86
30 85, 86
30:1-10 8, 109
30:1 14, 244
30:2 39, 110, 245, 258
30:7 115
30:8 39, 245, 258
30:10-12 103
30:10 8, 39, 85, 103, 109-111, 116, 123, 137, 157, 245, 258, 260-261
30:11 258
30:14 55
30:15 14, 244-245
30:16 53, 258
30:18 222, 244
30:19-20 232
30:19 152, 166, 244, 260
30:20 39, 53, 204
30:22-28 110
31-34 1, 5, 202, 204-206, 232-233, 250
31-33 237
31-32 119, 123-124, 135, 152, 158, 164, 207, 252, 264-265
31 5, 117-122, 125-126, 135, 137, 146, 148, 154, 156-157, 159-163, 167, 176, 181, 198, 207, 227, 240, 248, 250, 262-263
31:1-32:47 26, 117, 120-121, 180-181, 264
31:1-13 127, 146
31:1-8 128, 154
31:1-6 122
31:1 21, 38, 126, 160, 185, 232-233, 237
31:2-8 155
31:2-6 119, 126, 128-129
31:2-3 128, 130
31:2 128-129, 147, 155, 194, 222, 237
31:3 129-130, 134, 155, 181, 196
31:4 129
31:5 129
31:6 132-133, 155

31:7-9 127
31:7-8 119, 125-126, 128-134, 140, 148, 154, 156
31:7 5, 122, 126, 132-133, 153, 155, 204, 237
31:8 133, 155, 230
31:9-32:47 157
31:9-14 249
31:9-13 123-125, 128, 137, 140-142, 161, 163-164, 166, 179-180, 234, 260
31:9-12 157
31:9 1-3, 6, 8, 29, 84, 122-123, 125, 134-135, 137-141, 151, 156-158, 161-164, 199, 237, 248, 258, 260, 265
31:10-13 119, 122, 124, 126-127, 141-143, 145, 164, 230
31:10-11 145
31:10 123, 126, 140-142, 237
31:11-12 140
31:11 140, 145, 163, 173, 258
31:12-13 145
31:12 142-145, 163, 180, 258
31:13 139, 145, 180, 222
31:14-32:47 147, 264
31:14-29 179
31:14-23 21, 117, 122-123, 161
31:14-22 263
31:14-21 126
31:14-15 23, 148, 195, 237
31:14 13, 33, 35, 38-39, 117, 119-121, 125-128, 130, 133, 147-148, 153, 160, 202, 205, 237
31:15 148, 160
31:16-29 175
31:16-22 148, 157, 159, 176
31:16-21 13, 38, 119-120, 125-126, 154, 170, 174-175
31:16 83, 122, 125, 148-151, 157, 174, 194-195, 205, 232, 237
31:17 150, 175, 206
31:18 150, 174-175
31:19 150, 152-153, 157-158, 166, 176, 179, 248, 263
31:20-21 155
31:20 149, 151, 155, 174-175, 204
31:21 150-151, 155-156, 158, 166-167, 204, 206, 250
31:22-23 39
31:22 27, 37, 56, 106, 146, 150-151, 158-159, 162, 173, 248
31:23-25 127
31:23 13, 23, 33, 39, 120, 125-126, 130, 133, 153-156, 158, 160, 195, 237

31:24-39   179
31:24-30   156
31:24-29   124, 137, 157, 180, 249
31:24-27   122
31:24-26   122-123, 125, 156-158, 161, 163-164, 264
31:24-25   123
31:24   1-3, 6-7, 25, 29, 122-123, 135, 156-159, 161-163, 179, 184, 198-199, 234, 237, 248, 252, 256, 258, 260, 265
31:25-26   61-63, 125, 164
31:25   123, 126, 163, 165, 237
31:26-29   120, 153, 171-172, 174-175, 179, 194
31:26-28   126
31:26-27   180
31:26   141, 157, 158, 164-166, 172, 179, 227, 229, 248, 258-261
31:27-29   167, 170-172
31:27   166-168, 178, 207, 250
31:28-30   122, 124, 171
31:28   123, 141, 152, 166, 171-173, 175-176, 179, 233
31:29   167, 169-170, 172, 178, 195, 206-207, 232, 250
31:30-32:44   153, 173
31:30   119, 126, 151, 158, 161, 169, 171, 173, 233, 237, 248, 265
32   21, 27, 135, 206-207
32:1-43   126, 248
32:1   166, 173, 175
32:4   192, 207
32:5   169, 175-176, 208
32:6   207, 233
32:7   176, 208
32:8-9   233
32:8   176
32:9   232
32:12   175
32:13   175, 192
32:15   175, 192
32:18   192, 207
32:19   208
32:20   175, 177, 208
32:21   175, 207
32:22   176
32:25   160
32:26-27   177
32:26   176
32:28-29   207
32:28   171, 233
32:30   192

32:31   192
32:32-33   177
32:36   175, 233
32:39   178
32:40   176, 178
32:41-43   177
32:43   178, 208, 233
32:44-47   179
32:44-45   151, 237
32:44   123, 132, 134, 150-151, 161, 172, 178, 196, 233, 248, 265
32:45-47   123, 178, 180, 183
32:45-46   209, 232
32:45   25, 159, 178-180, 184, 198, 233-234, 252
32:46-47   258
32:46   7, 166, 178-180, 209, 237, 258
32:47-51   264
32:47   119, 178, 180, 192, 209, 222, 228, 232, 244, 264
32:48-34:12   183
32:48-34:10   197
32:48-52   18, 21, 183-188
32:48   35, 184, 237
32:49-52   13, 38, 125, 189, 193
32:49   185, 193, 216, 219, 222
32:50   186, 193-194, 224-225
32:51   186, 187, 189-192, 250
33-34   19, 23
33   21, 183, 206-207, 211-212, 215, 233
33:1-34:12   26, 185
33:1-34:7   192
33:1   17, 20, 23, 183-184, 192, 210-211, 214-215, 217, 233, 236-237
33:2-5   218
33:2   212
33:4   211, 232
33:5   211-212, 233
33:6-25   212
33:8-9   213
33:8   189, 212
33:9   213
33:10   232
33:13-17   213
33:13-16   232
33:13   213-214
33:15   213
33:16   213-214
33:22   213
33:24   212
33:26-29   218
33:28   215, 232
33:29   193, 212, 218, 233

34 23, 193, 219, 221, 223, 237, 250-251
34:1-6 193
34:1-4 23
34:1 5, 185, 193, 201, 216, 219
34:4 38, 125, 204, 219, 221-222, 232
34:5-6 224
34:5 193, 196, 217, 225-226
34:6 194, 197, 206, 217, 224-225, 230, 238
34:7 16, 128, 193, 208
34:8-12 194
34:8 195
34:9 23, 131, 195-196, 228, 245, 252
34:10-12 23
34:10 10, 21, 24-25, 161, 197, 199, 215, 221, 239, 251, 254
34:11 23
34:11-12 24, 253-254, 259
34:12 161

JOSHUA

1 154
1:6 130
1:8 76-77, 173, 199
1:9 130, 132
4 88
6:27 133
8:30-35 88, 249
8:31 227
8:32 74, 227
8:34 141
14:6 211
14:11 129
23 154
23:6 227
24 93, 167
24:1-2 172
24:22 152
24:25-26 106
24:25 245
24:26-27 249
24:26 167, 199
24:27 152, 167
24:31 195
24:32 226
27 93

JUDGES

1:1 195
2:7-10 195

2:10-11 195
2:11 195
5:4 101
6:32 134
7:1 134
13:6 211
13:8 211
16:7 208
16:8 208

1 SAMUEL

1:1 12
1:8 12
2:27 211
3:1 74
9:6 211
12 154
20:8 115

2 SAMUEL

7:12 205
11:14 84
11:15 84
23:1 200
24:1 200

1 KINGS

2:1 205
3:7 129
8:1-9 67
8:6 67
8:9 62
12:22 211
13:1 211
14:18 196
15:29 196
18:36 196
21:8 84
21:9 84
21:11 84

2 KINGS

2:1-12 225
4-8 211
5:5 84
5:6 84
5:7 84
9:7 196
9:36 196

10:1   84
10:2   84
10:6   84
10:7   84
10:10   196
11   154
11:18   31
14:25   196
17:13   196
17:23   196
19:14   84
20:12   84
21:10   196
22-23   77, 199
22   13, 247
22:20   224
23:1-3   106, 141
23:1-2   173
23:3   245
23:25   199, 247
24:2   196

ISAIAH

19:19-20   93
30:8   101, 262
37:14   84
39:1   84
50:1   84

JEREMIAH

1:1   10
3:1   83
3:8   84
7:25   196
8:8   72, 266
25:4   196
26:5   196
29:1   84
29:19   196
29:25   84
29:29   84
31:33   55
32   84
32:1-43   157
32:10   84
32:11   84-85
32:12   84
32:14   84, 263
32:16   84
32:44   84
34   115-116

34:10   115
34:18-19   115-116
34:18   115
34:19   115
35:15   196
36:6   77
36:8   77
36:13   77
36:14   77
36:18   74
44:4   196
48:48   159
51:64   159

EZEKIEL

1:15-16   1
1:16   1
16:8   115
17:3   115
17:24   208
21:3   208

HOSEA

9:10
12:3-15   230
12:11   231
12:12-15   231
12:12-13   231

AMOS

1:1   10
9:7   242

MICAH

6:1-8   216
6:4-5   216

HABAKKUK

2:2   29-30, 77, 262

PSALMS

1:2   77
37:31   55
40:4   157
62:10   47
72:20   159
78   157

90 211
119:11 55

JOB

1-2 13
2:9 193
19:23-24 101
19:23 85, 101
22:22 55
31:40 159

PROVERBS

3:3 41, 55
6:21 55
7:3 55
30:6 46

QOHELET

12:12-13 253
12:13 178, 181, 199

ESTHER

1:22 84
3:12-15 3
3:13 84
8:5 84
8:10 84
9:20 84
9:25 84
9:30 84

EZRA

3:2 211

NEHEMIAH

1:1 9-10

8:1-6 141
8:3 77
8:8 77, 141
8:9 141
8:13-18 141
8:18 77
9:3 77
10:30 115
13:1-2 217

1 CHRONICLES

22-29 154
23:14 211

2 CHRONICLES

15:12 115
22:17 84
30:16 211
34:18 77
34:28 224
34:31-32 245

2 MACCABEES

15:37-39 253
15:37 181

SIRACH

46:1 196
50:27 253

WISDOM

7:18 181

BARUCH

1:1 10

BIBLICAL INTERPRETATION SERIES

ISSN 0928-0731

1. VAN DIJK-HEMMES, F. & A. BRENNER. *On Gendering Texts.* Female and Male Voices in the Hebrew Bible. 1993. ISBN 90 04 09642 6
2. VAN TILBORG, S. *Imaginative Love in John.* 1993. ISBN 90 04 09716 3
3. DANOVE, P.L. *The End of Mark's Story.* A Methodological Study. 1993. ISBN 90 04 09717 1
4. WATSON, D.F. & A.J. HAUSER. *Rhetorical Criticism of the Bible.* A Comprehensive Bibliography with Notes on History and Method. 1994. ISBN 90 04 09903 4
5. SEELEY, D. *Deconstructing the New Testament.* 1994. ISBN 90 04 09880 1
6. VAN WOLDE, E. *Words become Worlds.* Semantic Studies of Genesis 1-11. 1994. ISBN 90 04 098879
7. NEUFELD, D. *Reconceiving Texts as Speech Acts.* An Analysis of 1 John. 1994. ISBN 90 04 09853 4
8. PORTER, S.E., P. JOYCE & D.E. ORTON (eds.). *Crossing the Boundaries.* Essays in Biblical Interpretation in Honour of Michael D. Goulder. 1994. ISBN 90 04 10131 4
9. YEO, K.-K. *Rhetorical Interaction in 1 Corinthians 8 and 10.* A Formal Analysis with Preliminary Suggestions for a Chinese, Cross-Cultural Hermeneutic. 1995. ISBN 90 04 10115 2
10. LETELLIER, R.I. *Day in Mamre, Night in Sodom.* Abraham and Lot in Genesis 18 and 19. 1995. ISBN 90 04 10250 7
12. TOLMIE, D.F. *Jesus' Farewell to the Disciples.* John 13:1-17:26 in Narratological Perspective. 1995. ISBN 90 04 10270 1
13. RYOU, D.H. *Zephaniah's Oracles against the Nations.* A Synchronic and Diachronic Study of Zephaniah 2:1-3:8. 1995. ISBN 90 04 10311 2
14. SONNET, J.-P. *The Book within the Book.* Writing in Deuteronomy. 1997. ISBN 90 04 10866 1
15. SELAND, T. *Establishment Violence in Philo and Luke.* A Study of Non-Conformity to the Torah and Jewish Vigilante Reactions. 1995. ISBN 90 04 10252 3
16. NOBLE, P.R *The Canonical Approach.* A Critical Reconstruction of the Hermeneutics of Brevard S. Childs. 1995. ISBN 90 04 10151 9
17. SCHOTTROFF, L.R & M.-T. WACKER (Hrsg.). *Von der Wurzel getragen.* Christlich-feministische Exegese in Auseinandersetzung mit Antijudaismus. 1996. ISBN 90 04 10336 8
18. BECKING, B. & M. DIJKSTRA (eds.). *On Reading Prophetic Texts.* Gender-Specific and Related Studies in Memory of Fokkelien van Dijk-Hemmes. 1996. ISBN 90 04 10274 4
19. BRETT, M.G. (ed.). *Ethnicity and the Bible.* 1996. ISBN 90 04 10317 1
20. HENDERSON, I.H. *Jesus, Rhetoric and Law.* 1996. ISBN 90 04 10377 5

21. RUTLEDGE, D. *Reading Marginally*. Feminism, Deconstruction and the Bible. 1996. ISBN 90 04 10564 6
22. CULPEPPER, R.A. (ed.). *Critical Readings of John 6*. (In preparation.)
23. PYPER, H.S. *David as Reader*. 2 Samuel 12:1-15 and the Poetics of Fatherhood. 1996. ISBN 90 04 10581 6
26. BRENNER, A. *The Intercourse of Knowledge*. On Gendering Desire and 'Sexuality' in the Hebrew Bible. 1997. ISBN 90 04 10155 1

DATE DUE

JUL 25 '99			
			Printed in USA

HIGHSMITH #45230